Pattern Recognition:
Statistical, Structural
and Neural Approaches

Pattern Recognition: Statistical, Structural and Neural Approaches

Robert J. Schalkoff

Clemson University

John Wiley & Sons, Inc.

New York • Chichester • Brisbane • Toronto • Singapore

Acquisitions Editor	Steven Elliot
Copy Editor	Genevieve Scandone
Production Manager	Linda Muriello
Senior Production Supervisor	Savoula Amanatidis
Illustration Coordinator	Sigmund Malinowski
Manufacturing Manager	Lorraine Fumoso

Recognizing the importance of preserving what has been written, it is a policy of John Wiley & Sons, Inc. to have books of enduring value published in the United States printed on acid-free paper, and we exert our best efforts to that end.

Library of Congress Cataloging in Publication Data:

Schalkoff, Robert J.
 Pattern recognition : statistical, structural and neural approaches / Robert J. Schalkoff.
  p. cm.
 Includes bibliographical references and index.
 ISBN 0-471-52974-5 (cloth)
 1. Pattern perception–Statistical methods. I. Title.
Q327.S27 1992
006.4–dc20   91-4751
                            CIP

Printed in the United States of America

10 9 8 7 6 5 4 3 2

Printed and bound by R.R. Donnelley & Sons, Inc.

To my sisters —
Mary and Ginny

About The Author

Robert J. Schalkoff is Professor of Electrical and Computer Engineering at Clemson University in Clemson, South Carolina. His primary research interests are in artificial intelligence and computer vision with a special emphasis on model-based image understanding, motion and stereo vision, and associated computer architectures. He is also the author of *Digital Image Processing and Computer Vision* (John Wiley & Sons, Inc., 1989) and *Artificial Intelligence: An Engineering Approach* (McGraw-Hill, 1990). He received the Ph.D. degree in Electrical Engineering from the University of Virginia in 1979.

Preface

The art of being wise is the art of knowing what to overlook.

The Principles of Psychology [1890], Chapter 22
William James 1842–1910

This book brings together an identifiable 'core' of pattern recognition (PR) ideas, techniques, and applications using statistical, syntactic and neural approaches. It is intended for beginning graduate/advanced undergraduate students as well as practicing engineers and scientists. It is the outgrowth of a graduate course taught in the Electrical and Computer Engineering Department at Clemson University. Like many similar medium-sized and 'mainstream' departments, we realized the need to introduce graduate students to the growing inventory of PR topics found in this book, including a structured introduction to neural networks for PR applications. The text is suitable for use in a one- or two-semester course and may be supplemented by individual student projects and readings from the current literature. Since there is more material than could comfortably be covered in a single semester, individual instructors may choose to emphasize or deemphasize specific topics.

As with most technical disciplines, the concept of 'pattern recognition' means different things to different people. PR researchers are typically fragmented into disjoint communities. It is my belief that PR is becoming a mature technology with roots in diverse areas such as estimation theory, formal languages, and optimization theory. In addition, the interfaces between pattern recognition and other technologies and application areas such as artificial intelligence and image processing, are quite fuzzy. All three PR approaches (statistical, syntactic, and neural) are currently receiving considerable attention and often share overlapping themes. The choice of one over another is a function of many variables, including constraints of the specific application and the background of the PR system designer. Therefore, I have attempted an exposition that illustrates the similarities and differences among the three approaches. Although statistical and syntactic pattern recognition are different, they share common ideas. An example is the use of formal models for pattern generation, which leads to formal solution procedures for classification/description. In addition, neural network-based approaches share a number of characteristics with 'traditional' pattern recognition techniques. They include hierarchical structures, clustering, pattern association, and learning or training.

I have also tried to emphasize an 'engineering' approach to PR, since I believe we should not be teaching PR as esoteric mathematics or as the 'art' of developing a set of problem-solving heuristics. An understanding of the underlying models and techniques and their respective limitations is a fundamental aspect of PR system design. Like many engineering and scientific disciplines, PR system design forces the designer to consider trade-offs between exact solutions to approximate models and approximate solutions to exact models. One of the caveats I stress to students is **'In PR problem formulations, you will get what you ask for in the solution,** *whether you recognize it or not.'* This allows students to appreciate a number of mathematical results that also appeal to intuition. Examples are as follows:

- When a statistical pattern recognition–based algorithm changes decision regions to account for a change in a priori probabilities.
- When a grammatical approach to describing the structure inherent in a pattern yields a context-sensitive grammar.
- When a feedforward-structure neural net, after training with a well-known algorithm, develops an internal layer that allows the attachment of semantics to the action of the internal units.

After completing this book, students should have a good grounding in the fundamentals of PR, exposure to three diverse PR approaches, and some perspective on the applicability of each approach. They should also be able to begin reading the current literature.

Opportunities abound for the application of pattern recognition techniques to present-day problems. Current examples are automated character recognition, digital image processing and analysis, and recognition and understanding of speech. In fact, many pattern recognition applications arise in situations where they are not expected. Examples of these are weather forecasting and stock market analysis. Individual instructors may wish to emphasize PR application in their respective research domains. My own experience with computer vision problems provided a wealth of examples, some of which are used in this text.

An attempt was made to keep the presentation balanced. The text has four main sections. Part 1 (Chapter 1) introduces the overall subject by asking the question What is pattern recognition? It provides an overview of pattern recognition concerns that are common to all approaches. The three approaches are then briefly introduced and compared. Part 2 (Chapters 2–5) concerns the statistical approach, beginning with a simple example and ending with unsupervised learning through clustering. Part 3

(Chapters 6–9) develops the syntactic or structural approach, beginning with a look at the representational capability of string grammars and corresponding recognition approaches (parsing), continuing with an exploration of higher dimensional representations and graphical approaches, and ending with an introduction to supervised learning (grammatical inference). Finally, Part 4 (Chapters 10–13) details the emerging neural approach, beginning with an overview of neural computing basics, an examination of pattern associators and feedforward nets and associated training algorithms, and concluding with unsupervised learning implementations. In each case, following development of the theory, examples are shown to illustrate the concepts. Each chapter contains a concluding section that cites relevant literature for more in-depth study of specific topics. Approximately 250 references are cited.

Some background in probability, linear algebra, and discrete mathematics is necessary to fully appreciate the topics considered in this book. The appendices document these and other fundamental background concepts and enable the book to be self-contained. In addition, numerous exercises are presented that will challenge and motivate the reader to further explore relevant concepts. Many of these exercises provide the bases for projects and thesis work. Instructors should contact the publisher regarding the availability of a solution manual.

This book completes a trilogy of books I have written over the last three years. The other two are *Digital Image Processing and Computer Vision* (John Wiley & Sons, Inc.) and *Artificial Intelligence: An Engineering Approach* (McGraw-Hill). They cover a broad area of computing technology that I believe (or hope) is likely to receive widespread attention as it continues to mature during the '90s.

Acknowledgments

A textbook does not just 'happen,' but rather requires a significant commitment from its author as well as a supporting environment. I have been quite fortunate in this regard. My wife, Leslie, functioned as 'the ultimate pattern recognition system' in transcribing pages of scribbling into an attractive TEX document. Students who used earlier versions of the notes provided both valuable feedback and enhanced motivation, since they proved that the educational objective of this book could be achieved. The environment in the Department of Electrical and Computer Engineering and the College of Engineering at Clemson University was also conducive to this task. The efforts of the professional staff at John Wiley and Sons, especially Steven Elliott and Savoula Amanatidis, deserve special thanks. Finally, in watching my daughter Katie grow, I realize there are lots of things we'll never want to automate.

Robert J. Schalkoff
Clemson, South Carolina

Contents

Part 1

Introduction and General Pattern Recognition Concerns

Pattern Recognition (PR) Overview 1

Knowledge is of two kinds. We know a subject ourselves, or we know where we can find information upon it.

From James Boswell, *Life of Johnson* 1791
Samuel Johnson 1709–1784

WHAT IS THIS BOOK ABOUT

Overview

Machine intelligence will be a dominant technology in the 1990s. Pattern recognition (PR) techniques are often an important component of intelligent systems and are used for both data preprocessing and decision making. Broadly speaking, pattern recognition (PR) is the science that concerns the description or classification (recognition) of measurements. There is little doubt that PR is an important, useful, and rapidly developing technology with cross-disciplinary interest and participation. PR is not comprised of one approach, but rather is a broad body of often loosely related knowledge and techniques. Historically, the two major approaches to pattern recognition are the statistical (or decision theoretic) and the syntactic (or structural) approaches. Recently, the emerging technology of neural networks has provided a third approach, especially for 'black box' implementation of PR algorithms. Since no single technology is always the optimum solution for a given PR problem, all three are explored in this text.

Each of the three interrelated pattern recognition approaches:

- Statistical Pattern Recognition (StatPR)
- Syntactic Pattern Recognition (SyntPR)
- Neural Pattern Recognition (NeurPR)

is defined in the following sections. Where appropriate, computational issues related to practical or even 'real-time' implementation of the corresponding PR systems is considered. In order to achieve this breadth of coverage, the scope of some PR topics is restricted.

'Engineering' Approaches to Pattern Recognition

An engineering approach to problem solving involves incorporating all available and relevant problem information in a structured fashion to formulate a solution. This includes the development or modification of models that perhaps incorporate structural and a priori information, including 'training' data.[1] Therefore, throughout this book, our examination of PR approaches will be guided by these three questions:

1. Are pattern recognition techniques suitable, or even applicable to the problem at hand? (Can the problem be solved?)
2. Can we develop or modify useful models for the situation and, if necessary, determine the model parameters?
3. If so, are there formal tools and heuristics that may be applied, and does a computationally *practical* solution procedure exist?

Relationship of PR to Other Areas

Pattern recognition techniques overlap with other areas, such as:
- (Adaptive) signal processing and systems
- Artificial intelligence
- Neural modeling
- Optimization/estimation theory
- Automata theory
- Fuzzy sets
- Structural modeling
- Formal languages

Pattern Recognition Applications

PR applications include:
- Image preprocessing, segmentation, and analysis
- Computer vision
- Seismic analysis
- Radar signal classification/analysis

---

[1]Pattern recognition (especially statistical) books are replete with the terms 'a priori' and 'a posteriori.' We will define 'a priori' as 'known before' (usually 'before' meaning 'before feature measurement') and 'a posteriori' to mean 'derived from subsequent measurements.'

- Face recognition
- Speech recognition/understanding
- Fingerprint identification
- Character (letter or number) recognition
- Handwriting analysis ('notepad' computers)
- Electrocardiographic signal analysis/understanding
- Medical diagnosis

PATTERN RECOGNITION, CLASSIFICATION, AND DESCRIPTION

Abstract Representation of Pattern Mappings

PR may be characterized as an *information reduction, information mapping,* or *information labeling* process. An abstract view of the PR classification/description problem is shown in Figure 1. We postulate a mapping between class-membership space, C, and pattern space, P. This mapping is done via a relation, G_i, for each class, and may be probabilistic. Each class, w_i, generates a subset of 'patterns' in pattern space, where the ith pattern is denoted p_i. Note, however, that these subspaces overlap, to allow patterns from different classes to share attributes. Another relation, M, maps patterns from subspaces of P into observations or measured patterns or features, denoted m_i. Using this concept, the characterization of many PR problems is simply that, given measurement m_i, we desire a method to *identify* and *invert* mappings M and G_i for all i. Unfortunately, in practice, these mappings are not functions. Even if they were, they are seldom 1:1, onto or invertible. For example, Figure 1 shows that identical measurements or observations may result from different p_i, which in turn correspond to different underlying classes. This suggests a potential problem with *ambiguity*. Nevertheless, it seems reasonable to attempt to model and understand these processes, in the hope that this leads to better classification/description techniques.

The abstract formulation of Figure 1 is well suited for modeling in both StatPR and SyntPR. Looking ahead, Figure 13 shows how more detailed formalizations of these approaches may be related to Figure 1. We may view the realized patterns in Figure 1 as basic 'world data,' which is then measured. Thus, another important aspect of Figure 1 concerns M. *This mapping reflects our choice of measurement system.* Measurement system design is an important aspect of PR system design, in the sense that good 'features' or 'primitives,' to be derived subsequently, probably require good, or at least adequate, measurements. It is unlikely that erroneous or incomplete measurements will facilitate good PR system performance. Finally, note that patterns that are generated by the same class (p_4 and p_1, from w_i, for example) and 'close' in pattern space, P, do not necessarily yield measurements (m_1 and m_3 in this case) that are also 'close.' This is significant when 'clustering' of measurement (or feature or primitive) data is used for measuring pattern similarity.

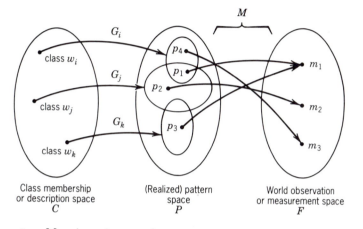

Figure 1: Mappings in an abstract representation of pattern genera-
tion/classification/interpretation systems.

Example Use of the Abstract Representation.   Consider a two-class problem where w_1
corresponds to the class 'apple' and w_2 corresponds to the class 'hand grenade.' In
realized pattern space, there will be some difference among the p_i resulting from apples, since not all apples are the same size, shape, weight, color, and so on. A similar
remark holds true for realizations of class w_2. Also, some realizations of 'apple' and
'hand grenade' share similar attributes (e.g., mass, volume, weight). Therefore, basing
our PR system on a measurement consisting simply of realized pattern *weight* is likely
to:

- (Mis)-classify some apples and hand grenades as the same.
- (Mis)-classify or distinguish between heavy apples and light apples (and similarly for w_2).

Ironically, at the same time we strive to understand and to 'undo' these mappings,
alternative (so-called black box) approaches, principally implemented by using neural
networks, are receiving increased attention. These black box approaches attempt to
eliminate the need for detailed information on both the mappings and inverses and,
instead, require a good set of training data (sample mappings between C and M) and
a trainable system.

Structure of a 'Typical' PR System

The structure of a typical pattern recognition system is shown in Figure 2. Notice that
it consists of a sensor (an image sensor or camera, for example), a feature extraction
mechanism (algorithm), and a classification or description algorithm (depending on
the approach). In addition, usually some data that have already been classified or
described are assumed available in order to train the system (the so-called training
set).

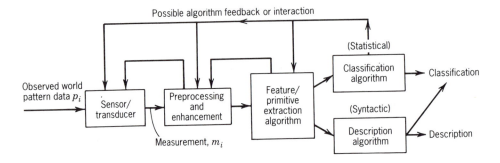

Figure 2: Typical pattern recognition system structures.

PATTERNS AND FEATURE EXTRACTION WITH EXAMPLES

Patterns and Features

Patterns. It comes as little surprise that much of the information that surrounds us manifests itself in the form of patterns. *The ease with which humans classify and describe patterns often leads to the incorrect assumption that this capability is easy to automate.* Sometimes the similarity in a set of patterns is immediately apparent, whereas in other instances it is not. Recognizing characters is an example of the former; economic forecasting illustrates the latter.

Pattern recognition, naturally, is based on *patterns*. A pattern can be as basic as a set of measurements or observations, perhaps represented in vector or matrix notation. Thus, the mapping M, from P to F in Figure 1, is an identity mapping. The use of measurements already presupposes some preprocessing and instrumentation system complexity. These measurements could be entities such as blood pressure, age, number of wheels, a 2-D line drawing, and the like. Furthermore, patterns may be converted from one representation to another.

The measurement, as shown in Figure 3, may be a two-dimensional image, a drawing, a waveform, a set of measurements, a temporal or spatial history (sequence) of events, the state of a system, the arrangement of a set of objects, and so forth.

Features. Broadly speaking, *features* are any extractable measurement used. Examples of low-level features are signal intensities. Features may be symbolic, numerical or both. An example of a symbolic feature is color; an example of a numerical feature is weight (measured in pounds). Features may also result from applying a *feature extraction algorithm or operator* to the input data. Additionally, features may be higher level entities: for example, geometric descriptors of either an image region or a 3-D object appearing in the image. For instance, aspect ratio and Euler number are higher level geometric features. Note that: (1) significant computational effort may be required in feature extraction; and (2) the extracted features may contain errors or

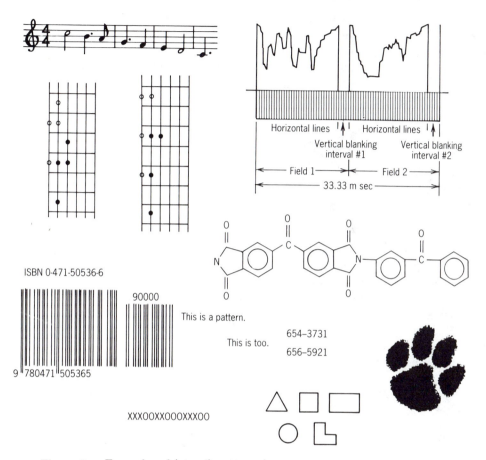

Figure 3:   Examples of (visual) patterns/measurements.

'noise.' Features may be represented by continuous, discrete, or discrete-binary variables. *Binary features* may be used to represent the presence or absence of a particular feature.

The related problems of *feature selection* and *feature extraction* must be addressed at the outset of any PR system design. The key is to choose and to extract features that (1) are computationally feasible; (2) lead to 'good' PR system success[2]; and (3) reduce the problem data (e.g., raw measurements) into a manageable amount of information without discarding valuable (or vital) information.

Feature Selection.   *Feature selection* is the process of choosing input to the PR system and involves judgment. It is important that the extracted features be relevant to the PR task at hand. In some cases there are mathematical tools that help in feature selection. In other cases, simulation may aid in the choice of appropriate features. Clearly,

---

[2]Perhaps in the form of small (mis)-classification errors.

restrictions on measurement systems may limit the set of possible features. Furthermore, features need not be low-level data. However, the level at which features are extracted determines the amount of necessary preprocessing and may also influence the amount of error that is introduced into the extracted features. For example, in medical applications the features may be *symptoms* and the classes might be states of health, including $w_1 =$ 'healthy,' $w_2 =$ 'has the flu,' and so forth.

Pattern Distortions—A Fundamental and Difficult Problem

Often, we seek classification, recognition, or description of a pattern that is invariant to some (known) changes or deviation in the pattern from the 'ideal' case. These deviations may be due to a variety of causes, including 'noise.' However, in many situations a set of patterns *from the same class* may exhibit wide variations from a single exemplar of the class. For example, humans are able to recognize (that is, classify) printed or handwritten characters with widely varying font sizes and orientations. Although the exact mechanism that facilitates this capability is unknown, it appears that the matching strongly involves structural analysis of each character. This is in contrast to a straightforward template matching or correlation approach (Appendix 5), which is usually unsuccessful in applications with significant pattern distortions.

Examples of pattern perturbations are shown in Figure 4. In this case, a careful choice of *invariant features* and pattern structure could be used for recognition. For example, in image processing PR applications, we often seek recognition of objects when the objects may be in arbitrary positions (Translated), angular orientations (Rotated), and Scale. Thus, RST invariant features [Casasent 1976], [Schalkoff 1989] are desired.

EXAMPLE 1: Feature Extraction Using Generalized Cylinders for 3-D Object Description and Classification

The classification of 3-D objects from visual (image) data is an important pattern recognition task. This task exemplifies many aspects of a typical PR problem, including feature selection, dimensionality reduction (3-D world information is mapped onto a 2-D image), and the use of qualitative and structural descriptors. Generalized cylinder (GC) [Agin/Binford 1976], [Biederman 1985] models of 3-D objects provide a framework for the following:

1. Models for class-specific generation of features;

2. Feature extraction; and

3. Structural approaches to building more complex 3-D objects.

The basis of GC models is the concept of a 'swept volume' of 2-D area along a 3-D trajectory. Specifically, a generalized cylinder is a solid whose axis is a 3-D space curve. Usually the axis is perpendicular to the cross section. For example, the typical cylinder or 'can' may be described by sweeping a circle along a line. We characterize a generalized cylinder by three parameters:

"Nominal" pattern   Dilation (magnification)   Displacement (translation)   Rotation

(a)

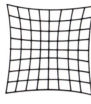 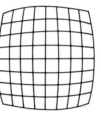

(b)

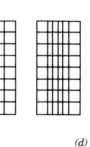

(c)

(d)

Figure 4:   Examples of pattern distortions (visual patterns).
     (a) Geometric distortions of visual (image) patterns-square.
     (b) Geometric distortions of grid pattern.
     (c) Geometric distortions of character patterns.
     (d) More extreme pattern distortions (missing parts and extra
       parts) using the patterns of parts (a) to (c).

1. A planar cross section;
2. A three-dimensional curve or 'spine'; and
3. A sweeping rule.

As shown in Figure 5, different 3-D objects may be generated by defining the following features:

1. A qualitative descriptor of the cross section edge curvature. This may be either straight (S) or curved (C).
2. The cross section degree of symmetry. Symmetry is defined as invariant under reflection and rotation (Symm++), invariant under reflection only (Symm+), or asymmetric (Asymm).
3. The change of cross section as a function of sweep. This may be constant (Const), expanding (Exp), contracting (Contr), expanding then contracting (Exp-Contr), or contracting then expanding (Contr-Exp).
4. The degree of curvature of the spine. This may be straight (S) or curved (C).

Edges: *S*
Symmetry: Symm + +
Cross-section-size Const
Axis: *S*

Edges: *C*
Symmetry: Symm + +
Cross-section-size: Const
Axis: *S*

Edges: *S*
Symmetry: Symm +
Cross-section-size: Exp
Axis: *S*

Edges: *C*
Symmetry: Symm +
Cross-section-size: Exp
Axis: *S*

Edges: *S*
Symmetry: Symm +
Cross-section-size: Exp
Axis: *C*

Edges: *C*
Symmetry: Symm +
Cross-section size: Exp
Axis *C*

Figure 5:   Example of feature extraction for 3-D figures.

Samples of generalized cylinder representations, together with corresponding qualitative features, are shown in Figure 5.

The generalized cylinder approach may be used in a hierarchical pattern representation scheme in which generalized cylinders are primitives and composition rules specify the relative orientations of the primitives [Schalkoff 1989].   ■

EXAMPLE 2: Generating RST Invariant Features and Application to 2-D Figure Recognition

Background.   A common PR application involves the recognition of 2-D shapes from visual (image) data. An example of several classes of shapes, hereafter referred to as regions, is shown in Figure 6. We show the approach and note the processing complexity required to achieve RST invariance.

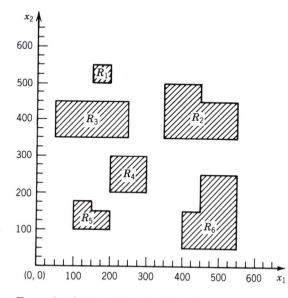

Figure 6:   Example of 2-D regions for RST feature extraction.

Moments are extracted features that are derived from the raw measurements and that, in 2-D, may be used to achieve rotation (R), scale (S), and translation (T) (or position) invariant. Observe from Figure 6 that several regions are scaled, rotated, and translated versions of one another.   ■

Feature Extraction

For simplicity, the strategy is shown for the continuous case. Given 2-D input data $f(x, y)$, a set of moment features [Hu 1961] is defined via

$$m_{pq} = \int_{-\infty}^{\infty} \int_{-\infty}^{\infty} x^p y^q f(x, y) dx\, dy \qquad p, q = 0, 1, 2 \dots \qquad (1-1)$$

So called *central moments*, μ_{pq} are defined via

$$\mu_{pq} = \int_{-\infty}^{\infty} \int_{-\infty}^{\infty} (x - \hat{x})^p (y - \hat{y})^q f(x, y) dx\, dy \qquad p, q = 0, 1, 2 \dots \qquad (1-2)$$

where $\hat{x} = m_{10}/m_{00}$ and $\hat{y} = m_{01}/m_{00}$. As shown in [Schalkoff 1989], the central moment-based features convey descriptive information about a region. Normalizing the μ_{pq} features yields

$$\eta_{pq} = \frac{\mu_{pq}}{\mu_{00}^{[(p+q)/2]+1}} \qquad p+q = 2,3\ldots \qquad (1-3)$$

From (1-3) a set of seven RST-invariant features, ϕ_1–ϕ_9, may be derived. They are shown in Table 1.1.

Table 1.1:   Moment-Based RST Invariant Features

$\phi_1 = \eta_{20} + \eta_{02}$

$\phi_2 = (\eta_{20} - \eta_{02})^2 + 4\eta_{11}^2$

$\phi_3 = (\eta_{30} - 3\eta_{12})^2 + (3\eta_{21} - \eta_{03})^2$

$\phi_4 = (\eta_{30} + \eta_{12})^2 + (\eta_{21} + \eta_{03})^2$

$\phi_5 = (\eta_{30} - 3\eta_{12})(\eta_{30} + \eta_{12})[(\eta_{30} + \eta_{12})^2 - 3(\eta_{21} + \eta_{03})^2]$
$\qquad + (3\eta_{21} - \eta_{03})(\eta_{21} + \eta_{03})[3(\eta_{30} + \eta_{12})^2 - (\eta_{21} + \eta_{03})^2]$

$\phi_6 = (\eta_{20} - \eta_{02})[(\eta_{30} + \eta_{12})^2 - (\eta_{21} + \eta_{03})^2] + 4\eta_{11}(\eta_{30} + \eta_{12})(\eta_{21} + \eta_{03})$

$\phi_7 = (3\eta_{21} - \eta_{03})(\eta_{30} + \eta_{12})[(\eta_{30} + \eta_{12})^2 - 3(\eta_{21} + \eta_{03})^2]$
$\qquad - (\eta_{30} - 3\eta_{12})(\eta_{21} + \eta_{03})[3(\eta_{30} + \eta_{12})^2 - (\eta_{21} + \eta_{03})^2]$

Numerical Results and Analysis

Table 1.2 shows ϕ_1–ϕ_9 corresponding to each of the six (binary) regions, R_1–R_6 in Figure 6. Note from Figure 6:

- R_1 and R_4, and R_2 and R_5, are *scaled* versions of one another;
- R_6 is a *rotated* version of R_2 and a *scaled and rotated* version of R_5.

Table 1.2:   Moment-Based Features ϕ_i for R_j $i = 1, 2, \ldots 7$; $j = 1, 2, \ldots 6$

Feature	R_1	R_2	R_3	R_4	R_5	R_6
ϕ_1	$1.67E-01$	$1.94E-01$	$2.083E-01$	$1.67E-01$	$1.94E-01$	$1.94E-01$
ϕ_2	$0.00E+00$	$6.53E-03$	$1.56E-02$	$0.00E+00$	$6.53E-03$	$6.53E-03$
ϕ_3	$0.00E+00$	$1.02E-03$	$0.00E+00$	$0.00E+00$	$1.02E-03$	$1.02E-03$
ϕ_4	$0.00E+00$	$4.56E-05$	$0.00E+00$	$0.00E+00$	$4.56E-05$	$4.56E-05$
ϕ_5	$0.00E+00$	$4.25E-09$	$0.00E+00$	$0.00E+00$	$4.25E-09$	$4.25E-09$
ϕ_6	$0.00E+00$	$1.70E-06$	$0.00E+00$	$0.00E+00$	$1.70E-06$	$1.70E-06$
ϕ_7	$0.00E+00$	$-8.85E-09$	$0.00E+00$	$0.00E+00$	$-8.85E-09$	$-8.85E-09$

Analysis

From Table 1.2 we observe the following:

- Comparing the ϕ_i for R_1 and R_4 and R_2 and R_5 we verify that the ϕ_i are invariant to S and T.
- Comparing the ϕ_i for R_2, R_5 and R_6 we verify that the ϕ_i are invariant to R and S.
- Noting that R_3 is a shape class that is not an RS or T variant of any other R_i, we verify that the ϕ_i for R_3 provide numerical features that allow discrimination *between classes*.

Extensions of this feature extraction and classification technique are shown in [Schalkoff 1989], Chapter 6.

What's Really Different Among Different Patterns?

Since the objective of *pattern recognition or classification* is to distinguish between different types of patterns, it is logical to investigate the basis for this discrimination ability. One intuitive answer is that different patterns (different pattern classes) are composed of different features or features with different numerical values. Unfortunately, this is not generally true. For example, consider a newspaper picture or so-called *halftone*. The picture consists of an array of dots, each being either 'white' or 'black.' If we consider these dots to be the basic features or primitives, we observe that all pictures are made up of the same features. However, in attempting to distinguish between a picture of a car and a picture of a boat, we note that the *spatial arrangements* of these features are decidedly different.

The Concept of Similarity. Much of StatPR, SyntPR, and NeurPR are based on the concept of *pattern similarity*. For example, if a pattern, x, is very similar to other patterns known to belong to class w_1, we would intuitively tend to classify x as belonging in w_1. *Quantifying similarity* by developing suitable *similarity measures* is often quite difficult. Universally applicable similarity measures that enable good classification are both desirable and elusive. Appendix 5 explores this concept further.

The Feature Vector and Feature Space

It is often useful to develop a geometric viewpoint of features, especially in the StatPR case. Features are arranged in a d-dimensional[3] *feature vector*, denoted $\underline{x}$, which yields a multidimensional measurement *space* or *feature space*. If each feature is an unconstrained real number, the feature space is R^d. In other instances, such as the artificial neural network units we consider, it is convenient to restrict feature space to a subspace of R^d. Specifically, if individual neuron outputs and network inputs are restricted to the range $[0, 1]$, for a d-dimensional feature vector, we have a pattern space that is a unit volume hypercube in R^d. Often classification is accomplished by partitioning feature space into regions for each class, as is shown below. Large feature vector dimensionality compounds feature extraction and application of direct pattern recognition approaches. For example, in image processing applications, it is impractical to use directly all the pixel intensities in an image as a feature vector, since a 512×512 pixel image yields a $262,144 \times 1$ feature vector!

Feature vectors are typically used in StatPR and NeurPR. Feature vectors are somewhat inadequate or, at least, cumbersome when it is necessary to represent relations between pattern components. Figure 7 shows how feature extraction is a common, yet different, problem for each PR application and approach.

---

[3]Note that often n is chosen as the dimension of the feature vector. To be consistent with other references, we use d and reserve n for other things, such as number of samples in the training set.

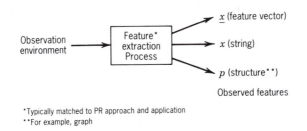

*Typically matched to PR approach and application
**For example, graph

Figure 7:   Input data preprocessing/feature extraction.

Scatter Plots.   Scatter plots are plots of sample feature vectors, $\underline{x}$, in feature space. An example is shown in Figure 8. Where applicable, they are excellent visualization tools for determining feature vector distribution in R^d, where $d \leq 3$. Scatter plots often facilitate identifying natural or obvious clustering of class-specific feature data and the partitioning of R^d into 'decision regions' for classification.

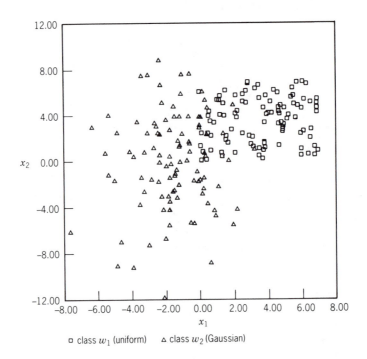

Figure 8: $c = 2$ class scatter plot example.

Definitions

Classification assigns input data into one or more of c prespecified classes based on extraction of significant features or attributes and the processing or analysis of these attributes. It is common to resort to probabilistic or grammatical models in classification.

Recognition is the ability to classify. Often we formulate PR problems with a $c+1$st class, corresponding to the 'unclassifiable' or 'don't know' or 'can't decide' class.

Description is an alternative to classification where a structural description of the input pattern is desired. It is common to resort to linguistic or structural models in description.

A *pattern class* is a set of patterns (hopefully sharing some common attributes) known to originate from the same source in C. The key in many PR applications is to identify suitable attributes (e.g., features) and to form a good measure of similarity and an associated matching process.

Preprocessing is the filtering or transforming of the raw input data to aid computational feasibility and feature extraction and minimize noise.

Noise is a concept originating in communications theory. In PR, the concept is generalized to represent a number of nonideal circumstances, including:

- Distortions or errors in the input signal/pattern (e.g., measurement errors)
- Errors in preprocessing
- Errors in feature extraction
- Errors in training data

Classifiers, Decision Regions and Boundaries, and Discriminant Functions

The concepts of decision regions are most applicable to StatPR and NeurPR. A *classifier* partitions feature space into class-labeled *decision regions*. In order to use decision regions for a possible and unique class assignment, these regions must cover R^d and be disjointed (nonoverlapping). An exception to the last constraint is the notion of fuzzy sets [Zadeh 1975]. The border of each decision region is a *decision boundary*. With this viewpoint, classification of feature vector $\underline{x}$ becomes quite simple: We determine the decision region (in R^d) into which $\underline{x}$ falls, and assign $\underline{x}$ to this class. Although the classification strategy is straightforward, the determination of decision regions is a challenge. It is sometimes convenient, yet not always necessary (or possible), to visualize decision regions and boundaries. Moreover, computational and geometric aspects of certain decision boundaries (e.g., linear classifiers that generate hyperplaner decision boundaries) are noteworthy.

In what follows, we also design a number of classifiers based on *discriminant functions*. In the c-class case, discriminant functions, denoted $g_i(\underline{x})$, $i = 1, 2, \ldots c$, are used to partition R^d as follows.

Decision Rule: Assign $\underline{x}$ to class w_m (region R_m), where $g_m(\underline{x}) > g_i(\underline{x}) \forall i = 1, 2, \ldots c$ and $i \neq m$.

Note that the case where $g_k(\underline{x}) = g_l(\underline{x})$ defines a decision boundary. Figures 9 and 10 show sample examples.

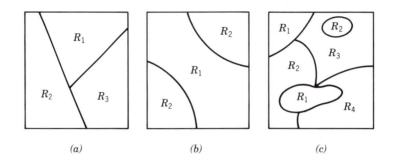

(a)   *(b)*   *(c)*

Figure 9: Sample decision regions (2-D example).
(a) Linear (piecewise).
(b) Quadratic (hyperbolic).
(c) (Relatively) general.

$$g_1(\underline{x}) = \| \underline{x} - \underline{x}_1 \|$$

$$g_2(\underline{x}) = \| \underline{x} - \underline{x}_2 \|$$

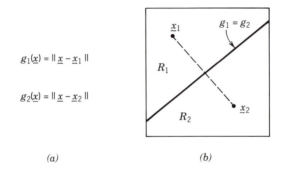

(a)   *(b)*

Figure 10: Discriminant function and corresponding decision regions (minimum distance classifier).
(a) Discriminant functions.
(b) Corresponding partition of R^2.

A particularly important discriminant function form is the *linear discriminant function*:

$$g_i(\underline{x}) = \underline{w}_i^T \underline{x} + w_{0i}$$

where $\underline{w}_i$ is a $d \times 1$ vector of weights used for class i. Appendix 6 shows that this function leads to decision boundaries that are hyperplanes. One important link between StatPR and NeurPR is the use of neural networks to implement discriminant functions.

TRAINING AND LEARNING IN PR SYSTEMS

Using A Priori Knowledge or 'Experience'

In each of the PR approaches we consider, it makes sense to employ the maximum amount of available information in designing the PR system. Intuitively, this would seem to lead to the best achievable system performance. We assume that a certain amount of a priori information, such as sample patterns with known class origin, is available to the PR system designer. In fact, it might appear quite foolish to attempt the design of a PR system without this information.[4]

A set of 'typical' patterns, where typical attributes or the class or structure of each is known, forms a database denoted the *training set* denoted H. In a general sense, the training set provides significant information on how to associate input data with output decisions (i.e., classifications or structural descriptions). Training is often associated (or loosely equated) with learning. The training set is used to enable the system to 'learn' relevant information, such as statistical parameters, natural groupings, key features, or underlying structure. In SyntPR, training samples may be used to learn or infer grammars.

Learning Curves (Improved 'Performance')

In areas such as artificial intelligence, learning takes on a more general connotation, somewhat analogous to the self-adaptation processes used by humans [Michalski et. al. 1986], [Schalkoff 1990, Chapter 18]. A learning system may adapt its internal structure to achieve a better response, perhaps on the basis of previous quantified performance. A performance measure could be the difference between desired and actual system output. This generic learning concept is related to the error-correction-based PR techniques we employ in developing linear discriminant functions in StatPR and the generalized delta rule in NeurPR. Both of these techniques are typical of gradient-descent techniques, where the system is modified following each experiment or iteration. This may lead to the typical 'learning curve' behavior in biological experiments, where $P(n)$ denotes the probability of the subject (animal or human) making the correct response in the nth trial of a learning experiment. A typical formula [Bolles 1979] to predict this behavior, which often matches experimental results, is

$$P(n) = 1 - [1 - P(1)](1 - \theta)^{n-1} \ n \geq 1$$

where θ is a learning parameter. This is shown in Figure 11. Unfortunately, the monotonically increasing performance shown in this figure is often difficult to achieve in practical PR systems.

Training Approaches

Training uses representative (and usually labeled) samples of types of patterns to be encountered in the actual application.[5] The training set is denoted H or H_i, where the subscript denotes a training set for a specific pattern class. In this context, *supervised*

---

[4]This is not always true. For example, see unsupervised learning (Chapter 5).

[5]An important extension of this definition, which is especially useful in grammatical inference and reasoning-based PR learning approaches, is that the training set for class w_i contains examples of patterns in w_i (positive exemplars) *as well as examples of patterns not in w_i (negative exemplars).*

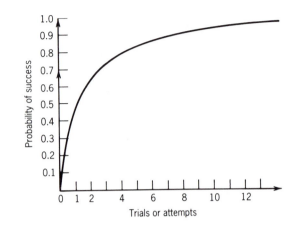

Figure 11:   Typical learning curve.

learning assumes a labeled (with respect to pattern class) set, whereas in *unsupervised* learning, the elements of H do not have class labels and the system must determine 'natural' partitions of the sample data.

Linear Separability of the Training Set.   Suppose we are given the labeled training set $H = \{\underline{x}_1, \underline{x}_2, \ldots \underline{x}_n\}$, where the class labeling partitions $H = \{H_1, H_2, \ldots H_c\}$. Sample $\underline{x}_i$ is assigned to partition H_j if the label on $\underline{x}_i$ is w_j. If a set of *linear discriminant functions* (also referred to as linear machines) can be used to correctly classify every element of H (or, equivalently, generate the decision regions that accomplish this), then a *linearly separable* problem results. A useful lemma is [Nilsson 1965] if H is linearly separable, then the partitions of H, that is, $H_1, H_2, \ldots H_c$, are *pairwise linearly separable*.

PATTERN RECOGNITION APPROACHES

Pattern recognition applications come in many forms. In some instances, there is an underlying and quantifiable *statistical basis* for the generation of patterns. In other instances, the underlying *structure* of the pattern provides the information fundamental for PR. In still others, neither of the above cases hold true, but we are able to develop and 'train' an architecture to correctly associate input patterns with desired responses. Thus, a given problem may allow one or more of these different solution approaches. When faced with solving a problem, one of the guiding principles an engineer or a scientist should apply is, loosely speaking, 'Use the right tool for the job!'

The Statistical Pattern Recognition Approach (StatPR)

Statistical (or 'decision-theoretic') PR assumes, as its name implies, a statistical basis for classification of algorithms. A set of characteristic measurements, denoted features, are extracted from the input data and are used to assign each feature vector to one of c classes. Features are assumed generated by a state of nature, and therefore the underlying model is of a state of nature or class-conditioned set of probabilities and/or probability density functions.

The Syntactic Pattern Recognition Approach (SyntPR)

Many times the significant information in a pattern is not merely in the presence or absence, or the numerical values, of a set of features. Rather, the interrelationships or interconnections of features yield important *structural* information, which facilitates structural description or classification. This is the basis of syntactic (or structural) pattern recognition. However, in using SyntPR approaches, we must be able to quantify and extract structural information and to assess structural similarity of patterns. One syntactic approach is to relate the structure of patterns with the syntax of a formally defined language, in order to capitalize on the vast body of knowledge related to pattern (sentence) generation and analysis (parsing).

Typically, SyntPR approaches formulate hierarchical descriptions of complex patterns built up from simpler subpatterns. At the lowest level, *primitive elements* or 'building blocks' are extracted from the input data. One discrepancy or distinguishing characteristic of SyntPR involves the choice of primitives. *Primitives must be subpatterns or building blocks, whereas features are any measurements.*

Structural PR Example.   Musical patterns are one of the best examples in which *structural information* is paramount. At the risk of being overly simplistic,[6] we observe that all (Western) music basically consists of the same elemental features—an octave is subdivided into distinct tones, and we use about 6 octaves. Therefore, the feature set for all types of music is about 72 distinct tones, which are common to all musical classes. It is the temporal arrangement and structure of these notes that defines the music.

Is SyntPR Dead?   It is probably worth asking this question, since there are PR observers who adamantly believe that SyntPR is a 'fading' field. It is true that the pattern representation capability of tractable formal grammars is somewhat limited, chiefly because of parsing difficulties. Advances in formal language research may alleviate this limitation. However, SyntPR encompasses a much broader spectrum of approaches, including representations such as trees and attributed graphs (Chapter 8). The SyntPR approach using graphical descriptions of structure appears to be gaining popularity, especially in areas like model-based vision and AI. Indeed, many applications exist where StatPR representational capabilities are limited and are surpassed by SyntPR capabilities. Examples might be speech recognition and handwriting analysis. Furthermore, recent studies indicate that powerful pattern representation capabilities may be achieved by combining StatPR and SyntPR in a syntactic-semantic approach [Fu 1986].

---

[6]Of course, timbre and other features also play a role.

The Neural Pattern Recognition Approach (NeurPR)

Modern digital computers do not emulate the computational paradigm of biological systems. The alternative of *neural computing* emerged from attempts to draw on knowledge of how biological neural systems store and manipulate information. This leads to a class of *artificial neural systems* termed *neural networks.* This study involves an amalgamation of research in many diverse fields such as psychology, neuroscience, cognitive science, and systems theory, and has recently received considerable renewed worldwide attention. Neural networks are a relatively new computational paradigm. It is probably safe to say that the advantages, disadvantages, applications, and relationships to traditional computing are not fully understood. Expectations (some might say 'hype') for this area are high. As shown in Chapters 11 to 13, neural networks are particularly well suited for pattern association applications. The notion that artificial neural networks can solve all problems in automated reasoning, or even all PR problems, is probably unrealistic. Neural networks are considered in this text as a means for implementing pattern recognition systems.

Comparing and Relating StatPR, SyntPR, and NeurPR

The boundaries between StatPR, SyntPR, and NeurPR are fuzzy and fading. They share common features and common goals. Often, given a specific PR problem, we choose one approach over another based on analysis of underlying *statistical* components (StatPR), underlying *grammatical* structure (SyntPR), as well as suitability of a *neural network* solution (and training ability), and perhaps lack of suitable statistical or structural models (e.g., 'black box').

In the StatPR or decision theoretic approach, the structure of the pattern is often deemed insignificant. However, the structure *could* be reflected by a suitable choice of features (e.g., a binary feature vector could indicate the presence or absence of observed relations). Similarly, the NeurPR approach is, in some cases, an implementation derived from StatPR and SyntPR approaches. When explicit structural information about the patterns is available, it makes sense to choose SyntPR. When this information is either unavailable or irrelevant, then StatPR may be used. Many practical PR applications fall between these two extremes. For example, an attributed grammar [Tsai/Fu 1980] provides a means to combine statistical and syntactic approaches. This is explored in Chapter 8.

Neural pattern classification is an emerging area with roots dating back approximately 30 years. It is still unclear whether we should consider NeurPR as a novel concept in pattern recognition (or computing) or merely a set of alternative techniques for the implementation of statistical or structural approaches. Table 1.3 and Figures 12 through 15 summarize the different PR approaches.

Examples of Pattern Recognition Approaches

The remainder of the text provides a detailed investigation of individual PR approaches. Three simple examples are shown here to give the reader a flavor of the approaches, as well as their differences.

Table 1.3:   Comparing StatPR, SyntPR, and NeurPR Approaches

	StatPR	SyntPR	NeurPR
1. Pattern Generation (Storing) Basis	Probabilistic Models	Formal Grammars	Stable State or Weight Array
2. Pattern Classification (Recognition/ Description) Basis	Estimation/ Decision Theory	Parsing	Based on (Predictable) Properties of NN
3. Feature Organization	Feature Vector	Primitives and Observed Relations	Neural Input or Stored States
4. Typical Learning (Training) Approaches			
Supervised:	Density/distribution estimation (usually parametric)	Forming grammars (heuristic or grammatical inference)	Determining NN system parameters (e.g., weights)
Unsupervised:	Clustering	Clustering	Clustering
5. Limitations	Difficulty in expressing structural information	Difficulty in learning structural rules	Often little semantic information from network

StatPR

EXAMPLE 3: Elementary Application of Statistical Pattern Recognition to Image Data (Remote Sensing)

Landsat Image Features and Land Type Determination.   Satellite-based sensors in orbit around the earth are one of the largest sources of quantitative image data. The acquired earth images, which may be spectrally distributed, contain information that has significant military, economic, and humanitarian application. For example, the identification of earth areas containing likely mineral deposits or the classification of areas on the basis of vegetation (i.e., specific crops) is possible. A comprehensive bibliography of remote sensing research is presented in [Land 1981].

A series of satellites used for earth remote sensing constitute the Landsat program, initiated in 1972 and somewhat defunct in 1990. Landsat satellites are equipped with multispectral scanner systems (MSS), which generate a feature vector for every pixel in the Landsat image, with the ith component of the feature vector representing the intensity response in a particular spectrum at this pixel location. For example, Table 1.4 shows nominal spectral parameters for the early generation Landsat sensors.

Useful applications of Landsat data are in land use classification and cartography. Development of a map that indicates type of land (e.g., sand, trees, mountains, and

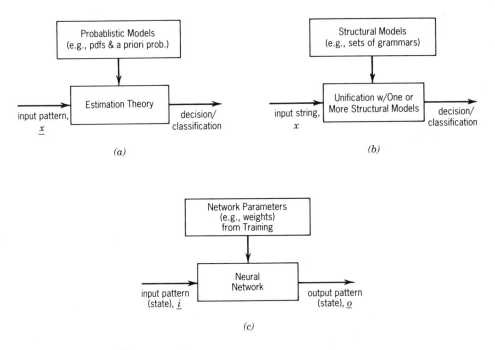

Figure 12:   PR approaches.
  (a) Statistical PR (StatPR) approach.
  (b) Syntactic PR (SyntPR) approach.
  (c) Neural network (NeurPR) approach.

water) imaged is desirable. Because of the different spectral responses of these types of land (e.g., the response of sand in the spectra shown in Table 1.4 is different from that of water), it is possible to postulate a class-specific model, train the model, and then allow the system to autonomously classify pixels into one of these regions. As shown in [Land 1981], experiments with Landsat image data, using these four features

Table 1.4:   Nominal Landsat Spectral
  Parameters for Image
  Point-Specific Features

Feature	Wavelength	Band
x_1	0.50–0.60μm	visible
x_2	0.60–0.70μm	visible
x_3	0.70–0.80μm	near IR
x_4	0.80–1.10μm	near IR

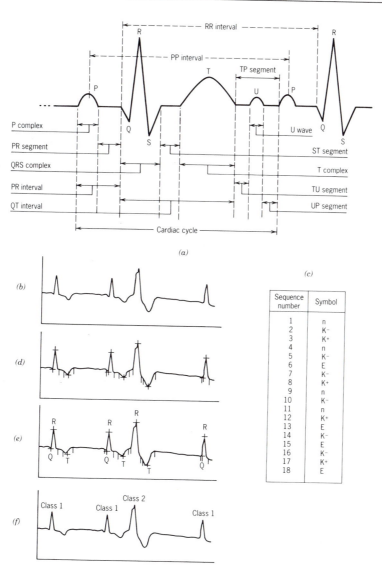

(a)

(b)

(c)

Sequence number	Symbol
1	n
2	K⁻
3	K⁺
4	n
5	K⁻
6	E
7	K⁻
8	K⁺
9	n
10	K⁻
11	n
12	K⁺
13	E
14	K⁻
15	E
16	K⁻
17	K⁺
18	E

(d)

(e)

(f)

Figure 13: Use of SyntPR for ECG waveform description and classification
(from [Trahanias/Skordalakis 1990]).
  (a) A cardiac cycle and its constituent patterns.
  (b) Input waveform.
  (c) Extracted primitives from waveform of (b).
  (d) Graphical display of extracted primitives from (c).
  (e) Recognized ECG cycles and constituent patterns from
      (d).
  (f) Classification of QRS complexes from ECG cycles of (e).

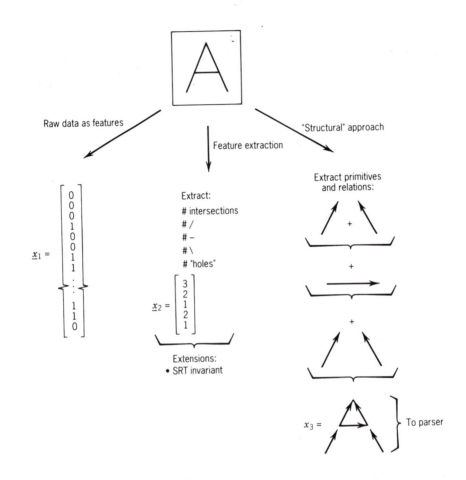

Figure 14: Example of PR approaches.
(a) Input pattern.
(b) Possible feature extraction approaches.

alone (following a training phase), yield a classification error of approximately 17%. Since we have considered only *spectral* features, it is natural to attempt even smaller error rates by extraction of other features, for example, *spatial* and *temporal* features.[7] Spatial features typically used in Landsat data classification, and more generally image segmentation, include *texture, context, shape, and structural relationships.* Note that generally an increase in classification accuracy requires a corresponding increase in the computational cost of the classification procedure. ■

---

[7]This leads to *contextual classification.*

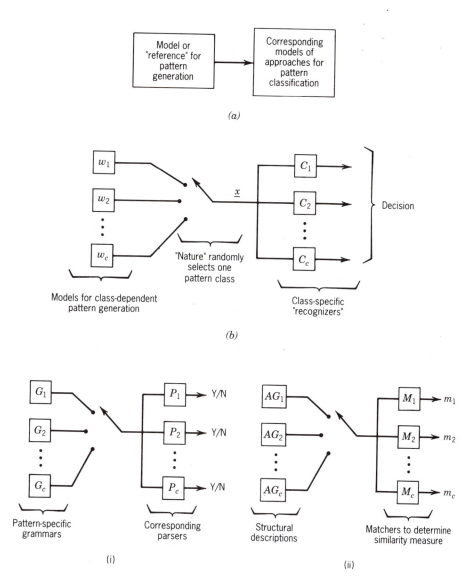

(a)

(b)

(c)

Figure 15:   Relating StatPR and SyntPR in the context of model-based PR.
(a) Overall structure.
(b) StatPR example.
(c) SyntPR examples.
(i) Grammatical approach.
(ii) Attributed-graph approach.

SyntPR

EXAMPLES 4 AND 5:

Suppose we are given an input pattern consisting of a string of characters, each of which is either $'a'$, $'b'$, or $'c'$. These characters may be assignments resulting from the preprocessing of raw input patterns, such as EKG waveforms [Trahanis/Skordalakis 1990] or speech signals. Two states of nature generate two classes of patterns, each characterized by its *structure*. Samples are shown below.

Table 1.5:   Typical Patterns (Strings)

Class 1	Class 2
ac	bc
abc	abc
$abbc$	$aabc$
$abbbc$	$aaabc$

Observe that the class of patterns generated by Class 1 is of the form $ab^n c$ $n \geq 0$ whereas the form *or structure* of Class 2 is $a^n bc$ $n \geq 0$. In addition, note that several patterns belonging to both classes may be generated. In a classification application of SyntPR, given a pattern such as $'aaabbc'$, the goal would be to determine which, if any, class could have produced this pattern.

Figure 13 (from [Trahanias/Skordalakis 1990]) illustrates the application of a syntactic approach to the analysis of electrocardiograms. To facilitate waveform analysis, chosen primitives are waveform positive and negative peaks, straight line segments, and parabolic segments. An alphabet of symbols $V_T = \{K^+, K^-, E, \Pi)$ is used to denote these primitives for a given wave. Primitive extraction thus yields a linguistic representation consisting of a sequence of these symbols, in a form similar to that shown in Table 1.5. Subsequences that comprise patterns are identified and classified, as shown in the figure.   ∎

EXAMPLE 6: Combinations of StatPR and SyntPR

Figure 14 shows a simple character recognition problem wherein a spectrum of PR approaches is possible. As shown, these approaches range from little feature extraction to extraction of complex primitives and accompanying spatial relations.

Figure 15 further relates the StatPR and SyntPR approaches from the viewpoint of model-based pattern generation and 'inversion' of this process in classification. The reader should compare the approaches shown in Figure 11 with the abstract PR formulation shown in Figure 1.   ∎

Procedures for PR System Engineering

In realistic applications, the design of an autonomous PR system is a complex, usually iterative and interactive task. Although it is impossible to provide an all-inclusive algorithmic procedure, the highly interrelated, skeletal steps outlined here reflect typical efforts and concerns.

Step 1: Study the classes of patterns under consideration to develop possible characterizations. This includes assessments of (quantifiable) pattern structure and probabilistic characterizations, as well as exploration of possible within-class and interclass similarity/dissimilarity measures. In addition, possible pattern deformations or invariant properties and characterization of 'noise' sources should be considered at this point.

Step 2: Determine the availability of feature/measurement data.

Step 3: Consider constraints on desired system performance and computational resources (e.g., parts/minute, classification accuracy).

Step 4: Consider the availability of training data.

Step 5: Consider the availability of suitable and known PR techniques (e.g., StatPR, SyntPR, and clustering).   an overall PR system structure.

Step 6: Develop a PR system simulation. This may involve choosing models, grammars, or network structures.

Step 7: Train the system.

Step 8: Simulate system performance.

Step 9: Iterate among the above steps until desired performance is achieved.

OTHER APPROACHES TO PR

'Black Box' Approaches

Both StatPR and SyntPR consider, to some extent, formal mechanisms to convey how patterns might be produced. In StatPR, statistical models are often used, whereas in SyntPR, structural or grammatical models are used.

Often, the quantitative aspects of a complex PR problem are largely unknown, defy quantification, and/or are so complex that detailed modeling is hopeless. An (engineering) alternative to handling problems of this type is to avoid modeling of the pattern-generating mechanism and, instead, to treat the problem from an input/output or 'black box' viewpoint. A black box system is specified by two things: (1) an internal computation; and (2) a stimulus/response (S-R) based training set (e.g., a set of input/output pattern pairs). For example, the human brain is, for purposes of present artificial intelligence implementations, a black box. We are able to observe and emulate intelligent behavior (including pattern recognition and classification) without a detailed set of algorithms that quantify the input–output characteristics of the brain. NeurPR often provides good examples of black box systems in cases where we do not care about the 'internal' semantics of the network but rather simply use training data to achieve good pattern mappings.

Note that under certain assumptions a StatPR approach may be viewed from the black box perspective. It is important to note that the black box implements a *computation*, but this computation may be structurally unrelated to the particular application. For example, the particular application may be reflected only in a choice of parameters used in the computation.

Reasoning-Driven Pattern Recognition

We could argue that all autonomous systems (in particular those that emulate human PR capability) make decisions based on *evidence*. This evidence may exist at varying levels; for example, it may consist of raw feature data (measured voltages, currents, temperatures, and the like), or at a higher level, perhaps as a result of preprocessing. Furthermore, the evidence need not simply come from external inputs; the use of stored information or knowledge may aid in the generation of evidence. The manipulation of evidence forms the basis of many approaches inherent in pattern recognition, learning machines, and expert systems.

Pattern Recognition and Artificial Intelligence.   Certain PR problems have a strong relationship to techniques of artificial intelligence (AI). Numerous research efforts to develop 'expert systems' for PR applications are underway ([Schalkoff 1990], Chapter 13). Consider, for example, the 'incomplete' pattern in Figure 16, which shows a small portion of an object. The human observer, through a somewhat difficult-to-quantify inference process, both recognizes and completes the pattern. We explore a somewhat reduced-order version of this process in the graphical (model-driven) approaches to SyntPR. We note in closing our brief discussion of reasoning-driven PR that emulation of human or biological processes is neither always possible nor desirable. For example, humans have mastered the concept of flight without emulating the mechanisms used by birds. One especially important area of PR and AI overlap is that of classifier design from labeled training data (PR) and the derivation of rules from large data sets [Bundy et. al. 1985], [Goodman/Smyth 1990]. In this case, a set of n labeled samples, each consisting of a d-tuple of features or attributes (which may be symbolic instead of numerical values, such as color) $a_1, a_2 \ldots a_c$ and a corresponding classification label, w_c, are assumed given. In the PR domain, the objective is to determine a *classifier*, whereas the AI objective is to use the data to infer a set of general *rules* that produce the desired class.[8]

OVERVIEW OF PR LITERATURE AND RESOURCES

Each of the following chapters contains a Bibliographical Remarks section that provides further references that are related to the specific chapter topics. What follows is a summary of general PR resources.

---

[8]This classifier may take any number of forms.

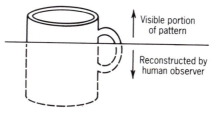

Figure 16:   Example of reasoning-driven PR.

Books

The field of PR is thoroughly covered in books devoted to this subject. However, the coverage is usually partitioned along StatPR, SyntPR, or NeurPR lines.

Statistical pattern recognition is explored in depth in books by [Duda/Hart 1973], [Devijer/Kittler 1982], [Fukunaga 1972], [Bow 1984], [Watanabe 1985], [Chien 1978], [Chen 1973], [Patrick 1972], [Young/Calvert 1974], [Sklansky 1973], [Agarwala 1977], [Jain/Dubes 1988], and [Therrien 1989].

Coverage of syntactic pattern recognition approaches are presented in [Fu 1 1982], [Tou/Gonzalez 1974], [Gonzalez/Thomason 1978], [Miclet 1986], and [Pavlidis 1977]. A unified view of StatPR and SyntPR is shown in [Fu 1980]. An interesting and heavily mathematically oriented approach, which explores StatPR and some aspects of reasoning-driven PR and PR applications in Artificial Intelligence, is presented in [Patrick/Fattu 1986].

Fundamental neural network architecture and application book references are [Anderson/Rosenfeld 1988], [Kohonen 1984], [Pao 1989], [Khanna 1990], and [Rummelhart/McClelland 1, 2 1986].

Journals

Work on various aspects of PR continues to cross-pollinate journals. Useful sources include the following:

- *Pattern Recognition* (letters)
- *Pattern Recognition* (journal)
- *IEEE Transactions on Systems, Man and Cybernetics*
- *IEEE Transactions on Pattern Analysis and Machine Intelligence*
- *IEEE Transactions on Acoustics, Speech and Signal Processing*
- *IEEE Transactions on Information Theory*
- *IEEE Transactions on Geoscience and Remote Sensing*
- *IEEE Transactions on Industrial Electronics*
- *IEEE Transactions on Neural Networks*
- *Optical Engineering* (SPIE)

- *Image and Vision Computing*
- *Neural Networks*
- *Applied Optics*

Conferences

Major related and periodic conferences include:

- International Conference on Pattern Recognition (sponsored by International Association for Pattern Recognition)
- IEEE Computer Vision and Image Processing Conference (formerly Pattern Recognition and Image Processing)
- International Joint Conferences on Neural Networks (IJCNN, cosponsored by IEEE).

EXERCISES

1.1   Distinguish between a pattern and a signal.

1.2   Suppose you were charged with the design of a PR system for character recognition. Suggest some RST invariant features.

1.3   Does a knowledge of *similarity* necessarily imply a knowledge of *dissimilarity*?

1.4   Distinguish between a feature and a measurement.

1.5   Show examples of features that are not primitives and vice versa.

1.6   Cite examples of applications where StatPR is more appropriate than SyntPR and vice versa.

1.7   Try to relate SyntPR with StatPR by using the SyntPR Example 2. What *features* of the pattern are useful for classification? Do you expect difficulty in statistically characterizing these features?

1.8   Repeat Example 2 (moment features for RST invariance) by using just region boundary data or the outline from Figure 6 as the raw data for moment calculations. Are the ϕ_i still RST invariant?

1.9   Again referring to Example 2 for the data of Figure 6, consider the use of a single, simpler feature for each R_i, namely,

$$D_i = \frac{A_{R_i}}{(P_{R_i})^2}$$

where A_{R_i} is the *area* of region R_i and P_{R_i} is the corresponding *perimeter*.

1.10   For the following set of characters

$$A \quad B \quad C \quad D \quad E$$

develop a set of features that allow unique identification of each character. (Hint: Consider possibilities such as total number of segments, number of straight segments, number of curved segments, number of enclosed regions, etc.) Discuss the feasibility of extracting these features.

1.11   Consider the recognition of the character 'E' in the presence of a reasonable set of pattern perturbations, including orientation, scale, script (handwritten) versus printed, and the like. What types of features would you extract to achieve recognition invariant to these distortions?

Part 2

Statistical Pattern Recognition (StatPR)

Introduction to Statistical Pattern Recognition

2

Since the measuring device has been constructed by the observer . . . we have to remember that what we observe is not nature in itself but nature exposed to our method of questioning.

Physics and Philosophy [1958]
Werner Karl Heisenberg, 1901–1976

INTRODUCTION TO STATISTICAL PATTERN RECOGNITION

The first part of our exploration of StatPR might appropriately be titled 'Part 1: What you would do to design a PR system, on a rigorous probabilistic basis, if you know a lot about the underlying problem characterizations.' This yields a formal and precise 'decision theoretic' approach, which may not be quite as simple or practical because of the necessary a priori information. Following this, we develop algorithms and approaches that facilitate extraction of the necessary information from a training set. Even though there are many cases in which the latter approach is not practical, it leads to more intuitive and practical alternatives.

Approaches to Developing StatPR Classifiers

In StatPR, we concentrate on developing *decision* or *classification strategies*, which form *classifiers*. Classifier design attempts to integrate all available problem information, such as measurements and a priori probabilities. Decision rules may be formulated in several interrelated ways, for example:

- By converting an a priori class probability $P(w_i)$ into a measurement-conditioned ('a posteriori') probability $P(w_i|\underline{x})$.

34

- By formulating a measure of expected classification error or 'risk,' and choosing a decision rule that minimizes this measure.

Both strategies lead to a partitioning of R^d and may be implemented via discriminant functions.

We begin our exploration of StatPR by considering a series of examples in order of increasing complexity and involving several 'typical' density forms. Recall that c denotes the number of classes and d denotes the dimension of feature space.

Simple Examples of Statistical Models and Applications

EXAMPLE 1: No Measurement, $c = 2$

Suppose we are given a $c = 2$ class problem where $P(w_1) = 0.7$ and $P(w_2) = 0.3$ with *no measurement* (and consequently no features), and are asked for a classification rule.[1] Denoting the probability of classification error as $P(\text{error})$, and defining $P(\text{error}) = P(\text{choose } w_2|w_1)P(w_1) + P(\text{choose } w_1|w_2)P(w_2)$, we are able to incorporate the given a priori information in the following decision rule: 'Always choose w_1, since $P(w_1) > P(w_2)$.' Notice that this leads to $P(\text{error}) = P(\text{choose } w_1|w_2)P(w_2) = (1)(0.3) = 0.3$. ■

EXAMPLE 2: Single Measurement, $c = 2$, Gaussian Densities, Equal A Priori Probabilities

Consider the case where $d = 1$, $c = 2$, $P(w_1) = P(w_2)$ and

$$p(x|w_i) = \frac{1}{\sqrt{2\pi}\sigma} exp\left\{ -\frac{1}{2}\left(\frac{x - \mu_i}{\sigma}\right)^2 \right\}$$

This is already a somewhat specialized case, since the variance and a priori probabilities for both classes are the same. Thus, only the class means (it is assumed $\mu_1 \neq \mu_2$) provide class-specific information. These are shown in Figure 1(a). We observe that Bayes rule yields $P(w_i|x) = p(x|w_i)\left[P(w_i)/p(x)\right]$, where $p(x)$ is the unconditional density function. Therefore, we adopt the decision rule: 'choose w_1 if $p(x|w_1) > p(x|w_2)$, otherwise choose w_2.' This leads to the decision regions defined by α, as shown in Figure 1(a).

Error Assessment.   This classification strategy may also be approached by a consideration of classification error. We formally define $P(\text{error})$ as

$$P(\text{error}) = P(\underline{x} \text{ is assigned to the wrong class})$$

For a $c = 2$ class problem, this may be expanded as:

$$P(\text{error}) = P(\text{choose } w_1 \text{ and } x \text{ actually from } w_2)$$

$$+P(\text{choose } w_2 \text{ and } x \text{ actually from } w_1)$$

---

[1]The reader may initially balk at attempting to solve such an apparently unpromising problem. However, it illustrates an important point.

$$= P(\text{error } |w_1)P(w_1) + P(\text{error } |w_2)P(w_2)$$
$$= P(\underline{x} \in R_2|w_1)P(w_1) + P(\underline{x} \in R_1|w_2)P(w_2)$$
$$= P(x < \alpha|w_2)P(w_2) + P(x > \alpha|w_1)P(w_1)$$
$$= P(w_2) \int_{-\infty}^{\alpha} p(\varsigma|w_2)d\varsigma + P(w_1) \int_{\alpha}^{\infty} p(\varsigma|w_1)d\varsigma$$

This is shown by the crosshatched regions in Figure 1(a). The exercises explore this further. ■

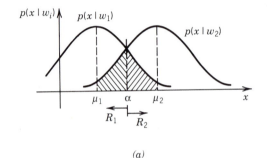

(a)

Figure 1(a):   Densities for Example 2.

Interpretation of Example 2 as a 'Minimum-Distance' Classifier.   The previous choice of α leads to the decision rule and partitioning of R^1 into R_1 and R_2, as is shown in Figure 1(a). For $P(w_1) = P(w_2)$, this may also be phrased as: 'Assign x to R_i, where x is closest to μ_i.' This is our first minimum distance classifier.

EXAMPLE 3:   Extended $c = 2$ $d = 2$ Classifier Design

Suppose we are charged with the design of an autonomous PR system to identify two types of machine parts. One part, which is denoted a 'shim,' is typically dark and has no surface intensity variation or 'texture.' Another part, denoted a 'machine bolt,' is predominantly bright and has considerable surface intensity variation. For illustration, we consider only texture and brightness as features, thus yielding a 2-D *feature space.* We also assume that these features are extractable from suitable raw measurements. Other possible features, such as shape, weight, and the like, may also be used. The problem, as formulated, is nontrivial since these features are only *typical* of each part type. There exist cases of shims that are bright and textured and bolts that are dark and have little texture, although they are *atypical*, that is, they do not occur often. More importantly, when features overlap, perfect classification is not possible. Therefore, we consider classification error, $P(\text{error})$, which indicates the likelihood that an incorrect classification or decision occurs. A more general cost or risk measure may be associated with a classification strategy.

Specifically, we define a 2×1 feature vector, $\underline{x}$, with element x_i, $i = 1, 2$, as a *feature* of the entities. Here we choose x_1 as measured brightness and x_2 as measured texture. We also define w_i as a *class*, or a 'state of nature,' where w_1 is taken to be shim and w_2 a bolt.

Thus, if the underlying class is w_1 (shims), we expect typical measurements of x_1 and x_2 (brightness and texture, respectively) to be small, whereas if the object under observation is from w_2 (bolts), we expect the values of x_1 and x_2 to be, on the average, large (or at least larger than those of w_1). This relationship is shown graphically in Figure 1(b). Of particular importance is the region where values of the features overlap. In this area errors in classification are likely.

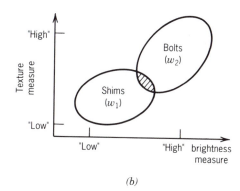

(b)

Figure 1(b):   Typical ranges of feature values for the 'shim–bolt' classification, Example 3.

The extracted features are arranged as a 2×1 feature vector, $\underline{x}^T = (x_1, x_2)$. $\underline{x}$ is one realization of a continuous random vector, $\underline{X}$. The case of discrete r.v.s is treated later. Suppose the *class conditioned probability density functions for the feature vector*, that is, $p(x_1, x_2 | w_i)$, or simply $p(\underline{x}|w_i)$ where $i = 1, 2$, are available. (This may be the result of training or learning experiments.) Finally, assume that something is known about the a priori (i.e., before measurement) likelihood of the occurrence of class w_1 or w_2; specifically assume the a priori probabilities $P(w_i), i = 1, 2$, are known.[2] For example, if we know that on a given day we inspect four times as many shims as bolts, then $P(w_1) = 0.8$ and $P(w_2) = 0.2$. In the absence of this information, an often reasonable assumption is that $P(w_1) = P(w_2)$, that is, the a priori probabilities of the states of nature are equal.

The statistical PR classification problem may now be cast succinctly as:

- Determine a strategy for classifying samples, based on the measurement of $\underline{x}$, such that *classification error is minimized*. ∎

'Generating' Feature Vectors with Density Functions.   In developing models that characterize the class-specific generation of feature vectors, we must be careful to observe the correct role of a (class-specific) density function. Density functions are charac-

---

[2]These are probabilities, not densities, since the w_i are considered realizations of a discrete random variable.

terizations of random vectors: they do not 'generate' random vectors. As shown in Appendix 2, $\underline{X}$ is generated by a mapping function and the outcome of an experiment [Papoulis 1984]. Often the loose jargon '$\underline{X}$ is generated by $p(\underline{x})$' is used. Rather, '$\underline{X}$ (partially) characterized by $p(\underline{x})$' is correct. Appendix 2 shows numerical methods for simulating r.v.s that may be characterized by a prespecified density function, $p(\underline{x})$.

To enable a rigorous solution of the problem, Bayes theorem is used. The a priori estimate of the probability of a certain class is converted to the a posteriori, or *measurement conditioned*, probability of a state of nature via

$$P(w_i|\underline{x}) = \frac{[p(\underline{x}|w_i)P(w_i)]}{p(\underline{x})} \qquad (2-1)$$

where

$$p(\underline{x}) = \sum_i p(\underline{x}|w_i)\,P(w_i) \qquad (2-2)$$

This is shown in Figure 2.

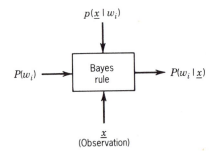

Figure 2:   Converting $P(w_i)$ to $P(w_i|\underline{x})$ via $\underline{x}$.

An Intuitive Classification Strategy.   Minimization of the previously defined classification error requires that a given realization or sample vector, $\underline{x}$, is classified by choosing the state of nature, w_i, for which $P(w_i|\underline{x})$ is largest. This is also intuitively reasonable. Notice in (2-1) the quantity $p(\underline{x})$ is common to all class-conditional probabilities; therefore, it represents a scaling factor that may be eliminated. Thus, in our shim–bolt example, the decision or classification algorithm is

$$\text{choose} \begin{cases} w_1 & \text{if } p(\underline{x}|w_1)P(w_1) > p(\underline{x}|w_2)P(w_2) \\ w_2 & \text{if } p(\underline{x}|w_2)P(w_2) > p(\underline{x}|w_1)P(w_1) \end{cases} \qquad (2-3)$$

Note also that any monotonically nondecreasing function of $P(w_i|\underline{x})$ may be used for this test.

Equation (2-3) is significant in that both a priori information $[P(w_i)]$ and measurement-related information $[p(\underline{x}|w_i)]$ are *combined* in the decision procedure. If $P(w_1) \neq$

$P(w_2)$, for example, this information may be explicitly incorporated in the decision process.

THE GAUSSIAN CASE AND CLASS DEPENDENCE

Gaussian Models for $p(\underline{x}|w_i)$

Gaussian models are popular because of their mathematical tractability. Consider a multidimensional Gaussian distribution:

$$p(\underline{x}) = (2\pi)^{-\frac{d}{2}}|\Sigma|^{-\frac{1}{2}} \exp\left[-\frac{1}{2}(\underline{x} - \underline{\mu})^T \Sigma^{-1}(\underline{x} - \underline{\mu})\right] \qquad (2-4)$$

where $\underline{x}$ is $d \times 1$ with mean vector $\underline{\mu}$ and covariance matrix Σ. The symmetry of the $d \times d$ covariance matrix allows complete specification of this distribution by $d + d(d+1)/2$ parameters, which may still prove computationally impractical for large d.

Introducing Class Dependence.   Assume that the class-conditional density functions are given by (2-4). The class dependence is obtained parametrically via *class specific mean vectors and covariance matrices*, that is, $\underline{\mu}_i$ and Σ_i.

DISCRIMINANT FUNCTIONS

Define a *discriminant function* for the ith class from (2-1) as

$$g_i(\underline{x}) = P(w_i|\underline{x}) \qquad (2-5)$$

Given a feature vector, $\underline{x}$, classification according to (2-1) and (2-3) is based on finding the largest discriminant function. Assuming equal a priori probabilities, this means choosing the class for which $p(\underline{x}|w_i)$ is largest. As indicated above, any monotonically increasing function of $g_i(\underline{x})$ is also a valid discriminant function. The log function meets this requirement, that is, an alternative discriminant function is

$$g_i'(\underline{x}) = \log\{p(\underline{x}|w_i)\} \qquad (2-6)$$

We now further simplify the model to illustrate the solution approach. In the Gaussian case with assumed equal covariance matrices (i.e., class dependence is only through the mean vectors, $\underline{\mu}_i$), (2-6) yields

$$g_i'(\underline{x}) = -\frac{1}{2}(\underline{x} - \underline{\mu}_i)^T \Sigma^{-1}(\underline{x} - \underline{\mu}_i) - \left(\frac{d}{2}\right)\log(2\pi) - \frac{1}{2}\log|\Sigma| \qquad (2-7)$$

The second and third terms in (2-7) are class-independent constant biases and may be eliminated. Observe, however, that Σ influences classification through the first term, which is the squared distance of feature vector $\underline{x}$ from the ith mean vector, $\underline{\mu}_i$, weighted by the inverse of the covariance matrix, Σ^{-1}. Appendix 6 considers various aspects of this quadratic term as a function of properties of Σ^{-1}. In the case where $\Sigma = I$, a Euclidean distance norm results. It is worthwhile to examine the quantity

$$d_i^2 = (\underline{x} - \underline{\mu}_i)^T \Sigma^{-1} (\underline{x} - \underline{\mu}_i) \qquad (2-8)$$

from (2-7). For a given $\underline{x}$, $g_i'(\underline{x})$ in (2-7) is largest when d_i^2 in (2-8) is smallest. Another viewpoint is that we are 'matching' $\underline{x}$ against each of the $\underline{\mu}_i$ and classifying based on the best match. Consider the case where $\Sigma = I$ in (2-8), we expand d_i^2 as

$$\| \underline{x} - \underline{\mu}_i \|^2 = \underline{x}^T \underline{x} - 2\underline{\mu}_i^T \underline{x} + \underline{\mu}_i^T \underline{\mu}_i \qquad (2-9)$$

This formulation yields our introduction to a *linear discriminant function or correlation detector* of the form:

$$g_i(\underline{x}) = \underline{w}_i^T \underline{x} + w_{i0} \qquad (2-10a)$$

where

$$w_{i0} = -\frac{1}{2}\underline{\mu}_i^T \underline{\mu}_i \qquad (2-10b)$$

and

$$\underline{w}_i = \underline{\mu}_i \qquad (2-10c)$$

Thus, each $\underline{\mu}_i$ may be thought of as a *template* for class w_i. An alternative view is that (2-10a) defines a matched filter (Appendix 5). As shown in the following, it is not necessary to constrain $\Sigma = I$ to achieve a linear discriminant function.

Generalized Results (Gaussian Case)

The form of the discriminant function in (2-7) leads to a multitude of extensions. In general, with class dependence introduced in $p(\underline{x})$ via $\underline{\mu}_i$ and Σ_i, a discriminant function of the form

$$g_i(\underline{x}) = -\frac{1}{2}(\underline{x} - \underline{\mu}_i)^T \Sigma_i^{-1} (\underline{x} - \underline{\mu}_i) - \left(\frac{d}{2}\right) \log(2\pi) - \frac{1}{2} \log |\Sigma_i| \qquad (2-11)$$

results. A key element of (2-11) is the quadratic term, which may be denoted $\| \underline{x} - \underline{\mu}_i \|^2_{\Sigma_i^{-1}}$. This scalar represents the square of the *Mahalanobis distance* from $\underline{x}$ to $\underline{\mu}_i$. A simpler interpretation is that $\| \underline{x} - \underline{\mu}_i \|_{\Sigma_i^{-1}}$ is a vector distance using a Σ_i^{-1} *norm*. For example, if $\Sigma_i = I$, then we are dealing with a Euclidean space.

Visualization of the surfaces in R^d where $\| \underline{x} - \underline{\mu}_i \|^2_{\Sigma_i^{-1}}$ is constant is important. As shown in Appendix 6, this quadratic term spawns a number of different surfaces, depending on Σ_i^{-1}.

Decision Surfaces for Specific Cases

The case where $\Sigma_i = I$ was introduced previously. From (2-11), the decision region boundaries are determined by considering classes pairwise and solving $g_i(\underline{x}) = g_j(\underline{x})$. Using (2-11) and the results of (2-10), we arrive at

$$(\underline{w}_i^T - \underline{w}_j^T)\underline{x} + (w_{i0} - w_{j0}) = 0 \qquad (2-12)$$

Defining $\underline{w} = \underline{w}_i - \underline{w}_j$ indicates that the decision regions in R^d are (pairwise) separated by hyperplanes that include the origin if $w_{i0} = w_{j0}$.

Let us consider a more general formulation, by defining a discriminant function, $g_i(\underline{x})$, which makes use of Bayes rule. Recalling that $P(w_i|\underline{x}) = p(\underline{x}|w_i)P(w_i)/p(\underline{x})$, a suitable form[3] is

$$g_i(\underline{x}) = \log\{P(w_i|\underline{x})p(\underline{x})\} = \log\{p(\underline{x}|w_i)\} + \log\{P(w_i)\} \qquad (2-13)$$

In the Gaussian case, neglecting the $(-d/2)\log(2\pi)$ bias, (2-13) becomes

$$g_i(\underline{x}) = -\frac{1}{2}\|\underline{x} - \underline{\mu}_i\|_{\Sigma_i^{-1}} -\frac{1}{2}\log|\Sigma_i| + \log\{P(w_i)\} \qquad (2-14)$$

If the components of $\underline{x}$ are uncorrelated with equal variances, $\Sigma_i = \sigma^2 I$, and eliminating the class-independent bias $(\log|\Sigma_i|)$ in (2-14) yields

$$g_i(\underline{x}) = -\frac{1}{2\sigma^2}(\underline{x} - \underline{\mu}_i)^T(\underline{x} - \underline{\mu}_i) + \log\{P(w_i)\} \qquad (2-15)$$

The loci of constant $\|\underline{x} - \underline{\mu}_i\|^2$ are therefore *hyperspheres*, each centered at the class mean, $\underline{\mu}_i$. In addition, (2-15) yields a direct mechanism to incorporate a priori probabilities in the discriminant function. It is left for the reader to show the decision boundaries in (2-15), as well as the influence of $P(w_i)$.

Uncorrelated Components, Unequal Variances.   When $\Sigma_i = \Sigma$ is diagonal with unequal σ_{ii}^2, that is,

$$\Sigma_i = \Sigma = \begin{pmatrix} \sigma_{11}^2 & 0 & 0 & \cdots & 0 \\ 0 & \sigma_{22}^2 & 0 & \cdots & 0 \\ & & \ddots & & \\ 0 & 0 & \cdots & 0 & \sigma_{dd}^2 \end{pmatrix}$$

therefore

$$\Sigma_i^{-1} = \begin{pmatrix} \dfrac{1}{\sigma_{11}^2} & 0 & 0 & \cdots & 0 \\ 0 & \dfrac{1}{\sigma_{22}^2} & 0 & \cdots & 0 \\ & & \ddots & & \\ 0 & 0 & \cdots & 0 & \dfrac{1}{\sigma_{dd}^2} \end{pmatrix}$$

---

[3]Notice that $p(\underline{x})$ is a scalar term, common to all classes.

The decision rule of (2-14) yields a weighted distance classifier. For example, if $\sigma_{11}^2 < \sigma_{22}^2, 1/\sigma_{11}^2 > 1/\sigma_{22}^2$, we would tend to put more emphasis on feature vector component x_1 than x_2. Equivalently, this is a way to account for our expectations that there will be more scatter in the x_2-direction of R^d than in the x_1-direction. Thus, we tolerate more deviation of x_2 from its mean than in x_1. Two additional results are left to the reader:

1. The loci of constant $p(x|w_i)$ for each class are hyperelliptical surfaces in R^d; and

2. A linear discriminant function formulation is possible.

$\Sigma_i = \Sigma$, *Not Diagonal.*   In this case, significant correlation exists between elements of Σ. Although we could work with this case directly, for visualization the diagonalization techniques of Appendices 1 and 2 are useful.

Decision Boundaries for $\Sigma_i = \Sigma$.   For simplicity, we assume $P(w_i) = (1/c) \; \forall i$. In this case, (2-14) reduces, through elimination of class-independent terms, to the equally useful discriminant function:

$$g_i(x) = -\parallel x - \mu_i \parallel_{\Sigma^{-1}}^2 \qquad (2-16)$$

Expanding (2-16) yields

$$g_i(x) = -(x - \mu_i)^T \Sigma^{-1} (x - \mu_i)$$

$$= -x^T \Sigma^{-1} x + 2\mu_i^T \Sigma^{-1} x - \mu_i^T \Sigma^{-1} \mu_i \qquad (2-17)$$

Again, (2-17) reduces to (note that Σ is symmetric)

$$g_i(x) = (\Sigma^{-1} \mu_i)^T x - \frac{1}{2} \parallel \mu_i \parallel_{\Sigma^{-1}}^2 \qquad (2-18)$$

which can be rewritten as

$$g_i(x) = w_i^T x - w_{i0} \qquad (2-19)$$

where

$$w_i = \Sigma^{-1} \mu_i \qquad (2-20a)$$

and

$$w_{i0} = +\frac{1}{2} \parallel \mu_i \parallel_{\Sigma^{-1}}^2 \qquad (2-20b)$$

It is important to note, therefore, that a linear discriminant function is applicable, and the decision surfaces are hyperplanes. The latter follows from using (2-19) and $g_i(x) = g_j(x)$ to define the surface:

$$w_i^T x - w_{i0} = w_j^T x - w_{j0} \qquad (2-21)$$

or

$$w_{ij}^T x - w_{ij0} = 0 \qquad (2-22a)$$

where

$$\underline{w}_{ij} = \underline{w}_i - \underline{w}_j = \Sigma^{-1}(\underline{\mu}_i - \underline{\mu}_j) \tag{2-22b}$$

$$w_{ij0} = w_{i0} - w_{j0} \tag{2-22c}$$

We investigate this further in Example 5.

Σ_i *Arbitrary*. Notice that in the previous formulations there was no class dependence reflected in Σ_i, that is, it was the same for all classes. When Σ_i is allowed to be class-dependent and nondiagonal (but with the constraint that it represent a covariance matrix and be invertable), the decision surfaces become more complex. The difficulty arises since each $g_i(\underline{x})$ contains a *class-specific quadratic term in $\underline{x}$* of the form $\underline{x}^T \Sigma_i^{-1} \underline{x}$. The decision surfaces defined by $g_i(\underline{x}) = g_j(\underline{x})$ therefore are general quartics in R^d (Appendix 6).

Modifications for General Σ_i. Several modifications to the general classification strategy are used to alleviate the computation of hyperhyperoid decision surfaces. Two are:

1. *Mixture normalization*, where we convert the given problem, with class-specific Σ_i, to another (different) problem where $\Sigma_i = \Sigma = \sum_{i=1}^{c} P(w_i)\Sigma_i$. This is a suboptimal solution, in the sense of classification error, but it leads to a more computationally practical form.

2. *Feature preprocessing*, using polynomial functions to preprocess the x_i and, in effect, compute the quadratic terms. Following this, a linear discriminant function may be used (Appendix 6).

A General Look at the StatPR Approach Structure

Figures 3 and 4 indicate the general structure of the StatPR approach that embodies the preceding solution procedure. 'Connecting' Figures 3 and 4 shows that, in this model-based context, we must 'invert' the pattern generation model to recover information concerning class w_i.

ADDITIONAL EXAMPLES

EXAMPLE 4: Uniform Densities, $c = 2, d = 1$

Consider a two-class problem where the underlying class densities are uniform, that is,

$$p(x|w_1) = \begin{cases} \dfrac{1}{a_2 - a_1} & \text{for } x\epsilon[a_1, a_2] \\ 0 & \text{otherwise} \end{cases}$$

and

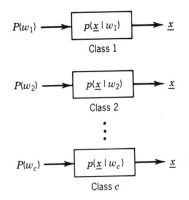

Figure 3:   Pattern vector statistical characterization.

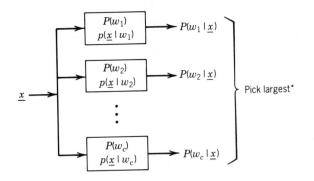

*With simple 0-1 risk measure

Figure 4:   Pattern vector classification approach.

$$
p(x|w_2) = \begin{cases} \dfrac{1}{b_2 - b_1} & \text{for } x\epsilon[b_1, b_2] \\[2mm] 0 & \text{otherwise} \end{cases}
$$

Assume equal a priori probabilities.

For the case of $a_1 < b_1 < a_2$, the density functions will overlap. Figure 5 shows several cases of possible feature overlap between classes. Note that in parts b to d a discriminant function and corresponding 'maximum' classification rule of the form $g_i(x) = p(x|w_i)$ will result in a nonzero classification error. ∎

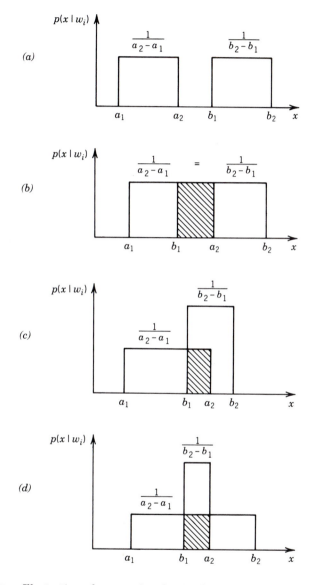

Figure 5:   Illustration of cases using density functions from Example 4.
(a) No overlap; perfect $[P(\text{error}) = 0]$ classification possible.
    Decision boundary is $a_2 \leq \alpha \leq b_1$.
(b) Possible overlap case
(c) Possible overlap case.
(d) Possible overlap case.

EXAMPLE 5: $c = 3, d = 2,$ **Gaussian Case**

Given the following three class situations for which a classifier is desired:

$$\Sigma_i = \Sigma = \begin{pmatrix} 1 & 0 \\ 0 & \frac{1}{2} \end{pmatrix}$$

$$\underline{\mu}_1 = \begin{pmatrix} 0 \\ 2 \end{pmatrix} \quad \underline{\mu}_2 = \begin{pmatrix} 4 \\ 1 \end{pmatrix} \quad \underline{\mu}_3 = \begin{pmatrix} 1 \\ 0 \end{pmatrix}$$

$$P(w_1) = P(w_2) = P(w_3)$$

$$p(\underline{x}|w_i) \sim N(\underline{\mu}_i, \Sigma_i)$$

Shape of PDF Contours.   Figure 6(a) shows the contours of the class-conditioned pdfs. Note that they are ellipses, as expected (Appendix 6). For example, since

$$\Sigma^{-1} = \begin{pmatrix} 1 & 0 \\ 0 & 2 \end{pmatrix}$$

computing $(\underline{x} - \underline{\mu}_i)^T \Sigma^{-1} (\underline{x} - \underline{\mu}_i) = k$, where k is an arbitrary (positive) constant, for each class yields the following:

for w_1 : $x_1^2 + 2(x_2 - 2)^2 = k$ or $\left(\dfrac{x_1}{\sqrt{2}}\right)^2 + \left(\dfrac{x_2 - 2}{1}\right)^2 = \dfrac{k}{2}$

for w_2 : $(x_1 - 4)^2 + 2(x_2 - 1)^2 = k$ or $\left(\dfrac{x_1 - 4}{\sqrt{2}}\right)^2 + \left(\dfrac{x_2 - 1}{1}\right)^2 = \dfrac{k}{2}$

for w_3 : $(x_1 - 1)^2 + 2x_2^2 = k$ or $\left(\dfrac{x_1 - 1}{\sqrt{2}}\right)^2 + \left(\dfrac{x_2}{1}\right)^2 = \dfrac{k}{2}$

Discriminant Functions.   From (2-19) and (2-20), we form $\underline{w}_i^T$ and w_{i0}:

$$g_1(\underline{x}) = (0 \quad 4)^T \underline{x} - 4 = 4x_2 - 4$$

$$g_2(\underline{x}) = (4 \quad 2)^T \underline{x} - 9 = 4x_1 + 2x_2 - 9$$

$$g_3(\underline{x}) = (1 \quad 0)^T \underline{x} - \frac{1}{2} = x_1 - \frac{1}{2}$$

Separating Hyperplanes.   Since $c = 3$, there are $(c^2 - c)/2 = 3$ separating hyperplanes given by (2-22). They are shown in Figure 6(b) and are computed as follows:

$$\underline{w}_{12} = \begin{pmatrix} -4 \\ 2 \end{pmatrix}$$

with accompanying hyperplane $H_{12} : 4x_1 - 2x_2 - 5 = 0$

$$\underline{w}_{23} = \begin{pmatrix} 3 \\ 2 \end{pmatrix}$$

with accompanying hyperplane $H_{23} : 6x_1 + 4x_2 - 17 = 0$ and

$$\underline{w}_{31} = \begin{pmatrix} -1 \\ 4 \end{pmatrix}$$

with accompanying hyperplane $H_{31} : 2x_1 - 8x_2 + 7 = 0$. Superimposing Figure 6(b) onto Figure 6(a) yields an excellent visual display of the manner in which the separating hyperplanes account for the orientation of the pdfs. This is shown in Figure 6(c). ■

EXTENSIONS

There are many extensions and ramifications to the previous StatPR presentation.

Training

One of the problems not addressed in the previous section is determination of the parameters for the class-conditioned probability density functions. In the case of Gaussian pdf models, a labeled set of *training samples*, that is, sets of labeled feature vectors with known class, are often used. This training set is denoted H and is used to estimate μ_i and Σ_i. This is treated from several viewpoints later. Large-dimension feature vectors, and consequently density functions, lead to situations wherein this approach is impractical. For example, in an image processing application, if we use the gray level measurements directly as features, an image with 100×100 pixel spatial resolution yields a 1000×1 feature vector and requires estimation of a 1000×1000 covariance matrix.

Alternative Classification Procedures

An alternative, which is related to the minimum distance classification approach, is the use of a nonparametric technique known as *nearest neighbor classification*. We illustrate the concept of a 1-nearest neighbor classification rule (1-NNR) first. Given a feature vector, $\underline{x}$, we determine the vector in H that is closest in distance to $\underline{x}$, denoted $\underline{x}'$. $\underline{x}$ is classified by assigning the class corresponding to $\underline{x}'$. A variation is the k-NNR, where the k samples in H that are nearest to $\underline{x}$ are determined, and the class of $\underline{x}$ is based on some measure of the labels of these samples (e.g., a voting scheme may be employed). This approach, although conceptually and computationally straightforward, may be shown to have a greater error rate than the minimum distance classifier.

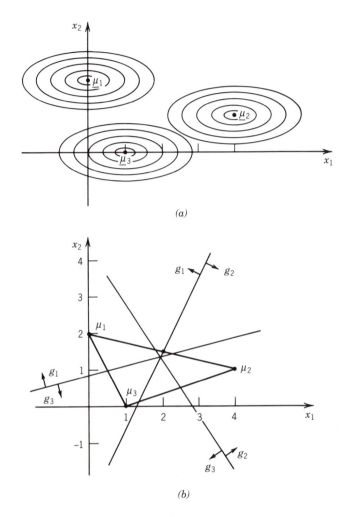

(a)

(b)

Figure 6:   Example 5: Densities and decision regions.
(a) Visualization of class-conditioned pdf contours.
(b) Separating hyperplanes.

However, the concept of classification based on nearness, or similarity, of features is significant.

Another nonparametric technique is to determine decision regions directly and to implement classification via *decision trees*. Both the NNR and decision trees are considered in Chapter 3.

Unsupervised Approaches

The previous approaches are predicated on the training set, H, being given. Consider the application of pattern recognition to *image segmentation*, that is, the classification of image pixels into groupings that represent some higher entity or information in the images. Unfortunately, it is rare to have either a statistical model to aid in this grouping or a training set. Therefore, so-called *unsupervised learning* techniques are applied.

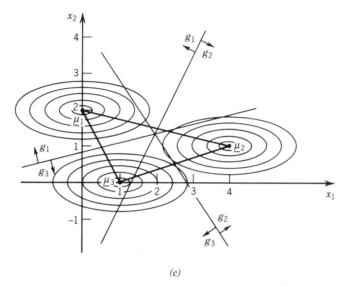

(c)

Figure 6 (cont.):   (c) Superposition of decision boundaries of (b) on pdf contours of (a) to show partitioning of R^2.

Two unsupervised learning approaches that embody more general measures of feature vector similarity and do not require H are known as *hierarchical clustering* and *partitional clustering*. A set of feature vectors is sequentially partitioned (or merged) on the basis of dissimilarity (or similarity). Thus, given only a similarity measure, we either aggregate feature vectors into a single class or sequentially subdivide feature vector partitions. These are considered in Chapter 5.

CLASSIFIER PERFORMANCE, RISK, AND ERRORS

One of the key advantages of statistical models is that direct characterizations of classification performance are possible. These characterizations, in turn, lead to guidelines or constraints on decision or classification strategies.

Measures of Classification Performance

In most practical PR formulations, a classification rule does not lead to perfect classification. One reason for this is the fact that features are common to two or more classes, that is, regions of support for $p(\underline{x}|w_i)$ overlap. In other words, associated with any decision rule is a *probability of classification error*. Therefore, we seek to formulate *measures of decision rule performance*. As we shall see, these may take into account things in addition to probability of a classification error, such as *significance of a classification error*.

Measures of classifier (decision rule) performance, once formulated, lead to classification strategies that minimize (or maximize) this measure. Often we speak of minimizing 'risk.' Different risk measures may lead to different classification strategies.

2-Class Example of a Classification Performance Measure.   Recall the Bayesian formulation for a simple $c = 2$ class (w_1 or w_2) problem in Examples 1 to 4 led to the intuitively appealing classification rule:

$$P(w_1|\underline{x}) \underset{w_2}{\overset{w_1}{\gtrless}} P(w_2|\underline{x}) \qquad (2-23)$$

It is important to note that (2-23) is a decision rule based on computation of a posteriori probabilities. It is possible for a vector $\underline{x}$ to yield $P(w_1|\underline{x}) > P(w_2|\underline{x})$, *but $\underline{x}$ could actually be from w_2* (or another class, i.e., in general $w_i \neq w_1$). Thus, we would choose w_1, with the probability of $\underline{x}$ actually belonging to another class given by $1 - P(w_1|\underline{x})$.

Another way to view this is to consider the *probability of a classification error, as a function of the measurement ($\underline{x}$), the true class, and the decision or classification rule*. Thus, in the $c = 2$ class case, we incur an error if we choose w_1 and the true class is w_2 or if we choose w_2 and the true class is w_1. Since we choose w_1 when, given $\underline{x}$, $P(w_1|\underline{x}) > P(w_2|\underline{x})$, from (2-23) the risk or error corresponding to this decision rule may be formulated as:

$$P(\text{error}|\underline{x}) = \begin{cases} P(w_1|\underline{x}) & \text{if we decide } w_2 \\ P(w_2|\underline{x}) & \text{if we decide } w_1 \end{cases} \qquad (2-24)$$

Expressing Conditional Error.   In order to assess classification performances, we consider several formulations for the unconditional $P(\text{error})$. In either case, we are characterizing the joint occurrence of: (1) a random variable $\underline{X}$ and an event A_i, that is,

$$P_{\underline{X}A}(\underline{x}, A_i) = P(\underline{X} \leq \underline{x} \cap \text{ event } A_i \text{ occurs}) \qquad (2-25a)$$

or (2) the joint occurrence of two random variables (at least one of which, i.e., w_i, is discrete):

$$P_{\underline{X}w}(\underline{x}, w_i) = P(\underline{X} \leq x \cap w = w_i) \qquad (2-25b)$$

Therefore, two error formulations are possible, depending on the 'conditioning.' The first is

$$P(\text{error}) = \int P(\text{error}, \underline{x})d\underline{x} \qquad (2-25c)$$

or the equivalent sum if $\underline{X}$ is discrete. The second is

$$P(\text{error}) = \sum_{i=1}^{c} P(\text{error} \cap w_i) = \sum_{i=1}^{c} P(\text{error} | w_i) P(w_i) \qquad (2-25d)$$

Both of these formulations are useful in classification error analysis. For example, in the continuous case we can write

$$P(\text{error}, \underline{x}) = P(\text{error} | \underline{x}) p(\underline{x}) \qquad (2-26)$$

Hence, using (2-25c),

$$P(\text{error}) = \int_{-\infty}^{\infty} \int_{-\infty}^{\infty} \cdots \int_{-\infty}^{\infty} P(\text{error} | \underline{x}) p(\underline{x}) d\underline{x} \qquad (2-27)$$

Therefore, if we always choose w_i (over all $\underline{x}$) such that $P(\text{error} | \underline{x})$ is smallest, we minimize (2-27). Notice that in the $c = 2$ class example of (2-23), the value of $P(\text{error} | \underline{x})$, as given by (2-24), is $P(w_i | \underline{x})$ *when we are wrong*. This makes some classification errors 'more wrong' than others. It is not clear that this is the best or most general measure of classification performance, as shown in the following example.

EXAMPLE 6: Why All Errors Are Not Equal (The 'Apple–Grenade' Problem)

Consider a somewhat drastic modification of our simple 2-feature, 2-class 'bolt–shim' classification problem presented earlier. Suppose now we are using the same features to classify the objects as either 'apple' or '(live) hand grenade,' and also using this classification decision for subsequent handling. In this example, assume apples are washed, cored, and coverted into applesauce by cutters and a high-powered press. Hand grenades are *carefully* packed and shipped to an armory. Clearly, the 'risk' encountered in misclassifying a live hand grenade as an apple and attempting to cut and press it might be much worse than sending an apple along in a case with hand grenades. ■

General Measures of Classification Risk

The Two-Class (c = 2) Case.   In this section, we formulate more general measures of classification performance and derive the classification rules that result from these measures. In the $c = 2$ case, our formulation is similar to the specification of receiver operating characteristics (ROCs), a problem familiar to communication and radar engineers [Van Trees 1968]. In ROC problems, the two classes correspond to 'valid-signal' (e.g., a message or perhaps a radar return) and 'noise' and the attempt is to develop strategies so that the incoming signal is correctly classified. Four possible cases may arise:

Case 1:   The incoming signal is a 'valid-signal' and we *correctly* classify it as such (a *detection*).

Case 2:   The incoming signal is a 'valid-signal' and we *incorrectly* classify it as noise (a *miss*).

Case 3:   The incoming signal is 'noise' and we *incorrectly* classify it as 'valid-signal.' This is a case of *a false alarm*.

Case 4:   The incoming signal is 'noise' and we *correctly* classify it as 'noise.'

Note, cases 1 and 4 represent desired ROC (classification) operation, whereas cases 2 and 3 represent errors in classification.

We formulate a *loss function*, *cost function*, or *risk function*, λ_{ij}, by defining a measure:

- λ_{ij} = cost or risk of choosing class w_i when class w_j is the true class. Intuitively, we would be inclined to design PR systems where the cost or risk of the wrong classification is higher than the cost or risk of a correct decision.

Formulation of λ_{ij}.   In the $c = 2$ (w_1 or w_2) case, there are four values of λ_{ij}, that is, λ_{11}, λ_{12}, λ_{21}, λ_{22}. λ_{11} and λ_{22} are the costs (or perhaps 'rewards' for a correct decision) whereas λ_{12} and λ_{21} are the costs of a classification error.

General Decision Rules.   In measuring overall classification risk or cost, the decision rule, the cost function, and the observations, $\underline{x}$ are considered. A *decision or classification* is denoted as α_i where α_i = the decision to choose class w_i. A *decision rule* is a mapping of the observed feature vector, $\underline{x}$, into a α_i through a decision rule $\alpha(\underline{x})$:

$$\alpha(\underline{x}) \rightarrow \{\alpha_1, \alpha_2, \ldots \alpha_c\} \qquad (2-28)$$

With this formulation, we can evaluate probabilities such as $P(\alpha_1 \cap w_1)$, that is, the probability that we choose α_1, when w_1 was the true class. Note

$$P(\alpha_i \cap w_j) = P(\alpha_i|w_j)P(w_j) \qquad (2-29)$$

Hence, an overall risk measure for the $c = 2$ case is

$$R = \lambda_{11}P(\alpha_1|w_1)P(w_1) + \lambda_{21}P(\alpha_2|w_1)P(w_1)$$
$$+\lambda_{12}P(\alpha_1|w_2)P(w_2) + \lambda_{22}P(\alpha_2|w_2)P(w_2) \qquad (2-30)$$

Of course, the $P(\alpha_i|w_j)$ terms depend on the chosen mapping $\alpha(\underline{x}) \rightarrow \alpha_i$, which in turn depends on $\underline{x}$. Thus, a measure of *conditional risk* associated with a $c = 2$ class decision rule is

$$R[\alpha(\underline{x}) \rightarrow \alpha_1] = R(\alpha_1|\underline{x}) = \lambda_{11}P(w_1|\underline{x}) + \lambda_{12}P(w_2|\underline{x})$$

for α_1 and

$$R[\alpha(\underline{x}) \rightarrow \alpha_2] = R(\alpha_2|\underline{x}) = \lambda_{21}P(w_1|\underline{x}) + \lambda_{22}P(w_2|\underline{x}) \qquad (2-31)$$

for α_2. For a c class decision problem, the expected risk is given by an application of the total probability theorem (Appendix 2):

$$R[\alpha(\underline{x})] = \int R[\alpha(\underline{x})|\underline{x}]p(\underline{x})d\underline{x} \qquad (2-32)$$

Minimizing the conditional risk, $R[\alpha(\underline{x})|\underline{x}]$ in (2-32) thus minimizes the expected risk. The lower bound on $R[\alpha(\underline{x})]$ is often referred to as the *Bayes risk*.

Minimizing $R[\alpha(\underline{x})]$ for c = 2. In order to minimize $R[\alpha(\underline{x})]$ for $c = 2$, since only two choices or classifications (α_1 or α_2) are possible, the decision rule is formulated as

$$R(\alpha_1|\underline{x}) \underset{\alpha_1}{\overset{\alpha_2}{\gtrless}} R(\alpha_2|\underline{x}) \qquad (2-33)$$

which is a generalization of (2-3). By using (2-31), (2-33) may be expanded into

$$\lambda_{11} P(w_1|\underline{x}) + \lambda_{12} P(w_2|\underline{x}) \underset{\alpha_1}{\overset{\alpha_2}{\gtrless}} \lambda_{21} P(w_1|\underline{x}) + \lambda_{22} P(w_2|\underline{x}) \qquad (2-34)$$

or

$$(\lambda_{11} - \lambda_{21}) p(\underline{x}|w_1) P(w_1) \underset{\alpha_1}{\overset{\alpha_2}{\gtrless}} (\lambda_{22} - \lambda_{12}) p(\underline{x}|w_2) P(w_2) \qquad (2-35)$$

Often, we choose $\lambda_{11} = \lambda_{22} = 0$, since there is no 'cost' or 'risk' in a correct classification. Assuming $(\lambda_{11} - \lambda_{21}) < 0$, (2-35) may be rewritten

$$\frac{p(\underline{x}|w_1)}{p(\underline{x}|w_2)} \underset{\alpha_2}{\overset{\alpha_1}{\gtrless}} \frac{(\lambda_{22} - \lambda_{12})}{(\lambda_{11} - \lambda_{21})} \frac{P(w_2)}{P(w_1)} \qquad (2-36)$$

Equation 2-36 is in the form of a likelihood ratio test, LRT, where the RHS is not simply the ratio of the a priori probabilities $P(w_2)/P(w_1)$ (as before), but rather this ratio weighted by $(\lambda_{22} - \lambda_{12})/(\lambda_{11} - \lambda_{21})$.

Ramifications of Choosing λ_{ij}. An investigation of different λ_{ij} choices in (2-36) raises some interesting issues. Suppose $\lambda_{11} = \lambda_{22} = 0$ and $\lambda_{12} = \lambda_{21} = 1$, that is, an incorrect classification 'costs' one unit. Then (2-36) becomes

$$\frac{p(\underline{x}|w_1)}{p(\underline{x}|w_2)} \underset{\alpha_2}{\overset{\alpha_1}{\gtrless}} \frac{P(w_2)}{P(w_1)} \qquad (2-37)$$

This is the same classification strategy as developed intuitively in (2-3).

Extensions to c classes. For c classes, with the loss function

$$\lambda_{ij} = \begin{cases} 0 & i = j \\ 1 & i \neq j \end{cases} \qquad (2-38)$$

all errors are *equally costly*. The conditional risk of decision α_i is based on generalizing (2-31)

$$R[\alpha(\underline{x}) \rightarrow \alpha_i] = \sum_{j=1}^{c} \lambda_{ij} P(w_j|\underline{x})$$

$$= \sum_{j \neq i} P(w_j|\underline{x}) = 1 - P(w_i|\underline{x}) \qquad (2-39)$$

To minimize the conditional risk in (2-39), the decision rule is therefore to choose the α_i that maximizes $P(w_i|\underline{x})$, that is, the w_i for which $P(w_i|\underline{x})$ is largest. This is intuitively appealing. Since $P(w_i|\underline{x})$ is the a posteriori probability, this results in the *maximum a posteriori probability* (MAP) classifier, which may be formulated as

$$P(w_i|\underline{x}) \overset{\alpha_i}{>} P(w_j|\underline{x}) \qquad \forall j \neq i \qquad (2-40)$$

As before, we would use Bayes rule to reformulate (2-40) in terms of class-conditioned density functions and a priori probabilities.

For general formulations of risk (through λ_{ij}) a decision rule that is a generalization of (2-40) results:

$$R(\alpha_i|\underline{x}) \overset{\alpha_i}{<} R(\alpha_j|\underline{x}) \quad \forall i \neq j \qquad (2-41)$$

EXAMPLE 7: Effects of λ_{ij} in $c = 2$ Cases

Suppose $P(w_1) = P(w_2)$ and $\lambda_{11} = -2$, $\lambda_{22} = -1$, $\lambda_{12} = 2$, and $\lambda_{21} = 4$, that is, a 'miss' is twice as costly as a 'false alarm.' Equation 2-36 becomes

$$\frac{p(\underline{x}|w_1)}{p(\underline{x}|w_2)} \overset{\alpha_1}{\underset{\alpha_2}{\gtrless}} \left(\frac{1}{2}\right) \frac{P(w_2)}{P(w_1)} \qquad (2-42)$$

The cost measures alone suggest that we have significant concern with correctly identifying vectors or signals from w_1. This may exemplify the 'friend' or 'foe' classification scenerio, where w_1 may correspond to 'foe.' ∎

BIBLIOGRAPHICAL REMARKS

A succinct review of statistical PR techniques is found in Chapter 1 of [Fu 1968]. Classic texts that emphasize the StatPR approach are [Duda/Hart 1973] and [Fukunaga 1972].

EXERCISES

2.1   Formulate suitable measures of λ_{ij} for the 'apple–grenade' problem (Example 6) and derive the resulting decision or classification strategy.

2.2   Consider a $c = 3$ class application where $\lambda_{ii} = 0$, and $\lambda_{12} = 1$, $\lambda_{13} = 1$, $\lambda_{21} = 2$, $\lambda_{23} = 2$, $\lambda_{31} = 4$, $\lambda_{32} = 4$. Formulate $R(\alpha_i|\underline{x})$ and determine the decision rule.

2.3   Show that a linear discriminant function that generates a hyperplane that bisects and is orthogonal to the line segment connecting points $\underline{x}_1$ and $\underline{x}_2$

(a) Is given by the equation

$$g(\underline{x}) = (\underline{x}_1 - \underline{x}_2)^T \underline{x} + \frac{1}{2}(\| \underline{x}_1 \|^2 - \| \underline{x}_2 \|^2)$$

(b) Generates the decision boundary $g(\underline{x}) = 0$.

2.4   Can a general, weighted distance measure of the form $\| \underline{x} - \underline{\mu}_i \|_{M_i}$ be cast as a correlation classifier? Consider the case where M_i is class specific as well as $M_i = M \quad \forall i$.

2.5   Verify (2-15).

2.6   **(a)** Show that the decision surfaces in (2-15) are hyperplanes whose locations are influenced by $P(w_i)$.

　　　(b) What happens if $P(w_i) = P(w_j) \quad \forall i, j$?

　　　(c) Repeat (b) for the case $P(w_i) > P(w_j)$.

2.7   Given class-dependent pdfs as follows:

$$p(\underline{x}|w_1) = \begin{cases} \frac{1}{9} & \text{for } 1 \le x_1 \le 4 \text{ and } 1 \le x_2 \le 4 \\ 0 & \text{elsewhere} \end{cases}$$

$$p(\underline{x}|w_2) = \begin{cases} 1 & \text{for } 2 \le x_1 \le 3 \text{ and } 2 \le x_2 \le 3 \\ 0 & \text{elsewhere} \end{cases}$$

where $\underline{x} = \begin{bmatrix} x_1 \\ x_2 \end{bmatrix}$.

Assume $P(w_1) = P(w_2) = \frac{1}{2}$.

　　　(a) Draw the decision regions.

　　　(b) Develop the classification strategy.

　　　(c) Compute the classification error.

2.8   For the case $\Sigma_i = \Sigma$ is diagonal with $\sigma_{ii}^2 \ne \sigma_{jj}^2$, show:

　　　(a) That the contours of constant density $p_i(\underline{x})$ are hyperellipses in R^d; and

　　　(b) A linear classifier is possible.

2.9   For the discriminant function developed in (2-13) show that

　　　(a) If $p(\underline{x}|w_1) = p(\underline{x}|w_2)$, then the observation $\underline{x}$ does not help classification and the decision is made solely using a priori probabilities $P(w_1)$ and $P(w_2)$.

　　　(b) If $P(w_1) = P(w_2)$ (equally likely a priori probabilities), then the decision is made solely on class-conditioned pdfs, i.e., solely based on the measurement data.

2.10   If Σ_i is nondiagonal and different for each class, can a diagonalization approach (linear transformation) be used?

2.11   Show in the $d = 2$-dimensional case that the loci of constant contours in the multivariate normal distribution *are ellipses* with the orientation of the principal axes along the e-vectors of Σ^{-1} and that the length of these axes are the corresponding e-values. Where is the origin of these ellipses?

2.12   Given a $d = 1$, $c = 2$ class case where $p(x|w_1)$ is Gaussian with mean $\mu_1 = 0$ and $\sigma_1^2 = 1$, and $p(x|w_2)$ is uniform with mean $\mu^2 = 2$ and $\sigma_2^2 = \frac{1}{3}$, and assuming equal a priori probabilities,

  (a) Plot $p(x|w_1)$ and $p(x|w_2)$.

  (b) Determine the classification strategy that minimizes classification error. What are discriminant functions $g_1(x)$ and $g_2(x)$?

  (c) Show the partitioning of R^1 for this case.

  (d) Compute the probability of classification error corresponding to the decision rule of part (c).

  (e) Repeat parts (b) to (d) for $P(w_1) = 2P(w_2)$.

  (f) Suppose the decision or classification rule is restricted to a *single threshold test*, i.e.,

$$\text{Choose} \begin{cases} w_1 & \text{if } x \leq \alpha \\ w_2 & \text{if } x > \alpha \end{cases}$$

  What value of α minimizes the classification error in this case? Show this error graphically, using the results of part (a).

  (g) Compute $P(\text{error})$ for the decision rule of part (f) and compare with the results of part (d).

2.13   Repeat ('no measurement') Example 1, but instead consider two 'randomized' decision rules:

  (a) We randomly choose w_1 or w_2, i.e., $P(\text{choose } w_1) = P(\text{choose } w_2) = \frac{1}{2}$.

  (b) We randomly choose w_1 or w_2 with $P(\text{choose } w_1) = 0.7$ $P(\text{choose } w_2) = 0.3$.

  Formulate the probability of an error in each case.

2.14   Repeat Example 2, but instead consider two uniform distributions with equal variances and $\mu_1 \neq \mu_2$. Show the plot of $p(x|w_i)$, as in Figure 1(a). Develop a classification rule and compute $P(\text{error})$.

2.15   For Example 2, show that *any choice of* α, other than $\alpha = (\mu_1 + \mu_2)/2$ yields a larger $P(\text{error})$. Relate this result to the shaded regions of Figure 1(a).

2.16   For cases (b) to (d) of Figure 5, compute the classification error.

2.17   Repeat Example 5 for the case $\Sigma_i = \Sigma = \begin{pmatrix} 1 & 0 \\ 0 & 1 \end{pmatrix}$. Specifically,

  (a) Plot the contours of constant $p(\underline{x}|w_i)$ for each class in R^2.

  (b) Calculate $g_i(\underline{x})$ for each class.

  (c) Express (b) in the form of a linear discriminant function for each class.

  (d) Determine and plot the $(c^2 - c)/2$ separating hyperplanes.

2.18   Show, in detail, how Bayes rule for probabilities, i.e.,

$$P(A|B)P(B) = P(B|A)P(A)$$

yields the useful pattern recognition formulation that mixes continuous and discrete random variables:

$$P(w_i|\underline{x}) = \frac{p(\underline{x}|w_i)P(w_i)}{p(\underline{x})}$$

2.19   Consider the ramifications of choosing the following risk weights:

   (a) $\lambda_{22} = \lambda_{11} = 2$, $\lambda_{12} = \lambda_{21} = 1$.

   (b) $\lambda_{22} = 0$, $\lambda_{11} = 2$, $\lambda_{12} = \lambda_{21} = 1$.

2.20   Is it possible to have a classifier, which partitions R^d, where some decision boundaries are hyperplanes, and others are more general quartic surfaces?

2.21   Consider a general $c = 4$ class problem where a classifier solution yielding decision regions R_1, R_2, R_3, and R_4 has been given.

   (a)   Show an equation for $P(\text{error})$.

   (b)   Show an equation for $P(\text{correct})$ [other than $1 - P(\text{error})$].

   (c)   Relate parts (a) and (b).

   (d)   Extend parts (a) and (b) to c classes.

Supervised Learning (Training) Using Parametric and Nonparametric Approaches

3

'Take some more tea,' the March Hare said to Alice, very earnestly. 'I've had nothing yet,' Alice replied in an offended tone: 'so I can't take more.' 'You mean you can't take less,' said the Hatter: 'it's very easy to take more than nothing.'

Alice's Adventures in Wonderland [1865], Chapter 7
Lewis Carroll [Charles Lutwidge Dodgson] 1832–1898

INTRODUCTION

In this chapter, we consider a number of PR system training approaches. Our first goal is the determination of $p(\underline{x}|w_i)$. This leads to or suggests additional approaches that use the training set for direct estimation of $P(w_i|\underline{x})$, as well as direct (but relatively speaking, suboptimal) approaches for classification without first estimating densities or probabilities. The k-NNR is an example of the latter approach.

PARAMETRIC ESTIMATION AND SUPERVISED LEARNING

Recall from the previous chapter that the StatPR formulation assumes knowledge of $p(\underline{x}|w_i)$ and $P(w_i)$ for each class. In addition, we needed to know a priori the *number* of classes. For Gaussian densities, for example, we would need to know $\underline{\mu}_i, \Sigma_i$, and so on, for $i = 1, 2, \ldots c$. Often this information is not available directly.

Instead, suppose we have a set of *design* or *training samples* representative of the type of features and underlying classes, with each labeled as to its correct class. This yields a training or learning problem. When the *form* of the densities is known, a *parameter estimation problem* results.

Approaches to Parameter Estimation

Two approaches are possible. In *maximum likelihood (ML)* estimation, we assume the parameters are fixed, but unknown.

- The ML approach seeks the 'best' parameter estimate in the sense that 'best' means the set of parameters that maximize the probability of obtaining the (given) training set.

Bayesian estimation on the other hand, models the parameters to be estimated as *random variables* with some (assumed) known a priori distribution. The training set samples are, in a sense, 'observations,' which allow conversion of the a priori information into an a posteriori density.

- The Bayesian approach uses the training set to update the training set-conditioned density function *of the unknown parameters.*

Uncertainty in the parameter estimates results from either approach. The Bayesian approach seeks a density that approximates an impulse. The ML approach seeks *parameter estimates* that maximize a likelihood function.

Supervised versus Unsupervised Learning

We call either parameter estimation approach *supervised learning.* By comparison, *unsupervised learning* uses sample feature vectors without class labels and is much more difficult. Unsupervised learning is treated later.

MAXIMUM LIKELIHOOD (ML) ESTIMATION

Formulation

Recall that ML estimation assumes the parameters to be estimated are *unknown, but constant.* The ML formulation assumes we have a training set (H) in the form of c subsets of samples or feature vectors $H_1 \ldots H_c$. Samples in H_i are assumed to be generated by the underlying density function for class i, $p(\underline{x}|w_i)$. It is assumed the parametric form of $p(\underline{x}|w_i)$ is known.

For notational simplicity, the set of parameters to be estimated for class i comprise parameter vector $\underline{\theta}_i$. For example, in the Gaussian case where $\underline{X} \sim N(\underline{\mu}_i, \Sigma_i)$, the components of $\underline{\theta}_i$ are the elements of $\underline{\mu}_i$ and Σ_i. We denote this dependence on $\underline{\theta}_i$ by writing $p(\underline{x}|w_i, \underline{\theta}_i)$ where it is understood that $\underline{\theta}_i$ is an unknown but fixed parameter vector (not a r.v.).

Use of the Training Set

We consider the training of each class separately. This makes sense when samples in H_i do not yield information about $\underline{\theta}_j$, $j \neq i$. For example, if all classes share a common covariance matrix, $(\Sigma_i = \Sigma)$, this is not an ideal strategy. It does, however, simplify the parameter estimation strategy. Figure 1 shows this distinction.

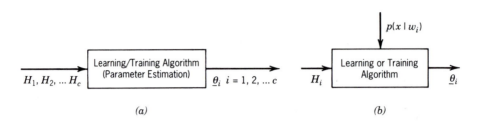

(a)   *(b)*

Figure 1:   Application of training sets in parametric supervised learning.
(a) Overall (*c*-classes).
(b) Cases where H_i only conveys information about w_i.

The Likelihood Function

Therefore, given H_i, the objective is to find $\hat{\underline{\theta}}_i$ that maximizes $p(H_i|\underline{\theta}_i)$, where $p(H_i|\underline{\theta}_i)$ is the *likelihood function*.[1] Suppose $H_i = \{\underline{x}_1, \underline{x}_2, \ldots \underline{x}_n\}$. If the $\underline{x}_k \in H_i$ are assumed independent, the joint parameter-conditioned pdf of H_i is

$$p(H_i|\underline{\theta}_i) = \prod_{k=1}^{n} p(\underline{x}_k|\underline{\theta}_i) \qquad (3-1)$$

The goal is to maximize $p(H_i|\underline{\theta}_i)$ with respect to parameter vector $\underline{\theta}_i$. This is shown in Figure 2. A straightforward approach[2] is to compute

$$\nabla_{\underline{\theta}_i} p(H_i|\underline{\theta}_i) = \underline{0} \qquad (3-2)$$

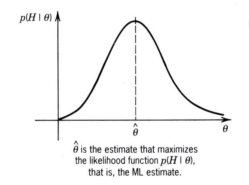

$\hat{\theta}$ is the estimate that maximizes
the likelihood function $p(H \mid \theta)$,
that is, the ML estimate.

Figure 2:   Likelihood function concept.

However, we can also maximize any monotonically increasing function of $p(H_i|\underline{\theta}_i)$. If f is such a function, it is often more convenient to solve:

---

[1] Now the terminology is more apparent. Notice that we find $\underline{\theta}_i$ to maximize the 'likelihood' of H_i.
[2] This assumes that $p(H_i|\underline{\theta}_i)$ is a differentiable function of $\underline{\theta}_i$.

$$\nabla_{\underline{\theta}_i} f(p(H_i|\underline{\theta}_i) = \underline{0} \tag{3-3}$$

One useful function is the natural logarithm function, that is, we work with $\log[p(H_i|\underline{\theta}_i)]$. Denoting the log of the likelihood function as

$$l(\underline{\theta}_i) = \log\{p(H_i|\underline{\theta}_i)\} \tag{3-4}$$

the independence assumption in (3-1) allows (3-4) to be rewritten

$$l(\underline{\theta}_i) = \sum_{k=1}^{n} \log\{p(\underline{x}_k|\underline{\theta}_i)\}$$

Using (3-3) yields the constraint on $\hat{\underline{\theta}}_i$:

$$\nabla_{\underline{\theta}_i} l(\hat{\underline{\theta}}_i) = \sum_{k=1}^{n} \nabla_{\underline{\theta}_i} \log\{p(\underline{x}_k|\underline{\theta}_i)\} = \underline{0} \tag{3-5}$$

We now digress to explore several uses of (3-5).

EXAMPLE 1: Estimating the Mean, $\underline{\mu}$, of a Gaussian pdf (Σ Assumed Known)

Here we assume $\underline{\mu}_i = \underline{\theta}_i = \underline{\mu}$, where

$$p(\underline{x}|\underline{\mu}) = \left\{1/\left[(2\pi)^d|\Sigma|\right]^{\frac{1}{2}}\right\} \exp[-\frac{1}{2}(\underline{x}-\underline{\mu})^T \Sigma^{-1}(\underline{x}-\underline{\mu})].$$

The training set sample $\underline{x}_k$ of H_i yields

$$\log\{p(\underline{x}_k|\underline{\mu})\} = -\frac{1}{2}(\underline{x}_k - \underline{\mu})^T \Sigma^{-1}(\underline{x}_k - \underline{\mu}) - \frac{1}{2}\log\{(2\pi)^d|\Sigma|\} \tag{3-6}$$

Forming (see Appendix 1) the gradient of (3-6)

$$\nabla_{\underline{\mu}} \log\{p(\underline{x}_k|\underline{\mu})\} = \Sigma^{-1}\underline{x}_k - \Sigma^{-1}\underline{\mu} \tag{3-7}$$

The ML estimator, $\hat{\underline{\mu}}$, therefore satisfies

$$\nabla_{\underline{\mu}} l(\hat{\underline{\mu}}) = \sum_{k=1}^{n}\{\Sigma^{-1}\underline{x}_k - \Sigma^{-1}\hat{\underline{\mu}}\} = \underline{0} \tag{3-8}$$

Since we assumed Σ is invertible[3], (3-8) becomes

$$\sum_{k=1}^{n} \underline{x}_k = n\hat{\underline{\mu}} \tag{3-9}$$

---

[3]The covariance matrix is symmetric and positive definite; this is guaranteed.

or

$$\underline{\hat{\mu}} = \frac{1}{n} \sum_{k=1}^{n} \underline{x}_k \qquad (3-10)$$

Thus, the ML estimate for the mean of a Gaussian distribution is the *sample mean*. This result, while rigorously developed, is intuitively appealing. ∎

EXAMPLE 2: Covariance Matrix Estimates

Without proof, we show the ML estimator for the covariance matrix

$$\hat{\Sigma} = \frac{1}{n} \sum_{k=1}^{n} (\underline{x}_k - \underline{\hat{\mu}})(\underline{x}_k - \underline{\hat{\mu}})^T \qquad (3-11)$$

The ML estimator for Σ is biased, since $E\{\hat{\Sigma}\} \neq \Sigma$. However, the following is an unbiased estimator:

$$\hat{\Sigma}_u = \frac{1}{n-1} \sum_{k=1}^{n} (\underline{x}_k - \underline{\hat{\mu}})(\underline{x}_k - \underline{\hat{\mu}})^T \qquad (3-12)$$

∎

Application to Other Densities. While conceptually straightforward, the ML approach is not directly applicable to a number of densities of interest. One example, explored in the exercises, is the uniform density.

THE BAYESIAN PARAMETER ESTIMATION APPROACH

Recall that for classification we needed $P(w_i|\underline{x})$ $i = 1, 2, \ldots c$. Our objective is, given H_i, to form $P(w_i|\underline{x}, H_i)$, where explicit dependence on H_i is shown. An application of Bayes rule yields

$$P(w_i|\underline{x}, H_i) = \frac{p(\underline{x}|w_i, H_i)P(w_i|H_i)}{p(\underline{x}|H_i)} \qquad (3-13a)$$

Also note the denominator of (3-13a) may be rewritten as

$$p(\underline{x}|H_i) = \sum_j p(\underline{x}|w_j, H_i)P(w_j|H_i) \qquad (3-13b)$$

Therefore, (3-13a) becomes

$$P(w_i|\underline{x}, H_i) = \frac{p(\underline{x}|w_i, H_i)P(w_i|H_i)}{\sum_j p(\underline{x}|w_j, H_i)P(w_j|H_i)} \qquad (3-14)$$

Equation 3-14 reinforces the idea that the classifier is conditioned on (and in some sense, 'as good as') the training set. Complicating (3-14) is the need to know $P(w_i|H_i)$ for $i = 1, 2, \ldots c$. A simplifying assumption is that this a priori probability is independent of a training set; therefore, $P(w_i|H_i) = P(w_i)$ and (3-14) becomes

$$P(w_i|\underline{x}, H_i) = \frac{p(\underline{x}|w_i, H_i)P(w_i)}{\sum_{j=1}^{c} p(\underline{x}|w_j, H_i)P(w_j)} \qquad (3-15)$$

Assuming that we know $P(w_i)$ $i = 1, 2, \ldots c$, (3-15) becomes useful if we can estimate the density $p(\underline{x}|w_i, H_i)$ $i = 1, 2, \ldots c$. This becomes our immediate goal.

Again assuming that H_i conveys information about only the parameters of class w_i, the notation is simplified and the corresponding estimation problem reduces to determining $p(\underline{x}|H_i)$. We assume the *functional form* of the density $p(\underline{x}|H_i)$ is known. Therefore, we need only estimate *a random vector* of parameters $\underline{\theta}_i$. This is in contrast to the ML approach, since $\underline{\theta}_i$ is itself a r.v., with assumed known a priori density $p(\underline{\theta}_i)$. The goal is to determine $p(\underline{x}|\underline{\theta}_i)$, where the training set serves to convert:

$$\underbrace{p(\underline{\theta}_i)}_{\text{a priori est. of density}} \xrightarrow{\quad H_i \quad} \underbrace{p(\underline{\theta}_i|H_i)}_{\text{a posteriori; after training set}}$$

Thus, H_i is used to refine $p(\underline{\theta}_i)$ to yield $p(\underline{\theta}_i|H_i)$. Ideally, H_i causes $p(\underline{\theta}_i)$ to approach a dirac delta function centered at the true value of $\underline{\theta}_i$. This is shown in the 1-D case in Figure 3.

Recall that our overall goal from (3-14) with the above assumption is to determine $p(\underline{x}|H_i)$, which is the *marginal density* of $p(\underline{x}, \underline{\theta}_i|H_i)$ w.r.t. $\underline{\theta}_i$, that is,

$$p(\underline{x}|H_i) = \int_{\underline{\theta}_i} p(\underline{x}, \underline{\theta}_i|H_i)d\underline{\theta}_i \qquad (3-16a)$$

We can write

$$p(\underline{x}, \underline{\theta}|H) = p(\underline{x}|\underline{\theta}, H)p(\underline{\theta}|H) \qquad (3-16b)$$

If we assume $\underline{x}$ (the feature vector to classify) is independent of H, the training set,

$$p(\underline{x}|\underline{\theta}, H) = p(\underline{x}|\underline{\theta}) \qquad (3-17)$$

Therefore, a very compact and intuitively appealing formulation results:

$$\underbrace{p(\underline{x}|H_i)}_{\text{desired class conditional density}} = \int_{\underline{\theta}_i} p(\underline{x}|\underline{\theta}_i) \underbrace{p(\underline{\theta}_i|H_i)}_{\text{density of } \underline{\theta}_i} d\underline{\theta}_i \qquad (3-18)$$

The intuitive idea is that H_i causes $p(\underline{\theta}_i|H_i)$ to peak sharply.[4] From the sifting property of impulses, if

$$p(\underline{\theta}_i|H_i) \to \delta(\hat{\underline{\theta}}_i) \qquad (3-19a)$$

where δ is the Dirac delta, then from (3-18)

$$p(\underline{x}|H_i) \approx p(\underline{x}|\hat{\underline{\theta}}_i) \qquad (3-19b)$$

---

[4]Ideally, an impulse causes the estimate $\underline{\theta}_i$ to have 'zero' variance.

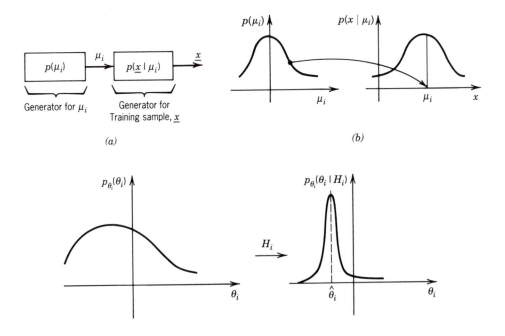

(c)

Note: if H_i determines θ_i exactly, then $p_{\theta_i}(\theta_i \mid H_i)$ is an impulse.

Figure 3:   Model for Bayesian approach to estimation of μ_i.
(a) 2-stage model.
(b) 1-D sketch of process in part (a).
(c) Using H_i to refine $p_{\theta_i}(\theta_i)$ (1-D example).

Since we don't really get this ideal peaking, (3-18) indicates that $p(\underline{x}|H_i)$ is the weighted average of $p(\underline{x}|\underline{\theta}_i)$ with the weighting being $p(\underline{\theta}_i|H_i)$.

EXAMPLE 3

The Bayesian approach for estimation of the mean of a normal density characterized by $\underline{\mu}_i$ and Σ_i is shown. Here $\underline{\theta}_i = \underline{\mu}_i$, and Σ_i is assumed known. For simplicity, the 1-D case is considered first. Samples in the training set H_i are characterized by

$$X \sim N(\mu_i, \sigma_i^2) \qquad (3-20)$$

where the unknown mean, μ_i, is a r.v. with density function $p(\mu_i)$. To reflect our initial uncertainty about μ_i, assume that our best guess of μ_i is its mean value (prior to H_i). Assume that μ_i is characterized by a normal distribution[5] with mean μ_0, and variance

---

[5]Other forms of the density should be considered. See [Patrick 1972].

σ_0^2. This leads to a two-step approach, as shown in Figure 3(c), where $\theta_i = \mu$ in this example. Using Bayes rule,

$$p(\mu|H) = \frac{p(H|\mu)p(\mu)}{p(H)} \qquad (3-21a)$$

Assuming independence of the samples in H, and noting that the denominator of (3-21a) is independent of μ,

$$p(\mu|H) = k_1 \left[\prod_{k=1}^{n} p(x_k|\mu) \right] p(\mu) \qquad (3-21b)$$

where scale factor $k_1 = 1/p(H)$. Incorporating the previously chosen density functions into (3-21b) yields, after some algebraic manipulations

$$p(\mu|H) = k_2 \, \exp\left[-\frac{1}{2}\left\{ \left[\sum_{k=1}^{n}\left(\frac{\mu - x_k}{\sigma}\right)^2 \right] + \left(\frac{\mu - \mu_0}{\sigma_0}\right)^2 \right\} \right] \qquad (3-21c)$$

$$= k_3 \, \exp\left\{ -\frac{1}{2}\left(\frac{n}{\sigma^2} + \frac{1}{\sigma_0^2}\right)\mu^2 - 2\left[\frac{\sum_{k=1}^{n} x_k}{\sigma^2} + \frac{\mu_0}{\sigma_0^2}\right]\mu \right\} \qquad (3-21d)$$

where k_2 and k_3 are constant (scaling) terms. The reader is encouraged to verify this derivation. Equation 3-21d indicates that the 'refined' density, $p(\mu|H)$ based on n samples, is Gaussian with parameters μ_n and σ_n^2. Also (see Appendix 2) $p(\mu|H)$ may be viewed as a density function of a r.v. formed as the *sum* of two Gaussian r.v.s, that is,

$$p(\mu|H) = \frac{1}{\sqrt{2\pi\sigma_n^2}} \exp\left\{ -\frac{1}{2}\left(\frac{\mu - \mu_n}{\sigma_n}\right)^2 \right\} \qquad (3-21e)$$

Completing the square of the exponent in (3-21c) and equating terms with (3-21e) yields

$$\frac{1}{\sigma_n^2} = \frac{n}{\sigma^2} + \frac{1}{\sigma_0^2} \qquad (3-21f)$$

and

$$\frac{\mu_n}{\sigma_n^2} = \frac{1}{\sigma^2}\sum_{k=1}^{n} x_k + \frac{\mu_0}{\sigma_0^2} \qquad (3-21g)$$

(3-21f) and (3-21g) yield a procedure to use the samples in H for updating μ_n and σ_n:

$$\mu_n = \frac{n\sigma_n^2}{\sigma^2}\left(\frac{1}{n}\sum_{k=1}^{n} x_k\right) + \left(\frac{\sigma_n^2}{\sigma_0^2}\right)\mu_0 = \frac{n\sigma_0^2}{n\sigma_0^2 + \sigma^2}\left(\frac{1}{n}\sum_{k=1}^{n} x_k\right) + \left(\frac{\sigma^2}{n\sigma_0^2 + \sigma^2}\right)\mu_0$$

$$(3-22)$$

where

$$\sigma_n^2 = \frac{\sigma_0^2\sigma^2}{n\sigma_0^2 + \sigma^2} \qquad (3-23)$$

The important *structure* of the estimation procedure for μ_n in (3-22) warrants further investigation. Notice that (3-22) incorporates the sample mean $\left(\frac{1}{n}\sum_{k=1}^{n} x_k\right)$ of H, and that (3-23) shows that $\sigma_n^2 \to 0$ as $n \to \infty$. For large n, $\sigma_n^2 \approx \sigma^2/n$, thus indicating that $p(\mu|H)$ approaches a narrow peak (ideally an impulse). Moreover, (3-22) and (3-23) illustrate how the initial guess of μ (i.e., μ_0) and its variance σ_n^2 (initially σ_0^2) are updated via H. Recall that we assumed that μ_0, σ_0^2, and σ^2 were assumed known. Thus, the Bayesian approach allows some (a priori) initial idea of parameter values (i.e., μ_0) and a measure of our confidence in these values (i.e., σ_0) to be incorporated directly into the formulation. ∎

Mean Vector $\underline{\mu}$; Multivariate Gaussian Case. This case follows by extension of the previous example and is left to the reader. The results are summarized and analyzed below. The mean estimator is

$$\underline{\mu}_n = \Sigma_0 \left(\Sigma_0 + \frac{1}{n}\Sigma\right)^{-1} \frac{1}{n}\sum_{k=1}^{n} \underline{x}_k + \frac{1}{n}\Sigma\left(\Sigma_0 + \frac{1}{n}\Sigma\right)^{-1} \underline{\mu}_0 \qquad (3-24)$$

and

$$\Sigma_n = \Sigma_0 \left(\Sigma_0 + \frac{1}{n}\Sigma\right)^{-1} \frac{1}{n}\Sigma \qquad (3-25)$$

We may assess the multidimensional results by analogy with the scalar case (considered in the exercises); however, matrix norms (Appendix 1) are employed. For example, in the computation of the mean estimate, μ_n, when $\| \Sigma_0 \| \gg \| \Sigma \|$, the value of the sample mean of H $\left(\frac{1}{n}\sum_{i=1}^{n} \underline{x}_i\right)$ is emphasized. Conversely, when $\| \Sigma \| \gg \| \Sigma_0 \|$, the value of $\underline{\mu}_0$ receives a relatively larger weighting. Similarly, when $\| \Sigma_0 \| \gg \| \Sigma \|$, $\Sigma_n \to \frac{1}{n}\Sigma$; conversely if $\| \Sigma \| > \| \Sigma_0 \|$, $\Sigma_n \to \Sigma_0$.

SUPERVISED LEARNING USING NONPARAMETRIC APPROACHES

A potential problem with the parametric approaches to supervised learning is that we require the underlying class-conditional pattern distributions (in both *form* and parameters).

Unfortunately, in practice, these two problems may arise:

1. We are not able to determine a specific form (e.g., Gaussian or uniform) for the distributions.
2. The form chosen does not fit one of the 'estimable' formulations.

For these reasons, we resort to *nonparametric learning techniques. Note that we still assume that a (labeled) training set, H_i, is available for each class.*

Nonparametric Approaches

1. *Estimation of density function $p(\underline{x}|w_i)$ (nonparametrically) directly.* For a d-dimensional feature space, this is a generalization of a multidimensional histogram

approach. We would need to study the properties and computational complexity of such an approach.

2. *Directly estimate (nonparametrically)* $P(w_j|\underline{x})$.
3. *Transform the feature space.* This is done in the hope that learning and classification will be easier in the transformed space. We consider this approach later.

General Aspects of Nonparametric Density Estimation

The probability of a vector $\underline{x}$ falling in region R is given by:

$$P(\underline{x} \in R) = \int_R p(\underline{x}')d\underline{x}' \triangleq P \qquad (3-26)$$

Thus, *over R, P* represents a smoothed or averaged measure of the density $p(\underline{x})$. For example, a reasonable assumption might be that $p(\underline{x})$ is constant over R. Therefore, to estimate $p(\underline{x})$, we could first estimate P.

The Basic Approach

Assume that n *independently drawn* samples from the pdf $p(\underline{x})$ that characterize class w_i are available in training set H_i. The probability that k out of n of these samples fall into region R is given by the *binomial distribution*:

$$P(k \text{ of } n \text{ vectors } \in R) = \binom{n}{k} P^k(1-P)^{n-k} \qquad (3-27)$$

where parameter P is from (3-26). The expected number of samples (of the n) falling in R, is the expected value, which in the case of the binomial distribution is

$$E\{k\} = nP \qquad (3-28)$$

This distribution peaks about its mean, nP. This is illustrated by the following example.

The Binomial Distribution and Properties.   The binomial distribution is given by

$$b(k, n, P) = \binom{n}{k} P^k(1-P)^{n-k} \qquad (3-29)$$

where $k = 0, 1, \ldots n$, and

$$\binom{n}{k} = \frac{n!}{(n-k)!k!} \qquad (3-30)$$

The reader is left to verify

$$\mu = nP$$

$$\sigma^2 = nP(1 - P) \tag{3-31}$$

Note also that the maximum variance as a function of P, from $d\sigma^2/dP = n - 2nP = 0$, yields $P = \frac{1}{2}$.

EXAMPLE 4: Application of the Binomial Distribution

Consider the 'coin toss problem' with $n = 6$. Assuming $P = \frac{1}{2}$, the following probabilities of outcomes (of 'heads') are calculated by using (3-29):

$$P(0 \text{ of } 6) = \frac{1}{64}$$
$$P(1 \text{ of } 6) = \frac{6}{64}$$
$$P(2 \text{ of } 6) = \frac{15}{64}$$
$$P(3 \text{ of } 6) = \frac{20}{64}$$
$$P(4 \text{ of } 6) = \frac{15}{64}$$
$$P(5 \text{ of } 6) = \frac{6}{64}$$
$$P(6 \text{ of } 6) = \frac{1}{64}$$

These are plotted in Figure 4. Note that the distribution is symmetric and peaks at $k = nP$. Here, $\sigma^2 = \frac{3}{2}$. ∎

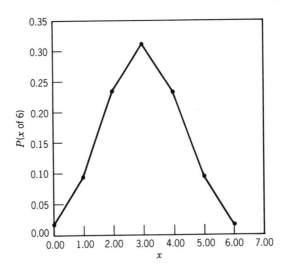

Figure 4: Binomial distribution example.

Significance and Application of the Previous Analysis. The previous analysis indicates that $P(k$ of n vectors $\in R)$ is large when $k \approx nP$. It is small otherwise. On this basis, we assume that it is likely that the *observed number* of vectors falling into R is the mean, that is, $k_{obs} = nP$. This means an estimator for P is $P = k_{obs}/n$. Assuming that $p(\underline{x})$ is constant over R (e.g., R is small), we approximate (3-26) as

$$P(\underline{x} \in R) = \int_R p(\underline{x}')d\underline{x}' \approx p(\underline{x})V \qquad (3-32)$$

where $\underline{x} \in R$ and

$$V = \int_R d\underline{x}' \qquad (3-33)$$

If we use the previous results:

$$p(\underline{x})V = \frac{k}{n} \qquad (3-34)$$

or

$$p(\underline{x}) \approx \frac{k/n}{V} \qquad (3-35)$$

Therefore, for class w_i, using training set H_i containing n samples, we denote the estimated pdf as

$$p_n(\underline{x}) = \frac{k_n/n}{V_n} \qquad (3-36)$$

where k_n of the n samples fall into region R with volume V_n.

We are concerned with the convergence (in several senses) of the result of (3-36) as $n \to \infty$.

Analysis of (3-35). The concerns regarding (3-35) are as follows:

1. If we fix $V_n \to V$ and let the number of samples, $n \to \infty$, the ratio k/n converges to P. However, over R, we still have the averaged version of $p(\underline{x})$.

2. Alternately, if we shrink $V \to 0$, we (theoretically) get less of an averaged value of $p(\underline{x})$, but (practically) R becomes so small that $k \to 0$, and we therefore (perhaps incorrectly) assume $p(\underline{x}) = 0$ for $\underline{x} \in R$. Even if $k \neq 0$, for small k, we suspect that estimates of $p(\underline{x})$ may vary considerably from region to region.

Therefore, given a fixed number of samples, n, in H_i, a trade-off exists between the volume V of d-dimensional region R, and the accuracy of the estimate of $p(\underline{x})$, and involves V versus n. This suggests that R cannot be allowed to become arbitrarily small.

Convergence of Estimates. For region R_n, we define

$$V_n = \int_{R_n} d\underline{x} \qquad (3-37)$$

The 'shape' of R_n may be chosen based on a priori knowledge of the density. Furthermore, k_n is the number of samples in R_n and $p_n(\underline{x})$ is the estimate of $p(\underline{x})$ over

R_n, where $\underline{x} \in R_n$ and $p_n(x)$ is given by (3-36). We explore the behavior of $p_n(\underline{x})$ as $n \to \infty$. Specifically, the conditions under which

$$\lim_{n \to \infty} p_n(\underline{x}) = p(\underline{x}) \tag{3-38}$$

are:

1. $\lim\limits_{n \to \infty} V_n = 0$ (There is no averaging in the limit.)

2. $\lim\limits_{n \to \infty} k_n = \infty$ (The relative frequency converges to a probability.) For example, note if $k_n \to c$ as $n \to \infty$, $p(\underline{x}) \to 0$.

3. $\lim\limits_{n \to \infty} (k_n/n) = 0$ [For $p(\underline{x})$ to be interpreted as a density, P(any single value of continuous r.v. $X) = 0$.]

Solutions that Achieve the Desired Convergences

1. *Shrinking Regions.* R^d is initially subdivided into regions, each with volume V_0. This volume is then shrunk as a function of n,

$$V_n = \frac{V_0}{f_w(n)} \tag{3-39}$$

where $f_w(\ )$ is a function that controls the size (and perhaps the shape) of the volume. For example, $f_w(n) = \sqrt{n}$. This leads to the *Parzen-Window (PW) method*.

2. *Growing Regions.* The number of samples desired in R_n is specified, that is,

$$k_n = f_k(n) \tag{3-40}$$

and R is grown or expanded until it includes k_n samples. For example, $f_k(n) = \sqrt{n}$. This approach gives rise to the k_n *nearest-neighbor method* $(k_n - NNR)$.

PARZEN WINDOWS

In this section, we follow the formulation of [Duda/Hart 1973]. Assume R_n is a d-dimensional hypercube in R^d with edge dimension h_n, that is, $V_n = (h_n)^d$ centered at $\underline{x}$. To facilitate analysis, define a *d-dimensional unit step function* or *unit hypercube* centered at $\underline{x} = 0$.

Unit Step Function $\phi(\underline{x})$

$$\phi(\underline{x}) = \begin{cases} 1 & |x_i| \leq \frac{1}{2} \quad i = 1, 2, \ldots d \\ 0 & \text{otherwise} \end{cases} \tag{3-41}$$

For example, for $d = 2$, a 2-D step or 'rect' function, is shown in Figure 5.[6] Notice that

---

[6]See Chapter 3 of [Schalkoff 1989] for applications of this function in 2-D signal processing.

$$\int_{R^d} \phi(\underline{x})d\underline{x} = 1 \qquad (3-42)$$

and

$$\phi_2(\underline{x}) = \phi\left(\frac{\underline{x} - \underline{x}^i}{h_n}\right) \qquad (3-43)$$

is a *translated and scaled* version of $\phi(\underline{x})$, where the origin or center of $\phi_2(\underline{x})$ is at $\underline{x}_i$. Also note the constraint from (3-43):

$$|x_j - x_j^i| \le \frac{1}{2}h_n \quad j = 1, 2, \dots d \qquad (3-44)$$

where x_j^i is the jth element of $\underline{x}_i$. A family of these step functions may then be developed to 'cover' or tesselate R^d, with side dimension h_n and volume h_n^d. An example is shown in Figure 6.

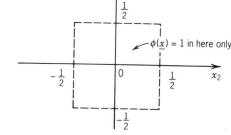

Figure 5:   Example of $\phi(\underline{x})$ in 2-D.

Notice that

$$\phi\left(\frac{\underline{x} - \underline{x}_i}{h_n}\right) = \phi\left(\frac{\underline{x}_i - \underline{x}}{h_n}\right) = 1 \qquad (3-45)$$

if $\underline{x}_i$ is within the hypercube with side dimension h_n, centered at $\underline{x}$. Therefore, $\phi(\underline{x})$ provides a useful tool to count samples in R. For a training set with n samples, the number of samples in the hypercube region centered at $\underline{x}$ is

$$k_n = \sum_{i=1}^n \phi\left(\frac{\underline{x} - \underline{x}_i}{h_n}\right) \qquad (3-46)$$

A More General Interpretation of $\phi(\underline{x})$ as an Interpolation Function.   Since (3-36) indicates $p_n(\underline{x}) = (k_n/n)/V_n$, the previous derivation yields

$$p_n(\underline{x}) = \frac{1}{n}\sum_{i=1}^n \frac{\phi\left[(\underline{x} - \underline{x}_i)/h_n\right]}{V_n} \qquad (3-47)$$

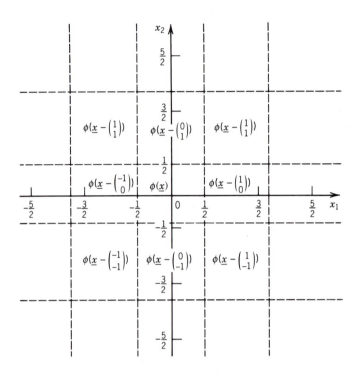

Figure 6:   Example of translated unit step (interpolation) functions, $\phi(\underline{x})$, used to tesselate R^2.

Equation 3-47 suggests that ϕ may be viewed as an *interpolation function* for $p_n(\underline{x})$, where samples $\underline{x}_i$ are available.[7] Defining

$$\delta_n(\underline{x}) = \frac{1}{V_n}\phi\left(\frac{\underline{x}}{h_n}\right) \qquad (3-48)$$

From (3-47), $p_n(\underline{x})$ therefore becomes the arithmetic sum of

$$p_n(\underline{x}) = \frac{1}{n}\sum_{i=1}^{n}\delta_n(\underline{x}-\underline{x}_i) \qquad (3-49)$$

Note that parameter h_n enters into (3-49) (through δ_n) in both ϕ and V_n. As $h_n \to 0$, $\delta_n(\underline{x})$ approaches a Dirac delta function. Two observations regarding the pdf estimator $p_n(\underline{x})$ in (3-49) are the following:

1. If h_n is large, $p_n(\underline{x})$ reflects a large amount of smoothing, since $\delta_n(\underline{x}-\underline{x}_i)$ is (relatively) insensitive to variations in $\underline{x}$.

---

[7] Recall that interpolation functions are used to determine function values between known, or sample, points.

2. If h_n is small, $\delta_n(\underline{x})$ peaks sharply at $\underline{x} = 0$. Therefore, $\delta_n(\underline{x} - \underline{x}_i)$ peaks at $\underline{x} = \underline{x}_i$, and $p_n(\underline{x})$ is the sum of n narrow 'pulses' centered around each of the samples $\underline{x}_i$. For a modest sized training set H_i, this may lead to unacceptable (and perhaps erratic) variations in $p_n(\underline{x})$.

$\phi(\underline{x})$ *as a Random Variable.*   Since $\underline{x}_i$ is (assumed to be) a r.v., $\phi(\underline{x} - \underline{x}_i)$, for fixed $\underline{x}$, is a function of a r.v. Under reasonable conditions (which we avoid here), $\phi(\underline{x} - \underline{x}_i)$ is therefore also a r.v., albeit a scalar r.v. Consequently, *the pdf estimate $p_n(\underline{x})$ is the sum of n r.v.s, and therefore a r.v. itself.* Recognizing this, we may wish to consider properties of $p_n(\underline{x})$, such as $E[p_n(\underline{x})]$ and $\mathrm{Var}\,[p_n(\underline{x})]$. In addition, as a function of n, $p_n(\underline{x})$ is a *sequence of r.v.s.*

Extension to More General Interpolation Functions

The choice of $\phi(\underline{x})$ in (3-47) yields a Zero Order Hold (ZOH) type of interpolator. ZOHs are familiar entities in discrete domain signal processing. More general choices of $\delta_n(\underline{x})$, which reflect a choice of alternative interpolation strategies, are both possible and desirable. For example, one such Gaussian interpolation function,

$$\delta_G(\underline{x}) = \frac{1}{(2\pi)^{\frac{d}{2}}} \exp\left\{-\frac{1}{2}\underline{x}^T\underline{x}\right\} \qquad (3-50)$$

is possible, and yields a 'smoother' interpolation strategy, with more central weighting of each sample, $\underline{x}_i$. In order to make the interpolation function of (3-50) sensitive to n (and perhaps control 'peaking'), a covariance matrix, Σ_n, which is parameterized by n, could be used. This is explored in the problems.

Convergence of the Mean of $p_n(\underline{x})$.   From (3-47), $p_n(\underline{x})$ is seen to be a function of the samples $\underline{x}_i, i = 1, 2, \ldots n$ in H_i. Presumably, these samples may be characterized by the true density $p(\underline{x})$. Therefore,

$$E[p_n(\underline{x})] = \frac{1}{n}\sum_{i=1}^{n} E\left\{\frac{1}{V_n}\phi\left[\frac{\underline{x} - \underline{x}_i}{h_n}\right]\right\} = \frac{1}{n}\cdot n\cdot\int\frac{1}{V_n}\phi\left[\frac{\underline{x} - \underline{\xi}}{h_n}\right]p(\underline{\xi})d\underline{\xi}$$

$$= \int \delta_n(\underline{x} - \underline{\xi})p(\underline{\xi})d\underline{\xi} = \delta_n(\underline{x}) * p(\underline{x}) \qquad (3-51)$$

where the operator $*$ represents a multidimensional convolution. Since we have already shown

$$\lim_{n\to\infty} \delta_n(\underline{x}) = \delta(\underline{x}) \qquad (3-52)$$

the sifting property of $\delta(\underline{x})$ yields

$$\lim_{n\to\infty} E[p_n(\underline{x})] = p(\underline{x}) \qquad (3-53)$$

Although we have not stressed them in the derivation, the following are required for (3-52) to hold true:

1. $p(\underline{x})$ is continuous.
2. $\phi(\underline{x}) \geq 0$.
3. $\int \phi(\underline{x})d\underline{x} = 1$.

k-NN NONPARAMETRIC ESTIMATION
A Problem with V_o

Recall that in the previous approach we shrunk the volume of the regions centered at $\underline{x}$ via approaches such as

$$V_n = \frac{V_0}{\sqrt{n}} \quad n > 0 \tag{3-54}$$

Therefore, the success of the nonparametric procedure is linked to initial region volume choice V_0. If V_0 is too small, R^d is subdivided into a large number of small regions. With a finite number of samples in H_i, many of the regions will not contain samples, and consequently the $\phi(\underline{x})$ functions will change erratically over $\underline{x}$. Conversely, if V_0 is too large, $p_n(\underline{x})$ will reflect a great deal of smoothing of the actual density, $p(\underline{x})$. Note that the above problem occurs since V_0, and consequently V_n, is independent of the actual sample values in H_i.[8] We refer to this approach as *iteration driven* volume determination.

A Data-Driven Approach.   Suppose, instead, that the cell volume V_n, $n > 1$, is allowed to be a function of the sample data. We formulate a *data-driven* approach to cell size determination. Given H_i, we form some number of regions (or volumes), each centered about a location $\underline{x} \in R^d$. The size of the region is then expanded until it encloses k_n samples, where $k_n = f(n)$. These samples are then the k_n nearest neighbors of location $\underline{x}$. If the density of training samples is high around $\underline{x}$, the region will be small. Conversely, a low density yields a large region. Note that a region cannot be infinite, since ultimately it will grow to border on neighboring regions.

Ramifications of the 'Region Growing' Approach.[9]   It is desired that

$$\lim_{n \to \infty} k_n \to \infty \tag{3-55}$$

so that the ratio k_n/n approaches (from a relative frequency viewpoint) the probability that a sample falls in a region with volume V_n, that is,

$$p_n(\underline{x}) = \frac{P(\underline{x} \text{ falls in } R(\underline{x}) \text{ with vol. } V_n)}{V_n} \tag{3-56}$$

For example, suppose $k_n = f(n) = \sqrt{n}$, that is,

$$p_n(\underline{x}) = \frac{k_n/n}{V_n} = \frac{1/\sqrt{n}}{V_n} \approx p(\underline{x}) \tag{3-57}$$

so rearranging (3-57) yields

---

[8]Note that it does depend on the number, n.

[9]This term is used frequently in image processing.

$$V_n = \frac{1}{\sqrt{n}p(\underline{x})} \qquad (3-58)$$

Notice that V_n is still a function of n, as in the previous formulation, *but is also weighted by* $p(\underline{x})$. Thus, if $p(\underline{x})$ is small in a region around $\underline{x}$, V_n will be large and vice versa. This is intuitively appealing.

Estimation of $P(w_i|\underline{x})$ Directly

Suppose we place a region of volume V and $\underline{x}$ and *capture k samples, k_i of which turn out to be labeled w_i.* We may approximate the joint density function of $\underline{x}$ and w_i by[10]

$$p_n(\underline{x}, w_i) = \frac{k_i/n}{V} \qquad (3-59)$$

as expected. From Bayes rule,

$$P_n(w_i|\underline{x})p_n(\underline{x}) = p_n(\underline{x}, w_i) \qquad (3-60)$$

or

$$P_n(w_i|\underline{x}) = \frac{p_n(\underline{x}, w_i)}{\sum_{j=1}^{c} p_n(\underline{x}, w_j)} = \frac{(k_i/n)/V}{\sum_{j=1}^{c}(k_j/n)/V} = \frac{k_i}{k} \qquad (3-61)$$

Thus, $P_n(w_i|\underline{x}) = k_i/k$, which is simply the fraction of samples ('captured') in R with label w_i.

Recalling that for the Bayes minimum error rate we select the largest $P(w_i|\underline{x})$, (3-61) requires we select the class *most frequently observed, that is, with the largest population* within the region centered at $\underline{x}$. The region size may be chosen via either the k-NNR or the Parzen window approaches. More importantly, however, this strategy leads to a powerful, commonly used and computationally simpler *direct classification strategy* commonly known as the *Nearest Neighbor Rule*.

EXAMPLES OF NONPARAMETRIC LEARNING

Figure 7 shows a 1-D example of the nonparametric approach. Notice that the density function estimate begins to approach the shape of the true density with increasing N. Figure 8 shows a 2-D example.

DIRECT CLASSIFICATION USING THE TRAINING SET [THE NEAREST NEIGHBOR RULE (NNR)]
The NNR Approach

The NNR technique represents a very practical approach for direct classification. *The NNR still requires and uses (directly) a priori information in the form of the training set.*

---

[10]Notice that here we use $k_i \leq k$ of the n in the numerator ratio. A relative frequency of occurrence interpretation of the joint density $p_n(\underline{x}, w_i)$, which corresponds to our previous strategy (3-36), is that we discard those $k - k_i$ samples that are not labeled w_i in forming the observed frequency k/n.

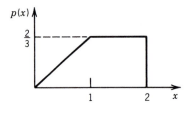

(a)

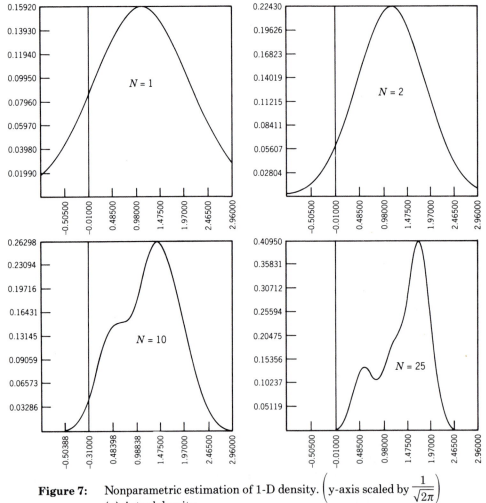

Figure 7:   Nonparametric estimation of 1-D density. $\left(\text{y-axis scaled by } \dfrac{1}{\sqrt{2\pi}}\right)$
(a) Actual density.

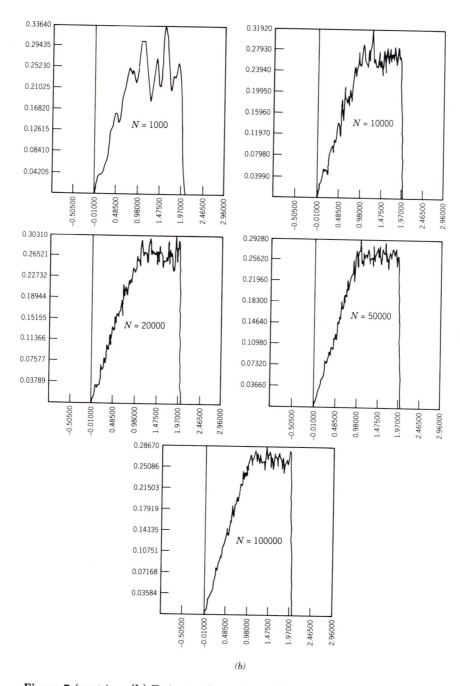

(b)

Figure 7 (cont.):   **(b)** Estimates for various values of N.

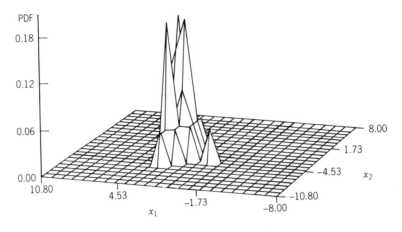

(a)

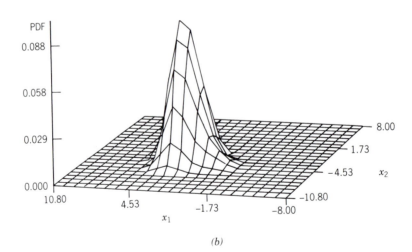

(b)

Figure 8:   Nonparametric estimation of 2-D density.
(a) Estimated pdf using 2-D rect, $\phi(\ \ )$, as interpolation function (30 samples).
(b) Estimated pdf using Gaussian interpolation function (30 samples).

Suppose we are given a (new) vector to classify, denoted $\underline{x}$, and a training set in the form of labeled samples:

$$H_n = \{\underline{x}_1, \underline{x}_2, \ldots \underline{x}_n\} \qquad (3-62)$$

where each $\underline{x}_i$ is labeled as to class membership. Suppose $\underline{x}'$ is the labeled sample in H_n nearest to $\underline{x}$. This implies a distance or similarity measure and requires further definition. The 1-NN rule (or NNR) is simple: $\underline{x}$ *is classified by assigning it the same label as the class of* $\underline{x}'$.

The NNR, instead of requiring underlying class distributions, requires that H_n be large and accurate. The underlying idea is quite simple: *samples that are 'close' in feature space likely belong to the same class.* The NNR rule is a suboptimal classification procedure when compared with the Bayesian approach, since in the asymptotic case $(n \rightarrow \infty)$

$$\text{error rate}_{NNR} > \text{error rate}_{Bayes} \qquad (3-63)$$

As we derive below,

$$\lim_{n \rightarrow \infty} \Rightarrow \text{error rate}_{NNR} < 2 * \text{error rate}_{Bayes} \qquad (3-64)$$

This suggests, in a sense, that the 1-NNR uses at least one half of the classification information in an infinite training set.

Why the 1-NNR Should Work.   Suppose $\underline{x}' \in H_n$ is the 1-NNR of $\underline{x}$, the class label of $\underline{x}'$ is θ', and the true class of $\underline{x}$ is w. The error in the 1-NNR rule is denoted e_{1NNR} and is defined as

$$e_{1NNR}(\underline{x}, \underline{x}') = P(w \neq \theta' | \underline{x}, \underline{x}') = \sum_i P(w = w_i, \theta' \neq w_i | \underline{x}, \underline{x}') \qquad (3-65)$$

With several assumptions concerning independence, (3-65) becomes

$$e_{1NNR}(\underline{x}, \underline{x}') = \sum_i P(w = w_i | \underline{x}) P(\theta' \neq w_i | \underline{x}') = \sum_i P(w = w_i | \underline{x})[1 - P(\theta' = w_i | \underline{x}')] \qquad (3-66)$$

Since $\underline{x}'$ is close to $\underline{x}$, if in the so-called large sample case we assume that the training set becomes so 'dense' in R^d that

$$\lim_{n \rightarrow \infty} \{P(\theta' = w_i | \underline{x}')\} = P(w = w_i | \underline{x}) \qquad (3-67)$$

(3-66) may be written as

$$e_{1NNR}(\underline{x}, \underline{x}') = \sum_i P(w = w_i | \underline{x})[1 - P(w = w_i | \underline{x})]$$

$$= \sum_i P(w = w_i | \underline{x}) - \sum_i [P(w = w_i | \underline{x})]^2 \qquad (3-68)$$

or

$$e_{1NNR}(\underline{x}, \underline{x}') = 1 - \sum_i [P(w = w_i | \underline{x})]^2 \qquad (3-69)$$

If there exists some class, w_m, such that

$$P(w_m|\underline{x}) = \overset{max}{i} \{P(w_i|\underline{x})\} \ i = 1, 2, \ldots c \tag{3 – 70}$$

when $P(w_m|\underline{x}) \approx 1$, the error rate in (3-69) will be small. This is easier to see if we note, for this class,

$$1 - [P(w_m|\underline{x})]^2 \approx 2[1 - P(w_m|\underline{x})] \tag{3 – 71}$$

In contrast, however, if all classes are equally likely, $P(w = w_i|\underline{x}) = 1/c$, and

$$e_{1NNR}(\underline{x}, \underline{x}') = 1 - \sum_{i=1}^{c} \left(\frac{1}{c}\right)^2 = 1 - \frac{1}{c} \tag{3 – 72}$$

For example, if $c = 2$ and $P(w = w_i|\underline{x}) = \frac{1}{2}$, then

$$e_{1NNR}(\underline{x}, \underline{x}') = \frac{1}{2} \tag{3 – 73}$$

An alternative and more intuitive interpretation of why the 1-NNR should work follows. Denote the sample-conditioned probability that $\theta' = w_i$ as $P(w_i|\underline{x})$. If

$$\lim_{n \to \infty} \{P(w_i|\underline{x}')\} = P(w_i|\underline{x}) \tag{3 – 74}$$

we can view the 1-NNR as a decision rule that, given $\underline{x}$ and $\underline{x}'$, selects class w_i with probability $P(w_i|\underline{x})$. In this sense, it is a randomized decision rule. Using the definition of w_m from (3-70), recall that the Bayes decision rule computes $P(w_i|\underline{x})$ $\forall i$ and *always* assigns $\underline{x}$ to w_m. Conversely, the 1-NNR selects w_i with $P(w_i|\underline{x})$. When $P(w_m|\underline{x})$ is large relative to other $P(w_i|\underline{x})$, for example, close to 1.0, the 1-NNR will approach the Bayes error rate.

Extensions to and Ramifications of the 1-NNR.   The 1-NNR uses the training set directly to implement a classifier. Classification capability is achieved by considering samples in H to be typical representations of each class and employing a similarity measure. One of the difficult problems, which we find is also prevalent in SyntPR, is the determination of a good, or even suitable, similarity measure. Appendix 5 shows examples of alternative choices. Thus, 'similar' patterns yield similar classification decisions (outputs). This operational structure is somewhat similar to the neural network pattern associator implementations we consider in Chapters 11 to 13.

The previous approach may be extended to the k-Nearest Neighbor Rule (k-NNR), where we examine the labels on the k-nearest samples in H and then classify by using a voting scheme. Often, in $c = 2$ class problems, k is chosen to be an odd number, to avoid 'ties.' Other significant concerns and possible extensions include the use of a reject option in instances where there is no clear 'winner,' and the finite sample size performance of the NNR.

Efficient Algorithms for Finding Nearest Neighbors.   Given a vector $\underline{x}_u$ and a training set H, whose cardinality may be large, the computational expense of finding the nearest neighbor of $\underline{x}_u$ may be significant. For this reason, frequent attention has been given to efficient algorithms. The computational savings are typically achieved by a preordering of samples in H, combined with efficient (often hierarchical) search strategies. Examples of these are documented in [Friedman et al. 1975], [Sethi 1981], and [Yunck 1976].

Example of 1-NNR and 3-NNR Classification.   Figures 9(a) and 9(b) illustrate the application of nearest neighbor classification.

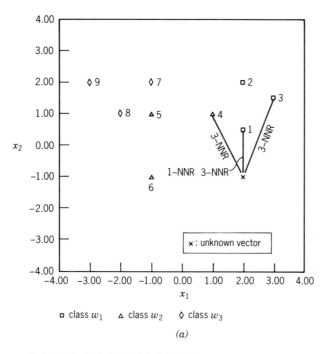

(a)

Vector to classify is: 2.000000 –1.000000

Sample No.	x_1	x_2	Class	Distribution to x	
1	2.000	0.500	w_1	1.500	(1–NNR)
2	2.000	2.000	w_1	3.000	
3	3.000	1.500	w_1	2.693	(3–NNR)
4	1.000	1.000	w_2	2.236	(3–NNR)
5	–1.000	1.000	w_2	3.606	
6	–1.000	–1.000	w_2	3.000	
7	–1.000	2.000	w_3	4.243	
8	–2.000	1.000	w_3	4.472	
9	–3.000	2.000	w_3	5.831	

Min distance: 1.500   Vector no.: 1   Class: w_1

(b)

Figure 9:   Example of 1-NNR.
(a) Graphical results.
(b) Numerical results.

Decision Trees. As shown in Chapter 1, once R^d is partitioned into decision regions the classification problem is trivial. Therefore, it is worthwhile to consider special, constrained partitions of R^d. One such case is when the decision boundaries are hyperplanes *and constrained to be parallel to the feature axes.* In such cases, a sequential classification procedure may be developed by considering successive partitions of R^d. The resulting procedure yields a *decision tree*–based classifier. Figure 10 illustrates theapproach. Algorithms to achieve these decision boundaries are considered in [Kanal 1979], [Friedman 1977], and [Sethi/Sarvarayudu 1982].

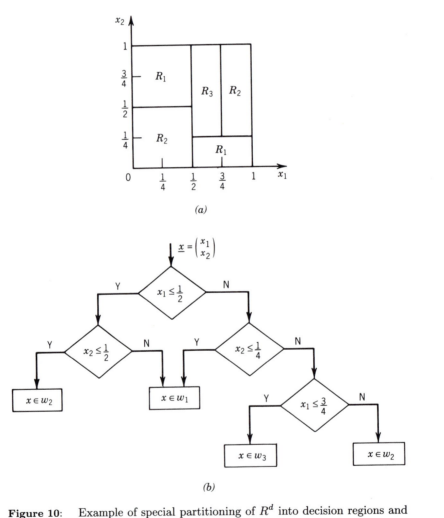

Figure 10: Example of special partitioning of R^d into decision regions and decision tree $(d = 2, c = 3)$.
(a) Decision regions in R^2 $(w_i \Leftrightarrow R_i)$.
(b) Decision tree.

BIBLIOGRAPHICAL REMARKS

Comprehensive presentations of parametric and nonparametric estimation approaches are found in [Duda/Hart 1973] and [Therrien 1989]. These sources, in turn, provide directions to, and interpretations of, the seminal estimation papers in this area, which date back to the 1940s. One of the seminal papers on the nearest neighbor approach is [Cover/Hart 1967]. Hierarchical classifier design and decision trees are considered in [Casey/Nagy 1984], [Sethi/Sarvarayudu 1982], [Wang/Suen 1984], [Kanal 1979], and [Henrichon/Fu 1969].

EXERCISES

3.1 Explain why the ML approach fails with a uniform distribution.

3.2 Derive (3-11).

3.3 Equation (3-50) indicated that $\delta_G(\underline{x})$ was an alternative interpolation function. Notice that n, and consequently V_n, does not enter into this formulation (i.e., there is no hypercube) since there is no limit to the extent of $\delta_G(\underline{x})$. How can we control the local effect of $\delta_G(\underline{x})$, possibly as a function of n?

3.4 Derive (3-18).

3.5 Compute $db(k, nP)/dk$ in (3-29) and find the maximum of b. Does intuition support this result?

3.6 Repeat Problem 3.5 with $P = \frac{1}{4}$. Compute σ^2 and compare the results with Figure 1.

3.7 Show that δ_n, defined in (3-48), has the properties:

  (a) $\int \delta_n(\underline{x} - \underline{x}_i)d\underline{x} = 1.0 \, \forall \, n$.

  (b) $\lim_{h_n \to 0} \delta_n(\underline{x} - \underline{x}_i) = \delta(\underline{x} - \underline{x}_i)$ where δ is the n-dimensional Dirac delta function.
     [Hint: it may be easier to consider $\delta_n(\underline{x})$ first.]

3.8 Show

$$\lim_{n \to \infty} \sigma_n^2(\underline{x}) = 0$$

where σ_n^2 is $\text{Var}[p_n(\underline{x})]$ in (3-36).

3.9 Derive (3-71) via a Taylor Series Expansion.

3.10 Given the following labeled samples $\underline{x} = (x_1, \ x_2)^T$ in R^2:

Class w_1 :		Class w_2 :		Class w_3 :	
2.491	2.176	4.218	−2.075	−2.520	0.483
1.053	0.677	−1.156	−2.992	−1.163	3.161
5.792	3.425	−4.435	1.408	−13.438	2.414
2.054	−1.467	−1.794	−2.838	−4.467	2.298
0.550	4.020	−2.137	−2.473	−3.711	4.364

Classify each of the following vectors, by using
  (a) The 1-NNR rule.
  (b) A 3-NNR rule.

$$
\begin{array}{rr}
2.543 & 0.046 \\
4.812 & 2.316 \\
-2.799 & 0.746 \\
1.079 & -1.735 \\
-3.787 & -1.400 \\
-7.429 & 2.329
\end{array}
$$

3.11 Show why

$$\hat{\Sigma} = \frac{1}{n}\sum_{i=1}^{n}(\underline{x}_i - \underline{\mu})(\underline{x}_i - \underline{\mu})^T$$

is a biased estimator for the covariance matrix.

3.12 Given the 2×1 sample vectors for a $c = 3$ class problem shown in Figure P.1, assume equal a priori probabilities and Gaussian density functions, and

(a) Estimate $\underline{\mu}_i$ and Σ_i for each class.

(b) Assuming $\Sigma_i = \Sigma$, for $i = 1, 2, 3$, use the pooled data to estimate Σ.

(c) Plot the samples and draw the decision regions. Assume equal a priori probabilities. Derive suitable discriminant functions for each class.

(d) Calculate the classification error based on the results of (a) to (c).

3.13 For the training set shown in Figure P.1, classify each of the vectors shown in Figure P.2, using the discriminant functions found in Problem 3.12.

Class w_1		Class w_2		Class w_3	
3.406	4.439	-4.256	-3.556	-4.306	4.967
3.811	4.893	-2.921	-2.543	-4.581	3.527
4.395	3.351	-2.962	-3.071	-3.606	3.334
5.340	2.770	-4.886	-5.544	-3.640	4.041
4.238	4.093	-2.452	-3.472	-2.899	4.127
4.249	3.562	-4.154	-3.769	-5.044	3.889
2.917	4.121	-5.018	-3.542	-3.501	4.047
4.992	4.851	-1.488	-3.488	-2.967	2.224
3.556	3.414	-4.680	-5.309	-3.466	4.475
4.437	3.178	-4.493	-5.967	-3.131	2.235
4.034	4.173	-4.162	-3.635	-4.114	2.561
4.326	5.138	-6.386	-3.763	-5.422	4.341
4.797	3.955	-3.136	-3.849	-4.450	4.243
1.962	2.517	-4.632	-4.351	-3.310	3.130
4.698	3.328	-5.684	-5.190	-3.607	3.318

Figure P.1: $(\underline{x}_i = [x_1 x_2]^T)$

$$
\begin{array}{rr}
4.7583 & 1.432 \\
-4.020 & -2.817 \\
-1.103 & 3.562
\end{array}
$$

Figure P.2: Data for classification $(\underline{x}_i = [x_1 \ x_2]^T)$.

3.14   (This makes an excellent project.) Given a r.v. $\underline{X}$, where $\underline{X} \sim N(\underline{\mu}, \Sigma)$ with $\Sigma = \begin{pmatrix} 1 & 0 \\ 0 & 4 \end{pmatrix}$ and $\underline{\mu} = \begin{pmatrix} 3 \\ -3 \end{pmatrix}$, develop a Parzen-window based nonparametric procedure to estimate $p(\underline{x})$. Specifically:

(a)   Generate a training set H_i (Box–Mullers approach from Appendix 2 may be useful) with several different choices of n.

(b)   Pick one or more suitable interpolation functions, $\phi(\underline{x})$.

(c)   Pick at least three choices for initial window dimensions. These should be related to your analysis of the given statistics.

(d)   Formulate $p_n(\underline{x})$ for each choice in (c).

(e)   Using (a), show (plot) $p_n(\underline{x})$ for each of the formulations in (d).

3.15   Repeat Problem 3.14 for the 1-D density shown in Figure P.3. Show plots at $n = 10$, 100, $1,000$, and $5,000$.

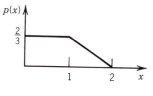

Figure P.3

3.16   Repeat Problem 3.15 for the 1-D density shown in Figure P.4.

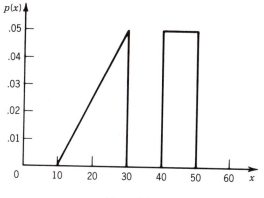

Figure P.4

3.17   Figure P.5 shows a two-class training set that summarizes the nine features of different flags. This is used to explore several classification/discrimination strategies. 'Type' refers to the classes and is not a feature. In this case, discrete variables 'union' (u) or 'confederate' (c) (some of which are binary) are used.

Flag	Stars	Bars	Stripes	Hues	Xcross	Icon	Humans	Word	Number	Type
Alabama	0	0	0	2	1	N	0	0	0	C
Arkansas	29	0	0	3	0	N	0	1	0	C
Connecticut	0	0	0	5	0	Y	0	4	0	U
Delaware	0	0	0	6	0	Y	2	4	2	U
Florida	0	0	0	6	1	Y	1	15	0	C
Georgia	13	1	0	3	1	Y	0	3	1	C
Illinois	0	0	0	6	0	Y	0	6	2	U
Iowa	0	2	0	5	0	Y	0	10	0	U
Louisiana	0	0	0	4	0	Y	0	4	0	C
Maryland	0	12	0	4	0	N	0	0	0	U
Massachusetts	1	0	0	4	0	Y	1	6	0	U
Mississippi	13	0	3	3	1	N	0	0	0	C
New Hampshire	9	0	0	5	0	Y	0	7	1	U
New Jersey	0	0	0	5	0	Y	2	3	1	U
New York	0	0	0	6	0	Y	2	1	0	U
N. Carolina	1	1	2	4	0	N	0	3	4	C
Ohio	17	0	5	3	0	N	0	0	0	U
Rhode Island	13	0	0	3	0	Y	0	1	0	U
S. Carolina	0	0	0	2	0	Y	0	0	0	C
Tennesee	3	2	0	3	0	N	0	0	0	C
Texas	1	1	2	3	0	N	0	0	0	C
Virginia	0	0	0	5	0	Y	2	4	0	C
Wisconsin	0	0	0	5	0	Y	2	2	1	U
Washington DC	3	0	5	2	0	N	0	0	0	U

Figure P.5

(a) Formulate a discriminant function that, using any combination of the 9 features, allows discrimination between class u and class c.

(b) If only *one* feature were allowed, which would you use? Assume the criterion is to maximize classification accuracy. What if only two were allowed?

(c) Assume the last ('Type') column in Figure P.5 is not given. Using the features given, are there any natural clusters of u or c type flags?

3.18 Suppose x is distributed uniformly with one endpoint fixed, i.e.,

$$p(x_k|\theta) = \begin{cases} \dfrac{1}{\theta} & 0 \le x \le \theta \\ 0 & \text{elsewhere.} \end{cases}$$

(a) For some given value of x, e.g., x_1, sketch $p(x_1|\theta)$ as a function of θ. This should help you to solve parts (b) and (c).

(b) Assuming n independent samples of x, compute the likelihood function $p(H|\theta)$. Hint: it is *not*

$$\overset{n}{\underset{i=1}{\pi}} \left(\frac{1}{\theta}\right)$$

Why?

(c) Show that the maximum likelihood estimate for θ, on the basis of n samples $\{x_1, x_2, \ldots x_n\}$, is the largest x_i. Does intuition support this?

(d) What if the problem generalized such that $x_k \in [\theta_{min}, \theta_{max}]$?

3.19 Show that the covariance matrix estimator

$$\hat{\Sigma}_{\underline{X}} = \frac{1}{n-1} \sum_{k=1}^{n} (\underline{x}_k - \hat{\underline{\mu}})(\underline{x}_k - \hat{\underline{\mu}})^T$$

is unbiased.

3.20 Discuss the similarities and differences between the maximum likelihood and Bayesian approaches to supervised parametric training (estimation). Illustrate your conclusions by considering two cases:

(a) The estimation of the mean μ of an (assumed) Gaussian density function; and

(b) The estimation of μ in the case of a uniform pdf.

3.21 **(a)** Verify the derivation of (3-21c) and (3-21d) from (3-21b).

(b) Verify (3-21e) to (3-21g).

3.22 Using (3-22) show what value of μ_n results in the following cases and analyze the result:

(a) $\sigma_0 = 0$;

(b) $\sigma_0 \neq 0$, $\sigma_0 \gg \sigma$.

3.23 Derive the Bayesian estimator for $\underline{\mu}$ in the multidimensional Gaussian case [(3-24) and (3-25)].

3.24 Show that an equivalent formulation of (3-24) is

$$\underline{\mu}_n = \left(\Sigma + \frac{1}{n}\Sigma_0^{-1} \right)^{-1} \left(\Sigma \frac{1}{n} \sum_{i=1}^{n} \underline{x}_i + \frac{1}{n}\Sigma_0^{-1}\underline{\mu}_0 \right)$$

3.25 Discuss the necessary modifications of the ML and Bayesian parameter estimation formulations in the case where *the samples in H are not independent*.

3.26 Consider a $d = 2$ dimensional, $c = 2$ class problem with Gaussian densities and a priori probabilities as follows:

$$\underline{\mu}_1 = \begin{pmatrix} 2 \\ 0 \end{pmatrix} \quad \underline{\mu}_2 = \begin{pmatrix} -2 \\ 0 \end{pmatrix}$$

$$\Sigma_1 = \Sigma_2 = \begin{pmatrix} 1 & 0 \\ 0 & \alpha \end{pmatrix} \quad \alpha > 0$$

$$\frac{P(w_1)}{P(w_2)} = r \quad r > 0$$

where α and r are variable parameters.

(a) For $\alpha = r = 1$, plot the contours of constant $p(\underline{x}|w_i)$ and the decision boundary.

(b) Repeat (a) for (i) $\alpha = 4$, $r = 1$, and (ii) $\alpha = 1$, $r = 4$. Show the change in orientation and location of the separating hyperplane.

(c) Compute the normal to the separating hyperplane as a function of α, and show how this makes intuitive sense.

3.27 The k-NNR, while intuitively appealing, requires significant computational effort in computing n distance measures when the number of samples n in the training set is large.

(a) By using a Euclidean distance measure, develop an approach for efficient computation of the 1-NN of $\underline{x}$. [Hint: partitioning of H is useful.]

(b) In the case of discrete binary feature vectors, develop an approach for computationally efficient determination of similarity by using the Hamming distance as a measure.

3.28 Consider the case of *class feature overlap* and its influence on the 1-NN classification rule. For example, if H contains $\underline{x}^{(w_1)} = (1 \quad 0)^T$ as well as $\underline{x}^{(w_2)} = (1 \quad 0)^T$, what happens to the 1-NN decision rule? How would this be handled in the Bayesian formulation?

3.29 Compare the following classification strategies:

(i) Bayesian

(ii) 'Direct' estimation of $P(w_i|\underline{x}) = k_i/k$

(iii) 1-NNR

in terms of

(a) Required a priori information and its use in the classification algorithm.

(b) Computational effort required for algorithm implementation.

(c) Error rates.

Linear Discriminant Functions and the Discrete and Binary Feature Cases

Art is the imposing of a pattern on experience, and our aesthetic enjoyment in recognition of the pattern.

Dialogues of Alfred North Whitehead [1953], Chapter 29
Alfred North Whitehead 1861–1947

INTRODUCTION

Linear Discriminant Functions

In this section we generalize the concept and utility of *linear discriminant functions (LDFs)*. Although LDFs are a fundamental concept in StatPR, they are also useful to introduce certain types of neural network structures and training formulations. Many StatPR models and associated classification strategies lead to discriminant functions that are of the form:

$$g_i(\underline{x}) = \underline{w}_i^T \underline{x} + w_{i0} \qquad i = 1, 2, \ldots c \qquad (4-1)$$

The decision regions are then separated by hyperplanes (Appendix 6). Conceptually, a d-dimensional feature vector, $\underline{x}$, is reduced to a single dimension or number that is then used for classification.[1] Throughout this chapter we consider the $c = 2$ class case, which may be extended by considering $c > 2$ classes pairwise.

Figure 1 summarizes the two major approaches considered in this chapter. The first involves projection of the d-dimensional data onto an appropriate line, thereby reducing the feature data to a single measurement. We show several approaches for

---

[1]This is one version of a problem in *Multiple Discriminant Analysis* where feature data are projected from R^d into R^q, where typically $q \ll d$.

determining the parameters of this line in order to obtain 'good' discrimination (classi-fication) ability. The second approach involves determination of a suitable separating hyperplane in R^d. Both iterative and 'batch' solutions for the determination of this plane from the sample data are considered. In either case, the solution structure re-mains the same irrespective of whether the underlying statistical characterizations and the Bayesian approach lead to such a solution; that is, we are forcing these structures on the solution.

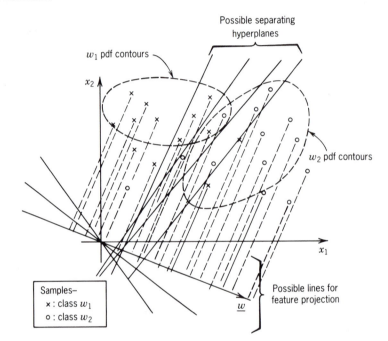

Figure 1:   The $d = 2$ example of chapter objectives.

Fisher's Linear Discriminant

The Fisher approach [Fisher 1936] is based on *projection* of d-dimensional data onto a *line*. The hope is that these projections onto a line will be well *separated by class*. Thus, the line is oriented to maximize this class separation. The real utility of this type of an approach is when the size of the feature vector is very large, for example $d = 50, 100$, or larger. We begin with a $c = 2$ class example. The given training set

$$H = \{\underline{x}_1, \underline{x}_2, \dots \underline{x}_n\} = \{H_1, H_2\} \qquad (4-2)$$

is partitioned into $n_1 \leq n$ training vectors in subset H_1, corresponding to class w_1, and $n_2 \leq n$ training vectors in set H_2, corresponding to class w_2, where $n_1 + n_2 = n$. The feature vector projections are formed via

$$y_i = \underline{w}^T \underline{x}_i = <\underline{w}, \underline{x}_i> \quad i = 1, 2, \dots n \qquad (4-3)$$

If we further constrain $\| \underline{w} \| = 1$, each y_i is the projection of $\underline{x}_i$ onto a line *in the direction of $\underline{w}$*. Note that this line always goes through the origin in R^d. The problem is to choose the direction of $\underline{w}$, given H, such that y_i from H_1 and y_i from H_2 fall into (ideally) distinct clusters along the line, denoted Y_1 and Y_2. Ideally, if $y_i \in Y_1$, then $\underline{x}_i \in H_1$ and if $y_i \in Y_2$, then $\underline{x}_i \in H_2$.

Measures of Projected Data Class Separation.   One *measure of separation* of the projections is the *difference of the means of the projections*. For example, $|\mu_{Y_1} - \mu_{Y_2}|^2$ is such a measure, where, using (4-3)

$$\mu_{Y_i} = E\{y_i | \underline{x}_i \in w_i\} = E\{\underline{w}^T \underline{x}_i | \underline{x}_i \in w_i\} \qquad (4-4)$$

This measure may be shown to be related to the H_1, H_2 sample means through $\underline{w}$:

$$\underline{m}_i = \frac{1}{n_i} \sum_{\underline{x}_i \in H_i} \underline{x}_i \qquad (4-5a)$$

Thus, the *projection mean* for each class is a scalar, given by

$$\bar{m}_i = \frac{1}{n_i} \sum_{\underline{x}_i \in H_i} \underline{w}^T \underline{x}_i = \frac{1}{n_i} \sum_{y_i \in \underline{y}_i} y_i$$

$$= \underline{w}^T \frac{1}{n_i} \sum_{\underline{x}_i \in H_i} \underline{x}_i = \underline{w}^T \underline{m}_i \qquad (4-5b)$$

where $\underline{m}_i$ is the sample mean of the vectors in H_i. The difference of the projection means using sample data is therefore

$$|\bar{m}_1 - \bar{m}_2| = |\underline{w}^T (\underline{m}_1 - \underline{m}_2)| \qquad (4-5c)$$

The difference between the means of the projected data alone is insufficient for a good classifier, as is shown in Figure 2. Although we want well-separated (class) projections, *they should not be intermingled*. To achieve this, we need to consider variances of y_i in Y_i *relative* to the means. Therefore, a better class separation measure is the ratio (difference of means)/(variance of within-class data). For example, a reasonable criterion in the $c = 2$ case is

$$J(\underline{w}) = \frac{(\mu_{Y_1} - \mu_{Y_2})^2}{\sigma_{Y_1}^2 + \sigma_{Y_2}^2} \qquad (4-6a)$$

or, in the case of sample data,

$$J(\underline{w}) = \frac{(\bar{m}_1 - \bar{m}_2)^2}{\hat{\sigma}_1^2 + \hat{\sigma}_2^2} \qquad (4-6b)$$

where $\hat{\sigma}_i^2$ is a measure of within-class scatter of the projected data. Instead of using variances in (4-6b), we could define the within-class scatter of the projection data as

$$\bar{s}_i^2 = \sum_{y \in Y_i} (y - \bar{m}_i)^2 \qquad (4-7a)$$

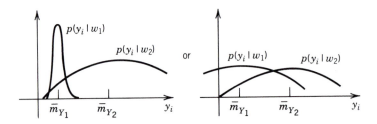

Figure 2:   The importance of defining good separation measures for projected data.

Recall that $\hat{\sigma}^2 = [1/(n-1)] \sum_{i=1}^{n} (x_i - m_i)^2$ is an unbiased variance estimator. Therefore, for n_i samples in H_i (from w_i)

$$\bar{s}_i^2 \approx (n_i - 1)\hat{\sigma}_i^2 \qquad (4-7b).$$

Fisher showed that a reasonable measure of projected data separability is the criterion function that is a scaled version of (4-6b):

$$J(\underline{w}) = \frac{(\bar{m}_1 - \bar{m}_2)^2}{\bar{s}_1^2 + \bar{s}_2^2} \qquad (4-8)$$

The value of $\underline{w}$ that maximizes (4-6a), (4-6b), or (4-8) is used in a linear discriminant function (of the form $\underline{w}^T \underline{x}$) to yield *Fisher's linear discriminant*. To proceed further, it is necessary to rewrite J in (4-8) as an *explicit function* of $\underline{w}$. Notice $\underline{w}$ influences *both* the numerator and the denominator of (4-8), since both m_i and s_i are functions of y_i. We therefore have created an optimization problem, that is, to determine the direction of $\underline{w}$ such that the criterion of (4-8) is maximum.

Solution for Criteria of (4-6a) (Exact Means and Covariances Known).   Denoting the mean and covariance of the d-dimensional vectors in class w_i as $\underline{\mu}_i$ and Σ_i respectively, it is straightforward to show

$$\mu_{Y_i} = \underline{w}^T \underline{\mu}_i \qquad i = 1, 2 \qquad (4-9a)$$

and

$$\sigma_{Y_i}^2 = \underline{w}^T \Sigma_i \underline{w} \qquad i = 1, 2 \qquad (4-9b)$$

A maximum of (4-6a) is found by setting $\partial J/\partial \underline{w} = \underline{0}$. This requires

$$\frac{\partial J}{\partial \underline{w}} = \frac{\partial J}{\partial \mu_{Y_1}} \frac{\partial \mu_{Y_1}}{\partial \underline{w}} + \frac{\partial J}{\partial \mu_{Y_2}} \frac{\partial \mu_{Y_2}}{\partial \underline{w}} + \frac{\partial J}{\partial \sigma_{Y_1}^2} \frac{\partial \sigma_{Y_1}^2}{\partial \underline{w}} + \frac{\partial J}{\partial \sigma_{Y_2}^2} \frac{\partial \sigma_{Y_2}^2}{\partial \underline{w}} = 0 \qquad (4-9c)$$

Equation 4-9c together with (4-9a) and (4-9b) yields the constraint on the optimal $\underline{w}$, denoted $\hat{\underline{w}}$:

$$\frac{2(\mu_{Y_1} - \mu_{Y_2})}{\sigma_{Y_1}^2 + \sigma_{Y_2}^2} (\underline{\mu}_1 - \underline{\mu}_2) - \frac{2(\mu_{Y_1} - \mu_{Y_2})^2}{(\sigma_{Y_1}^2 + \sigma_{Y_2}^2)^2} (2\Sigma_1 + 2\Sigma_2)\hat{\underline{w}} = \underline{0} \qquad (4-9d)$$

or

$$\hat{\underline{w}} = \frac{1}{2}k(\Sigma_1 + \Sigma_2)^{-1}(\underline{\mu}_1 - \underline{\mu}_2) \qquad (4-9e)$$

where

$$k = \frac{\sigma_{Y_1}^2 + \sigma_{Y_2}^2}{\mu_{Y_1} - \mu_{Y_2}} \qquad (4-9f)$$

is merely a scale term that affects only $\| \underline{w} \|$. Equation 4-9e is intuitively pleasing and bears a striking similarity to Bayesian results in the Gaussian case (Chapter 2). Therefore, by estimating Σ_i and $\underline{\mu}_i$ from H_i, the direction of $\hat{\underline{w}}$ may be determined.

Solution for Criterion of (4-8), Based on Sample Data.   An alternative procedure is now shown. Defining a *scatter matrix* S_i as

$$S_i = \sum_{\underline{x} \in H_i} (\underline{x} - \underline{m}_i)(\underline{x} - \underline{m}_i)^T \qquad i = 1, 2 \qquad (4-10a)$$

and

$$S_W = S_1 + S_2 \qquad (4-10b)$$

the denominator of (4-8) may be formulated as

$$\bar{s}_1^2 + \bar{s}_2^2 = \underline{w}^T S_W \underline{w} \qquad (4-10c)$$

Similarly, the numerator of (4-8), using (4-5c), may be rewritten in terms of the sample means as

$$(\bar{m}_1 - \bar{m}_2)^2 = \underline{w}^T (\underline{m}_1 - \underline{m}_2)(\underline{m}_1 - \underline{m}_2)^T \underline{w} = \underline{w}^T S_B \underline{w} \qquad (4-10d)$$

where S_B is the *between-class scatter matrix*. Since S_B is the outer product of a vector with itself, it has rank one. Therefore, (4-8) becomes

$$J(\underline{w}) = \frac{\underline{w}^T S_B \underline{w}}{\underline{w}^T S_W \underline{w}} \qquad (4-11a)$$

where the sample data in H_1 and H_2 are used to determine S_W and S_B. Forming $\partial J / \partial \underline{w} = \underline{0}$ leads to

$$S_W \hat{\underline{w}} (\hat{\underline{w}}^T S_B \hat{\underline{w}})(\hat{\underline{w}}^T S_W \hat{\underline{w}})^{-1} = S_B \hat{\underline{w}} \qquad (4-11b)$$

which yields a *generalized eigenvector problem*, where the scalar term $(\hat{\underline{w}}^T S_B \hat{\underline{w}})(\hat{\underline{w}}^T S_W \hat{\underline{w}})^{-1} = \lambda$. Thus, we seek a solution to

$$\lambda S_W \hat{\underline{w}} = S_B \hat{\underline{w}} \qquad (4-11c)$$

If S_W^{-1} exists, a simple solution for the *direction* of $\hat{\underline{w}}$ is

$$\hat{\underline{w}} = (S_W^{-1} S_B) \hat{\underline{w}} \qquad (4-11d)$$

and a solution for $\underline{w}$ may be found by solving for an e-vector of $(S_W^{-1} S_B)$. An alternative solution is based on the fact that $S_B \hat{\underline{w}}$, in (4-11b), has direction $\underline{m}_1 - \underline{m}_2$, since $(\underline{m}_1 - \underline{m}_2)(\underline{m}_1 - \underline{m}_2)^T \hat{\underline{w}} = (\underline{m}_1 - \underline{m}_2)k$. Therefore,

$$\hat{\underline{w}} = S_W^{-1}(\underline{m}_1 - \underline{m}_2) \qquad (4-12)$$

Figure 3 shows an example of the Fisher approach in the $c = 2$ class case.

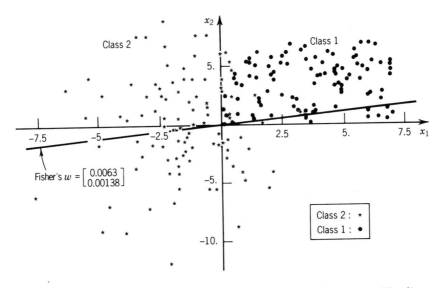

Figure 3: An example of Fisher's linear discriminant function. The line onto which feature data are projected is shown. (The line passes through the origin.)

DISCRETE AND BINARY CLASSIFICATION PROBLEMS

Classification Procedures for Discrete Feature Data

Previous formulations assumed continuous-valued features. When features are modeled as realizations of discrete random variables, density functions are replaced by probabilities (Appendix 2). Therefore, Bayes rule in the case of a discrete feature vector becomes

$$P(w_j|\underline{x}) = \frac{P(\underline{x}|w_j)P(w_j)}{P(\underline{x})} \qquad (4-13)$$

where

$$P(\underline{x}) = \sum_{i=1}^{c} P(\underline{x}|w_j)P(w_i) \qquad (4-14)$$

The overall StatPR approach remains unchanged. The definition of conditional risk $R(\alpha_i|\underline{x})$ and the Bayes decision rule that minimizes overall risk is still to select action α_i for which $R(\alpha_i|\underline{x})$ is minimum, where

$$R(\alpha_i|\underline{x}) = \sum_{j=1}^{c} \underbrace{\lambda(\alpha_i|w_j)}_{\text{cost or loss function}} P(w_j|\underline{x}) \qquad (4-15)$$

To minimize average probability of error, that is, the *error rate*, a 0-1 loss function λ, where

$$\lambda = \begin{cases} 0 & i = j \\ 1 & i \neq j \end{cases} \qquad (4-16)$$

yields the decision or classification rule:

$$P(w_i|\underline{x}) \overset{w_i}{>} P(w_j|\underline{x}) \quad \forall j \neq i \qquad (4-17)$$

Thus, obvious discriminant function choices are

$$g_j(\underline{x}) = P(w_j|\underline{x}) \quad j = 1, 2, \dots c \qquad (4-18)$$

or

$$g_j'(\underline{x}) = P(\underline{x}|w_j)P(w_j) \qquad (4-19)$$

The latter result is from application of Bayes rule, since $P(\underline{x})$ is common to all classes and therefore has no influence. Alternately,

$$g_j''(\underline{x}) = \log[P(\underline{x}|w_j)] + \log[P(w_j)] \qquad (4-20)$$

Formulation for the Binary Case

In this case, the features are not only discrete, but also binary. A *specific feature is either present or not*, that is, we have $x_i \in \{0,1\}$. This case[2] is typical of many PR problems, and yields a feature vector:

$$\underline{x} = \begin{pmatrix} x_1 \\ x_2 \\ \vdots \\ x_d \end{pmatrix} \qquad (4-21)$$

where $x_i \in \{0,1\}$. An alternative binary formulation, which often appears in neural network applications, is the case of *bilevel* features, that is, $x_i \in \{-1,1\}$. We consider only the $\{0,1\}$ case in this section.

---

[2]Recognizing *binary patterns* is one aspect of logic circuits, including sequential circuits, sequence detectors, and combinatorial logic and is also fundamental in certain neural network applications.

In the $c = 2$ class case, where $x_i \in \{0, 1\}$, we define

$$p_i = P(x_i = 1 | w_1)$$

$$q_i = P(x_i = 1 | w_2) \qquad i = 1, 2, \ldots d \qquad (4-22)$$

p_i is the probability that feature i is 'present,' given class w_1. If $p_i > q_i$, we expect feature x_i to assume value '1' more frequently for vectors generated by w_1 than by w_2.

Classification Procedures for the Binary Case

To make the problem tractable, the assumption of *conditional independence* of the d components of $\underline{x}$ is often used. This facilitates classification and estimation formulations, although at the expense of accurate modeling in some instances. Therefore,

$$P(\underline{x}|w_1) = \prod_{i=1}^{d} P(x_i|w_1) \qquad (4-23)$$

where

$$P(x_i|w_1) = \begin{cases} p_i \text{ if } x_i = 1 \\ \\ (1 - p_i) \text{ if } x_i = 0 \end{cases} \qquad (4-24)$$

a formulation that uses the conditional independence assumption is

$$P(\underline{x}|w_1) = \prod_{i=1}^{d} p_i^{x_i} (1 - p_i)^{1-x_i} \qquad (4-25)$$

and, correspondingly,

$$P(\underline{x}|w_2) = \prod_{i=1}^{d} q_i^{x_i} (1 - q_i)^{1-x_i} \qquad (4-26)$$

From

$$P(\underline{x}|w_1) \underset{w_2}{\overset{w_1}{\gtrless}} P(\underline{x}|w_2) \qquad (4-27)$$

the likelihood ratio (LR), denoted δ, assuming equal a priori probabilities, is used for classification in the form:

$$\delta = \frac{P(\underline{x}|w_1)}{P(x|w_2)} \underset{w_2}{\overset{w_1}{\gtrless}} 1 \qquad (4-28)$$

The previous results allow δ in (4-28) to be expanded as

$$\delta = \frac{\prod_{i=1}^{d} p_i^{x_i} (1 - p_i)^{1-x_i}}{\prod_{i=1}^{d} q_i^{x_i} (1 - q_i)^{1-x_i}} = \prod_{i=1}^{d} \left(\frac{p_i}{q_i}\right)^{x_i} \left(\frac{1 - p_i}{1 - q_i}\right)^{1-x_i} \qquad (4-29)$$

A discriminant function formulation for a $c = 2$ class case is

$$g(\underline{x}) = g_1(\underline{x}) - g_2(\underline{x}) = P(w_1|\underline{x}) - P(w_2|\underline{x}) \qquad (4-30)$$

and the corresponding decision region is shown in Figure 4. Alternately, using Bayes rule, (4-30) leads to an equally valid discriminant function:

$$g'(\underline{x}) = P(\underline{x}|w_1)P(w_1) - P(\underline{x}|w_2)P(w_2) \qquad (4-31)$$

Therefore, the overall LRT for the $c = 2$ case becomes

$$g'(\underline{x}) \underset{w_2}{\overset{w_1}{\underset{<}{\gtrless}}} 0 \qquad (4-32)$$

or

$$\frac{P(\underline{x}|w_1)P(w_1)}{P(\underline{x}|w_2)P(w_2)} \underset{w_2}{\overset{w_1}{\underset{<}{\gtrless}}} 1 \qquad (4-33)$$

Applying the log function to both sides yields the decision rule:

$$\log\left(\frac{P(\underline{x}|w_1)}{P(\underline{x}|w_2)}\right) + \log\left(\frac{P(w_i)}{P(w_2)}\right) \underset{w_2}{\overset{w_1}{\underset{<}{\gtrless}}} 0 \qquad (4-34)$$

Expanding (4-34) using (4-25) and (4-26) defines the discriminant function $g''(\underline{x})$ where

$$g''(\underline{x}) = \sum_{i=1}^{d} \log\left\{\left(\frac{p_i}{q_i}\right)^{x_i}\left(\frac{1-p_i}{1-q_i}\right)^{1-x_i}\right\} + \log\left(\frac{P(w_1)}{P(w_2)}\right)$$

$$= \sum_{i=1}^{d} \left\{x_i \log\left(\frac{p_i}{q_i}\right) + (1-x_i)\log\left(\frac{1-p_i}{1-q_i}\right)\right\} + \log\left(\frac{P(w_1)}{P(w_2)}\right) \qquad (4-35)$$

Notice that $g''(\underline{x})$ may be reformulated as

$$g''(\underline{x}) = \sum_{i=1}^{d} w_i x_i + w_0 = \underline{w}^T \underline{x} + w_0 \qquad (4-36)$$

where

$$w_i = \log\frac{p_i(1-q_i)}{q_i(1-p_i)} \quad i = 1, 2, \ldots d \qquad (4-37)$$

and

$$w_0 = \left\{\sum_{i=1}^{d} \log\left(\frac{1-p_i}{1-q_i}\right)\right\} + \log\left(\frac{P(w_1)}{P(w_2)}\right) \qquad (4-38)$$

This yields a linear form. The above formulation fails in several cases, for example, p_i (or q_i) $= 1$. For instance, if $p_i = 1$ and $q_i = 0$, we can simply use feature x_i alone for error-free classification. Alternately, if $p_i = q_i = 1$, then this feature provides no discrimination ability between w_1 and w_2.

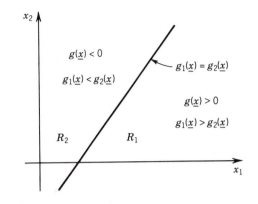

Figure 4:   An example of decision regions in $d = 2$ case from LRT of (4-30).

An Analysis of $g''(\underline{x})$.   The LR test is

$$g''(\underline{x}) \underset{w_2}{\overset{w_1}{\gtrless}} 0 \tag{4 – 39}$$

Since each element of $\underline{x}$, that is, $x_i \in \{0, 1\}$, is multiplied by w_i, each weight w_i measures the 'significance' of $x_i = 1$ (since $x_i = 0$ contributes nothing to $\underline{w}^T \underline{x}$). Consider the following cases and the corresponding discriminant function weights:

Case 1:

$$p_i = q_i \Rightarrow w_i = 0 \tag{4 – 40}$$

No new information for classification results from this feature, since a 1 in x_i is equally likely from either class.

Case 2:

$$p_i > q_i \Rightarrow w_i > 0 \tag{4 – 41}$$

and $w_i x_i$ for $x_i = 1 > 0$. This makes sense since, if we have a 1 in x_i, we should tend toward w_1. Alternately, this *adds* or provides positive reinforcement in $w^T \underline{x}$ for w_1.

Case 3:

$$p_i < q_i \Rightarrow w_i < 0 \tag{4 – 42}$$

Here $w_i x_i < 0$ for $x_i = 1$, thus providing negative reinforcement for w_1, or positive reinforcement for w_2.

Nonparametric Estimation of $P(\underline{x}|w_i)$

To apply the previously derived classification rules, we need estimates over all possible values $\underline{x}$ (where $x_i \in \{0, 1\}$) of $P(\underline{x}|w_i)$ $i = 1, 2, \ldots c$ for each class. It is appropriate to question how large this set of values is. For d components of $\underline{x}$, each $x_i \in \{0, 1\}$ and thus has 2 values; therefore, there are 2^d probabilities for each class. This may be a significant problem. For example, when $d = 10$, there are $2^{10} = 1024$ probabilities to estimate. A simplification is to assume any two components x_i and xj in $\underline{x}$ are independent. Then

$$P(\underline{x}|w_i) = \prod_{i=1}^{d} P(x_i|w_i) = \prod_{i=1}^{d} p_i^{x_i}(1 - p_i)^{1-x_i} \qquad (4-43)$$

from before, where $p_i = P(x_i = 1|w_i)$ and $1 - p_i = P(x_i = 0|w_i)$. We therefore need, for each class, only to estimate p_i, $i = 1, 2, \ldots d$. With this assumption, there exists a trade-off. In the general formulation there are 2^d probabilities with statistically dependent x_i permitted, whereas the simplified formulation requires estimation of d probabilities with the constraint that x_i must be statistically independent.

TECHNIQUES TO DIRECTLY OBTAIN LINEAR CLASSIFIERS

The Concept of Linear Separability

Viewing the samples of a $c = 2$ class training set as points in R^d, we note that some configurations of feature vectors are separable by a (possibly non-unique) hyperplane. Although this is not true for an arbitrary configuration of samples (this is considered in the exercises), the computational and conceptual advantages of a linear decision boundary often motivate us to consider its application, even at the expense of increased classification error rates vis-à-vis using the exact (non-planar) decision surfaces.

DEFINITION: **Linear Separability**

If a hyperplanar decision boundary exists that correctly classifies all the training samples for a $c = 2$ class problem, the samples are said to be linearly separable.

Recall (Appendix 6) that this hyperplane, denoted H_{ij}, is defined by parameters $\underline{w}$ and w_0 in a linear constraint of the form:

$$g(\underline{x}) = \underline{w}^T x - w_0 = 0 \qquad (4-44)$$

$g(\underline{x})$ separates R^d into positive and negative regions R_p and R_n, where

$$g(\underline{x}) = \underline{w}^T \underline{x} - w_0 = \begin{cases} > 0 & \text{if } \underline{x} \in R_p \\ 0 & \text{if } \underline{x} \in H_{ij} \\ < 0 & \text{if } \underline{x} \in R_n \end{cases} \qquad (4-45)$$

Design of Linear Classifiers

Assume a $c = 2$ class training set $H = \{\underline{x}_i\}$ $i = 1, 2, \ldots n$, which may be partitioned into H_1 and H_2, where H_i consists only of samples labeled w_i. The goal is to determine plane H_{12} where, for each $\underline{x}_i$ in H,

$$w_{12}^T x_i - w_0 = \begin{cases} > 0 & \text{if } x_i \in H_1 \\ < 0 & \text{if } x_i \in H_2 \end{cases} \tag{4-46}$$

This plane is characterized by $d + 1$ parameters, namely the d elements of w_{12} (the normal) and w_0. Defining

$$w = \begin{pmatrix} w_{12} \\ -w_0 \end{pmatrix} \tag{4-47a}$$

and converting each x_i in H to a $(d+1) \times 1$ vector by adding '1' as the $(d+1)$st element yields the standard homogeneous coordinate representation (see, for example, [Riesenfeld 1981], [Schalkoff 1989]) as follows:

$$\hat{x}_i = \begin{pmatrix} x_i \\ 1 \end{pmatrix} \tag{4-47b}$$

Noting that $w^T \hat{x}_i$ is a scalar quantity allows (4-46) to be rewritten as

$$\hat{x}_i^T w = \begin{cases} > 0 & \text{if } \hat{x}_i \in H_1 \\ < 0 & \text{if } \hat{x}_i \in H_2 \end{cases} \tag{4-48}$$

A desirable modification to (4-48) is to replace each homogeneous vector $\hat{x}_i$ in H_2 by its negative. This conversion therefore yields the single constraint:

$$\hat{x}_i^T w > 0 \qquad i = 1, 2, \ldots n \tag{4-49}$$

Considering all the 'converted' elements of H yields the matrix formulation of (4-49) as

$$Aw > 0 \tag{4-50}$$

where the $n \times (d+1)$ matrix A consists of the converted vectors from the training set as:

$$A = \begin{pmatrix} \hat{x}_1^T \\ \hat{x}_2^T \\ \vdots \\ \hat{x}_n^T \end{pmatrix} \tag{4-51}$$

A 'Batch' (Pseudoinverse) Solution. Equation 4-50 is a set of n *linear inequalities.* Many solution procedures exist, including linear programming. A solution is developed that is based on converting (4-50) into a linear constraint, by defining a vector of user-chosen 'offsets', b, as

$$\underline{b} = \begin{pmatrix} b_1 \\ b_2 \\ \vdots \\ b_n \end{pmatrix} \qquad b_i > 0 \qquad\qquad (4-52)$$

Thus, (4-50) becomes

$$A\underline{w} = \underline{b} \qquad\qquad (4-53)$$

and a solution for the parameters of the separating plane, $\underline{w}$, is obtained via forming the pseudoinverse of A

$$\hat{\underline{w}} = A^\dagger \underline{b} \qquad\qquad (4-54)$$

The Solution Region in R^{d+1}.   Another approach for solving the system of linear inequalities given by (4-48) or, equivalently, (4-49) is to view these equations as n constraints in $(d+1)$-dimensional space. Each equation of the form of (4-49) together with a user-chosen offset or 'margin' may be written as

$$\hat{\underline{x}}_i^T \underline{w} - b_i > 0 \qquad i = 1, 2, \ldots n \qquad\qquad (4-55)$$

From Appendix 6, each of the n linear inequality constraints in (4-55) may be visualized, *by viewing $\hat{\underline{x}}_i^T$ as the normal vector to a $(d+1)$-dimensional hyperplane that partitions R^{d+1}*. A requirement for a solution is that the solution vector $\underline{w}$ must lie in the positive half R_p of R^{d+1}, at a distance of $|b_i|/\parallel \hat{\underline{x}}_i^T \parallel$ from the boundary. Moreover, the intersection of the n half spaces of R^{d+1} defined by (4-55) is the overall *solution region* for $\underline{w}$. In problems that are not linearly separable, this region does not exist. Conversely, in linearly separable solutions with non-unique separating planes, this region contains an infinite number of solution points. In addition, by setting the margins $b_i = 0, \quad i = 1, 2, \ldots n$, we find the largest solution region from solving

$$\hat{\underline{x}}_i^T \underline{w} > 0 \quad i = 1, 2, \ldots n \qquad\qquad (4-56)$$

Iterative (Descent) Procedures.   By using a gradient approach (Appendices 1 and 4), an iterative procedure to determine $\underline{w}$ may be found. The form is

$$\underline{w}^{(n+1)} = \underline{w}^{(n)} - \alpha_n \frac{\partial J(\underline{w})}{\partial \underline{w}}\Big|_{\underline{w}=\underline{w}^{(n)}} \qquad\qquad (4-57)$$

where α_n controls the adjustment at each iteration. The iteration procedure requires a stopping criterion. Examples are

$$\parallel \underline{w}^{(n+1)} - \underline{w}^{(n)} \parallel < \epsilon \qquad\qquad (4-58a)$$

where ϵ is a user-chosen tolerance, or

$$n = n_{max} \qquad\qquad (4-58b)$$

where n_{max} is the (predetermined) maximum number of iterations, or

$$J(\underline{w}^{(n)}) \leq J_T \tag{4-58c}$$

where J_T is an error threshold and $J(\underline{w})$ is a measure of classification error. Often we design $J(\underline{w})$ with the minimum value $J(\underline{w}) = 0$ for perfect classification.

Error Forms.   Many forms for the error $J(\underline{w})$ are possible. For example, a vector $\underline{w}$ where

$$\hat{\underline{x}}_i^T \underline{w} < 0 \tag{4-59}$$

misclassifies sample $\hat{\underline{x}}_i^T$. Therefore, one error measure, the *Perceptron Criterion Function*, is

$$J_p(\underline{w}) = -\sum_{\hat{\underline{x}} \in X_{ERR}(\underline{w})} (\hat{\underline{x}}_i^T \underline{w}) \tag{4-60}$$

where $X_{ERR}(\underline{w})$ is the set of *samples misclassified by* $\underline{w}$. Note that this set will vary from iteration to iteration in the solution procedure. If $X_{ERR}(\underline{w}) = \emptyset$, then $J_p(\underline{w}) = 0$, and the minimum of the error function is obtained.

Since

$$\nabla_{\underline{w}} J_p(\underline{w}) = -\sum_{\hat{\underline{x}}_i \in X_{ERR}(\underline{w})} \hat{\underline{x}}_i \tag{4-61}$$

the iterative procedure of (4-57) becomes

$$\underline{w}^{(n+1)} = \underline{w}^{(n)} + \alpha_n \sum_{\hat{\underline{x}}_i \in X_{ERR}(\underline{w}^{(n)})} \hat{\underline{x}}_i \tag{4-62}$$

Notice that when $X_{ERR}(\underline{w}^{(n)}) = \emptyset$, the adjustments to $\underline{w}^{(n)}$ cease.

Training by Sample and Training by Epoch.   Equation 4-62 suggests that at each iteration the entire set of samples misclassified by $\underline{w}^{(n)}$ be used to form the correction at the next iteration. This represents a consideration of the entire training set for each adjustment of $\underline{w}$ and, thus, *training by epoch*. Another alternative is to *adjust $\underline{w}$ as soon as a single classification error is made*. This represents *training by sample*, and may be viewed as a 'correct as soon as possible' strategy. It is often unclear whether training by epoch or training by sample is preferable, and this concern carries over into our training of certain similar neural network structures in Chapter 12. In the case of training by sample, (4-62) becomes

$$\underline{w}^{(n+1)} = \underline{w}^{(n)} + \alpha_n \hat{\underline{x}}_i \tag{4-63}$$

where $\hat{\underline{x}}_i$ is the first sample misclassified by $\underline{w}^{(n)}$.

Procedures to Find Both $\underline{w}$ and $\underline{b}$.   In the previous procedures, it was necessary to choose the 'margin' vector $\underline{b}$. We consider a procedure [Ho/Kashyap 1965] based on iterative refinement of both $\underline{w}$ and $\underline{b}$ that is derived from the approach of (4-53). Choosing an error measure as

$$J_H(\underline{w}, \underline{b}) = \| A\underline{w} - \underline{b} \|^2 = (A\underline{w} - \underline{b})^T (A\underline{w} - \underline{b}) \tag{4-64}$$

we assume that the problem is linearly separable, so that vectors $\hat{\underline{w}}$ and $\hat{\underline{b}}$ exist that yield $J_H(\hat{\underline{w}}, \hat{\underline{b}}) = 0$. Forming the gradients of J_H with respect to parameters $\underline{w}$ and $\underline{b}$ (Appendix 1) yields

$$\nabla_{\underline{w}} J_H(\underline{w}, \underline{b}) = 2A^T A\underline{w} - 2A^T \underline{b} = 2A^T(A\underline{w} - \underline{b}) \qquad (4-65)$$

$$\nabla_{\underline{b}} J_H(\underline{w}, \underline{b}) = 2\underline{b} - 2A\underline{w} = -2(A\underline{w} - \underline{b}) \qquad (4-66)$$

Equations 4-65 and 4-66 are the basis of a set of coupled equations that are iteratively applied to obtain both $\underline{w}$ and $\underline{b}$.

Setting $\nabla_{\underline{w}} J_H(\underline{w}, \underline{b}) = \underline{0}$ in (4-65), with a prechosen margin vector $\underline{b}$, leads to a pseudoinverse solution for $\underline{w}$. Using this $\underline{w}$ in (4-66) provides a mechanism for adjustment of $\underline{b}$. Therefore, a procedure is as follows:

1. Choose an initial $\underline{b}$, that is, $\underline{b}^{(1)}$. Solve for $\underline{w}^{(n)}$ from

$$A^T A\underline{w}^{(n)} = A^T \underline{b}^{(n)} \qquad (4-67)$$

2. Use a gradient descent procedure with (4-66) to update $\underline{b}^{(n)}$ to form $\underline{b}^{(n+1)}$. A direct formulation is

$$\underline{b}^{(n+1)} = \underline{b}^{(n)} - \rho \nabla_{\underline{b}} J_H(\underline{w}^{(n)}, \underline{b}^{(n)}) \qquad (4-68a)$$

Using (4-66), (4-67) becomes

$$\underline{b}^{(n+1)} = \underline{b}^{(n)} + \rho(A\underline{w}^{(n)} - \underline{b}^{(n)}) \qquad (4-68b)$$

Recall that the role of $\underline{b}$ is that of a vector of positive 'margins.' Therefore, a variation on (4-68b) is to consider only corrections to $\underline{b}^{(n)}$ that increase these margins. This may be accomplished by defining $\underline{c}^{(n)}$ as a vector that retains only the positive parts of correction vector $(A\underline{w}^{(n)} - \underline{b}^{(n)})$. Elements of $(A\underline{w}^{(n)} - \underline{b}^{(n)})$ that are negative yield corresponding values of 0 in $\underline{c}^{(n)}$. Thus, the ith element of $\underline{c}^{(n)}$, denoted $c_i^{(n)}$, is given by

$$c_i^{(n)} = \begin{cases} (A\underline{w}^{(n)} - \underline{b}^{(n)})_i & \text{if } (A\underline{w}^{(n)} - \underline{b}^{(n)})_i > 0 \\ 0 & \text{if } (A\underline{w}^{(n)} - \underline{b}^{(n)})_i \leq 0 \end{cases} \qquad (4-69)$$

An alternative way to form $c_i^{(n)}$, as defined in (4-69), is

$$c_i^{(n)} = \frac{1}{2}\left[(A\underline{w}^{(n)} - \underline{b}^{(n)})_i + |(A\underline{w}^{(n)} - \underline{b}^{(n)})_i|\right] \quad i = 1, 2, \ldots d+1 \quad (4-70)$$

3. Use $\underline{b}^{(n+1)}$ to form $\underline{w}^{(n+1)}$ from (4-67). Check stopping criteria, for example, convergence of $\underline{b}^{(n+1)}$. If converged, stop, otherwise go to step 2 to update $\underline{b}^{(n+1)}$.

Stopping Criteria. Like most iterative algorithms, the procedure outlined in (4-67) through (4-70) requires suitable stopping criteria. These may be based on:

1. Convergence of $\underline{b}^{(n)}$.

2. Convergence of $\underline{w}^{(n)}$.

3. $n \leq n_{max}$.

4. $J(\underline{w}^{(n)}, \underline{b}^{(n)}) \leq J_{THRESH}$.

Figure 5 shows an example of the approach, using the same data as in Figure 3.

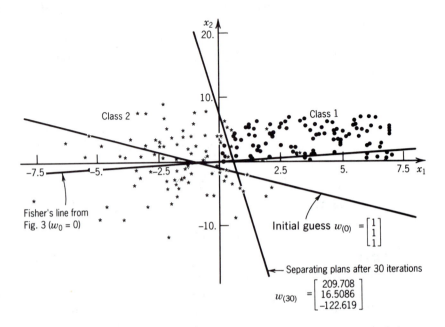

Figure 5:   A separating plane obtained by using the iterative approach (same data as Figure 3).

BIBLIOGRAPHICAL REMARKS

The computational advantages (in both implementation and training) and ease of visualization of linear classifiers account for their popularity. Seminal works include [Fisher 1936], [Nilsson 1965], [Widrow/Hoff 1960], [Ho/Kashyap 1965], and [Fukunaga/Olsen 1970]. An extensive consideration of the development of linear discriminant functions for minimum error is found in [Fukunaga 1972]. A good summary of the concept of linear separability as related to threshold logic and switching theory is in [Glorioso/Colon-Osorio 1980].

In Chapters 11 and 12, we explore extensions of linear classifiers to layers of linear (and semilinear) classifiers that achieve complex decision boundaries, and therefore merge StatPR-based linear classifiers with the structure of several types of neural networks.

EXERCISES

4.1   Under what conditions is the Bayesian classifier of Chapter 2 the same as the result of (4-9e)?

4.2   As shown by Cover [Cover 1965], of the 2^n possible dichotomies of n points in R^d, the fraction of these that are achievable using a hyperplane (so-called linear dichotomies) is given by the function:

$$f(n, d) = \begin{cases} 1 & n \leq d+1 \\ \dfrac{2}{2^n} \displaystyle\sum_{i=0}^{d} \binom{n-1}{i} & n > d+1 \end{cases}$$

   (a)   Show that at $n = 2(d+1)$ (this is sometimes referred to as the capacity of a d-dimensional hyperplane), $f(n, d) = \frac{1}{2}$. Thus, half the possible dichotomies are achievable with a linear discriminant function.

   (b)   Plot $f(n, d)$ for $0 \leq n \leq 4(d+1)$. This is a family of curves, indexed by d. Show curves for $d = 1, 10, 100$.

   (c)   What happens at $d = \infty$?

4.3   For the data in Figure P.1, we desire to apply Fisher's linear discriminant to separate $c = 2$ classes.

   (a)   Calculate the within- and between-class scatter matrices, S_W and S_B.

   (b)   Compute $\underline{w}$.

   (c)   Compute the projection means and variances for $i = 1, 2$.

   (d)   Compute the classification error (using H) using the results of (b).

Class w_1		Class w_2	
−0.253	1.832	1.188	−2.550
1.130	3.181	1.658	−2.604
−2.812	3.775	4.192	−0.281
0.543	−0.010	2.081	−0.941
−2.309	−0.414	2.208	−1.102

Figure P.1:   Data for Fisher's linear discriminant and iterative hyperplane determination $\underline{x} = (x_1 \; x_2)^T$.

4.4   For the data for classes w_1 and w_2 shown in Figure P.1, use the iterative procedure of (4-67) to (4-70) to generate the optimum discriminant function. Show the set of samples misclassified at each step, as well as the sequence of weight vectors. Plot $J(\underline{w}^{(n)})$ vs. n.

4.5   A d-dimensional hyperplane H in the form of a linear machine

$$g(\underline{x}) = \underline{w}^T \underline{x} = 0$$

divides R^d into regions R_1 and R_2, depending on whether $g(\underline{x}) > 0$ or $g(\underline{x}) < 0$, respectively. The purpose of this problem is to consider the geometrical significance of this partitioning when several layers of these linear machines are applied.

(a) For the case where feature vector $\underline{x}$ yields output $\underline{x}_0$ as

$$\underline{x}_0 = \overset{d \times d}{A} \; \underline{x}$$

show how this mapping of R^d into R^d can be visualized as the parallel arrangement of d linear classifiers in a single layer.

(b) For the case

$$\underline{x}_0 = A_q A_{q-1} \ldots A_1 \underline{x}$$

show how this may be visualized as q layers of linear machines.

(c) What is the significance of the case

$$\underline{x}_0 = A_2 A_1 \underline{x}$$

where A_1 is $n \times d$, $n > d$, A_2 is $c \times n$, $c < n$ and $c < d$?

4.6 Table P.1 shows an $n = 24$ training set H for a $c = 3$ class ('decision'), $d = 4$ feature discrete classification problem.

Table P.1: Decision Table for Fitting Contact Lenses

Value of attribute				Decision†	Value of attribute				Decision†	Value of attribute				Decision†
a	b	c	d	δ	a	b	c	d	δ	a	b	c	d	δ
1 1	1	1	1	3	9 2	1	1	1	3	17 3	1	1	1	3
2 1	1	1	2	2	10 2	1	1	2	2	18 3	1	1	2	3
3 1	1	2	1	3	11 2	1	2	1	3	19 3	1	2	1	3
4 1	1	2	2	1	12 2	1	2	2	1	20 3	1	2	2	1
5 1	2	1	1	3	13 2	2	1	1	3	21 3	2	1	1	3
6 1	2	1	2	2	14 2	2	1	2	2	22 3	2	1	2	2
7 1	2	2	1	3	15 2	2	2	1	3	23 3	2	2	1	3
8 1	2	2	2	1	16 2	2	2	2	3	24 3	2	2	2	3

†The reader is asked not to be tempted to use this decision table to deturmine whether or not (s)he is suitable for contact lenses as there are many factors, not mentioned here, that may radically influence the decision.
Source: From Cendrowska, J., "PRISM An Algorithm for Inducing Modular Rules," *Int J. Man-Machine Studies,* Vol. 27, 1987, pp. 349–370.

(a) Use H to directly estimate $P(w_i|\underline{x})$ for each class.

(b) Develop a similarity measure and show a decision or classification rule based on a nearest neighbor rule.

(c) For each of the classes considered pairwise, use a descent procedure to determine a linear classifier that provides a hyperplanar boundary between decision regions. Are the data linearly separable?

4.7 Show an iterative solution formulation of (4-53).

4.8 Show the applicability of the stopping criteria in (4-58a) through (4-58c) in cases where:

(a) A separating hyperplane does not exist.

(b) The problem is linearly separable with a non-unique solution.

4.9 Cite and discuss relative advantages and disadvantages of training by sample versus training by epoch.

4.10   Show how the solution of (4-63), which is equivalent to adding a scalar multiple of a misclassified vector to $\underline{w}^{(n)}$, leads to a solution vector and why this makes intuitive sense.

4.11   Assume that a problem is linearly separable.

   (a)   Show that choice of the margin vector $\underline{b} = \underline{0}$ may lead to a 'marginal' solution, in the sense that the resulting hyperplane may be very close to several samples and therefore ill-posed to handle errors or vectors that are perturbed versions of those in H.

   (b)   Show that injudicious choice of $\underline{b}$ may lead to a formulation with no solution.

4.12   Derive (4-65) and (4-66).

4.13   **(a)**   Discuss direct use of (4-68b), without the constraint on only positive corrections to $\underline{b}^{(n)}$. (Hint: Consider $\underline{b}^{(1)} = \underline{0}$.)

   (b)   Comment on an alternative variation on (4-68b), in which $\underline{b}^{(n+1)}$ is adjusted using (4-68b), but with the additional constraint that no element of $\underline{b}$ can become negative.

4.14   Extend the $c = 2$ class discrete classification problem of (4-13) to (4-42) to the case of *ternary* measurements, i.e., $x_i \in \{-1, 0, 1\}$. Is a linear discriminant function still possible? If so, how do the w_i reflect knowledge of $P(x_i = -1|w_1)$, $P(x_i = 0|w_1)$, etc.?

4.15   **(a)**   Derive (4-9a) and (4-9b).

   (b)   Derive (4-9d).

4.16   Relate the result of (4-9e) to the Bayesian results from Chapter 2 (include mixture normalization).

4.17   Derive (4-11b). Hint: Rewrite $J(\underline{w})$ as $(\underline{w}^T S_B \underline{w}) J(\underline{w}) = \underline{w}^T S_B \underline{w}$ and differentiate each side w.r.t. $\underline{w}$. Recall that S_B and S_W are symmetric.

4.18   Discuss the difference in the solutions in (4-9e) and (4-12).

4.19   In this chapter, we have considered both the 'optimal' projection of d-dimensional data onto a line (Fisher's approach) and the determination of a separating hyperplane in R^d (e.g., the iterative approach). Discuss conditions under which the line determined by Fisher's approach will be orthogonal to the plane determined by the iterative procedure. Is this result intuitively appealing?

4.20   Referring to (4-6a) or (4-6b), what would be the effect of instead choosing $J(\underline{w}) = (\mu_{y_1} - \mu_{y_2})^2$ or $J(\underline{w}) = (\bar{m}_1 - \bar{m}_2)^2$, respectively, and maximizing this measure?

(Problems 4.21 and 4.22 illustrate some aspects of gradient descent procedures. Readers may wish to review Appendix 4 prior to attempting these problems.)

4.21   For $A = \begin{pmatrix} 1 & -1 \\ 2 & -2 \end{pmatrix}$ $\underline{b} = \begin{pmatrix} -1 \\ 4 \end{pmatrix}$ with $E = \| A\underline{x} - \underline{b} \|$ compute E and determine $\nabla_{\underline{x}} E$. Formulate a gradient descent procedure to determine an $\underline{x}$ that minimizes E. Discuss the significance of these results.

4.22   Repeat Problem 4.21 for:

$$A = \begin{pmatrix} 1 & -1 \\ 2 & 1 \\ 1 & 1 \end{pmatrix} \qquad \underline{b} = \begin{pmatrix} -1 \\ 4 \\ 2 \end{pmatrix}$$

Notice in this case that $\underline{b} \in R^3$ and $R(A) \neq R^3$; therefore $\underline{b} \notin R(A)$, where $R(A)$ is the range of matrix A or the span of its columns.

Unsupervised Learning and Clustering 5

Appearances to the mind are of four kinds. Things either are what they appear to be; or they neither are, nor appear to be; or they are, and do not appear to be; or they are not, and yet appear to be. Rightly to aim in all these cases is the wise man's task.

Discourses, Book 1, Chapter 27
Epictetus c. 50–120

FORMULATION OF UNSUPERVISED LEARNING PROBLEMS

A Modified Training Set

Suppose we are given a PR problem with one additional aspect: instead of a labeled training set, we are given an unlabeled set of *typical* features. Denote this unlabeled training set H_u. For each sample, $\underline{x} \in H_u$, the class origin or label is unknown. Three desirable attributes of H_u are:

- The cardinality of H_u is large;
- All classes are represented in H_u; and
- Subsets of H_u may be formed into natural groupings or 'clusters,' where each cluster most likely corresponds to an underlying pattern class. (This attribute of H_u is strongly influenced by our choice of features.)

Unsupervised learning approaches attempt to develop a representation for the given sample data. They are even applicable in the supervised case where we are given a labeled set and desire a mathematical model that reflects multiple modes of the data.[1] Instead of working with multimodal densities, we may attempt to determine

---

[1] Recall the often-used assumption that the class-conditioned pdfs are unimodal.

regions in feature space where unimodal densities are applicable. This may be done by using a mixture density. One popular and somewhat obvious approach is *clustering* or *mode separation*.

Thus, in unsupervised learning, our objective is to *define the classes*. One may question the wisdom or prospects of success of such an apparently unpromising problem. There is little doubt that the general problem of PR system design using only unlabeled sample data is challenging. Figures 1 and 2 illustrate problem extremes.

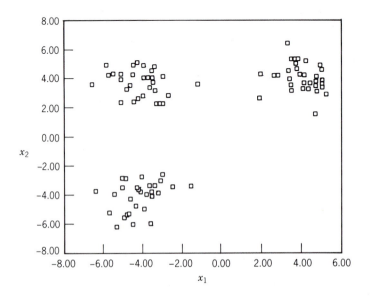

Figure 1: The case where samples in H_u naturally cluster.

We first investigate a formal approach to the unsupervised learning problem, which, although of limited mathematical tractability, provides insight into a number of less formal but intuitive and practical approaches.

How Could Such a Problem Arise?

- We are able to obtain samples, but unable to label them.
- Over time the characteristics of the class-specific pattern generating systems are changing; therefore, it is necessary to continuously learn or *adapt*.

Unsupervised Learning Approaches

We consider two major approaches:

- A parametric strategy based on known functional forms for underlying class-conditioned distributions, which involves *combined classification* and *parameter estimation*.

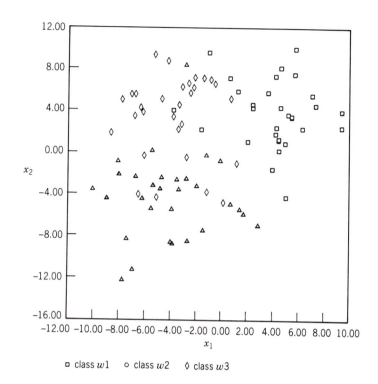

x_2

x_1

□ class $w1$ ○ class $w2$ ◊ class $w3$

Figure 2:   The case where 'natural clusters' are not apparent.

- A nonparametric approach, which involves *partitioning the unlabeled data into subsets.*

Whereas the first approach is a straightforward extension of previous StatPR formulations, the second approach is suboptimal, but practical and tractable. It is commonly used. We note that the second approach is also reflected in several self-organizing neural approaches considered in Chapter 13.

Combined Classification and Parameter Estimation (Overview).   As before, let $\underline{\theta}_i$ be the parameter vector for the ith class. Assume that we know a priori the following:

1. c (the number of classes).
2. $P(w_i)$ $i = 1, 2, \ldots c.$
3. $p(\underline{x}|w_i, \underline{\theta}_i)$ in form only.
4. H_u.

Our goal is to find $\underline{\theta}_i$, $i = 1, 2, \ldots c$. We present a summary of the approach here.

The Mixture Density Concept and Formulation.   Assume that all the samples in H_u are generated by a single *mixture density*:

$$p(\underline{x}|\underline{\theta}) = \sum_j p(\underline{x}|w_j, \underline{\theta}_j) P(w_j) \qquad (5-1)$$

Assume that $p(\underline{x}|\underline{\theta})$ is the only information that may be directly inferred from H_u. Notice that the mixture density is a weighted sum of individual (often unimodal) densities. An example is shown in Figure 3. *It is critical to note that the mixture density formulation does not imply that the vectors in H_u are the sums of realization of random vectors with the respective component densities.* For example, the density function characterizing the sum of Gaussian random variates is not the summation of their densities.

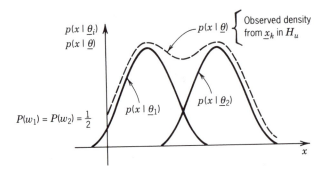

Figure 3: The mixture density concept (1-D example).

Therefore, given the functional form of $p(\underline{x}|\underline{\theta})$, our immediate goal becomes that of determining $\underline{\theta}$, from which we work backwards to find the $\underline{\theta}_i$. It is not always possible to undo or invert the combination in (5-1). The question of *identifiability* [Duda/Hart 1973] arises in this formulation.

Assuming that the n samples are independent, the joint density of the training set is derived from the mixture density:

$$p(H_u|\underline{\theta}) = \Pi_{k=1}^n p(\underline{x}_k|\underline{\theta}) \qquad (5-2)$$

To find the ML estimate, $\hat{\underline{\theta}}$, we seek a value of $\underline{\theta}$ that maximizes (5-2). In the case where $p(H_u|\underline{\theta})$ is unimodal and $p(\underline{x}_k|\underline{\theta})$ is differentiable with respect to $\underline{\theta}$, we may choose a convenient monotonically increasing function of $p(H_u|\underline{\theta})$, denoted f, and form

$$\nabla_{\underline{\theta}} f[p(H_u|\underline{\theta})] = \underline{0} \qquad (5-3)$$

to arrive at a constraint on $\hat{\underline{\theta}}$. The log function is an obvious choice for f; therefore, (5-3) becomes

$$\nabla_{\underline{\theta}}\{\log[p(H_u|\underline{\theta})]\} = \nabla_{\underline{\theta}} \sum_{k=1}^n \log[p(\underline{x}_k|\underline{\theta})] = \sum_{k=1}^n \nabla_{\underline{\theta}} \log[p(\underline{x}_k|\underline{\theta})] = \underline{0} \qquad (5-4)$$

Since the differentiation formula

$$\frac{\partial}{\partial x} \log\{u(x)\} = \frac{1}{u(x)} \frac{\partial u(x)}{\partial x} \qquad (5-5)$$

applies to each element of the vector in (5-4), using (5-1) and taking the derivative with respect to $\underline{\theta}_i$ yields

$$\underline{g} \equiv \nabla_{\underline{\theta}_i}\{\log[p(H_u|\underline{\theta})]\} = \sum_{k=1}^{n} \left\{ \frac{1}{p(\underline{x}_k|\underline{\theta})} \nabla_{\underline{\theta}_i} \left\{ \sum_{j=1}^{c} p(\underline{x}_k|w_j, \underline{\theta}_j)P(w_j) \right\} \right\}$$

$$= \underline{0} \qquad i = 1, 2, \ldots c \qquad (5-6)$$

Assuming functional independence of $\underline{\theta}_i$ and $\underline{\theta}_j$, that is,

$$\nabla_{\underline{\theta}_i} p(\underline{x}_k|w_j, \underline{\theta}_j) = \underline{0} \quad \text{unless } i = j \qquad (5-7)$$

Bayes rule allows us to form

$$P(w_i|\underline{x}_k, \underline{\theta}) = \frac{p(\underline{x}_k|w_i, \underline{\theta}_i)P(w_i)}{p(\underline{x}_k|\underline{\theta})} \qquad (5-8)$$

so g becomes

$$\underline{g} = \sum_{k=1}^{n} \frac{1}{p(\underline{x}_k|\underline{\theta})} \nabla_{\underline{\theta}_i}\{p(\underline{x}_k|w_i, \underline{\theta}_i)P(w_i)\} = \sum_{k=1}^{n} \frac{P(w_i)}{p(\underline{x}_k|\underline{\theta})} \nabla_{\underline{\theta}_i}\{p(\underline{x}_k|w_i, \underline{\theta}_i)\}$$

$$= \sum_{k=1}^{n} \frac{P(w_i|\underline{x}_k, \underline{\theta})}{p(\underline{x}_k|w_i, \underline{\theta}_i)} \nabla_{\underline{\theta}_i}\{p(\underline{x}_k|w_i, \underline{\theta}_i)\}$$

'Reversing' (5-5) yields

$$\underline{g} = \sum_{k=1}^{n} P(w_i|\underline{x}_k, \underline{\theta})\nabla_{\underline{\theta}_i}\{\log[p(\underline{x}_k|w_i, \underline{\theta}_i)]\} \qquad (5-9)$$

From the definition of the ML estimate, we arrive at the constraint equation for $\hat{\underline{\theta}}_i$:

$$\sum_{k=1}^{n} P(w_i|\underline{x}_k, \hat{\underline{\theta}})\nabla_{\underline{\theta}_i}\{\log[p(\underline{x}_k|w_i, \hat{\underline{\theta}}_i)]\} = \underline{0} \qquad (5-10)$$

In (5-10) $\hat{\underline{\theta}}$ is the mixture density parameter vector corresponding to the $\hat{\underline{\theta}}_i$.

This result, although difficult to apply directly in a number of cases, leads to a family of iterative strategies that facilitate unsupervised learning. We show this by considering the Gaussian case.

Example Using Gaussian Densities (Unknown Mean Vector Only). Assume the only unknowns are the mean vectors, $\underline{\mu}_i$, $i = 1, 2, \ldots c$. Thus, $\underline{\theta}_i$ and $\underline{\theta}$ consist of the elements of $\underline{\mu}_i$ and $\underline{\mu}$, respectively. The mixture density is formed as the sum of Gaussian densities, that is, for each class

$$p(\underline{x}_k|w_i, \underline{\mu}_i) = (2\pi)^{-\frac{d}{2}}|\Sigma_i|^{-\frac{1}{2}} \exp\left\{-\frac{1}{2}\left[(\underline{x}_k - \underline{\mu}_i)^T\Sigma_i^{-1}(\underline{x}_k - \underline{\mu}_i)\right]\right\} \qquad (5-11)$$

Taking the log of (5-11), differentiating, and using (5-10) yields

$$0 = \sum_{k=1}^{n} P(w_i|\underline{x}_k, \hat{\underline{\mu}})\Sigma_i^{-1}(\underline{x} - \hat{\underline{\mu}}_i) \qquad i = 1, 2, \ldots c \qquad (5-12)$$

Premultiplying both sides by Σ_i yields

$$\sum_{k=1}^{n} P(w_i|\underline{x}_k, \hat{\underline{\mu}})(\underline{x}_k - \hat{\underline{\mu}}_i) = \underline{0} \qquad i = 1, 2, \ldots c$$

or

$$\hat{\underline{\mu}}_i = \frac{\sum_{k=1}^{n} P(w_i|\underline{x}_k, \hat{\underline{\mu}})\underline{x}_k}{\sum_{k=1}^{n} P(w_i|\underline{x}_k, \hat{\underline{\mu}})} \qquad i = 1, 2, \ldots c \qquad (5-13)$$

Analysis of the Result.   The result in (5-13) illustrates several points.

1. $\underline{\mu}_i$ is formed as a weighted summation of the $\underline{x}_k$, where the weight for each sample is $P(w_i|\underline{x}_u, \hat{\underline{\mu}})/\sum_{k=1}^{n} P(w_i|\underline{x}_k, \hat{\underline{\mu}})$. For samples where $P(w_i|\underline{x}_k, \hat{\underline{\mu}})$ is zero (or small), little is contributed to μ_i. This is intuitively appealing and suggests the obvious—namely form μ_i using only samples in w_i.

2. Equation (5-13), as formulated, is difficult to apply directly. Substitution for $P(w_i|\underline{x}_k, \underline{\mu})$ [which is a function of $p(\underline{x}_k|w_i, \underline{\mu}_i)$, $P(w_i)$, and $p(\underline{x}_k|\underline{\mu})$] does little to help, but suggests an iterative procedure. Provided that we can obtain reasonable initial estimates of $\hat{\underline{\mu}}_i(0)$, $i = 1, 2, \ldots c$, these may be updated via:

$$\hat{\underline{\mu}}_i(m+1) = \frac{\sum_{k=1}^{m} P[w_i|\underline{x}_k, \hat{\underline{\mu}}(m)]\underline{x}_k}{\sum_{k=1}^{n} P[w_i|\underline{x}_k, \hat{\underline{\mu}}(m)]} \qquad i = 1, 2, \ldots c \qquad (5-14)$$

Note that this involves updating the class means by readjustment of the weights on each sample at each iteration. This procedure is similar to the c-means clustering algorithm we consider later.

CLUSTERING FOR UNSUPERVISED LEARNING AND CLASSIFICATION

The Clustering Concept and the Search for 'Natural Clusters'

The previous procedure culminating in (5-14), represents a rigorous, probabilistically based procedure for combined classification and parameter estimation.

Alternately, we could consider designing a self-consistent procedure following the generic strategy:

1. Convert a set of unlabeled samples H_u into a *tentative* training set H_T.
2. Using H_T, apply a supervised training procedure and develop corresponding discriminant functions/decision regions.
3. Use the results of step 2 on H_u, that is, reclassify H_u. If the results are consistent with H_T, stop; otherwise go to 1 and revise H_T.

Notice that what we need is a mechanism that 'clusters' data by observing similarity. As shown later, there exist neural networks with this feature.

In many PR applications involving unsupervised learning, features naturally fall into easily observed groups. This is shown in Figure 1. However, the more difficult case of Figure 2 is also prevalent. Unfortunately, a solution procedure to handle the latter is not obvious. In this context, clustering may be conceptualized as 'how do I build my fences?'

Insights for Clustering from (5-8) in the Gaussian Case.   In the Gaussian case with equal $P(w_i)$ (5-8) becomes

$$P(w_i | \underline{x}_k, \underline{\theta}) = \frac{k_1 |\Sigma_i|^{-\frac{1}{2}} \exp -\frac{1}{2} \left\{ \| \underline{x}_k - \underline{\mu}_i \|^2_{\Sigma_i^{-1}} \right\}}{p(\underline{x}_k | \underline{\theta})} \qquad (5-15)$$

Note that (5-15) is large when

$$\| \underline{x}_k - \underline{\mu}_i \|^2_{\Sigma^{-1}} \qquad (5-16)$$

is small. This suggests a procedure for assigning $\underline{x}_k$ to class w_m $m \in \{1, c\}$ where (5-16) is smallest. *It is therefore another nearest neighbor approach*, and yields the *c-means* or *'Basic' Isodata* algorithm.

The c-means Algorithm

1. Choose the number of classes, c.
2. Choose $\hat{\underline{\mu}}_i, \hat{\underline{\mu}}_2, \ldots \hat{\underline{\mu}}_c$. These are initial guesses.
3. Classify each $\underline{x}_k$.[2]
4. Recompute the estimates for $\hat{\underline{\mu}}_i$ using the results of 3.
5. If the $\hat{\underline{\mu}}_i$ are consistent, STOP; otherwise go to step 1, 2, or 3.

Notice that the essence of this approach is to achieve a self-consistent partitioning of the data. The choice of initial parameters [c and $\underline{\mu}_i(o)$] is still a challenging issue. This spawns an area of study concerning *cluster validity*.

Figure 4 shows examples of the *c*-means algorithm for the $c = 2$ class case. The trajectory of the $\underline{\mu}_i$, as a function of the iteration, is shown.

The criterion of (5-15) and (5-16) suggest that each sample is compared with a 'representative' of the ith cluster, namely $\underline{\mu}_i$. Those that are close to $\underline{\mu}_i$ are seen to form a natural grouping, falling within some distance of (and centered around) $\underline{\mu}_i$.

---

[2]This spawns a number of possible variants ranging from simple 1-NNR approaches to Bayesian formulations (the latter may require more than knowledge of the $\underline{\mu}_i$).

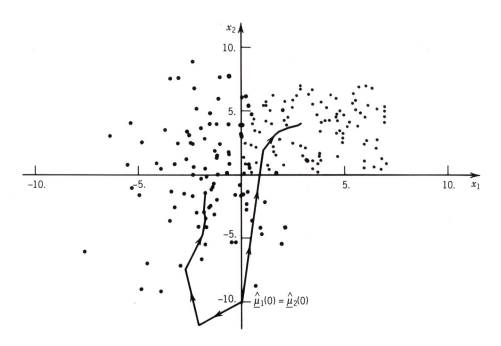

Figure 4: The example of c-means algorithm, $c = 2$, $d = 2$ case. Trajectory of $\hat{\underline{\mu}}_i$ shown. (Figure courtesy of R. D. Ferrell.)

There exist many other clustering measures that are also intended to produce 'natural clusters.'

Learning Vector Quantization (LVQ)

A strategy known as *Learning Vector Quantization (LVQ)* [Makhoul et al. 1985] is used to both quantize input pattern vectors into reference or 'codebook' values and to use these reference values for classification. It is frequently applied in signal processing applications such as speech recognition. The strategy bears a strong semblance to the c-means algorithm, previously described, and the self-organizing neural networks of Chapter 13. The basic algorithm assumes that an a priori known set of reference vectors $\{\underline{\mu}_i | i = 1, 2, \ldots c\}$ is available. Note that several $\underline{\mu}_i$ may correspond to a single class. A set of labeled samples $H = \{\underline{x}_j | j = 1, 2, \ldots n\}$ is used for further refinement. A simple similarity measure (e.g., Euclidean distance) is used.

At each iteration, indexed by k, the $\underline{\mu}_i$ are updated by H using the following strategy:

1. For each element of H, that is, $\underline{x}_j$, find the $\underline{\mu}_i$ that is closest to $\underline{x}_j$. Denote this vector $\underline{\mu}_c$.

2. Update the $\underline{\mu}_c(k)$ to form $\underline{\mu}_c(k+1)$ using $\underline{x}_j$ as follows:

$$\underline{\mu}_c(k+1) = \underline{\mu}_c(k) + \alpha(k)[\underline{x}_j - \underline{\mu}_c(k)] \qquad (5-17a)$$

   (a) IF $\underline{x}_j$ is correctly classified, that is, it is labeled with the class corresponding to $\underline{\mu}_c$,

      THEN continue with the next element of H

      ELSE ($\underline{x}_j$ is incorrectly classified), so update $\underline{\mu}_c(k)$ as follows:

$$\underline{\mu}_c(k+1) = \underline{\mu}_c(k) - \alpha(k)[\underline{x}_j - \underline{\mu}_c(k)] \qquad (5-17b)$$

   (b) $\underline{\mu}_i(k+1) = \underline{\mu}_i(k)$ for $i \neq c$ $(5-17c)$

Here $\alpha(k)$ is an iteration-dependent parameter used to control convergence of the algorithm. For stability, $0 < \alpha(k) < 1$, and $\alpha(k)$ is constrained to decrease monotonically with k.

The adjustment strategy of (5-17) is intuitively appealing. Correct classifications lead to a refinement of $\underline{\mu}_c$ in a direction toward $\underline{x}_j$, whereas incorrect classification (or quantization) moves $\underline{\mu}_c$ in the opposite direction, and $\underline{\mu}_i$ not close to $\underline{x}_j$ are not changed. Convergence and other ramifications of LVQ and other clustering algorithms are considered in [Anderberg 1973], [Linde et al. 1980], and [Gray/Karnin 1982].

Formal Characterization of General Clustering Procedures

Clustering Similarity Measures. In general, we desire a clustering measure, $d(\underline{x}_i, \underline{x}_j)$, such that

$$d(\underline{x}_i, \underline{x}_j) = \begin{cases} \text{'large'} & \text{when } \underline{x}_i \text{ and } \underline{x}_j \text{ belong in different clusters;} \\ \text{'small'} & \text{when } \underline{x}_i \text{ and } \underline{x}_j \text{ belong in the same cluster.} \end{cases} \qquad (5-18a)$$

We may interpret this as a distance measure, for example, $d(\underline{x}_i, \underline{x}_i) = 0$. By using measure $d(\underline{x}_i, \underline{x}_j)$, we can develop a skeletal threshold-based clustering procedure:

$$\text{assign } \underline{x}_i \text{ and } \underline{x}_j \text{ to} \begin{cases} \text{the same cluster} & \text{if } d(\underline{x}_i, \underline{x}_j) \leq d_T \\ \text{different clusters} & \text{if } d(\underline{x}_i, \underline{x}_j) > d_T. \end{cases} \qquad (5-18b)$$

Of course, determination of d_T is critical. If d_T is large (i.e., we are fairly loose in our assessment of similarity), we end up with a few, 'widespread' clusters. Conversely, if d_T is small (we are fairly critical), we may end up with many sparse clusters. Thus, the clustering problem involves choosing $d(\underline{x}_i, \underline{x}_j)$ and d_T and classifying all elements of H_u such that:

- $d(\underline{x}_i, \underline{x}_j)$ is 'small' for all pairs $(\underline{x}_i, \underline{x}_j)$ in the same cluster.
- $d(\underline{x}_i, \underline{x}_j)$ is 'large' when $\underline{x}_i$ and $\underline{x}_j$ are in different clusters.

This involves a consideration of *inter-* and *intracluster similarity,* which in turn relies on general distance or similarity measures. Appendix 5 considers several possibilities.

Efficient algorithms for finding nearest neighbors are fundamental to the c-means and LVQ algorithms. The computational effort and related efficient algorithms for finding nearest neighbors are cited in Chapter 3, under the heading DIRECT CLASSIFICATION USING THE TRAINING SET.

Objectives. A *partition*, denoted P, of a set H, is a set of disjoint subsets of H, that is, $P = \{H_1, H_2, \ldots H_m\}$ with $H_i \cap H_j = \phi$ unless $i = j$ and $\cup_{j=1}^{m} H_j = H$. We desire a *partition* of H_u

$$H_u = \{H_1, H_2, \ldots H_m\} \tag{5 - 19}$$

where m is chosen such that a clustering function, J_e, is extremized (minimized or maximized). J_e reflects both intra- and intercluster similarity measures.

There are

$$\frac{1}{c!} \sum_{k=1}^{c} \binom{c}{k} (-1)^{c-k} k^n \approx \frac{c^n}{c!} \tag{5 - 20}$$

possible partitions of n vectors into c nonempty subsets. For example, given the apparently innocuous case of $n = 100$ vectors and $c = 10$ sets, there are approximately $10^{100}/10! \approx 3 \times 10^{93}$ possible partitions. Clearly, exhaustive search procedures are impractical.

Clustering Strategies

Clustering may be achieved through a number of strategies, including iterative and hierarchical approaches. Hierarchical strategies may further be subdivided into agglomerative (merging of clusters) or devisive (splitting of clusters). Hierarchical strategies have the property that not all partitions of the data are considered, and therefore are particularly attractive in that the measure of (5-20) is considerably reduced. However, when the number of samples is large, hierarchical clustering may be inappropriate. For example, notice that in an agglomerative procedure, two samples, once in the same class, remain in the same class throughout subsequent cluster merging. This may lead to resulting data partitions being suboptimal.

Overall Clustering Criterion Functions. Developing appropriate similarity measures $d(\underline{x}_i, \underline{x}_j)$ is paramount in clustering. For a given partition of H_u, denoted P, we develop measures of the 'goodness' of the overall clustering via families of *clustering criterion functions*, $J(P)$. If

$$J(P_1) < J(P_2) \tag{5 - 21}$$

P_1 is a better partition than P_2. Our goal, once a suitable $J(P)$ is defined, is to find P_m such that

$$J(P_m) = \overset{min}{P} \left(J(P) \right) \tag{5 - 22}$$

in a computationally efficient manner. This is a problem in discrete optimization.

Sum of Squared Error (SSE) Criterion.   We briefly show one of the more popular clustering metrics. Given n_i samples in H_i, with sample mean $\underline{m}_i$, where

$$\underline{m}_i = \frac{1}{n_i} \sum_{\underline{x}_k \in H_i} \underline{x}_k \qquad (5-23)$$

the SSE criterion, J_{SSE} is defined as

$$J_{SSE}(P) = \sum_{i=1}^{c} \sum_{\underline{x}_k \in H_i} \| \underline{x}_k - \underline{m}_i \|^2 \qquad (5-24)$$

J_{SSE} thus indicates the total 'variance' for a given partition.

'Cluster-Swapping' Approaches

The c-means algorithm gave no indication or guidance as to how clusters in partition P_k should be reorganized to yield P_{k+1}. Using $J_{SSE}(P)$, we develop a variant on the c-means iterative algorithm that indicates a 'good' cluster reorganization strategy, where 'good' means

$$J_{SSE}(P_{k+1}) \leq J_{SSE}(P_k) \qquad (5-25)$$

For illustration, our reorganization strategy is restricted to the movement of a single vector $\underline{x}_j$ from H_i to H_j, denoted $H \overset{\underline{x}_j}{\to} H_j$. The revised clusters in P_{k+1} are denoted H_i' and H_j'. The reader can easily show

$$\underline{m}_j' = \frac{1}{n_j + 1} \sum_{\underline{x}_k \in H_j} \underline{x}_k = \ldots = \underline{m}_j + \frac{\underline{x}_j - \underline{m}_j}{n_j + 1} \qquad (5-26)$$

and therefore the criterion due to the change in subset H_j, denoted $J_{SSE}(H_j')$, *increases* to

$$J_{SSE}(H_j') = \sum_{\underline{x}_k \in H_j'} \| \underline{x}_k - \underline{m}_j' \|$$

$$= \ldots = J_{SSE}(H_j) + \frac{n_j}{n_j + 1} \| \underline{x}_j - \underline{m}_j \|^2 \qquad (5-27)$$

Similarly, $J_{SSE}(H_i')$ *decreases* to

$$J_{SSE}(H_i') = J_{SSE}(H_i) - \left(\frac{n_i}{n_i - 1}\right) \| \underline{x}_j - \underline{m}_i \|^2 \qquad (5-28)$$

Therefore, $H_i \overset{\underline{x}_j}{\to} H_j$ decreases $J_{SSE}(P_k)$ if

$$\left(\frac{n_j}{n_j + 1}\right) \| \underline{x}_j - \underline{m}_j \|^2 < \left(\frac{n_i}{n_i - 1}\right) \| \underline{x}_j - \underline{m}_i \|^2 \qquad (5-29)$$

Extended Example: A Hierarchical Clustering Procedure

Consider a hierarchical clustering procedure in which clusters are merged so as to produce the smallest increase in the sum-of-squared error at each step. The ith cluster or partition, denoted H_i, contains n_i samples with sample mean $\underline{m}_i$. It is shown in what follows that the smallest increase results from merging the pair of clusters for which the measure M_{ij}, where

$$M_{ij} = \frac{n_i n_j}{n_i + n_j} \parallel \underline{m}_i - \underline{m}_j \parallel^2 \qquad (5-30)$$

is minimum. Recall the SSE is given by

$$J_e = \sum_{i=1}^{c} \sum_{\underline{x} \in H_i} \parallel \underline{x} - \underline{m}_i \parallel^2 \qquad (5-31)$$

that is, J_e measures the total squared error incurred in representing the n samples $\underline{x}_1, \ldots \underline{x}_n$ by c cluster means $\underline{m}_1 \ldots \underline{m}_c$.

The *change* in the SSE after merging clusters i and j is

$$\triangle J_e = - \left(\sum_{\underline{x} \in H_i} \parallel \underline{x} - \underline{m}_i \parallel^2 + \sum_{\underline{x} \in H_j} \parallel \underline{x} - \underline{m}_j \parallel^2 \right) + \sum_{\underline{x} \in H_i \ or \ H_j} \parallel \underline{x} - \underline{m}_{ij} \parallel^2 \qquad (5-32)$$

where

$$\underline{m}_i = \frac{1}{n_i} \sum_{\underline{x} \in H_i} \underline{x} \qquad \underline{m}_j = \frac{1}{n_j} \sum_{\underline{x} \in H_j} \underline{x} \qquad (5-33)$$

and

$$\underline{m}_{ij} = \frac{1}{n_i + n_j} \sum_{\underline{x} \in H_i \ or \ H_j} \underline{x} \qquad (5-34)$$

Note that $\underline{m}_{ij} \neq (\underline{m}_i + \underline{m}_j)/2$ unless $n_i = n_j$, since

$$\underline{m}_{ij} = \frac{1}{n_i + n_j}(n_i \underline{m}_i + n_j \underline{m}_j) \qquad (5-35)$$

Clearly we want $\triangle J_e$ to be a minimum. Breaking the last term in (5-32) into parts yields

$$\triangle J_e = \sum_{\underline{x} \in H_i} \parallel \underline{x} - \underline{m}_{ij} \parallel^2 - \overbrace{\sum_{\underline{x} \in H_i} \parallel \underline{x} - \underline{m}_i \parallel^2}^{J_i} + \sum_{\underline{x} \in H_j} \parallel \underline{x} - \underline{m}_{ij} \parallel^2 - \underbrace{\sum_{\underline{x} \in H_j} \parallel \underline{x} - \underline{m}_j \parallel^2}_{J_j} \qquad (5-36)$$

Recalling that $\parallel \underline{\varsigma} \parallel^2 = <\underline{\varsigma}, \underline{\varsigma}>$, we get

$$\triangle J_e = \sum_{\underline{x} \in H_i} \left[-2 \left(\underline{m}_{ij}^T - \underline{m}_i^T \right) \underline{x} + \left(\underline{m}_{ij}^T \underline{m}_{ij} - \underline{m}_i^T \underline{m}_i \right) \right]$$

$$+ \sum_{\underline{x} \in H_j} \left[-2 \left(\underline{m}_{ij}^T - \underline{m}_j^T \right) \underline{x} + \left(\underline{m}_{ij}^T \underline{m}_{ij} - \underline{m}_j^T \underline{m}_j \right) \right] \qquad (5-37)$$

A little algebra and (5-33) yield

$$\triangle J_e = n_i (\underline{m}_{ij} - \underline{m}_i)^T (\underline{m}_{ij} - \underline{m}_i) + n_j (\underline{m}_{ij} - \underline{m}_j)^T (\underline{m}_{ij} - \underline{n}_j) \qquad (5-38)$$

or

$$\triangle J_e = \frac{n_i n_j}{(n_i + n_j)} \parallel \underline{m}_j - \underline{m}_i \parallel^2 = \frac{n_i n_j}{(n_i + n_j)} \parallel \underline{m}_i - \underline{m}_j \parallel^2 \qquad (5-39)$$

Analysis.   Notice that if $n_i = n_j = n$ for all pairs of clusters i, j, then the rule says to merge clusters whose means are closest in the sense of Euclidean distance. Otherwise, we weight our hierarchical clustering decision based on the number of points in each cluster. For example, if three clusters i, i' and j are such that $\parallel \underline{m}_i - \underline{m}_j \parallel = \parallel \underline{m}_{i'} - m_j \parallel$ but $n_i < n_{i'}$, that is, the ith cluster has fewer vectors than the i'th, we would choose to merge the ith and jth since $k/[1 + (k/n_i)]$ is always smaller than $k/[1 + (k/n_{i'})]$ if $n_i < n_{i'}$. As n_i and $n_{i'}$ get large, however, this difference becomes small.

BIBLIOGAPHICAL REMARKS

Interested readers should consult [Duda/Hart 1973], pages 190–210 for an in-depth presentation of the combined classification and parameter estimation problem. Clustering continues to be a popular approach in unsupervised learning [Dubes/Jain 1980]. Clustering applications in image analysis, for example, include [Coleman/ Andrews 1979] and [Bryant 1979]. Iterative algorithms involving cluster splitting and merging are shown in [Schalkoff 1989]. The popularity of clustering has spawned a sizable and varied library of clustering algorithms [Blashfield et al. 1982], one of the most popular being the squared-representation error-based ISODATA approach [Dubes/Jain 1976]. Other background references for clustering include [Forgy 1965] and [Hartigan 1975]. Background material may be found in [Fukunaga 1972] and [Patrick 1972]. A dedicated architecture for implementation of clustering is shown in [Ni/Jain 1985].

EXERCISES

5.1   Referring to the training set data for $c = 2$ in Figure P.1,

   (a)   Plot these data.

   (b)   Are the data linearly separable?

(c)   Use the Ho-Kayshap procedure to find $\underline{a}_k$ and $\underline{b}_k$ for this case. Show explicitly all assumptions and iterative formulations. Plot $\underline{a}_k$ and tabulate $\underline{b}_k$ for several values of k.

$$\underline{x} = (x_1 \quad x_2)^T$$

unsupervised	x_1	x_2	supervised
$n = 12$	3.353	4.716	$w_1 (n = 6$ samples)
pool of	1.877	−1.257	for Exercise 1
data for	4.403	4.358	
Exercise 2	3.529	7.579	
	3.007	9.977	
	4.025	3.545	
	−2.460	−3.124	$w_2 (n = 6$ samples)
	−3.458	3.432	for Exercise 1
	−3.375	−8.403	
	−3.842	−7.374	
	−2.227	2.416	
	−0.247	−5.085	

Figure P.1:   Sample data for simulation exercise.

5.2   Consider the $n = 12$ samples in Figure P.1 as unlabeled training data.

(a)   Using (i) the SSE criterion and (ii) the iterative optimization procedures, find J_e for cases of

(i) $c = 2$
(ii) $c = 3$

(b)   Consider instead an agglomerative hierarchical clustering procedure. Choose the distance measure:

$$d_{min}(H_i, H_j) = \underline{x} \in H_1, \quad \underline{x}' \in H_2 \| \underline{x} - \underline{x}' \|$$

(i)   Begin with $c = 12$ and show the clustering algorithm results.
(ii)   Plot a dendogram for part (i).
(iii)   Repeat parts (i) and (ii) for a distance measure as suggested in (5-39):

$$d_e(H_i, \ H_j) = \frac{n_i n_j}{n_i + n_j} \| \underline{m}_i - \underline{m}_j \|$$

(iv)   Compare the results of part (iii) with those of part (a).

5.3   Prove that (5-1) is a valid density function.

5.4   Show $\triangle J_e \geq 0$ in (5-32), i.e., the SSE must *increase*.

5.5   For the data shown in Figure P.3,

(a)   Plot a scatter diagram of the data.
(b)   Use a hierarchical unsupervised learning procedure to classify the data.
(c)   Classify each of the samples shown in Figure P.2, using
(i)   the 1-NNR rule;

(ii)   the 3-NNR rule.

$$
\begin{array}{rr}
3.992 & -0.016 \\
1.334 & 0.657 \\
-3.291 & -7.170
\end{array}
$$

Figure P.2:   Samples to be classified.

−0.473	3.612	3.077	4.906
6.164	0.479	0.574	0.010
3.425	0.325	1.476	1.579
−0.449	4.075	4.732	−2.447
5.052	4.080	−2.294	−1.341
0.276	0.293	1.429	1.553
4.097	2.073	−3.056	2.012
1.702	3.138	−4.539	−4.270
4.235	1.154	−3.438	−2.073
3.725	7.659	−4.046	−0.997
2.094	−0.011	−5.633	−4.268
3.260	3.501	−2.679	−3.708
1.845	4.541	−4.001	−4.356
3.288	1.237	−3.856	−2.827
−1.915	−1.464	−4.973	−2.999
1.724	3.848	−2.601	−4.634
−0.788	1.008	−2.665	−2.026
0.271	−4.467	−4.552	−2.046
2.150	−2.828	−0.496	−4.021
2.649	−1.553	−0.366	−1.062
2.882	0.837	0.282	−2.030

Figure P.3:   Data for unsupervised learning $(\underline{x}_i = [x_1 \ x_2]^T)$.

5.6   Referring to the $n = 24$ training set for the $c = 3$ class problem of Table P.1, used in Exercise 4.6 of Chapter 4, assume that the classification or 'decision' is not known (i.e., we are given H_u) and develop and apply a clustering approach. How well do your unsupervised learning results correspond to the labeled training set data?

5.7   **(a)**   For the training set H_1 shown in Figure P.3, estimate the number of classes and suitable forms and statistics for each class.

   (b)   Repeat for the data of Figure P.4.

$$
\begin{array}{rr}
5.910 & 6.414 \\
5.626 & 6.800 \\
0.657 & 5.445 \\
-8.335 & 0.030 \\
-4.175 & 1.924 \\
2.398 & 2.676 \\
-1.745 & 2.221 \\
-4.380 & 8.718 \\
-3.044 & -4.301
\end{array}
$$

Figure P.4: H_u for Exercises 5.7 and 5.8.

5.8   An interesting clustering approach is known as the *maximin* (maximum/minimum distance) approach [Batchelor/Wilkins 1969]. Assuming that c clusters are desired, where c is initially unknown, with n unlabeled samples, $\underline{x}_1, \underline{x}_2, \ldots \underline{x}_n$, a Euclidean distance measure, i.e., $d(\underline{x}_i, \underline{x}_j) = \| \underline{x}_i - \underline{x}_j \|$ is used. Basically, the algorithm is as follows:

Step 1:   Arbitrarily assign a sample, say $\underline{x}_1$, to w_1.

Step 2:   Find the sample farthest from $\underline{x}_1$, and assign it to w_2. We now have $n = 2$ classes.

Step 3:   *Of the currently defined classes,* find the class closest to the remaining samples (denoted w_{c1}) and store the corresponding *minimum distances* as the set $D_{w_{c1}}$. Find the *maximum* distance in $D_{w_{c1}}$ and assign the corresponding sample to w_{n+1}.

Step 4:   Repeat step 3 until the maximum distance found is 'significantly less' than previously found maximum distances.

(a)   Discuss the effect of the choice of the initial sample in step 1 on the resulting partitions.

(b)   Explain how the stopping criteria in step 4 are reasonable.

(c)   Apply the procedure to the set of vectors shown in Figure P.4.

(d)   Comment on the computational complexity of this procedure for large n.

5.9   This problem makes an excellent project in unsupervised learning. Use a random number generator to generate 100 $d = 2$ dimensional samples from each of $c = 2$ classes to form unlabeled samples in set H_u. Choose the class-dependent statistics such that there is some class overlap. Apply the c-means algorithm to these data, with the cases $c = 2, 3, 4$. For each case:

(a)   Choose $\underline{\mu}_i(0)$, $i = 1, 2, \ldots c$. Use some judgment to get 'reasonable' starting values.

(b)   Use the 1-NNR for sample classification.

(c)   Choose, and justify, a stopping criteria.

(d)   Plot $\underline{\mu}_i(k)$, $k > 0$ (k is the iteration number).

(e)   Use the SSE measure, J_{SSE} from (5-24) to get an idea of the 'goodness' of your clusters.

(f)   Revise your choice of $\underline{\mu}_i(0)$ (pick 'slightly unreasonable' initial values, for contrast) and repeat parts (b) and (d).

(g)   Analyze your results.

5.10   This problem investigates hierarchical clustering approaches. H_u is shown in Figure P.4.

(a)   Considering each sample to initially represent a separate class, apply the merging criteria of (5-30), until $c = 1$.

(b)   Use the results of (a) and the SSE measure, J_{SSE} from (5-24), to calculate $J_{SSE}(c)$ for $c = 1, 2, \ldots 9$.

(c)   Considering all of H_u to be a single class (i.e., starting with $c = 1$), use (5-29) to develop a cluster splitting/swapping approach. Note: stop at $c = 3$, and use (5-29) initially to determine the members of w_2 and w_3 by removing them from w_1. Then swap among w_1, w_2, and w_3 using (5-29).

5.11   In the c-means algorithm, how might we choose or determine the following:

    (a) c (the number of classes).

    (b) $\mu_i(0)$ $i = 1, 2, \ldots c$.

    Consider iterative approaches.

5.12   For the data shown in Chapter 3, Figure P.5, apply several clustering approaches (assuming the pooled data are unlabeled). Compare your results with the actual (known) clusters.

5.13   This problem considers the 'follow the leader' sequential clustering algorithm [Hartigan 1975]. Basically the algorithm is as follows:

    1. Select the first member of H_u as the first cluster exemplar or template, denoted $\underline{t}^0$.

    2. Compare the next element of H_u, denoted $\underline{x}^n$, with previous templates, $\underline{t}^i$ for $i = 1, 2, \ldots k$ (where k previous clusters have been formed). If the distance between $\underline{x}^n$ and $\underline{t}^i$ is less than some preselected threshold, it is clustered with $\underline{t}^i$. Otherwise, $\underline{x}^n$ is the template for a new cluster. This test is repeated over the entire set of unlabeled samples.

    Note that the number of clusters formed grows as H_u is processed, and the strategy is strongly influenced by the choice of similarity measure, threshold, and ordering of H_u. Apply this algorithm to the data shown in Figures P.3 and P.4 using a Euclidean distance measure and several different thresholds.

5.14   The following unsupervised learning problem involves scores from a comprehensive exam (200 points maximum), which were obtained as follows:

$$H_u = \{186,\ 177,\ 155,\ 146,\ 160,\ 137,\ 195,\ 139,\ 165\} \qquad (P.14-1)$$

It is known a priori that there are $c = 2$ classes (corresponding to PASS or FAIL).

    (a) Using a hierarchical clustering approach, we begin with each sample initially defining a separate class. Define a similarity measure that enables classes to be merged (e.g., scores 137 and 139 are likely candidates for initial merging and seem to define a 'fail' cluster). Show the overall results.

    (b) Repeat (a) using J_{SSE} and a cluster swapping procedure.

    (c) Compare the results of (a) and (b) with a simple thresholding procedure, i.e.,

$$class(\underline{x}_i) = \begin{cases} PASS & \text{if } \underline{x}_i \geq T \\ \\ FAIL & \text{if } \underline{x}_i < T \end{cases} \qquad (P.14-2)$$

5.15   Cite several examples of applications wherein it is possible to obtain feature vector samples, but labeling is impossible (or difficult).

5.16   How reasonable is the assumption that precedes (5-11), that is, that the mean vector is unknown but Σ_i is known? Can you think of a situation when this might occur?

5.17   Equation (5-24) approaches clustering using a squared error criterion. Suggest alternative clustering criterion functions and indicate where they might be applicable.

Part 3

Syntactic Pattern Recognition (SyntPR)

Overview

6

High thoughts must have a high language.

Frogs [405 B.C.], l. 1058
Aristophanes c., 450–385 B.C.

SYNTACTIC PATTERN RECOGNITION (SYNTPR) OVERVIEW

Statistical pattern recognition attempts to classify patterns (or entities) based on a set of extracted features and an underlying statistical (perhaps ad hoc) model for the generation of these patterns. It might be nice if all PR problems could be approached by using a single straightforward procedure, namely: (1) determine feature vector, x; (2) train system; and (3) classify patterns. Unfortunately, for many realistic problems, this is not the case. As mentioned in Chapter 1, many patterns contain structural or, more generally, relational information, that is difficult or impossible to quantify in feature vector form.

The premise of syntactic pattern recognition (SyntPR) is that the *structure* of an entity is paramount, and that it may be used for classification and description. This could be accomplished, for example, by defining suitable and distinct grammars that reflect the structure of each pattern class. Elements of a SyntPR system are shown in Figure 1. Readers may wish to refer to Chapter 1, Figure 15, parts (b) and (c), to relate the arrangement of Figure 1 with that of the StatPR approach.

SyntPR is used for both classification and description. Classification may be based on measures of pattern structural similarity. For example, each pattern class could be defined according to a common structural representation or description. However, there exist situations where each possible structural description defines a unique class. In this case, a quantitative description of pattern structure is still desirable even though the objective is not classification. An example is found in image interpretation

128

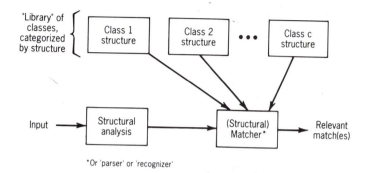

Figure 1:   Using SyntPR for classification (with explicit characterization of structure).

applications, where each image has a unique structural description, and therefore an infinite number of structural classes, each composed of a single member, exist.

QUANTIFYING STRUCTURE IN PATTERN DESCRIPTION AND RECOGNITION

Structure-based PR assumes pattern 'structure' is quantifiable. This structure quantification is shown using two approaches:

1. Formal grammars; and
2. Relational descriptions (principally graphs).

These tools allow structurally quantitative pattern representation, which facilitates recognition, classification, or description. A class of procedures for *syntactic recognition*, including *parsing* (for formal grammars) and *relational graph matching* (for attributed relational graphs) are then developed.

Hierarchical Approaches

Although it is not mandatory, many SyntPR techniques are based on generation and analysis of complex patterns by a hierarchical decomposition into simpler patterns. An example is the written (English) language, where a paragraph may be decomposed into sentences, sentences may be decomposed into words, words may be decomposed into letters, and letters may be decomposed into strokes.

Complex patterns are often best treated by successive decomposition into more manageable entities. Continuing the previous example, to generate a paragraph using a grammar, one need not begin with the problem of generating the entire paragraph, but instead should first consider the generation of appropriate strokes, which form letters, which form words, and so on. In addition, in analyzing a paragraph it is not necessary (or common) to attempt an analysis of the paragraph as a whole; one first decomposes the paragraph into sentences, then words, then letters, and so on, thereby 'reversing' the process of hierarchical generation of the paragraph.

Relational Models

In some SyntPR approaches, the *properties and relationships* of observed features are used to build more complex structure-based models. Often the relational information in these models is the only significant information, since many other pattern classes share the same low-level features.

GRAMMAR-BASED APPROACH AND APPLICATIONS

In this section we consider the use of structural descriptions in a number of application areas, including natural language processing, line drawing analysis, and 3-D 'blocks world' descriptions. We first develop a general and formal mathematical description of the notion of a *language*. It is worth noting that *the descriptors 'language' and 'sentence' connote a far broader meaning than 'spoken words.'* For example, they include computer programming languages as well as languages used to describe music and the structure of 2-D, 3-D, and time-varying patterns.

Using Formal Linguistics to Model and Describe Patterns

The syntax rules of formal grammars may be used to generate patterns (possibly from other patterns) with constrained structural relations. A grammar may therefore serve to model a class-specific pattern-generating source that generates all the patterns with a class-specific structure. Furthermore, it is desirable to have each class-specific grammar derivable from a set of sample patterns, that is, training must be considered. This raises the issue of *grammatical inference*, which is addressed in Chapter 9.

Suitability of Grammar-Based Approaches for SyntPR.   The use of formal grammars in SyntPR applications is reasonable if a *decomposition* of the entity under consideration *into a set of elements (primitives)* that lend themselves to automatic identification or extraction is possible. The entity has a discernible structure that may be employed in the solution process, and tractable grammars that capture this structure are available.

Languages.   In very general terms, a language is a mechanism that permits the expression of general ideas. Although this definition is too broad for our purposes, it tends to illustrate our representational objective. Languages are generated by grammars. In some instances, grammar specification may occur intuitively (or heuristically). We begin a study of formal definitions of grammars and parsing approaches with a simple example.

EXAMPLE 1: Sentence Formation as Productions (Rewrite Rules)

Consider the following sentence:

'The quarterback throws accurately.' $(6-1)$

Let us temporarily ignore the significance of the capital letter at the beginning and the period at the end and concentrate on the formation and structure of this sentence. The sentence was produced by using the following sequence of 'rewriting' rules.

1. <sentence>
2. <noun phrase> <verb phrase>
3. <article[1] > <noun> <verb phrase>
4. the <noun> <verb phrase>
5. the quarterback <verb phrase>
6. the quarterback <verb> <adverb>
7. the quarterback throws <adverb>
8. the quarterback throws accurately $(6-2)$

Note also the gradual elimination of intermediate and relatively nonspecific entities such as 'noun' and 'adverb.' The sequence that led to the production of the sentence of (6-1) could be cataloged according to the above sequence of rewrites or substitutions. ■

Structural Analysis and Description Applications

Structural analysis is an algorithmic approach common to many applications, including

1. Compilation of high-level languages.   The languages are written by using a set of reserved words (primitives) and rules (productions) for combining these reserve words to form programs according to the syntax of the language. For example, in Pascal this may be shown in BNF (Backus Naur Form[2]) as:

$$function - identifier ::= identifier$$

$$identifier ::= letter\{letter - or - digit\}$$

$$letter ::= a|b|c|\ldots|z|\ldots|A|\ldots|Z$$

$$digit ::= 0|1|2|3|4|\ldots|9$$

$$letter - or - digit ::= letter|digit$$

where the BNF meaning of the symbol

::= means 'is defined as,'

| means 'or,' and

{} indicates items that may be repeated zero or more times.

A compiler or interpreter for a high-level language attempts to generate lower

---

[1] Also referred to as a 'determiner,' may be adverb or adjective.
[2] Or Backus normal form.

level machine instructions by determining the desired structure of the input high-level language program through *parsing* the input or source code.

2. Understanding of natural language. The autonomous understanding of natural language (i.e., speech) is an active area of current research [Carbonell/Hayes 1987]. Applications for this capability include 'keyboardless' document preparation (the system user verbally dictates the input, in contrast to typing), voice actuated machine control (freeing the operator's hands and eyes for other tasks), and operatorless telephone information and reservation systems.

This task fits a structural PR approach, since these basic extracted words (primitives) are combined by the speaker according to the grammar (allowable productions) of the particular language. It is useful to note that the use of and often correct interpretation of grammatically incorrect or imprecise (i.e., ambiguous) sentences makes this task quite challenging. The process of generating and then determining the structure of a sentence using the PROLOG language is shown in [Schalkoff 1990].

One of the most popular examples of simplistic natural language analysis is Weizenbaum's ELIZA program, which emulates conversation with a Rogerian psychologist. Figure 2 shows an example of a conversation with ELIZA. (Note: In Figure 2, 'D' indicates 'doctor,' or program *output*, 'P' indicates 'patient' or user *input*.) ELIZA's responses are not determined through understanding of user input, but rather *a simple pattern-matching approach is used to determine system response*. The program recognizes particular patterns in the user input and then selects and modifies one of a stored set of replies for response. This behavior is evident in the 'shallow' conversation of Figure 2.

3. Music representation. The perceived audio *structure* and *repetition* inherent in music suggests that it is made up of carefully ordered patterns. This becomes even more evident when one views a transcription of a musical composition (i.e., sheet music). Patterns of notes or primitives (e.g., scale fragments) are clearly evident. Thus, music, like spoken language, may be viewed as a language. Numerous authors have attempted to apply the theory of formal grammars to music interpretation and composition [Holtzman 1981], [Roads 1979]. Furthermore, music representation is a good example of the use of *hierarchical data structures*. Figure 3 shows this structure.

4. Description and interpretation of image (visual) data. A good overview of image interpretation research is found in [Bolc 1984]. An application related to formal grammars, structural analysis and description, and parsing is the development of automated systems that allow a human operator to converse, in natural language, with an image or pictorial database system equipped with both image and language understanding capability. This PR capability is useful for systems such as automated weather forecasting, satellite imagery interpretation, pictorial information archiving, and medical diagnosis assistance. Major software components of these systems are: (1) a *preprocessor and parser* to determine the structure of the input phrase; (2) a *translator, query generator*, and *evaluator* which, together with the (3) *analyzer*, take the output of (1) and, through the (4) *answer generator*, query the pictorial database and formulate the system response in natural language form. This is shown in Figure 4.

D: I am at your service; just tell me anything that troubles or concerns you.
P: I am having a great deal of trouble writing a Pattern Recognition textbook.

D: Is it because you are having a great deal of trouble writing a Pattern Recognition textbook that you came to me?
P: Yes.

D: Is there something bothering you?
P: The work in the Pattern Recognition textbook.

D: I am not sure I understand you fully.
P: I hate to write Pattern Recognition texts.

D: What else do you hate?
P: Rogerian therapists.

D: Please go on.
P: Rogerian therapists are for fools.

D: Suppose Rogerian therapists were not for fools.
P: Yes

D: Why are you so sure?
P: No.

D: Can you be more informative?
P: No.

D: Very well.
P: Tell me how to write a Pattern Recognition text.

D: Are you still having a great deal of trouble writing a Pattern Recognition textbook?
P: Yes

D: I see.
P: This doesn't seem to be leading anywhere.

D: What does that suggest to you?
P: This program is not as intelligent as it seems.

D: Possibly that is for the better.
P: I agree.

D: You say you agree?
P: Yes.

D: I understand.
P: Goodbye.

D: I hope I have been of some service. Let's get together again sometime.

Figure 2:   An example of Eliza language 'understanding' program (Rogerian therapist).

ELEMENTS OF FORMAL GRAMMARS[3]

Definitions and Conventions

We begin with *string grammars*, where P is used to generate sentences that consist of linear or 1-D strings of terminals. Note that this does not restrict the representation to 1-D, as shown in the following section.

---

[3]The reader may wish to review the notion of sets in Appendix 3.

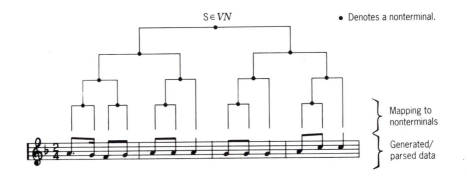

Figure 3:   Structure of a simple musical phrase in terms of terminals and nonterminals. Note hierarchical structure.

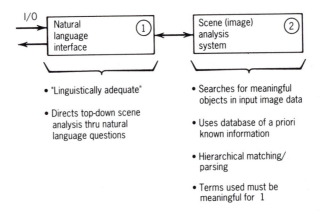

Figure 4:   An example of an image analysis program with natural language interface.

Strings.   An alphabet (V) is a finite, nonempty set of *symbols*, for example:

$$V = \{a, b, c, \ldots z\} \qquad (6-3)$$

The concatenation of a and b, denoted $a \circ b$, produces a sequence of two symbols simply denoted hereafter as ab. A *string* (or sentence[4]) over V is either a single symbol from V or a sequence of symbols formed by concatenation of zero or more symbols from V. Therefore, from V above, 'a', 'ab', 'az', and '$azab$' are strings or *sentences* over V. The length or number of symbols in string s is denoted $|s|$. A string has a natural ordering of elements from left to right. Often it is convenient to denote a string like $x = aaa \ldots a$, where a symbol (or sequence of symbols) is repeated n times as $x = a^n$.

---

[4]This requires careful interpretation.

The Null String and Closure.   The empty string or 'empty sentence', denoted ϵ or λ, has the property that for any string

$$x \circ \epsilon = \epsilon \circ x = x \qquad (6-4a)$$

and also

$$|\epsilon| = 0 \qquad (6-4b)$$

Denoting

$$V \circ V = V^2 \qquad (6-5)$$

as the set of all strings of length 2 derivable from V, and

$$V \circ V \circ V = V^3 \qquad (6-6)$$

as the set of all strings of length 3, we may continue this process up to V^n. Finally, we define V^+ as

$$V^+ = V \cup V^2 \cup V^3 \cup \ldots \qquad (6-7)$$

V^+ is the set of all nonempty sentences producible using V. Adding the empty string to V^+ produces V^*, that is,

$$V^* = \{\epsilon\} \cup V^+ \qquad (6-8)$$

V^* is denoted the *closure (set)* of V, and $V^+ = V^* - \{\epsilon\}$ is often called the *positive closure* of V. The sentences produced using these sets need not be finite in length.

Grammar and Languages Using Strings

Grammars are used with V to give some meaning to a subset of strings, $L \subseteq V^*$, principally by recording structure. L is called a *language*. Another viewpoint is that a grammar (defined below), which generates a language also restricts the production of strings from V. Note that often the cardinality[5] of V^*, denoted $|V^*|$ is such that $|V^*| = \infty$.

Union, Concatenation, Iterates, and Substrings.   Given two languages, L_1 and L_2, over some alphabet V (i.e., $L_1 \subseteq V^*$ and $L_2 \subseteq V^*$),

  1. The *union* of L_1 and L_2 is

$$L_1 \cup L_2 = \{s | s \in L_1 \text{ or } s \in L_2\} \qquad (6-9a)$$

  2. The *concatenation*, denoted $\circ$, of L_1 and L_2 is

$$L_1 \circ L_2 = \{s | s = s_1 s_2 \text{ where } s_1 \in L_1 s_2 \in L_2\} \qquad (6-9b)$$

  3. The *iterate* of L_1, denoted $L_1^{iterate}$ is

$$L_1^{iterate} = \{s | s = s_1 s_2 \ldots s_n, \ n \geq 0 \text{ and } s_i \in L_1\} \qquad (6-10)$$

---

[5]See Appendix 3. Here we use the same notation to denote the length of a string and the cardinality of a set, since it should be clear which entity (string or set) is being referenced.

For strings $x, y \in V^*$, string y is a *substring* of x if V^* contains strings u and v such that

$$x = uyv \tag{6-11}$$

Grammars.   A *grammar* consists of the following four entities:

1. A set of terminal or primitive symbols (primitives), denoted V_T (or, alternately, Σ)[6]. In many applications, the choice of the terminal set or primitives is difficult and has a large component of 'art,' as opposed to 'science.'

2. A set of *nonterminal symbols, or variables*, which are used as intermediate quantities in the generation of an outcome consisting solely of terminal symbols. This set is denoted as V_N (or, alternately, N).

3. A set of *productions, or production rules or rewriting rules* that allow the previous substitutions. It is this set of productions, coupled with the terminal symbols, that principally gives the grammar its 'structure.' The set of productions is denoted P.

4. A starting (or root) symbol, denoted S. $S \in V_N$. In example #1, $S =<$ *sentence* $>$.

Note that V_T and V_N are disjoint sets, that is, $V_T \cap V_N = \emptyset$.
Thus, using the above definitions, we formally denote a grammar, G, as the four-tuple:

$$G = (V_T, V_N, P, S) \tag{6-12}$$

Constraining Productions.   Given V_T and V_N, the productions, P, may be viewed as mappings. Different types of grammars place restrictions on these mappings. For example, it is reasonable[7] to constrain elements of P to the form

$$A \rightarrow B \tag{6-13a}$$

where

$$A \in (V_N \cup V_T)^+ - V_T^+ \tag{6-13b}$$

and

$$B \in (V_N \cup V_T)^* \tag{6-13c}$$

Thus, A must consist of at least one member of V_N, (i.e., a nonterminal), and B is allowed to consist of any arrangement of terminals and nonterminals. This is a partial characterization of *phrase structure grammar*.

Grammar Application Modes

A grammar may be used in one of two modes:

1. *Generative.* The grammar is used to create a string of terminal symbols using P; a *sentence* in the language of the grammar is thus generated.

---

[6]Unfortunately, few texts are consistent in this notation. These conventions probably represent the best common denominator of all the variants found in the literature.

[7]A type $\emptyset$ language does not require this.

2. *Analytic.* Given a sentence (possibly in the language of the grammar), together with specification of G, one seeks to determine:

   (a) If the sentence was generated by G; and, if so,

   (b) The structure (usually characterized as the sequence of productions used) of the sentence.

How a Grammar-Based Language Reduces the Number of Possible Class Patterns. Any subset $L \subseteq V_T^*$ is a *language*. If $|L|$ is finite, the language is called finite; otherwise it is infinite. Typically, simply specifying V_T yields an infinite language. Furthermore, the number of possible languages is nondenumerable. Therefore, for a grammar, and consequently a language, to have practical application in PR, some restrictions or constraints must be placed on L, through grammar G. In addition, compact or efficient representations of L are often obtained through specification of G.

The *language generated by grammar* G, denoted $L(G)$, is the set of all strings that satisfy the following constraints:

   1. Each string consists solely of terminal symbols from V_T of G; and
   2. Each string was produced from S using P of G.

The use of graphical constructs for a grammar in either the generative or analytic mode is common. In the generative mode we may show a *derivation tree* (Chapter 7, Figure 1), whereas in the analytic mode we may use a *parse tree*.

Grammar Types and Productions

Definitions. Throughout this chapter, specifically to characterize the productions of different types of grammars, we will use the following formal notation:

   1. Symbols beginning with a capital letter (e.g., S_1 or S) are elements of V_N.
   2. Symbols beginning with a lowercase letter (e.g., a or b) are elements of V_T.
   3. n denotes the length of string s, that is,

$$n = |s| \qquad (6-14)$$

   4. Greek letters (e.g., α, β) represent (possibly empty) strings, typically comprised of terminals and/or nonterminals.

Types of String Grammars. Constraints on the production or rewrite rules, P, in string grammar G are explored by considering the 'general' production form:

$$\alpha_1 \rightarrow \beta_2 \qquad (6-15)$$

which means string α_1 'is replaced by' string β_2. In general, α_1 and β_2 may contain terminals and/or nonterminals. Four types of grammars have been delineated by [Chomsky 1957]:

<u>Type 0; T_0</u> (Free or Unrestricted[8])

A T_0 grammar has no restrictions on the rewrite rules and is of little practical significance. However, one interesting and allowable aspect of a T_0 grammar is the

---

[8]'Unrestricted' will have a different connotation when used in describing stochastic grammars in Chapter 7.

possibility of 'erasing productions,' since the constraint $|\alpha_1| \leq |\beta_2|$ does not exist. This is an especially interesting concept when considering grammars that produce pattern variations that include deletions of subpatterns.

Type 1; T_1 (Context-Sensitive)

In a T_1 grammar, the production restrictions using the form of (6-15) are

$$\beta_2 \neq \epsilon \qquad (6-16)$$

and

$$|\alpha_1| \leq |\beta_2| \qquad (6-17)$$

Typically, this grammar restricts productions to the form:

$$\alpha\alpha_i\beta \rightarrow \alpha\beta_i\beta \qquad (6-18)$$

meaning β_i replaces α_i *in the context of α and β*, where $\alpha, \beta \in (V_N \cup V_T)^*, \alpha_i \in V_N$, and $\beta_i \in (V_N \cup V_T)^* - \{\epsilon\}$. Equation 6-17 requires $|\alpha\alpha_i\beta| \leq |\alpha\beta_i\beta|$. Note that α or β (or both) may equal ϵ.

Type 2; T_2 (Context Free) CFG

In a T_2 grammar, the production restrictions, using (6-15) are

$$\alpha_1 = S_1 \in V_N \qquad (6-19)$$

that is, α_1 *must be a single nonterminal* for every production in P, and

$$|S_1| \leq |\beta_2| \qquad (6-20a)$$

An alternate characterization of a T_2 grammar is that every production must be of the form:

$$S_1 \rightarrow \beta_2 \qquad (6-20b)$$

where $\beta_2 \in (V_N \cup V_T)^* - \{\epsilon\}$. Note that (6-15), (6-19), and (6-20) *restrict* productions to the replacement of S_1 by string β_2 *independently of the context in which S_1 appears.*

T_2 grammars can generate a string of terminals or nonterminals or both in a single production. Moreover, since productions of the form $A \rightarrow \alpha A \beta$ are allowed, T_2 grammars are *self-embedding*. It is also worth noting that:

- Context-free grammars are important because they are the most descriptively versatile grammars for which effective (and efficient) parsers are available.
- *The production restrictions _increase_ in going from context-sensitive (T_1) to context free (T_2) cases.*

Type 3; T_3 (Finite-State or Regular)

Regular grammars are extremely popular. The production restrictions in a T_3 grammar are, using (6-15), those of a T_2 grammar, plus the additional restriction that *at most one nonterminal symbol is allowed on each side of the production*, that is,

$$\alpha_1 = S_1 \in V_N \qquad (6-21)$$

$$|S_1| \leq |\beta_2| \qquad (6-22)$$

and productions are restricted to

$$A_1 \to a \qquad\qquad (6-23a)$$

or

$$A_1 \to aA_2 \qquad\qquad (6-23b)$$

Equation 6-23 shows the only allowed production forms in this type grammar. A_1 and A_2 are $\in V_N$ and a is $\in V_T - \{\epsilon\}$. Finite state grammars are useful when analysis (parsing) is to be accomplished with finite state machines [Hopcroft/Ullman 1969].

Finite-state (FS) grammars have many well-known characteristics that explain their popularity, including simple graphical representations and known tests for equivalence. The reader should observe, on the basis of the stated constraints, that there are context-free grammars that are not regular grammars.

Graphical Representations of FSGs.   Every FSG has a corresponding graphical representation. Rules for formation of the graph are straightforward:

1. The nodes (with one exception) correspond to elements of V_N. This includes S, the start symbol. A special *terminal node*, denoted T, is also used.
2. An arc from node A_i to node A_j, labeled a, exists for each production of the form $A_i \to aA_j$.
3. An arc from node A_i to node T, labeled a, exists for each production of the form $A_i \to a$.

Thus, the out-degree of node T is zero, and the in-degree of node S is zero.

Example of a FSG Graphical Representation.   Given a FSG, $G_{FSG} = \{V_T, V_N, P, S\}$ where

$$V_T = \{a, b\} \qquad V_N = \{S, A_1, A_2\}$$

$$P = \{S \to aA_2$$

$$S \to bA_1$$

$$A_1 \to a$$

$$A_1 \to aA_1$$

$$A_2 \to b\} \qquad\qquad (6-24a)$$

The corresponding graph is shown in Figure 5.

Recognizing Strings Using the Graphical Representation of a FSG (A Prelude to Parsing).

LEMMA 1: Given a FSG, G, a string $x = x_1, x_2, \ldots x_n$, where $x_i \in V_T$, is an element of $L(G)$ if there exists *at least one* path $x_1, x_2, \ldots x_n$ from S to T in the graphical representation of the FSG.   ■ $(6-24b)$

Other Production Constraints in String Grammars

Phrase Structure Grammars.   A *phrase structure grammar* (PSG[9]) constrains productions as follows:

---

[9]This was hinted at previously in discussing P.

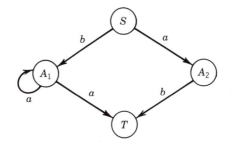

Figure 5:   The graphical representation of sample FSG of (6-24a).

$$\alpha \to \beta \tag{6-25}$$

$$\alpha \neq \epsilon \tag{6-26}$$

or, more specifically,

$$\alpha \in \{V_T \cup V_N\}^* - \{\epsilon\} - \{V_T\} \tag{6-27}$$

Thus, string α must consist of at least one element of V_N. The constraint on β is

$$\beta \in \{V_T \cup V_N\}^* \tag{6-28}$$

Regular Languages.   A language is *regular* if the following holds:
1. L is finite; *OR*
2. $L \in L_1 \cup L_2$ where L_1 and L_2 are regular; *OR*
3. $L \in L_1 \circ L_2$ (concatenation) and L_1 and L_2 are regular; *OR*
4. $L \in L_1^{iterate}$ where L_1 is regular.

Right- and Left-Linear Languages.   Subclasses of context-free grammars, known as linear grammars, are important. A *right-linear language*, denoted $LR(k)$, is generated by a right-linear grammar, where P has the following production restrictions:

$$A \to bC \tag{6-29a}$$

or

$$A \to b \tag{6-29b}$$

where

$$A \in V_N \tag{6-29c}$$

$$b \in V_T \cup \{\epsilon\} \tag{6-29d}$$

Notice that if (6-29d) is restricted to $b \in V_T$, a right-linear grammar becomes a FSG. Similarly, a *left-linear language*, denoted $LL(k)$, constrains P to productions of the form:

$$A \to Ab \tag{6-30a}$$

or

$$A \to c \tag{6-30b}$$

Description/Recognition Trade-offs and a Hierarchy of Classes of Languages Generated.
In progressing from a T_0 to a T_4 grammar, notice that as production restrictions increase, representational power decreases. A strong case can often be made for the use of context-sensitive grammars in pattern structural description. For example, structural representation applications such as spoken or written sentences are naturally handled via context-sensitive grammars. However, in parsing strings in a T_1 grammar, the number of contextual possibilities for each of the rewrite rules would need to be considered. The number of recognition steps in such a parser becomes combinatorially explosive. Generating sentences by using CFGs may result in syntactically correct sentences with nonsense meanings (or semantics). Parsing complexity in a T_2 grammar is a linear function of the number of rewrite rules in a derivation. Similarly, a CFG, while perhaps more descriptively versatile than a FSG, requires a parser that is more complex than a finite-state machine.

If we denote $L(T_i)$ as the class of language generated by grammar T_i, the above restrictions indicate

$$L(T_3) \subset L(T_2) \subset L(T_1) \subset L(T_0) \qquad (6-31)$$

Figure 6 summarizes these concerns.

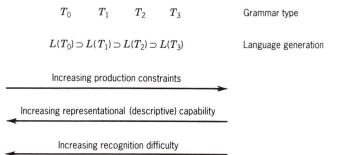

Figure 6:   The trade-offs between representational capability and recognition difficulty in $T_0 - T_4$ grammars.

The Non-uniqueness of G, Given L.   Grammars generate languages; however, there is no unique relationship between a given language and a grammar. In other words, a language L may be generated by several different grammars, that is, $L = L(G_1) = L(G_2)$. This raises interesting questions in the design of grammars for structural description as well as for the *training* of grammar-based PR systems. These concerns parallel questions in training StatPR systems, where often the form of various density functions (and their corresponding parameters) must be inferred from training set H.

Additional Introductory Concepts

Derivations versus Productions.   As we have shown previously, rewrite rules or productions are designated by using a simple right arrow: '$\rightarrow$.' These define *allowable* *replacements*. In order to show the specific use of a production to generate a new string x_n, from x, or a so-called *derivation*, the $\Rightarrow$ symbol is used. Thus, $A \to c$ defines a production, whereas $x \Rightarrow x_n$ denotes the use of this production to convert string x into string x_n.

Recursive and Definite Grammars. G is *recursive* if it allows at least one derivation of the form:

$$S_1 \Rightarrow \alpha S_1 \beta \tag{6 – 32}$$

where $S_1 \in V_N$ and $\alpha, \beta \in (V_T \cup V_N)^*$. A recursive grammar, G_R, generates a $L(G_R)$ where $|L(G_R)| = \infty$. Recursive grammars often yield compact representations for class-specific pattern generation. If G is not recursive, G is said to be a *definite* grammar. $|L(G)|$ is finite for a definite grammar.

Equivalence of Grammars.   Two grammars, G_1 and G_2 are *equivalent* iff $L(G_1) = L(G_2)$. Grammar equivalence has the following ramifications:

- If G_1 and G_2 are finite-state grammars, an algorithm to determine if they are equivalent exists [Hopcroft/Ullman 1969].
- If G_1 and G_2 are CFGs, a general algorithm to test for equivalence does not exist [Fu/Booth 1986].

Another important observation is that two different and nonequivalent grammars may generate one or more identical strings.

Covering.   A grammar $G_1 = \{V_T^1, V_N^1, P^1, S^1\}$ *covers* grammar $G_2 = \{V_T^2, V_N^2, P^2, S^2\}$ if there exists a function f that maps elements of V_N in G_2 (denoted V_N^2) into elements of V_N in G_1 (denoted V_N^1) such that:

1. $S^1 = f(S^2)$; and
2. P^1 may be obtained by applying f to every nonterminal element of P^2.

An important consequence is that if G_1 covers G_2, then $L(G_2) \subseteq L(G_1)$. This is of use in grammatical inference.

EXAMPLE 2: Context-Sensitive, Context-Free, and Finite-State (Regular) Grammar Productions

Context-Free.

$$S \to aAa$$
$$A \to a$$
$$A \to b \tag{6 – 33a}$$

Context-Sensitive.

$$S \to SC$$
$$CB \to Cb$$
$$aB \to aa$$
$$bB \to bb \tag{6 – 33b}$$

Finite-State.

$$S \rightarrow aA_1$$

$$S \rightarrow bA_1$$

$$A_1 \rightarrow a$$

$$A_1 \rightarrow b \qquad\qquad (6-33c)$$

■

Normal Forms.   Normalization achieves standardization while preserving certain desired characteristics. Languages may be normalized. Consider the pattern-generating capability of two grammars, G_1 and G_2, where

$$L(G_1) = L(G_2) \qquad\qquad (6-34a)$$

G_1 (or G_2) may be considerably simpler in form, (or perhaps easier to parse). For example, it is often preferable to consider *cycle-free* grammars, which do not allow derivations of the form $x \Rightarrow x_1 \Rightarrow x_2 \ldots \Rightarrow x$. Such a derivation is a *cycle* and serves no useful purpose. Another important application is comparison of class-specific language-generating grammars, G_1 and G_2, to determine if

$$L(G_1) \neq L(G_2) \qquad\qquad (6-34b)$$

so that certain patterns produced are unique to one language. The normalization of CFGs are useful.

Chomsky Normal Form (CNF).   A CFG is in Chomsky Normal Form (CNF) [Moll et al. 1988] if each element of P is in one of the following forms:

$$A \rightarrow BC \quad \text{where } A, B, C \in V_N$$

$$A \rightarrow a \quad \text{where } A \in V_N, a \in V_T \qquad\qquad (6-35)$$

LEMMA 2. For any CFG, G, there exists an equivalent[10] G' in CNF.   ■

Ambiguity.   A sentence generated by a grammar is *ambiguous* if there is more than one parse tree for it. A grammar is ambiguous if it generates one or more ambiguous sentences. Unfortunately, ambiguity is difficult to detect in the process of developing a grammar. There is no algorithm that, given a CFG, can determine whether it is ambiguous in finite time. However, sufficient conditions can be developed and applied to the design of a grammar such that the resulting grammar is unambiguous [Tremblay/Sorenson 1985].

Examples of Ambiguity.
- 'Flying over New York, I saw the Statue of Liberty.'
- $8 \times 4 + 3 \div 6$
- Optical illusions (visual ambiguity)

---

[10]$L(G) = L(G')$.

EXAMPLES OF STRING GENERATION AS PATTERN DESCRIPTION

EXAMPLE 3: 2-D Line Drawing Description Grammar [Shaw 1970]

Several examples of the descriptive capability of string grammars are presented. The first example shows the application of a grammar-based approach to the description of line drawings, which assumes a preprocessed (via a sequence of steps involving noise minimization, edge detection, enhancement, and connection) image that results in a line drawing of some object or set of objects appearing in a scene. This line drawing is the input to our grammatically based analysis of the scene.

A Line Drawing (Cylinder) Description Grammar.   We consider the cylinder description grammar, G_{cyl}, as follows:

$$G_{cyl} = (V_T^{cyl}, V_N^{cyl}, P^{cyl}, S^{cyl}) \qquad (6-36a)$$

where

$$V_T^{cyl} = \{t, b, u, o, s, *, \neg, +\} \qquad (6-36b)$$

(as described in Figure 7)

$$V_N^{cyl} = \{Top, Body, Cylinder\} \qquad (6-36c)$$

$$P^{cyl} = \{Cylinder \rightarrow Top * Body$$

$$Top \rightarrow t * b$$

$$Body \rightarrow \neg u + b + u\} \qquad (6-36d)$$

We use the following interpretations of the productions in (6-36d):

+ represents head to tail concatenation
* represents head-head and tail-tail attachment
¬ represents head and tail reversal
→ means 'may be replaced by'

and

$$S^{cyl} = Cylinder \qquad (6-36e)$$

This grammar allows the representation of the class of cylinders shown in Figures 7 and 8. Note the use of 2-D directed features with standardized 'attachment points' denoted head and tail (H, T). In this grammar, the set of terminals, V_T, is composed of *both* the pattern primitives and the symbols used to denote interconnection. (Interconnection precedence, using parentheses, may also augment V_T.)

The above grammar is useful for two applications:

1. Classification of line drawings. The problem, for example, of discriminating between a line drawing of a cube and of a cylinder is handled. It translates into the problem, given a suitable string description, denoted s_x, of the line drawing of a scene, and given the cylinder and cube grammars G_{cyl} and G_{cube} respectively, of determining whether $s_x \in L(G_{cyl}), s_x \in L(G_{cube})$, or $s_x \in$ some other language. This would be accomplished via parsing.

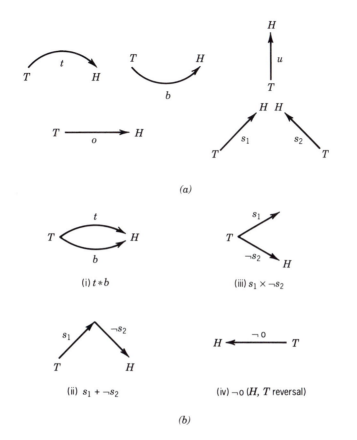

Figure 7:   **(a)** Picture description grammar primitives showing
attachment points (H, T).

(b) Attachment and other operator examples.
(i) $t * b$
(ii) $s_1 + \neg s_2$
(iii) $s_1 \times \neg s_2$
(iv) $\neg o$ $(H, T$ reversal).

2. Determining the *structure* of the entity under observation, perhaps for descriptive purposes, or perhaps as a prelude to some operation on the structure (such
as moving it). In this example, the identity and spatial relationship of 'side,'
'top,' and perhaps the shape of the entity (i.e., cylindrical or cubical) is useful;
again, a parse of the description provides this. It is also crucial to note that the
structural description and recognition of an entity avoids many of the problems caused by varying orientations, that is, it should be possible to recognize
a cylinder in any orientation. Conversely, the approach (i.e., the grammars)
could be revised to be directionally as well as entity sensitive; in this case a

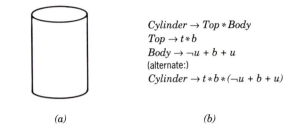

$$Cylinder \to Top * Body$$
$$Top \to t * b$$
$$Body \to \neg u + b + u$$
(alternate:)
$$Cylinder \to t * b * (\neg u + b + u)$$

(a) *(b)*

Figure 8: A sample line drawing: the grammar-based approach.
(a) Cylinder line drawing.
(b) Productions.

description of the entity as well as its corresponding orientation may be obtained. This is a considerably more difficult problem to formulate than mere 2-D 'signal processing.' ∎

EXAMPLE 4: Character Description Using PDL

Figure 9 introduces a four-class set of patterns that are recognized as 'block' versions of the uppercase alphabet characters 'A,' 'C,' 'P,' and 'F.' We use a subset of the PDL for description of these characters. Note that only sample descriptions are shown in Figure 9(b); other class or character-specific descriptions are possible (this is expanded in the exercises). Note that this problem is considered again in several ways in the NeurPR framework of Chapters 11 and 12. ∎

EXAMPLE 5: Object Description Using Projected Cylinder Models

Figure 10 shows a grammar in CNF form for composition of generalized cylinders to describe the 2-D projections (images) of 3-D objects. Figure 5 (Chapter 1) shows the basic primitives and relevant properties. Further details may be found in [Schalkoff 1989]. ∎

Extended Example 6: Blocks World Description

In this section a grammar is developed to describe and classify situations involving stacks of blocks on a table. Although the example is simple, it illustrates the use of structural analysis for both pattern description and pattern recognition. We restrict ourselves to the situation shown in Figure 11. Initially, our goal is to distinguish '2-blocks' situations from '3-blocks' cases as shown in the figure. Clearly, the difference between the two situations is the *structure* of the blocks arrangement. We adopt the following constraints:

1. There is no unique naming of blocks.[11]
2. There are always four blocks.
3. The bottom block of a stack must reside on the table.

---
[11] Extensions to this are left as a (challenging) exercise for the reader.

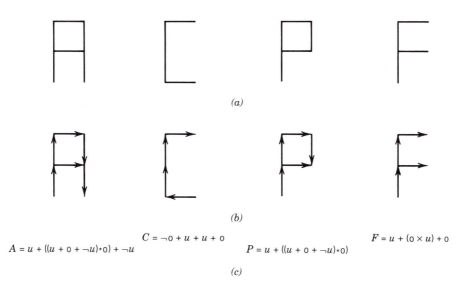

(a)

(b)

$$C = \neg o + u + u + o$$
$$A = u + ((u + o + \neg u) \cdot o) + \neg u \qquad\qquad P = u + ((u + o + \neg u) \cdot o)$$
$$F = u + (o \times u) + o$$

(c)

Figure 9:   A four-character example and sample PDL descriptions.
(a) Pattern data.
(b) Primitive representation and interconnection.
(c) Corresponding descriptions.

A Grammatical Approach.   We develop grammars G_2 and G_3, to describe the 2-blocks and 3-blocks cases, respectively. It is important to note the context-sensitive nature of G_3.

G_2 *(2-blocks).*   (Note: In V_T, $+$ means 'also' and $\uparrow$ means 'on top of.')

$$V_T = \{table,\ a\_block,\ +,\ \uparrow\}$$

$$V_N = \{DESC,\ LEFT - STACK,\ RIGHT - STACK\}$$

$$S = DESC \in V_N$$

$$P = \{$$

$$DESC \rightarrow LEFT - STACK + RIGHT - STACK$$

$$DESC \rightarrow RIGHT - STACK + LEFT - STACK$$

$$LEFT - STACK \rightarrow a\_block \uparrow a\_block \uparrow table$$

$$RIGHT - STACK \rightarrow a\_block \uparrow a\_block \uparrow table \ \} \qquad (6-37)$$

G_3 *(3-blocks).* V_T, V_N and S are the same as G_2.

$$P = \{$$

$$DESC \rightarrow LEFT - STACK + RIGHT - STACK$$
$$LEFT - STACK + RIGHT - STACK \rightarrow$$
$$a\_block \uparrow table + a\_block \uparrow a\_block \uparrow a\_block \uparrow table$$
$$LEFT - STACK + RIGHT - STACK \rightarrow$$
$$a\_block \uparrow a\_block \uparrow a\_block \uparrow table + a\_block \uparrow table\}$$

$$(6 - 38)$$

object :: = object-name root

root :: = part

part :: = part-name cylindar carries

cylindar :: = cyl-name edges symmetry cross-section-size axis aspect ratio

carries :: = NIL I (subpart carries)

subpart :: = subpart-name attachment part

attachment :: = where how by-what

object-name :: = identifier

part-name :: = identifier

subpart-name :: = identifier

cyl-name :: = identifier

edges :: = S I C

symmetry :: = Symm + + I Symm + I Asymm

cross-section-size :: = Const I Exp I Exp-Contr

axis :: = S I C

aspect-ratio :: = Long I Normal I Short

where :: = Same-axis-top I Sams-axis-bottom
        I Right-side-top I Right-side-middle I Right-side-bottom
        I Left-side-top I Left-side-middle I Left-side-bottom

how :: = Perpendicular I Acute-angle I Obtuse-angle

by-what :: = By-the-top I By-the-bottom

Figure 10:   The grammar for object description using 2-D features and attributed primitives from Chapter 1, Figure 5 (BNF).

Distinguishing Between 2-blocks and 3-blocks Cases—Parsers and Graph Structural Matching (Prelude to Chapter 8).   The simplicity of the G_2 and G_3 grammars enables a parsing approach to classification. Alternately, as shown in Figure 11, the 2-block and 3-block cases each yields a graphical representation that is isomorphic to all others, regardless of block names. Therefore, we may use this *structural* information to distinguish between the two cases. Note, however, that the graphical approach provides

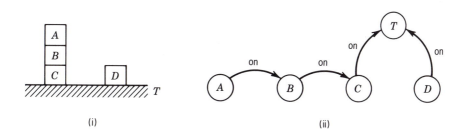

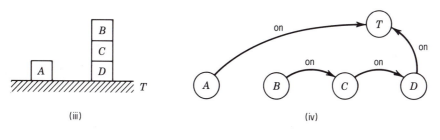

(a)

Figure 11:   The 2-blocks versus 3-blocks descriptions.
(a) '3-blocks' class.
(i) Example
(ii) Graphical representation of (i)
(iii) Alternate example (same class)
(iv) Graphical representation corresponding to (iii).

a vehicle for *structural feature extraction*, which may also facilitate classification. For example, as shown in Figure 11:

- In- or out-degree of any graph node is not a distinguishing feature.
- Both G_2 and G_3 representations have 4 blocks, 1 table and 4 'on' relations in common.
- The longest path length (3 in the 3-block case; 2 in the 2-block case) provides a suitable distinguishing feature. ■

Remarks on the Heuristic Generation of Grammars

The previous examples illustrated primitive selection and grammar generation. Many concerns arise in this process, including the following:

1. Primitive selection. Different primitives lend themselves to the design of different grammars.
2. Grammars, particularly those designed in an ad hoc manner, may generate 'superfluous' sentences, including strings that are also producible by another class-specific grammar.

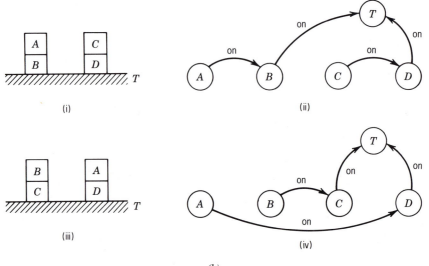

(b)

Figure 11 (cont.):   **(b)** '2-blocks' class.
      (i) Example
      (ii) Corresponding graphical representation
      (iii) Alternate example (same class)
      (iv) Graphical description corresponding to (iii).

3. The choice of grammar type, while important, is often secondary to achieving adequate descriptive power.

4. As a result of concerns 1 to 3, the designing of a grammar or set of grammars is typically an iterative process.

BIBLIOGRAPHICAL REMARKS

Early attempts to characterize languages via a taxonomy are due to [Chomsky 1957]. Useful introductions to formal grammars are [Hopcroft/Ullman 1969], [Aho/ Ullman 1972], and [Moll et al. 1988]. [Fu 1 1982], [Gonzalez/Thomason 1978], and [Miclet 1986] are devoted entirely to SyntPR. A comprehensive summary of approaches related to the PDL application is [Rosenfeld 1979]. An extended example of the utility of SyntPR in an image interpretation application is [Don/Fu 1985].

EXERCISES

6.1   Given $V = \{a, b\}$, show V^2, V^3, and V^4.

6.2   Distinguish between, or relate, a phrase structure grammar and
    (a) A free grammar.
    (b) A context-sensitive grammar.

6.3   Which of the following are true?

    (a)   A regular grammar is a context-free grammar.

    (b)   A regular grammar is a free grammar.

    (c)   A context-free grammar is a context-sensitive grammar.

    (d)   A context-sensitive grammar is a context-free grammar.

6.4   For each of the grammars shown in (6-15) through (6-30)

    (a)   Derive a table that compares the restrictions on each.

    (b)   Design an example of the grammar.

6.5   This exercise, as does Example 6, provides some familiarity with context-sensitive grammars.

    (a)   Show that the following grammar [Fu 1974] can be used to generate the language of equilateral triangles, that is, $L(G) = \{a^n b^n c^n \quad for \quad n > 1\}$

$$S \rightarrow aSBA | aBA$$

$$AB \rightarrow BA$$

$$bB \rightarrow bb$$

$$bA \rightarrow bc$$

$$cA \rightarrow cc$$

$$aB \rightarrow ab$$

    (b)   Using the results of (a), develop a similar formulation in the PDL. Assume that unit-length primitives with the necessary $0°, 60°$, and $120°$ orientations are available.

6.6   If every production of a CFG has the form

$$A_1 \rightarrow \alpha B_1 \beta$$

or

$$A_1 \rightarrow \alpha$$

where $\alpha, \beta \in V_T^*$, $A_1, B_1 \in V_N$, and α and β are not *both* the empty string, a *linear grammar* results. What restrictions on a linear grammar yield $LR(k)$ and $LL(k)$ grammars?

6.7   Using the definition in Exercise 6.6, show an example of a CFG that is not a linear grammar.

6.8   Suppose you are given the language L, where $L = \{a^n b | n = 1, 2, \ldots\}$. Derive three different types of grammars that generate L.

6.9   Define a grammar that produces the language

$$L = \{a^n b^{n+1} | n > 0\}$$

6.10   For each of the grammars in Example 2, show $L(G)$.

6.11   Convert the production in G

$$S \to ABC$$

into those that would appear in G', where G' is defined in (6-35).

6.12   Given $V_T = \{a, b\}$ and $V_N = \{F, G\}$, determine $(V_N \cup V_T)^*$ and $(V_N \cup V_T)^* - V_T^*$.

6.13   Use the sample FSG given in (6-24a), together with Lemma 1 (6-24b) and Figure 5 to determine if

(a) $x^{(1)} = ab$

(b) $x^{(2)} = baa$

(c) $x^{(3)} = bab$

are elements of $L(G_{FSG})$.

6.14   Given a grammar G_{BIN}, where

$$G_{BIN} = \{V_T^{BIN}, V_N^{BIN}, P^{BIN}, S^{BIN}\}$$

with

$$V_T^{BIN} = \{0, 1\}$$

$$V_N^{BIN} = \{S\} = S^{BIN}$$

$$P^{BIN} = \{S \to 0$$

$$S \to 0S$$

$$S \to 1$$

$$S \to 1S$$

$$S \to \epsilon\}$$

(a)   Determine $L(G_{BIN})$.

(b)   Using the definitions and constraints presented in this chapter, determine all types of grammars that G_{BIN} could be classified as.

6.15   For the FSG productions shown in (6-33c)

(a)   Determine $L(G)$.

(b)   How does $L(G)$ change if the productions are changed to

$$S \to aA_2$$

$$S \to bA_1$$

$$A_1 \to a$$

$$A_2 \to b$$

6.16   (a)   Revise G_2 and G_3 so that each of the four blocks in the description has a unique name.

(b)   What types of grammars result?

6.17   What types of grammars are blocks grammars G_2 and G_3 in (6-37) and (6-38)?

6.18   Extend G_2 and G_3 to allow *any number* of stacks, with the constraint that there be *exactly one* 2-block and 3-block stack, respectively. This should allow any number of total blocks (≥ 5) as well as stacks of height 4, 5, etc.

6.19   Repeat Exercise 6.18, but require *at least one* 2- or 3-block stack in each string produced by G_2 or G_3, respectively.

6.20   Using the G_2 and G_3 grammars developed in Exercises 6.18 and 6.19, develop and show examples of several syntactic recognition strategies for each class.

6.21   Referring to character description Example 4, derive $G_A, G_C, G_P,$ and G_F and graphically show $L(G_A)$, $L(G_C)$, $L(G_P)$, and $L(G_F)$.

6.22   Using the PDL, develop G_{RECT}, the grammar that generates all rectangles. Is $L(G_{RECT})$ finite? Can $L(G_{RECT})$ be expressed in closed form?

6.23   Develop G_A, where the character 'A' is shown in Figure P.1.

Figure P.1:

6.24   Referring to Figure 9 (Example 4), note the structural similarity of the 'block' versions of characters 'A' and 'P'. How is this similarity reflected in G_A and G_P? (The results of Exercise 6.21 may be useful here.)

6.25   This exercise considers an alternative to the PDL. Refer to the primitives and sample relations shown in Figure P.2, with

$$V_T = \{b,\ u,\ o,\ \uparrow_L,\ \uparrow_R,\ \downarrow_L,\ \downarrow_R\}$$

where $\uparrow_L, \ldots, \downarrow_R$ denote 'connected to above on the left' through 'connected to below on the right.'

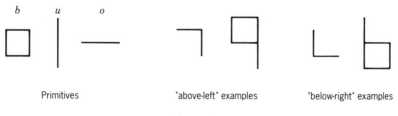

Figure P.2

(a)   Develop G_A, G_C, G_P, G_F and show examples of descriptions in $L(G_A), \ldots L(G_F)$.

(b)   Are $\uparrow_L$ and $\downarrow_R$ both necessary?

6.26   A student was asked to design a grammar to produce squares with varying side lengths (units are in dimensions of u or o) and responded with the following solution:

$$G_{SQ} = \{V_T^{SQ}, V_N^{SQ}, P^{SQ}, S^{SQ}\}$$

$$V_T^{SQ} = \{o, u, \neg, +\}$$

$$V_N^{SQ} = \{Square, \quad Side1, \quad Side2, \quad Side3, \quad Side4\}$$

$$P^{SQ} = \{$$

$$Side1 \rightarrow o|Side1 + o$$

$$Side2 \rightarrow \neg u|Side2 + \neg u$$

$$Side3 \rightarrow \neg o|Side3 + \neg o$$

$$Side4 \rightarrow u|Side4 + u$$

$$Square \rightarrow Side1 + Side2 + Side3 + Side4\}$$

$$S^{SQ} = \{Square\}$$

(a)   What is wrong with this strategy? [Show examples of both desired productions (squares) and undesired productions.]

(b)   Suggest modifications necessary to achieve the stated objective.

Syntactic Recognition via Parsing and Other Grammars

7

The speech of man is like embroidered tapestries, since like them this too has to be extended in order to display its patterns, but when it is rolled up it conceals and distorts them.

From Plutarch, *Lives, Themistocles*, sec 29
Themistocles c. 528–462 B.C.

RECOGNITION OF SYNTACTIC DESCRIPTIONS

The previous chapter considered the generation of syntactic or structural pattern descriptions using formal grammars. In this chapter, the 'inverse' of this problem is considered. Given the description of a pattern as a string produced by a class-specific grammar, the objective is to determine to which $L(G_i)\, i = 1, 2, \ldots c$ the string belongs.

Recognition by String Matching

A somewhat obvious approach to classification or recognition of entities using syntactic descriptions is a matching procedure. Consider the c-class case. Class-specific grammars $G_1, G_2, \ldots G_c$ are developed. Given an unknown description, x, to classify, it is necessary to determine if $x \in L(G_i)$ for $i = 1, 2, \ldots c$. Suppose that the language of each G_i could be generated and stored in a class-specific *library* of patterns. By matching x against *each pattern in each library*, the class membership of x could be determined. String matching metrics are considered in Appendix 5. The reader may recognize this procedure as a variant of the 1-NNR rule for feature vectors, where a matching metric using strings instead of vectors is employed.

Computational Complexity/Efficiency Concerns. There are several shortcomings to the previously described procedure. First, often $|L(G_i)| = \infty$; therefore the cataloging or library-based procedure is impossible. Second, even if $L(G_i)$ for each i is denumerable, it usually requires very large libraries. Consequently, the computational effort in matching is excessive. Third, it is an inefficient procedure. Alternatives that employ efficient search algorithms, prescreening of the data, the use of hierarchical matching, and prototypical strings are often preferable. *Note that in SyntPR, the similarity measure(s) used must account for the similarity of primitives as well as similarity of structure.*

Recognition by Parsing

Parsing is a fundamental concept related to the syntactic or structural approach, whose objective is to determine if the input pattern (string) is *syntactically well formed* in the context of one or more prespecified grammars. Parsing is accomplished by parsers, which are often referred to as syntax analyzers. To construct a parser for any language, it is first necessary to quantify the language as described in Chapter 6 and (6-13).

Different parsing methods are usually associated with restricted classes of grammars. For example, we have already seen a parser 'in disguise,' in considering the use of the graphical representation of a FSG for recognition (Chapter 6, Figure 5). In what follows, the use of the CYK parsing algorithm on a CFG grammar in Chomsky normal form is shown. Constraining the type of grammar to be parsed often yields efficient or practical parser complexities; however, this may be at the expense of representational flexibility.

PARSING

Fundamental Concepts

Parser Hierarchical Structures.   To be efficient, the parser could be of hierarchical structure. For example, the initial decomposition of the sentence to be parsed should be in terms of smaller entities (such as phrases). Following this, the parsing of the phrases could occur.

Graphical Constructs: The Derivation Tree.

EXAMPLE 1: Grammar G_1

Consider the following grammar, G_1:

$$G_1 = (V_T, V_N, P, S)$$

where

$$V_T = \{the, program, crashes, computer\}$$

$$V_N = \{SENTENCE, ADJ, NP, VP, NOUN, VERB\}$$

$$P = \Big\{$$

$$(i) SENTENCE \rightarrow NP + VP$$

$$(ii) NP \rightarrow ADJ + NOUN$$

$$(iii) VP \rightarrow VERB + NP$$

$$(iv) NOUN \rightarrow computer | program$$

$$(v) VERB \rightarrow crashes$$

$$(vi) ADJ \rightarrow the \quad \Big\}$$

In P the symbol $+$ stands for 'concatenation of,' but may be thought of in terms of 'string summation', that is, the joining of two strings. Similarly, the symbol $\rightarrow$ stands for 'may be replaced by.' The symbol $|$ has the meaning 'or,' from the BNF syntax.

$$S \rightarrow SENTENCE$$

Given the productions and symbols (terminal and nonterminal) above, the 'context-free' nature of our productions is significant. The grammar enforces syntax, not semantics.

As a prelude to the development of a parser for grammar G_1, let us enumerate the steps used to construct the sentence:

'the program crashes the computer'

This is a valid sentence in the language of G_1. Figure 1 shows this sequence and is referred to as a *derivation tree*. The process starts at the topmost portion of the tree with the root or starting symbol S ($\in V_N$) and terminates with the final substitutions of terminals (constants $\in V_T$) at the leaves of the tree. The productions occur by traversing the tree from the root to the leaves. Proceeding from the top of the derivation tree, we notice that in all but the last substitutions (which yield the leaves), nonterminals (noun phrases, verb phrases, verbs, adjectives, and nouns) are involved in the productions. Notice that the structure of the resulting sentence is determined completely by the tree, regardless of the order of substitutions used to generate successor nodes. ■

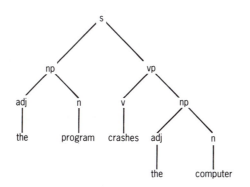

Figure 1:   Derivation tree example.

An Abstract View of the Parsing Problem

Given a string of terminals comprising a sentence x, and a grammar G, specified as

$$G = (V_T, V_N, P, S) \tag{7-1}$$

we construct a triangle of the form shown in Figure 2. The process of filling the interior of this triangle with a tree of productions that link S to x is called a parse. If we are successful, we have determined that x is a member of $L(G)$. If we fill the interior of the triangle from the top down (i.e., from the root of the tree), a *top-down parse* results. Alternately, if we work from the bottom (x) up, that is, begin with the terminal symbols, a *bottom-up parse* results. Note that a bottom-up parse (so-called *parse tree*) may be obtained from a derivation tree, where the productions, P, are applied in reverse order. Thus

- *Bottom-up parsing* proceeds from terminals toward S.
- *Top-down parsing* proceeds from S toward the terminals. It is an attempt to obtain a derivation of x.

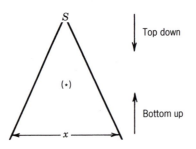

(·) Interior to be filled with valid productions

Figure 2:   Parsing.

From Parsing (Structure) to Deeper Meaning.   Parsing (particularly when applied to spoken/written languages) provides a potential first step in recognizing the structure and, consequently, *meaning* of an input sentence. A parsed sentence may subsequently be converted into a 'deeper' representation (e.g., a conceptual graph [Sowa 1984], [Schalkoff 1990]) forming the basis for a higher level interpretation.

Parsing/Generation Similarities.   Although generation and parsing of a string are strongly related, it is not a 'two-way street.' Application of a grammar in the generative mode is usually far easier than in the analytic mode, that is, parsing. Two concerns are the following:

1. *In practice, the parser must determine the extent of the elements that comprise non-terminals.* This is not simple, given a sophisticated grammar. It also suggests that parsing is accomplished with a contextual component, which makes sense, since the parser ultimately seeks the 'structure' of the entity it is parsing.

2. *The parser must find a use for all of x,* that is, it cannot simply identify parts of the string with some structure and discard the rest. Thus, in a sense, the string must be 'consumed' in the parse.

Parsing Computational Complexity.   It is of significant practical importance that *a grammar should enable an efficient parser.* We now seek a way to satisfy these constraints. Parsing of sentences in formal languages involves the matching of substructures to form and to recognize an overall or global structure. The potential search complexity suggests that other a priori information (including heuristics) may be useful in the development of practical parsers.

The Decidability Problem.   Given $L(G_i)$ and a string x, we ask the following:

$$x \stackrel{?}{\in} L(G_i) \qquad\qquad (7-2)$$

If so, pattern x is classified in class i. More importantly, we consider the effort required to answer this question. If there exists an algorithm that answers this question in a finite amount of time, the parsing problem is said to be *fully decidable*.

Parsing Approaches

Top-Down Parsing.   In this approach, we proceed from the start symbol, S, to the terminals. Several approaches [Tremblay/Sorenson 1985] are:

1. Top-Down with Full-Backup (TDFB) (brute force): This is a depth-first expansion of nonterminals starting with the leftmost nonterminal in the expansion of the goal.
2. Recursive Descent (RD): This approach allows no backup; it may not work on all grammars. It utilizes binary-valued and recursive *functions* to recognize substrings that correspond to expansion of a specific nonterminal.
3. Top-Down with Limited Backup (TDLB).

Bottom-Up Parsing ('Brute Force').   We might envision top-down parsing as the speculative application of productions, beginning with S. The alternative bottom-up approach may be viewed as the speculative 'reversing' of productions. Given x, we construct series or sequences of intermediate strings from $(V_N \cup V_T)^+$ by 'reversing' corresponding series of productions.

'Reversing' a Production.   Given a production, $P1$

$$P1: A \rightarrow \alpha \qquad\qquad (7-3)$$

where A is a nonterminal and α is a string of terminals and nonterminals, 'reversing' $P1$ means locating an occurrence of α in one of the strings in the sequence, and replacing α by A. In a realistic application, the combinatorial explosion of choices in the sequence are often a barrier to practical application. For example, given $\alpha = a$, the string $x = aaaa$, and $P1$, possible (one-step) 'reverses' are

$$A\,a\,a\,a$$
$$a\,A\,a\,a$$
$$a\,a\,A\,a$$
$$a\,a\,a\,A$$

Bottom-up approaches, therefore, attempt to speculatively 'contract' the given string into nonterminals, whereas top-down are speculative (or tentative) expansions.

Comparing Parsing Approaches.   It is difficult to comparatively assess top-down and bottom-up approaches. There are grammars that are more efficiently parsed with top-down parsers and others where bottom-up parsers are more efficient. Therefore, the choice is often grammar-dependent. In addition, transformation or normalization of a given grammar may affect parsing efficiency. Unfortunately, brute force top-down and bottom-up parsing approaches have a computational complexity that, in general, may grow exponentially with $|x|$. For this reason, we seek enhancements or alternatives that yield more practical utility.

THE COCKE–YOUNGER–KASAMI (CYK) PARSING ALGORITHM

The Approach

The CYK algorithm is a parsing approach that will parse string x in a number of steps proportional to $|x|^3$. *The CYK algorithm requires that the CFG be in Chomsky Normal Form (CNF).* Recall from Chapter 6 that in CNF each production is either $A \rightarrow BC$ or $A \rightarrow a$. With this restriction, the derivation of any string involves a series of binary decisions.

The CYK Table

Given string $x = x_1, x_2, \ldots x_n$, where $x_i \in V_T$, $|x| = n$, and a grammar G, we form a triangular table with entries t_{ij} indexed by i and j where $1 \leq i \leq n$ and $1 \leq j \leq (n - i + 1)$. The origin is at $i = j = 1$, and entry t_{11} is the lower left-hand entry in the table. t_{1n} is the uppermost entry in the table. This structure is shown in Figures 3(a) and 3(b).

Building the CYK Table.   The CYK parse table is built, starting from location $(1, 1)$. *If a substring of x, beginning with x_i and of length j, can be derived from a nonterminal, this nonterminal is placed into cell (i, j).* If cell $(1, n)$ contains S, the table contains a valid derivation of x in $L(G)$. It is convenient to list the x_i, starting with $i = 1$, under the bottom row of the table.

EXAMPLE 2: **Sample Operation of the CYK Algorithm**[1]

Sample Grammar Productions.

$$S \rightarrow AB | BB$$

$$A \rightarrow CC | AB | a$$

---

[1]This is a modified example of that shown in [Moll et al. 1988], p. 65.

$$B \rightarrow BB|CA|b$$

$$C \rightarrow BA|AA|b \qquad\qquad (7-4a)$$

There are six forms for the derivation of $x = aabb$.

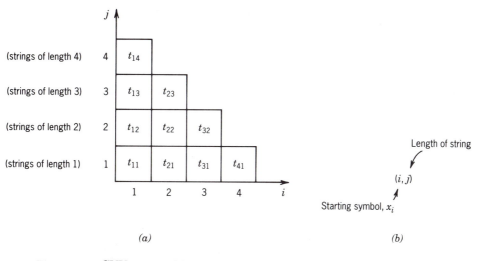

(a)

Length of string

(i, j)

Starting symbol, x_i

(b)

Figure 3:   CYK parse table.
   (a) Example of table for $|x| = n = 4$.
   (b) Structure of cell entries.

Construction of the Parse Table for Example 2.   Construction of a sample parse table is shown in Figure 4(a). Recall that cell entry (i, j) corresponds to the possibility of producing a string of length j, starting with symbol x_i. The table is formed from the bottom row $(j = 1)$ upwards. Entries for cells $(1, 1)$, $(2, 1)$, $(3, 1)$ and $(4, 1)$ are relatively easy to determine, since they each correspond to production of a single terminal. The process for $j > 1$ is more complicated.

   For the second $(j = 2)$ row of the table, all nonterminals that could yield derivations of substrings of length 2, beginning with x_i, $i = 1, 2, 3$, must be considered. For example, cell $(1, 2)$ corresponds to production of a two-terminal long string beginning with 'a.' Alternately, it is only necessary to consider nonterminals that produce AA, as shown in the $j = 1$ row of the table. From Figure 4(a), only nonterminal 'C,' in the production $C \rightarrow BA|AA|b$, satisfies this and so nonterminal C is placed in cell $(1, 2)$. The remainder of the $j = 2$ row is formed similarly.

   Forming the third and fourth $(j = 3$ and $j = 4$, respectively) rows of the table is slightly more complicated. For example, cell $(1, 3)$ corresponds to strings of length 3, beginning with terminal x_1 ('a' in this case). This requires examination of cells $(1, 1)$ and $(2, 2)$, corresponding to producing the desired string with 1 nonterminal followed

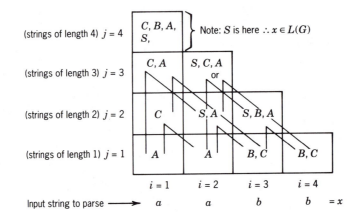

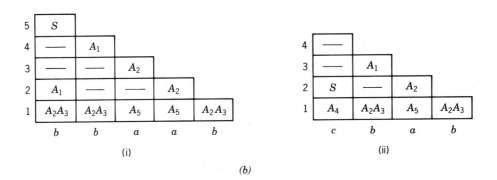

Figure 4: Sample parse tables using CYK algorithm.
(a) Table for parse of string $x =$'aabb' using productions of (2-4a).
(b) Parse tables using productions of (2-4c).
(i) $x =$'bbaab' (succeeds).
(ii) $x =$'cbab' (fails).

by 2 nonterminals (denoted $\{1+2\}$ hereafter) as well as cells $(1, 2)$ and $(3, 1)$ (denoted the $\{2+1\}$ derivation). For the former, it is necessary to consider production of 'AS' or 'AA,' and nonterminal 'C' is applicable. For the latter, the production of 'CB' and 'CC' is considered, yielding nonterminal 'A.' Thus from (7-4a), cell $(1, 3)$ contains nonterminals 'C' and 'A.' Similarly, for cell $(2, 3)$, cells $(2, 1)$, and $(3, 2)$ (the $\{1+2\}$ derivation) as well as $(2, 2)$ and $(4, 1)$, (the $\{2+1\}$ derivation) must be considered.

Finally, formation of cell $(1, 4)$ is considered. Possible cell pairings to consider are summarized below:

$(1, 1)$ and $(2, 3)$ $\{1 + 3\} \rightarrow AS, AC, \underline{AA} : C$

$(1, 2)$ and $(3, 2)$ $\{2 + 2\} \rightarrow CS, CB, \underline{CA} : B$

$(1, 3)$ and $(4, 1)$ $\{3 + 1\} \rightarrow CB, \underline{CC}, \underline{AB}, AC : A, S$

Cell pairings that yield a possible nonterminal are shown underlined. Thus, $(1, 4)$ contains nonterminals C, B, A, S. Since this includes the starting symbol, the parse succeeds and '*aabb*' is a valid string in the language of this grammar. Note that since the grammar is in CNF, it is never necessary to consider more than two-cell pairings (although as we increase j, the number of possible pairings increases). ∎

EXAMPLE 3: **Further Illustration of Parsing**

Suppose we are given the following FSG:[2]

$$S \rightarrow bA_1 | cA_2$$

$$A_1 \rightarrow bA_2$$

$$A_2 \rightarrow b | aA_2 \qquad\qquad (7 - 4b)$$

Converting (7-4b) to CNF yields

$$S \rightarrow A_3 A_1$$

$$A_3 \rightarrow b$$

$$S \rightarrow A_4 A_2$$

$$A_4 \rightarrow c$$

$$A_1 \rightarrow A_3 A_2$$

$$A_2 \rightarrow b$$

$$A_2 \rightarrow A_5 A_2$$

$$A_5 \rightarrow a \qquad\qquad (7 - 4c)$$

Parse tables for strings $x = bbaab$ and $x = cbab$ are shown in Figures 4(b)(i) and 4(b)(ii), respectively. Note that the existence of an empty cell [other than $(1, n)$] does not necessarily lead to a failure to parse. ∎

(AUGMENTED) TRANSITION NETWORKS (ATNs) IN PARSING

Transition Networks

In Chapter 6 we saw how the graphical representation of a finite state grammar led directly to a parsing procedure. Transition networks extend this concept. A transition network (TN) is a digraph used to show the (context free) productions of a grammar. TNs are used to facilitate parsing and, as an important practical matter, easily

---

[2]This grammar is also used in Chapter 9 to illustrate grammatical inference.

map into finite state machines. A TN consists of a set of nodes, representing *states*, and a set of labeled arcs, representing either nonterminals (classes of words such as nouns, verbs, and determiners in our examples) or terminals (specific words such as dog, computer, etc.). A TN parses an input string by starting at an initial state, denoted S, and sequentially checking each word in the input string against the label of each arc emanating from the present node. When a match is found, the attention focuses on the new node, or state, of the parse, and the matching process is repeated until a node representing the goal state (a successful parse) is reached. Goal states are typically indicated by a node labeled 'end' (or a double circle.) Thus, the TN parses by 'consumption' of the input string. Furthermore, when the parser is in a specific state, the existence of several arcs emanating from this node indicates that several productions are potentially applicable. Thus, an arc represents a condition under which the arc may be traversed. Note that a TN may be employed recursively, thus providing a space-efficient parsing machine. Productions (P) of G map directly into elements of the TN. Figure 5 shows corresponding TN elements for the productions of G_1.

Given a TN to be parsed, parsing of an input string proceeds by traversing the TN to a goal state, while 'consuming' the input string. An arc may be traversed under one of the following conditions:

1. The arc is labeled with a terminal and the next entry in the input string is the same terminal. This terminal is 'consumed.'

2. The arc is labeled with a nonterminal. In this instance, control passes to one or more TNs related to this nonterminal.

If the parser reaches a state (node) in the TN where no outgoing arc is applicable, a failure is encountered. This invokes *backtracking*, which may be implemented in a number of ways. If we simply backtrack to the previous node (i.e., the last TN state), we are employing depth-first search in the parsing procedure.

Augmented Transition Nets (ATNs)

An ATN is derived from the basic TN by adding several features, especially recursion. Arcs in ATNs may be labeled with the names of other TNs. These arcs are used to let an arc 'call' or pass control (and the string) to another TN. For example, in an ATN corresponding to the TNs of Figure 5 (part 1), the nonterminal arc labeled np is not simply traversed, but rather TN 'np' (part 2) is called or used to check for a noun phrase in the input string. This allows the parser to progress to a new node, that is, consider a new production, without 'consuming' additional input.

Other features of ATNs distinguish them from TNs. This includes the embedding of *conditional tests* and *corresponding actions* (e.g., jump to another ATN under certain conditions) to an arc. Actions include the ability to record previous actions (i.e., 'take notes') and refer to these notes at a later point. This includes attaching linguistic properties or features to a node.

Production   Corresponding TN

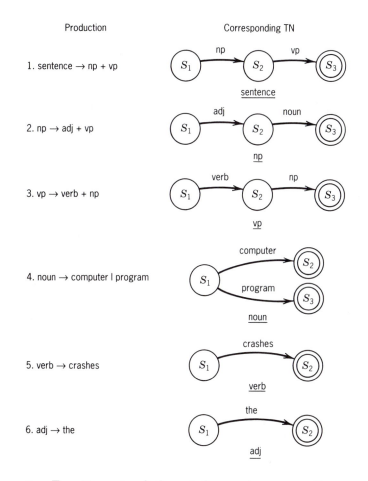

1. sentence → np + vp

2. np → adj + vp

3. vp → verb + np

4. noun → computer I program

5. verb → crashes

6. adj → the

Figure 5:   Transition network elements for sample grammar G_1.

HIGHER DIMENSIONAL GRAMMARS

Introduction

Grammars other than string grammars exist and are characterized by their terminals and nonterminals (as opposed to constraints on P). These are useful in 2-D and higher dimensional pattern representation applications, in that the structure of the productions involving terminals and nonterminals is greater than one dimensional. Higher dimensional grammars also facilitate relational descriptions. Productions in higher dimensional grammars are usually more complex, since rewriting rules embody operations more complex than simple 1-D string modifications. For example, in 2-D cases standard 'attachment points' are defined. Two of the more popular are *tree grammars* and *web grammars* [Fu 1 1982]. Not surprisingly, there is little correlation between the dimension of the *grammar* used for pattern generation and the dimensionality of the pattern space. For example, a 1-D grammar may be used for 2-D or 3-D patterns, as we have seen in the PDL.

Tree Grammars

Introduction to Tree-Based Descriptions.   One commonly encountered higher-dimensional grammar is a *tree grammar*. A tree is basically a directed, acyclical graph. More formal aspects of trees are defined below and in Appendix 3.

Trees store pattern information in two ways:

1. Through nodes, which may store pattern primitive or substructure information; and

2. Through arcs, which reflect relational information between the parent node and successors.

Trees are especially useful for structural representations that involve hierarchical decomposition, since the descriptions become compact. Another important property of tree structures is the ability to build or describe complex patterns using primitives with multiple (> 2) 'connection points.' Recall that the PDL, for example, allowed connection (although several different *types* of connection) at only two points, denoted head or tail. Tree grammars extend this capability, since a node may have out-degree > 2. If a complex pattern may be naturally represented in tree form, it is also natural to consider its generation via a tree grammar. Figure 6 shows a general tree representation (a 'universal tree domain').

Sample Tree Representations.   Figures 7 and 8 show two uses of trees for describing patterns. The basis of tree representations is a set of nodes, arranged in a tree structure, where the node relationships indicate hierarchical structure. The first is an alternative to the PDL that describes line drawings of cubes. The second, adapted from [Schalkoff 1989], shows a hierarchical (tree) representation or decomposition of image data at varying image resolutions. Note that a clear relation between nodes (of primitive type black, white, or gray) at different resolution levels exists.

Traversing and Describing Trees

In traversing, that is, enumerating all the nodes of a general tree, there are any number of possible paths that may be taken. Each different path or traversal yields a possibly different ordering of the nodes 'visited.' For example, the concepts of depth-first and breadth-first traversals of trees are often utilized to illustrate search algorithms. By associating an alphabet (set of symbols), perhaps ordered or ranked in some way, with a tree, a hierarchical coding or description of the tree may be developed. Consider the alphabet $V = I^{(+)} \cup \{.\}$ where $I^{(+)} = \{0, 1, 2, \ldots\}$ and the symbol '.' is used to denote node descendents. $I^{(+)}$ is the set of nonnegative integers (I^+ includes 0).

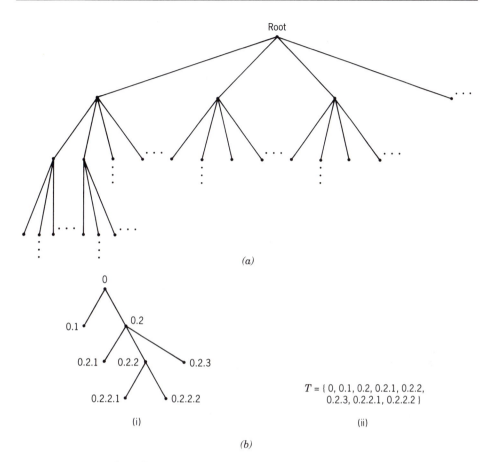

(a)

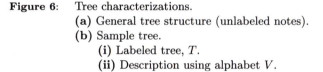

$T = \{\, 0, 0.1, 0.2, 0.2.1, 0.2.2,$
$0.2.3, 0.2.2.1, 0.2.2.2 \,\}$

(i)   (ii)

(b)

Figure 6:   Tree characterizations.
   (a) General tree structure (unlabeled notes).
   (b) Sample tree.
         (i) Labeled tree, T.
         (ii) Description using alphabet V.

Each node of a given tree may then be labeled with a string from V, with the structure of the tree preserved in the node labels. Furthermore, by simply enumerating the set of node labels, the tree is described. An example is shown in Figure 6(b).

Tree Similarity.   Comparison of trees, as is the case in comparison of vectors and strings, is a fundamental operation in SyntPR. One approach is by developing a similarity measure. Given trees T_1 and T_2, denote this measure $d(T_1, T_2)$. To make this comparison computationally feasible, we will work with string descriptions of the corresponding trees. Therefore, we digress to consider more generalized symbolic descriptions of trees. Once these descriptions are available, a set of similarity measures may be developed [Boorman/Olivier 1973], [Selkow 1977], [Lu 1979].

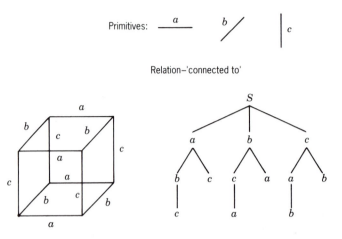

Figure 7:   Tree representation of a cube.

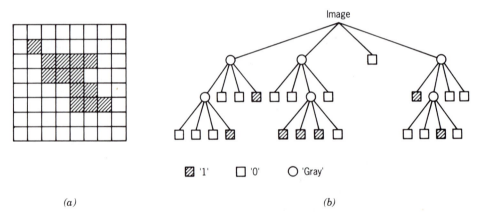

(a)   *(b)*

Figure 8:   Quadtree representation of binary image.
(**a**) 8 × 8 image.
(**b**) Resulting quadtree.

Ordering the Nodes in Trees.   Trees may be partitioned into subtrees.[3] To formally characterize tree grammars, we need a means to constrain the allowable trees that may be generated. This could include interconnection of trees and possible replacements or rewriting using trees.

The notions of alphabets and *ranked alphabets* are introduced and used to relate symbols (node labels) to trees, thus yielding the concept of *labeled trees*. A tree is labeled if there exists a mapping of nodes onto an alphabet. The notion of an alphabet

---

[3] A subtree is formally defined in Appendix 3.

was defined in Chapter 6. In order to quantify rewriting of trees, a ranked alphabet is introduced. A ranked alphabet is a pair (V, r), where V is an alphabet and $r \subseteq V \times I^{(+)}$. r is therefore a relation or mapping between V and the set of nonnegative integers. For example, if $V = \{a, b, c, \ldots z\}$, a sample relation r is

$$r = \{(a, 1), (b, 2), (c, 3), \ldots (z, 26)\} \qquad (7-5)$$

Often, if symbol x is the first element of a number of elements of r, for instance, $(x, 2), (x, 3), (x, 4)$, that is, the second element of r can assume values 2, 3, and 4, we denote this as the set $r(x) = \{2, 3, 4\}$. To achieve one tree-grammar representation technique, V is used to label the set of nodes of a tree, and r is used to denote the out-degree of each node. Leaves or terminal nodes of a tree correspond to members of r whose second element is zero. Thus, given a specific node x, the mapping $r(x)$ indicates the number of descendants of x.

DEFINITION: Tree Grammar.

A tree grammar (TG or G_T) is a four-tuple

$$G_T = \{V, r, P, S\} \qquad (7-6)$$

where $V = V_T \cup V_N$ is the grammar alphabet (both terminals and nonterminals), P is a set of productions involving trees, and $S \subset T_V$, where T_V is the set of 'starting' or 'root' trees. $T_V \subseteq V_N$ and is often a set of single-node trees.

Productions and Derivations with Trees

The replacement or rewriting rules used to form productions in string grammars are relatively straightforward. For tree grammars, however, simply writing productions in the form $T_i \rightarrow T_j$, indicating that tree T_j replaces or is 'rewritten by' tree T_i, has no meaning until we define what it means for a tree to 'replace' another tree. This type of production, where T_i and T_j are defined over (V, r), must be carefully considered. For this reason, elements of P are often shown graphically. For example, the concept of a tree 'replacing' another tree could correspond to rewriting of a (sub)tree with nodes initially labeled with nonterminals by a tree of exactly the same structure, but with nodes labeled by terminal symbols. Figure 9(a) illustrates this case. Therefore, productions may be shown using notation $T_i \rightarrow T_j$, where T_i and T_j are symbolic or graphical descriptions of trees and $\rightarrow$, as in string grammars, indicates replacement. An alternative is *expansive production forms*, where productions are constrained to the form shown in Figure 9(b), that is, the only form permitted is

$$X \rightarrow x X_1 X_2 \ldots X_n \qquad (7-7)$$

where $X, X_1, \ldots X_n \in V_N$, $x \in V_T$, and $n \in r(x)$. $r(x) = 0$ is a special case of (7-7), indicating that the expansion is terminated.

Derivations using G_T are denoted using an extension of string grammars, by the form

$$T_\alpha \overset{a}{\Rightarrow} T_\beta \qquad (7-8)$$

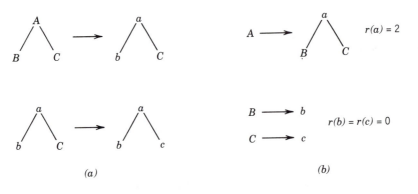

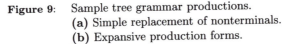

(a)   (b)

Figure 9:   Sample tree grammar productions.
(a) Simple replacement of nonterminals.
(b) Expansive production forms.

where T_α and T_β are trees. Equation 7-8 denotes a derivation corresponding to the derivation of tree T_β from tree T_α. For (7-8) to make sense, the significance of the 'at node a' designation in the notation of (7-8) must be understood. This requires P to contain a production $T_i \to T_j$ and T_i to be a subtree of T_α at node a which, when replaced by T_j, yields tree T_β.

$L(G_T)$.   By analogy with string grammars, we require descriptions in $L(G_T)$ to ultimately consist solely of terminals and any tree to be derived using P. The set of trees with (all) nodes in V_T is denoted T_{V_T}. Therefore,

$$L(G_T) = \{T | T \in T_{V_T} \cap T_i \Rightarrow T \qquad for\ T_i \in S\} \qquad (7-9)$$

EXAMPLE 4: Using Tree Grammars for Motion Description

Figure 10 shows an expansive tree grammar, denoted G_M, used to formulate tree-based structural descriptions of a 2-D trajectory. Terminals, nonterminals, and productions are shown in the figure. The reader may wish to compare these descriptions with that obtained from the PDL. ■

STOCHASTIC GRAMMARS AND APPLICATIONS

The previous consideration of formal grammar application to SyntPR assumed that:

1. $L(G_i) \cap L(G_j) = \emptyset$, that is, the languages were disjoint; and
2. 'Errors' in the sentences produced by a grammar did not occur.

Furthermore, there was no way in which to incorporate a priori information concerning the likelihood of a pattern class. This information could be of use in parsing, for example, if some probability measure such as $P(G_i)$ were available.

In practice, one or both of these assumptions may be invalid. For example, (structural) descriptions may contain 'noise' or pattern deformation, perhaps because of

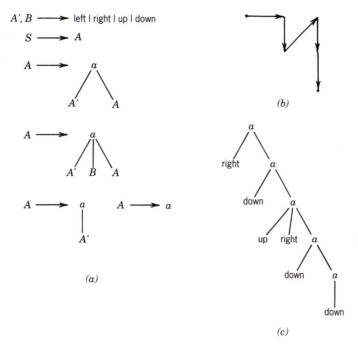

Figure 10:   Tree grammar to generate 2-D motion description.
(a) Productions.
(b) Sample trajectory.
(c) Tree description corresponding to (b).

errors in the primitive extraction process. For this reason, the use of *stochastic grammars* for pattern description may be useful. Although a detailed exploration of this area is beyond the scope of this text (see the Bibliographical Remarks), a quick summary of stochastic grammars is shown.

Stochastic Grammars

A stochastic grammar is defined as the four-tuple

$$G_s = \{V_N, V_T, P_s, S_s\} \qquad (7-10)$$

The major distinctions between a stochastic grammar and the string grammars we have previously considered are the characterization of productions P_s and the characterization of the starting symbol S_s. P_s is a set of *stochastic productions* each of the form:[4]

$$\alpha_i \overset{p_{ij}}{\to} \beta_j \qquad (7-11)$$

where p_{ij} is the probability that α_i is replaced with β_j.

---
[4]An alternate notation is $p_{ij} : \alpha_i \to \beta_j$.

Thus, the notion of a production is generalized by the addition of a corresponding probability. Because of the stochastic nature of the productions, a string x, produced by G_s is therefore viewed as the outcome of a sequence of trials. In addition, S_s is a modification of S, where the choice of $S \in V_N$ is characterized by a probability distribution.

Derivations in a Stochastic Language

The derivation of a sentence in a stochastic language may be viewed as a sequence of probabilistic events. For example, consider the following derivation of string x using n productions:

$$S_s = \alpha_0 \Rightarrow \alpha_1 \Rightarrow \alpha_2 \ldots \Rightarrow \alpha_n = x \qquad (7-12)$$

Denote the ith production $\in P_s$ as p^i, $i = 1, 2, \ldots m$, and let $t_{k-1,k}$ denote the label or name of the production used to rewrite α_{k-1} as α_k, $k = 1, 2, \ldots n$. Thus, $t_{k-1,k} = p^i$ is an event with an associated probability. The overall sequence used to generate x therefore has a corresponding probability.

The probability of generating x by the stochastic production sequence $t_{0,1}, t_{1,2}, \ldots t_{n-1,n}$ is given by the joint probability $P(t_{0,1} \cap t_{1,2} \cap \ldots \cap t_{n-1,n})$, which (Appendix 2) may be rewritten as

$$P(t_{0,1} \cap t_{1,2} \cap \ldots t_{n-1,n}) =$$

$$P(t_{n-1,n}|t_{n-2,n-1}, \ldots t_{1,2}, t_{0,1})P(t_{n-2,n-1}|t_{n-3,n-2}, \ldots, t_{1,2}, t_{0,1})$$

$$\ldots P(t_{1,2}|t_{0,1})P(t_{0,1}) \qquad (7-13)$$

If the conditional probabilities in (7-13) are replaced by unconditional probabilities, that is,

$$P(t_{k-1,k}|t_{k-2,k-1}, \ldots) = P(t_{k-1,k}) \qquad (7-14)$$

an *unrestricted* stochastic grammar results.[5] This is equivalent to assuming that in generating x, the probability of applying the next production is independent of the previously chosen sequence. This assumption simplifies (7-14) to

$$P(t_{0,1}, t_{1,2}, \ldots t_{n-1,n}) = \prod_{q=1}^{n} P(t_{q-1,q}) \qquad (7-15)$$

Proper Stochastic Grammars. If all elements of P_s are of the form

$$A_i \xrightarrow{p_{ij}} \beta_j \qquad (7-16)$$

where $A_i \in V_N$, $\beta_j \in (V_N \cup V_T)^+$, and if there are n_i possible β_j for each nonterminal A_i, with

---

[5]This is not the same as the nonstochastic type 0 grammar considered in Chapter 6. Unfortunately, the notation is the same.

$$\sum_{k=1}^{n_i} p_{ik} = 1 \qquad\qquad (7-17)$$

the stochastic grammar is said to be *proper*.

The Characteristic Grammar.   Notice that a stochastic grammar differs from a non-stochastic grammar only in the attachment of probabilities to each production. Removing these probability characterizations from the productions in a stochastic grammar G_s yields the corresponding *characteristic grammar* G_c (or simply G). On this basis, stochastic grammars may be classified as stochastic Type 0, stochastic Type 1, and so on, according to the classification of their corresponding characteristic grammar.

Stochastic Languages.   The *stochastic language* generated by G_s is an extension of $L(G_c)$ in that it consists of the set of all derivable strings together with their accompanying probabilities. Formally,

$$L(G_s) = \left\{ (x, p(x)) | x \in V_T^+, \quad S_s \overset{p_j}{\Rightarrow} x, \quad j = 1, 2, \ldots k \quad and \quad p(x) = \sum_{j=1}^{k} p_j \right\}$$
$$(7-18)$$

Notice that (7-18) allows G_s to be *ambiguous*, in that there is the possiblity of $k > 1$ derivations of x.

BIBLIOGRAPHICAL REMARKS

The relationship between certain classes of grammars and parsing automata is shown in [Hopcroft/Ullman 1969]. Although we have considered only the CYK algorithm, an equally important procedure is Earley's algorithm [Aho/Ullman 1972], which does not require the grammar in CNF. Furthermore, parallel parsing algorithms and VLSI implementations have been developed for Earley's algorithm [Chiang/Fu 1984]. Transition network grammars applied to natural language parsing is shown in [Woods 1970]. A comprehensive look at grammars and parsers from the compiler-writing point of view is [Tremblay/Sorenson 1985]. Early work on the description [Shaw 1969] and parsing [Shaw 1970] of pictorial data is illustrative. The relationship between certain types of tree and string grammars is shown in [Gonzalez/Thomason 1978]. This reference, together with [Fu 1982], also shows examples of other higher dimensional grammars, including web, plex, and graph grammars, as well as stochastic grammars. In addition, both references consider parsing approaches in detail. A simple introduction to the merging of grammars and probabilities is [Booth/Thompson 1973]. The use of multidimensional grammars for applications in n dimensions has been considered using *array grammars* [Rosenfeld 1973], [Wang 1980]. An array grammar generates a language of n-dimensional arrays of symbols, with a set of productions consisting of subarray substitutions. Another example of a class of 2-D grammars is mosaic grammars [Ota 1975]. The language of a mosaic grammar is easily visualized as all patterns of equally sized, but different 'colored' (or featured) tiles, which form a 2-D mosaic.

EXERCISES

7.1   Suppose a matching procedure is used for string pattern classification. For a c-class problem, assume that

$$|L(G_i)| = s_i \qquad i = 1, 2, \ldots c$$

and

$$E\{|l_j^i|\} = n_i$$

where l_j^i is the jth string in the library for the ith class (the E denotes expectation or simply 'average').

(a) For a brute-force match, estimate the number of symbolic comparisons that are required to classify x, where $E\{|x|\} = \alpha$.

(b) Consider several modifications to the matching procedure that lead to an efficient computational procedure, such as presorting, computing partial matches, etc. Revise your estimate from part (a), and show examples of each.

7.2   An unrestricted stochastic grammar assumed that $P(t_{k-1,k}|t_{k-2,k-1}, t_{k-3,k-2}, \ldots)$ $= P(t_{k-1,k})$.

(a) Discuss the pros and cons of the reasonableness of this assumption.

(b) What significance might be attached to

(i) $P(t_{k-1,k}|t_{k-2,k-1}) < P(t_{k-1,k})$,

(ii) $P(t_{k-1,k}|t_{k-2,k-1}) > P(t_{k-1,k})$.

7.3   In this problem we extend the PDL grammar of Chapter 6 (Figures 7 and 8) into a stochastic grammar and show the utility of such an extension by generating 'noisy' geometric figures.

(a) Develop a nonstochastic grammar G^{SQ}, which generates squares with side length $n = 3$ (where terminals u and o have length $= 1$), i.e., for

$$L(G^{SQ}) = \left\{ (o+)^n (\neg u+)^n (\neg o+)^n (u+)^{n-1} u | n = 3 \right\} \qquad (P.3 - 1)$$

(b) Revise the grammar of (a) such that each (partial) derivation of the form $A \Rightarrow$ $o + o + o$ in P is replaced by the pair of stochastic productions in P_s:

$$A \xrightarrow{\frac{2}{3}} o + o + o$$

$$A \xrightarrow{\frac{1}{3}} o + \neg s_2 + s_1 \qquad (P.3 - 2)$$

Show sample derived figures with their corresponding probabilities.

(c) Repeat parts (a) and (b) for side length $n \geq 3$, i.e.,

$$L(G^{SQ}) = \left\{ (o+)^n (\neg u+)^n (\neg o+)^n (u+)^{n-1} u | n \geq 3 \right\} \qquad (P.3 - 3)$$

7.4   Referring to Chapter 6, Exercise 6.21,

(a) Convert these G_i to CNF.

(b) Show parse tables for samples of $L(G_A)$, $L(G_c)$, $L(G_p)$, and $L(G_F)$ using G_A, G_c, G_p, and G_F.

7.5 Referring to Chapter 6, Exercise 6.22,

(a) Convert G_{RECT} to CNF.

(b) Generate several strings ϵ $L(G_{RECT})$ and show corresponding parse tables.

(c) For several strings that are not in $L(G_{RECT})$, show examples of attempted parses.

7.6 (a) Using the grammar of (7-4b) (Example 3), show a parse table for $x = caab$.

(b) If the parse succeeds, show a sequence of productions that yields x in both (i) the original form (7-4b) and (ii) CNF form (7-4c).

7.7 Suppose the tree description approach of Figure 6(b) is used for trees T_1 and T_2, yielding set-based descriptions T_1^s and T_2^s, of the form of Figure 6(b)(ii). Show why it is not possible, in general, to determine if T_1 is a subtree of T_2 (or vice versa) by simply checking if $T_1^s \subset T_2^s$ (or vice versa).

7.8 Which of the five trees shown in Figure P.1 (a) to (e) are elements of $L(G_M)$, where G_M is the motion description grammar of Figure 10?

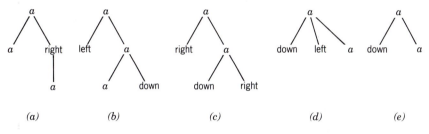

(a)   (b)   (c)   (d)   (e)

Figure P.1:

7.9 Develop a tree grammar for the blocks world (Chapter 6) representation.

Graphical Approaches to SyntPR

> *Facts which at first seem improbable will, even on scant explanation, drop the cloak which has hidden them and stand forth in naked and simple beauty.*
>
> *Dialogues Concerning New Sciences* [1638], Day I
> Galileo Galilei 1564–1642

GRAPH-BASED STRUCTURAL REPRESENTATIONS

Graph theory is a well developed branch of discrete mathematics. In this chapter we show how graph-based structural representations may be used to facilitate pattern recognition. Graphical alternatives for structural representation are natural extensions of higher dimensional grammars, where the need for parsers is replaced by the need to match. This, in turn, requires measures of *graph similarity*.

From Digraphs to Semantic Nets to Relational Graphs

As shown in Appendix 3, *directed graphs or digraphs* are valuable tools for representing relational information. Here we represent graph G as $G = \{N, R\}$ where N is a set of nodes (or vertices) and R is a subset of $N \times N$, indicating arcs (or edges) in G. An extension of the unlabeled digraph is the *semantic net*. We hereafter refer to a semantic net wherein nodes represent subpatterns and primitives, and arcs represent relations between these subpatterns and primitives as a *relational graph*.

EXAMPLE 1: Blocks-World Representations

Figure 11 in Chapter 6 introduced an example of a digraph used to represent the structure of block configurations. Figure 1 shows additional examples using the blocks-world example. Here, no distinction is made in 'naming' nodes, that is, we do not distinguish between 'block A' and 'block B.' They are merely 'blocks.' A single relation, ('on,' or 'supported-by') is used to describe the structure of the blocks configuration. This example is continued in the problems.   ■

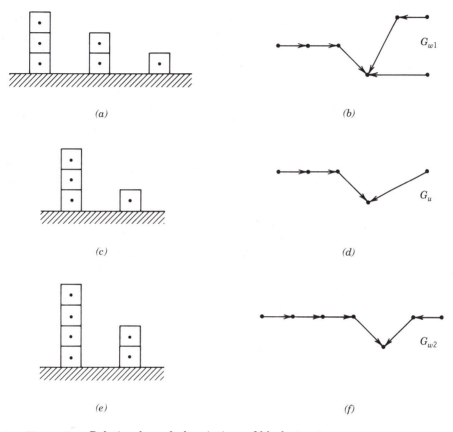

(a)   *(b)*

(c)   *(d)*

(e)   *(f)*

Figure 1:   Relational graph descriptions of block structures.
(**a**) Structural example (class w_1).
(**b**) Relational graph (prototype; G_{w_1}).
(**c**) Alternate structure (to classify).
(**d**) Relational graph corresponding to (c). (Used for classification; G_u). Note subisomorphism with G_{w_1} in (b) and G_{w_2} in (f).
(**e**) Structural example (class w_2).
(**f**) Relational graph corresponding to (e) (prototype; G_{w_2}).

Application of Relational Graphs to PR

One way to recognize structure using graphs is to let each pattern (structural) class be represented by a prototypical relational graph. An unknown input pattern is then converted into a structural representation in the form of a graph, and this graph is then *compared* with the relational graphs for each class.[1]

Graphical Descriptions for Pattern Classification.   Suppose, in a $c = 3$ class problem, prototypical relational graphs G_{w_1}, G_{w_2}, and G_{w_3} are available. Given new pattern data to classify, a relational graph is extracted from the data and denoted G_u. A classification strategy could be based upon comparisons of G_u with G_{w_1}, G_u with G_{w_2}, and G_u with G_{w_3}. By analogy with StatPR, this could be viewed as inputting G_u into a set of $c = 3$ (graph) discriminant functions, each of which is based on G_{w_i}, $i = 1, 2, \ldots c$, and a suitable measure of similarity. Whichever graph pair is closest, or more similar, would yield a larger discriminant function value, and the pattern would be classified accordingly.

Extensions to this approach could involve matching G_u with a library of prototypical patterns for each class. Note that this is analogous to a k-NN approach in StatPR. Since matching or similarity measures in this instance are based on both nodes (features) and arcs (relations), to make the matching process efficient the selection and use of critical features [Lowe 1987] is important.

Comparing Relational Graph Descriptions.   Seldom do the observed data *exactly* match a stored relational representation. Therefore, the concept of *similarity* of two representations must be explored. For example, it is often the case that not all the relational data for a given model are present in the observed data. One strategy, therefore, might be simply to require that the observed data match a portion of the relational model. In this comparison or matching process, there are two extremes:

Case 1:   Any feature or relation not present in both graphs yields a match failure. This is an overly conservative measure.

Case 2:   Any single match of a feature or relation yields success. This is an overly optimistic approach, which, at best, causes ambiguity.

A realistic matching strategy is somewhere in between these extremes.

Graphical Approaches vis-à-vis Formal Grammars.   Since we developed the grammatical approach to SyntPR, a fair question is 'Why not always use that approach?' Two cases seem to favor the graphical approach:

1. When the training set is too small to correctly infer pattern class grammars.

2. When each pattern could be considered a prototype of its pattern class.

The Adjacency Matrix.   A digraph G with p nodes may be converted to an *adjacency matrix* via the following procedure:

1. Number each node and thereby develop a set of numbered graph nodes indexed by $[1, \ldots p]$.

2. To represent the existence or absence of an edge (or arc) between any two nodes in G, form an adjacency matrix with entries:

---

[1]Notice that 'compared' does not necessarily mean matched verbatim.

$$ADJ[i,j] = \begin{cases} 1 & \text{if } G \text{ contains an edge from node } i \text{ to node } j \\ 0 & \text{otherwise} \end{cases} \qquad (8-1)$$

A 2-D data structure (specifically a $p \times p$ binary matrix) results and is useful for computer implementation. Note that the implied directionality of the digraph precludes the adjacency matrix from being, in general, symmetric. In addition, the adjacency matrix, if sparse, occupies a lot of memory and stores a little information. In cases where a relation is symmetric, the arcs are bidirectional and yield an *undirected graph*.

GRAPH ISOMORPHISM

Uniqueness of Digraph-Based Structural Description and Isomorphism

Homomorphism and Isomorphism.   Consider two graphs:

$$G_1 = \{N_1, R_1\} \qquad (8-2a)$$

and

$$G_2 = \{N_2, R_2\} \qquad (8-2b)$$

A *homomorphism* [Johnsonbaugh 1986] from G_1 to G_2 is a function f from N_1 to N_2 with the property that if node $v_1 \in N_1$ is adjacent to node $w_1 \in N_1$ in G_1 [that is, $(v_1, w_1) \in R_1$] then $f(v_1) \in N_2$ and $f(w_1) \in N_2$ are adjacent in G_2 (that is, $[f(v_1), f(w_1)] \in R_2$). Thus, G_1 and G_2 are *homomorphic* if

$$(v_1, w_1) \in R_1 \Rightarrow [f(v_1), f(w_1)] \in R_2 \qquad (8-2c)$$

A stricter test is that of *isomorphism*, where f is required to be 1:1 and onto. The digraph for a specific relation is not unique, since two digraphs may be isomorphic. This is a consequence of the arbitrary labeling of nodes to represent specific elements of set A. The *structure* of the graphs resulting from any choice of nodes (or 'vertices') will be the same, however. Formally, G_1 and G_2 are *isomorphic* if

$$(v_1, w_1) \in R_1 \Leftrightarrow [f(v_1), f(w_1)] \in R_2 \qquad (8-2d)$$

A far less rigorous but intuitive characterization of isomorphism is simply to say that a relabeling of nodes yields the same graph structure. Appendix 3 further discusses the isomorphism concept.

Unfortunately, determining graph isomorphism is computationally expensive. A PR classification application compounds this difficulty, since we must compare (determine the possible isomorphism of) the observed graph with *each* of the class-specific or prototypical graphs. Every known algorithm for testing graph isomorphism requires exponential or factorial time (in the worst case). No polynomial-bound algorithms are known. Fortunately, there are suboptimal approaches that are more practical [Read/Corneil 1977].

Determining Isomorphism

Given two graphs G_1 and G_2, each with p nodes,[2] a straightforward procedure to determine isomorphism is as follows:

1. Label the nodes of each graph with labels $1, 2, \ldots, p$.
2. Form an adjacency matrix for each graph. (Note that these are *unique*.) Call these M_1 and M_2, respectively.
3. If $M_1 = M_2$, G_1 and G_2 are isomorphic. This requires that we check each of the p^2 elements of M_1 against those of M_2. This requires $O(p^2)$ operations (matches or compares).
4. Since the initial labeling of G_1 is arbitrary, to test for isomorphism we need to consider all the $p!$ possible labelings on G_2 and apply the test in step 3. This makes the computational complexity of the overall process $O(p^2 \cdot p!)$, which is tolerable only for small values of p.

The complexity in step 4 spawns a search of polynomial complexity $O(p^k)$, where $k \in I$ is the number of alternatives. An example of computing the isomorphism of two graphs via node labeling and the adjacency matrix is shown in Figure 2.

Problems with Isomorphism as a Similarity Measure.   We should suspect that in practical problems, not all existing relations for a given class will be observed. This could be due to effects such as noise, or perhaps allowable *structural deformations*. In other words, the observed pattern may be some variant of an exact or idealized pattern.

- In most practical problems, isomorphism is too rigorous or critical a test. Isomorphism determination procedures allow only *exact matching*; therefore, no error correction capability is possible.

Determining Lack of Isomorphism.   The isomorphism determination procedure described above hinted that certain basic tests (e.g., equal number of vertices) may be applied to rule out the isomorphism of G_1 and G_2. Thus, an alternative procedure to determine whether G_1 and G_2 are *not isomorphic* is to find at least one property that isomorphic graphs must share and G_1 and G_2 do not.

Invariants under Graph Isomorphism.   A property that is preserved under graph isomorphism is termed an *invariant*. For example, the following are obvious invariants:

1. number of nodes.
2. number of arcs.

In addition to those cited above, the following are useful invariants:

1. in-degree i of a vertex.
2. out-degree j of a vertex.
3. degree k[3] of a vertex (for undirected graphs only).
4. closed path (or cycle or circuit) of length l.

---

[2]Note that if the number of nodes is not the same, the test immediately fails.
[3]Total number of undirected arcs incident on the vertex.

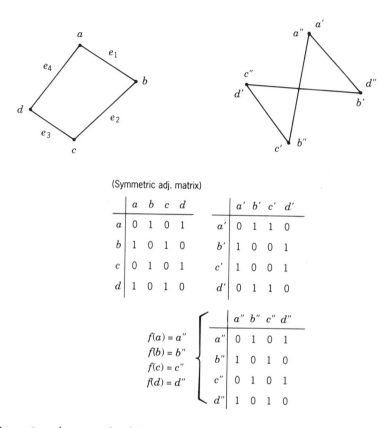

(Symmetric adj. matrix)

	a	b	c	d
a	0	1	0	1
b	1	0	1	0
c	0	1	0	1
d	1	0	1	0

	a'	b'	c'	d'
a'	0	1	1	0
b'	1	0	0	1
c'	1	0	0	1
d'	0	1	1	0

$$f(a) = a''$$
$$f(b) = b''$$
$$f(c) = c''$$
$$f(d) = d''$$

	a''	b''	c''	d''
a''	0	1	0	1
b''	1	0	1	0
c''	0	1	0	1
d''	1	0	1	0

Figure 2:   An example of isomorphism of two undirected graphs, $p = 4$.

Subisomorphism. G_1 and G_2 are called *subisomorphic* if a subgraph of G_1 is isomorphic to a subgraph of G_2. Clearly, this is a less restrictive structural match than that of isomorphism. If G_1 and G_2 are isomorphic, they are also subisomorphic. Determining subisomorphism is also computationally expensive. In the worst case, the isomorphism of all pairs of subgraphs must be considered. Cliques and maximal cliques (described later) help to facilitate this. The problem of determining the isomorphism of subgraphs is equivalent to determining the *inclusion* of one graph in another. For example, referring to Figure 1, note that G_u is subisomorphic to G_{w_1}, as well as to G_{w_2}.

Extensions to the Elementary Graph Matching Approach

Matching Measures That Allow Structural Deformations.   To allow structural deformations, numerous match or 'distance' measures have been proposed. These include [Sanfeliu/Fu 1983] [Shapiro/Haralick 1985]:

1. Extraction of *features* from G_1 and G_2, thereby forming feature vectors, $\underline{x}_1$ and $\underline{x}_2$, respectively. This is followed by the use of StatPR techniques to compare $\underline{x}_1$ and $\underline{x}_2$. Note the features are *graph features*, as opposed to direct pattern features.

2. Using as a matching metric *the minimum number of transformations necessary to transform G_1 (the input) into G_2 (the reference)*. Common transformations include:

   (a) Node insertion.

   (b) Node deletion.

   (c) Node splitting.

   (d) Node merging.

   (e) Vertex insertion.

   (f) Vertex deletion.

Some of the practical difficulties with these approaches are as follows:

1. The computational complexity (again!) considering the number of possibilities if an exhaustive procedure is used; and

2. Designing an adequate distance measure such that relational graphs with *allowed* structural deformations are considered similar, whereas those that represent different classes are considered dissimilar.

A Formal Characterization of the Relational Graph Similarity Problem[4]

Relational Description.   Given a set of nodes X, a corresponding relational description is defined as a set of (binary) relations

$$D_X = \{R_1, R_2, \ldots R_n\} \qquad (8-3a)$$

where each $R_i \subseteq X \times X$. In the more general case, where R_i are higher order relations,

$$R_i \subseteq X^{n_i} \qquad (8-3b)$$

where $n_i \in I$ and X^k denotes

$$\underbrace{X \times X \times \ldots X}_{k \ times}$$

or the set of all ordered k-tuples of X.

Given two node sets A and B, with $|A| = |B|$, and corresponding relational descriptions D_A, D_B, where $D_A = \{R_1, R_2, \ldots R_n\}$ and $D_B = \{S_1, S_2, \ldots S_n\}$, we seek a measure of the similarity of the description.

---

[4]Nonattributed graph case. This section follows the format of [Shapiro/Haralick 1985].

Composition.   Defining $R \subseteq A^n$ and $S \subseteq B^n$, the *composition* $R \circ f$ maps n-tuples of R into n-tuples of B^n as follows:

$$R \circ f = \{(b_1, b_2, \ldots b_n) \in B^n | \exists (a_1, a_2, \ldots, a_n) \in A^n\}$$

$$\text{with } f(a_i) = b_i \qquad i = 1, 2, \ldots, n \tag{8 - 4}$$

f is required to be a 1:1, onto mapping.[5]

Structural Error.   Using composition, the *structural error* based upon the ith relation (R_i) in D_A and the ith relation (S_i) in D_B is

$$E^i(f) = |R_i \circ f - S_i| + |S_i \circ f^{-1} - R_i| \tag{8 - 5}$$

Thus, $E^i(f)$ simply measures the number of elements in R_i that are not in S_i and the number of elements of S_i that are not in R_i. This is a relatively obvious measure.

The *total structural error* for this mapping is therefore simply the sum over all relations,

$$E(f) = \sum_{i=1}^{n} E^i(f) \tag{8 - 6}$$

and therefore the *relational distance* between D_A and D_B is defined as

$$RD(D_A, D_B) = \overset{min}{f} \; E(f) \tag{8 - 7}$$

Clearly, the minimum of $RD(D_A, D_B)$ is zero. If an f may be found such that D_A is isomorphic to D_B, then $RD(D_A, D_B) = 0$.

Extensions of Relational Graphs (Attributed Graphs)

The representational capability of relational graphs is limited, since it is possible that not all the relevant problem information may be mapped into a set of nodes and vertices. In addition, directly matching relational graphs yields computationally expensive PR procedures. For example, continuous numerical pattern features, allowed in StatPR, are not directly representable. This is partially owing to our (heretofore) concentration on structure. In addition, other node-specific *symbolic properties* (e.g., color) are not representable without cumbersome extensions to the graph (e.g., adding a node for each 'color' and arcs from each node to the appropriate color with the label 'has'). These types of representations may be more efficiently treated 'locally,' by extending the relational graph concept.

Relational Graphs with Attributes (Attributed Graphs).   In addition to representing pattern structure, the representation may be extended to include *numerical and per-*

---

[5] $f : X \to Y$ is 1:1 (or injective) if for each $b \in B$, there is *at most* one $a \in A$ such that $f(a) = b$. An alternative characterization is that if $a, a' \in A$, then $f(a) = f(a') \to a = a'$. A function which is 1:1 and onto is also called a bijection.

haps symbolic attributes of pattern primitives (i.e., relational graph nodes). In this context, we develop an extended representation where an entity has (observed)

- Features or properties
- Relations with other entities

An *attributed graph*, as defined below, results.

DEFINITION: Attributed Graph.

An attributed graph, G_i, is a 3-tuple and is defined as follows:

$$G_i = \{N_i, P_i, R_i\} \qquad (8-8)$$

where

N_i *is a set of nodes*

P_i *is a set of properties of these nodes*

and

R_i *is a set of relations between nodes. [An alternative viewpoint is that R_i indicates the labeled arcs of G_i, where if an arc exists between nodes a and b, then R_i contains element (a, b).]*

Attributed Graph Assignments. Suppose we are given two attributed graphs G_1 and G_2, with node sets N_1 and N_2, respectively. Denote $p_q^i(n)$ as the value of the qth property of node n of graph G_i. We use a *similarity measure*, and nodes $n_1 \in N_1$ and $n_2 \in N_2$ are said to form an *assignment* if

$$p_q^1(n_1) \overset{s}{\sim} p_q^2(n_2) \qquad (8-9)$$

where the $\overset{s}{\sim}$ denotes similarity. An example might be 'same color.' Denoting this assignment (n_1, n_2), if (8-9) holds true for all p_q,[6] we say the *feature set* for node n_1 in N_1 is similar to the feature set for node n_2 in N_2. This allows a comparison of *feature or node similarity.* Therefore, an assignment is a pairing (n_1, n_2), where $n_1 \in N_1$ and $n_2 \in N_2$.

In addition, we must consider the relational information. Denote $r_j^i(n_x, n_y)$ as the jth relation involving nodes n_x and n_y of the ith attributed graph. Note n_x and $n_y \in N_i$. In comparing G_1 and G_2, two assignments (n_1, n_2) and (n_1', n_2') are considered *compatible*, denoted $\overset{c}{\sim}$, if

$$r_j^1(n_1, n_1') \overset{c}{\sim} r_j^2(n_2, n_2') \quad \forall j \qquad (8-10)$$

This is shown in Figure 3.

Isomorphism and Subisomorphism of Attributed Graphs. Two attributed graphs G_1 and G_2 are isomorphic if there exists a set of 1:1 assignments of nodes in G_1 to nodes in G_2 such that all assignments are compatible. G_1 and G_2 are subisomorphic if a subgraph of G_1 is isomorphic to a subgraph of G_2.

---

[6]This requires consideration of what to do with features that are not common to nodes n_1 and n_2.

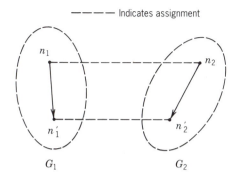

Figure 3:   Assignments and compatibility.

A STRUCTURED STRATEGY TO COMPARE ATTRIBUTED GRAPHS

Relaxing Requirements for Pattern Isomorphism and Subisomorphism

For the same reasons cited above when we consider relational graphs, a less critical test of the matchability of attributed graphs G_1 and G_2 is desired. Similar matching metrics may be developed.

An alternative, as shown below, is to develop suitable similarity (or 'distance') measures between attributed graphs G_1 and G_2. These measures require, as does the isomorphism test, a series of pairings of nodes in G_1 with nodes in G_2. Thus, the measures may provide an assessment of the goodness of the match, but they do not indicate how to attempt 'good' node pairings. For this reason, a three-step strategy is used:

1. Compute the match graph (MG).
2. Find maximal cliques in the MG. These provide a starting point for 'good' candidate matches.
3. Define and use a similarity measure to assess the similarity between G_1 and G_2 using each of the maximal cliques of the MG.

This strategy is shown in Figure 4.

Match Graphs (MGs)

A graph is *connected* if, given any two nodes, a path (set of arcs) exists between them. Loosely speaking, a graph is connected if we could 'pick up' any node and the graph would 'hang together.' A disconnected graph would fall into separate components. A *totally connected* graph has a direct path or connection between any two distinct nodes. A *clique* of a graph G is a totally connected subgraph. A *maximal clique* is not included in any other clique.

Given attributed graphs G_1 and G_2, we form a *match graph* MG with the following characteristics:

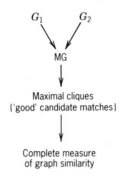

Figure 4:   A relational matching strategy.

1. Nodes of the MG are *assignments* (node pairings) from G_1 and G_2, respectively,
2. An arc in the MG exists between two nodes if the corresponding assignments are compatible. Compatible may be defined as *not incompatible*, in order to handle two node assignments where $r_q^1 = r_q^2 = \emptyset$.

Recursive Procedure to Find Cliques [*cliques* (X, Y)]

Input:

    X: a clique, expressed as a set of nodes (possibly empty).

    Y: set of nodes representing a graph or subgraph.

Output: the set of all maximal cliques in Y that include X.

    PROCEDURE cliques (X, Y);
    BEGIN

                Form $Y - X$;
                IF a node y in $Y - X$ is connected to every element of X,
                THEN return cliques $(X \cup \{y\}, Y) \cup cliques(X, Y - \{y\})$
                ELSE return X.

    END

EXAMPLE 2: Finding Cliques

Consider the match graph shown in Figure 5, with

$$Y = \{a, b, c, d\} \qquad (8 - 11)$$

We start with node set X initially empty, that is, $X = \emptyset$ so

$$Y - X = Y \qquad (8 - 12)$$

We find a node in Y, denoted y, such that y is connected to all elements of X. Suppose, that to get the algorithm example started we choose $X = \{d\}$.[7] Then we continue to use the algorithm recursively to find *cliques* $(\{d\}, Y)$, with $Y - X = \{a, b, c\}$.

---

[7]Note that $X = \{a\}$, $X = \{b\}$, and $X = \{c\}$ would also need to be investigated.

Cliques $(\{d\}, Y) = cliques\ (\{d, b\}, Y) \cup cliques\ (\{d\}, \{a, c, d\})$, since $y = b$ is connected to all nodes in X (currently $\{d\}$). Now to find *cliques* $(\{d, b\}, Y)$, we form $Y - \{d, b\} = \{a, c\}$, and $y = c$ satisfies the algorithm. Therefore, *cliques* $(\{d, b\}, Y) = cliques\ (\{d, b, c\}, Y) \cup cliques\ (\{d, b\}, \{a, b, d\})$. Furthermore, *cliques* $(\{d\}, \{a, c, d\}) = cliques\ (\{d, c\}, \{a, c, d\}) \cup cliques\ (\{d\}, \{a, d\})$, since c satisfies the algorithm.

Now, $Y - \{d, b, c\} = \{a\}$, so the reader should verify
$$cliques\ (\{d, b, c\}, Y) = \{d, b, c\}$$
$$cliques\ (\{d, b\}, \{a, b, d\}) = \{d, b\}$$
$$cliques\ (\{d, c\}, \{a, c, d\}) = \{d, c\}$$
$$cliques\ (\{d\}, \{a, d\}) = \{d\}$$

Therefore
$$cliques\ (\{d\}, \{a, c, d\}) = \{d, c\}$$
$$cliques\ (\{d, b\}, Y) = \{d, b, c\}$$

So *cliques* $(\{d\}, Y) = \{d, b, c\}$. This is visually apparent from Figure 5. ∎

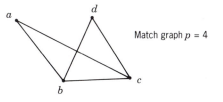

Match graph $p = 4$

Figure 5:   The sample MG for maximal clique-finding algorithm.

OTHER ATTRIBUTED GRAPH DISTANCE OR SIMILARITY MEASURES

Design and Selection of Similarity Measures

A similarity measure between two attributed graphs G_1 and G_2 is desired. As mentioned previously, two approaches are possible:

1. Extract features from G_1 and G_2 (e.g., number and degree of vertices, path lengths for R_i, etc.), form respective feature vectors x_1 and x_2, and employ matching. For example, $\| \underline{x}_1 - \underline{x}_2 \|_R$, where R is a suitable norm (Appendix 5), could be an appropriate measure.

2. Determine the minimum number of 'modifications' to G_1 required to transform it into G_2 (or vice versa). These may involve node insertion (creation) or deletion,[8] as well as edge insertion or deletion.

This number of transformations may be considered a measure of distance or similarity, where a pair of graphs with a smaller distance measure than another pair may be considered more similar.

---

[8]Note that since we are considering the matching of *attributed* graphs, some node pairings from G_1 and G_2 may have inconsistent *properties*. In this case, we could develop a cost of property 'modification,' or alternately, delete a node with certain properties and insert another with modified properties.

Assessment of the Similarity Measures. The first measure is straightforward, but relies (as do all similar PR problems) on the determination and extraction of good features and a suitable R, so when $\| \underline{x}_1 - \underline{x}_2 \|_R$ is small, the two relational descriptions are close. This is easier said than done. The second measure is intuitively appealing but computationally expensive.

Transforming G_i into G_j

Generalized Measure. Here we consider a set of *comparisons, transformations,* and *associated costs* in deriving a measure $D(G_i, G_j)$. Desirable attributes of $D(G_i, G_j)$ are the following:

1. $D(G_i, G_i) = 0$
2. $D(G_i, G_j) > 0$ if $i \neq j$
3. $D(G_i, G_j) = D(G_j, G_i)$
4. $D(G_i, G_j) \leq D(G_i, G_k) + D(G_k, G_j)$ $\qquad\qquad (8-13)$

Property 4 is referred to as the triangle inequality. Property 3 requires $w_{ni} = w_{nd}$ and $w_{ei} = w_{ed}$, where w_{ni} is the cost of node insertion, w_{nd} is the cost of node deletion, w_{ei} is the cost of edge insertion, and w_{ed} is the cost of edge deletion.

Node Matching Costs. Since nodes possess attributes and therefore even without considering relational constraints 'all nodes are not equal,' a similarity measure between node p_i of G_i and node q_j of G_j is required. Denote this cost $f_n(p_i, q_j)$. For candidate match between G_1 and G_2, denoted x, with p nodes, the total cost is

$$c_n(x) = \sum f_n(p_i, q_j) \qquad\qquad (8-14).$$

where the summation is over all corresponding node pairs, under node mapping x.

Overall Cost. For a candidate match configuration (i.e., some pairing of nodes and subsequent transformations), the overall cost for configuration x is

$$D_S(x) = w_{ni}c_{ni} + w_{nd}c_{nd} + w_{bei}c_{bei} + w_{bed}c_{bed} + w_n c_n(x) \qquad\qquad (8-15)$$

and the distance measure D is defined as

$$D = \overset{min}{x} \{D_s(x)\} \qquad\qquad (8-16)$$

Extended Example 3: Structural Unification Using Attributed Graphs

The Basic Problem. Consider the 'library' of stored 2-D patterns shown in Figure 6, together with a new (unknown) pattern to classify. Each 2-D pattern is built from a set of connected line segments. A structural approach based on attributed relational graphs is used.

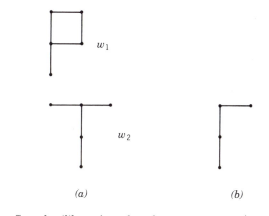

(a)   (b)

Figure 6:   Sample 'library' and unknown pattern (structure-based approach).
(**a**) Library.
(**b**) New pattern (to classify).

Choosing Features.   For each pattern, a label is placed on each line segment, thus specifying an attribute that indicates segment orientation. In specifying nodes, '◇' indicates a vertically oriented segment, whereas '○' indicates a segment with a horizontal orientation. These attributed segments form *nodes* in the AG for each pattern. A single symmetric (undirected) relation of 'attached' is used.

Attributed Graphs.   Attributed graphs for each of the labeled patterns are shown in Figure 7. Attributed graphs AG_{l_1}, AG_{l_2}, and AG_u correspond to labeled patterns l_1, l_2, and u, respectively.

Simple Relational Comparisons.   Several of the previously mentioned matching approaches could be used to compare AG_u with AG_{l_1} and AG_{l_2}. This includes

- Determining subisomorphism.
- Using features extracted from the AG, for example, number of nodes of each type and number of arcs.

Developing the Match Graphs.   Comparing AG_u and AG_{l_1}, assignments are

$$(a, a''), (b, b''), (b, c''), (c, a'')$$
$$(d, b''), (d, c''), (e, b''), (e, c'')$$

The corresponding MG is shown in Figure 8.
    Comparing AG_u and AG_{l_2} yields the assignments:

$$(a', a''), (b', a''), (c', b''), (c', c''), (d', b''), (d', c'').$$

The corresponding MG is shown in Figure 9.

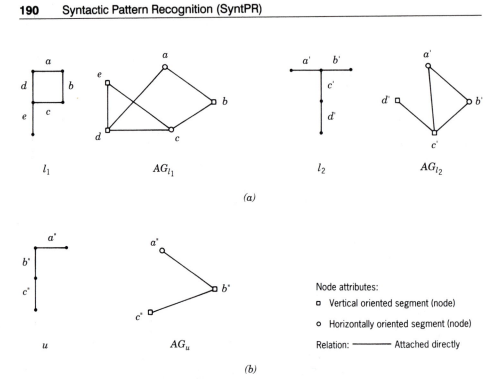

(a)

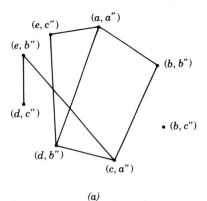

(b)

Figure 7: AGs corresponding to patterns of Figure 6.
(a) Library.
(b) Pattern to classify.

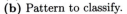

(a)

(b)

(c)

Figure 8: MG and resulting clique—1st match.
(a) Match graph for $AG_{l_1}-AG_u$ comparison.
(b) Maximal clique.
(c) Visual appearance of (b).

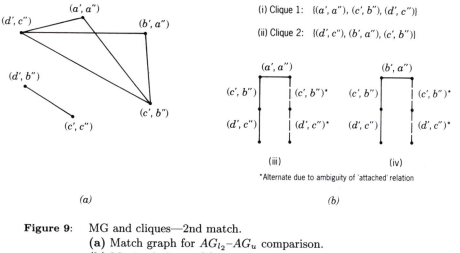

(a)

(b)

(i) Clique 1: $\{(a', a''), (c', b''), (d', c'')\}$

(ii) Clique 2: $\{(d', c''), (b', a''), (c', b'')\}$

(iii)   (iv)

*Alternate due to ambiguity of 'attached' relation

Figure 9:   MG and cliques—2nd match.
   (a) Match graph for AG_{l_2}–AG_u comparison.
   (b) Maximal cliques (2).
      (i) Clique 1: $\{(a', a''), (c', b''), (d', c'')\}$
      (ii) Clique 2: $\{(d', c''), (b', a''), (c', b'')\}$.
      (iii) Visual appearance of (i).
      (iv) Visual appearance of (ii).

Results.   As shown in Figures 8 and 9, each MG has at least one maximal clique of cardinality = 3. Using these cliques as the basis for node mappings, a visual assessment of the pattern structural similarities is shown.   ■

BIBLIOGRAPHICAL REMARKS

Graph-based structural representations are well-suited to a number of applications. Matching of simple (nonattributed) graphs, however, is difficult [Read/Corneil 1977]. Matching of relational graphs is considered in [Sanfeliu/Fu 1983], [Ullman 1976], [Nev 1982], and [Shapiro/Haralick 1985]. A computationally efficient algorithm for subisomorphism that combines tree search with relaxation is shown in [Cheng/Huang 1981]. Furthermore, matching measures for incomplete or distorted attributed graphs are considered in [Tsai/Fu 1983]. The attributed graph concept may be related to the grammatical approach of Chapter 6 through the concept of *attribute grammars* [Knuth 1968], [Sebesta 1989]. From a generic viewpoint, attribute grammars are grammars with sets of attribute values associated with elements of V_T and V_N. This provides an interesting extension as well as increased representational capability in production or rewrite rules, since the attributes of symbols must be taken into account. An application is shown in [Bunke 1982]. Finally, the mathematical basis and alternate formulations to the important and recurring PR problem of *constraint satisfaction* are shown in further detail in Chapter 7 of [Schalkoff 1989].

EXERCISES

8.1   For each of the seven geometric figures shown in Figure P.1, develop the corresponding attributed graph.

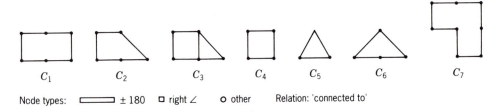

C_1 C_2 C_3 C_4 C_5 C_6 C_7

Node types: ⊏⊐ ± 180   ◻ right ∠   ○ other   Relation: 'connected to'

Figure P.1:

8.2   Develop the match graph (MG) for

    (i) C_1 and C_2

    (ii) C_2 and C_3

    (iii) C_3 and C_4

    (iv) C_2 and C_6

    (v) C_5 and C_5

    (vi) C_1 and C_7

    (vii) C_2 and C_7

For parts (ii) and (iii), find maximal cliques and show that they make sense.

8.3   Using the metric of (8-7), compute the relational distance between descriptions for each of the cases in Exercise 8.2. (Note: This will involve (a) ignoring node attributes and (b) possibly adding 'dummy' nodes.)

8.4   Referring to Exercise 8.3, consider an alternative relational distance measure based on the cost of transforming G_i into G_j, where G_i is the graph for C_i.

    (a)   Develop suitable transformations and associated cost.

    (b)   Develop an overall cost.

    (c)   Using this cost, repeat Exercise 8.3.

8.5   **(a)**   Denoting $P_1 = P_2 = \phi$, show how (8-10) reduces to the same constraint as the test for isomorphism in relational graphs.

    (b)   Show how $R_1 = R_2 = \phi$ reduces the test for isomorphism to that of simple pattern feature vector matching.

8.6   Repeat the solution procedure shown in Example 2 by using (8-11) and Figure 5 for *cliques* $(\{a\}, Y)$.

8.7   Use the two matching approaches suggested in Simple Relational Comparisons to compare AG_u with AG_{l_1} and AG_{l_2}.

8.8   Repeat the comparison of AG_{l_1} and AG_{l_2} with AG_u shown in Figure 6, but instead use the 'graph transformation cost' approach.

8.9 In relational matching approaches, once a suitable similarity metric is chosen, a threshold for similarity must be determined. One approach is to use the similarity metric to pairwise compare library AGs, with the assumption that they will yield similarity measures in the 'dissimilar' range. A threshold for considering two AGs similar would therefore be below these interclass (dis)similarity measures. Derive the MG for a comparison of AG_{l_1} with AG_{l_2}.

8.10 Is the sum of the number of nodes and the number of arcs an invariant under graph isomorphism?

8.11 In considering graph matching, the extraction and comparison of graph features was considered. A somewhat obvious choice of a useful feature might be the number of possible subisomorphisms, since each subisomorphism, to some extent, reflects structural similarity. Explore the pros and cons of this approach, using examples to support your reasoning.

8.12 Develop appropriate costs and apply the 'transformation cost' approach to G_{w_1} and G_u as well as G_{w_2} and G_u in Figure P.1. For reference, compute the 'transformation cost' between G_{w_1} and G_{w_2}.

8.13 Simply using the cardinality of the largest maximal clique of the MG as a measure of similarity can lead to difficulties. Denote $|G|$ as the number of nodes of graph G and $m(G_1, G_2)$ as the cardinality of the largest maximal clique in the MG corresponding to graphs G_1 and G_2. Explore this by using the following three examples:

Example P.13-1	**Example P.13-2**	**Example P.13-3**
$|G_u| = 6$	$|G_u| = 6$	$|G_u| = 20$
$|G_{w_1}| = 8$	$|G_{w_1}| = 8$	$|G_{w_1}| = 8$
$|G_{w_2}| = 8$	$|G_{w_2}| = 20$	$|G_{w_2}| = 18$
$m(G_u, G_{w_1}) = 3$	$m(G_u, G_{w_1}) = 3$	$m(G_u, G_{w_1}) = 3$
$m(G_u, G_{w_2}) = 5$	$m(G_u, G_{w_2}) = 5$	$m(G_u, G_{w_2}) = 5$

Learning Via Grammatical Inference 9

A man's mind stretched by a new idea can never go back to its original dimensions.

Oliver Wendell Holmes, Jr.

LEARNING GRAMMARS[1]

Problem Overview

In SyntPR applications, it is often assumed that the necessary grammar(s) are 'available,' perhaps because of efforts of the PR system designer in formulating V_N, P, and so on for each class. If this is true, training is unnecessary.

In other (and realistic) applications, it is desired that the necessary grammar(s) can be directly inferred from a set of sample patterns. This problem of learning grammar(s) from a training set of sample sentences concerns the process of *grammatical inference* (GI). Thus, GI is a (supervised) learning approach in SyntPR. Note that grammatical inference is of interest to those involved in application areas besides PR, for instance, the design of programming languages [Crespi-Reghizzi et al. 1973]. We restrict our interest in grammatical inference to special types of string grammars useful in PR.

Difficulties in Structural Learning

It is important to restate a limitation noted previously:

- *There is not a unique relationship between a given language and some grammar.*

---

[1] Readers may wish to review the definitions and properties of specific grammar types before beginning this section.

194

Alternatively, the same language may be generated by several different grammars. Thus, the question 'which grammar will the system learn?' arises. This lack of uniqueness forces us to employ additional constraints or place restrictions on the grammar to be learned.

PROBLEM FORMULATION

Characterizing the Grammar Source, Ψ

As shown in Figure 1, we assume a *sentence source* Ψ, which is characterized by a single (to be determined) grammar, G. Ψ generates strings in $L(G)$ of the form $x = x_1, x_2, \ldots x_p$, where $x_i \in V_T$. We denote the ith string by $x^{(i)}$.

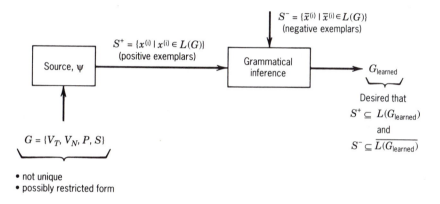

Figure 1:   Grammatical inference model and objectives.

Concerns Related to the Training Set

Positive and Negative Exemplars.   Training data are available in the form of the Ψ-generated $x^{(i)}$, described previously. These are denoted *positive exemplars* of strings in $L(G)$. However, suppose we also are able to obtain sample strings $\bar{x}$, which are *not in* $L(G)$. These *negative exemplars*, although perhaps difficult to obtain, are nonetheless valuable training information. On this basis, the training set for G becomes

$$H = \{S^+, S^-\} \tag{9-1}$$

where

$$S^+ = \{x^{(i)} | x^{(i)} \in L(G)\} \tag{9-2a}$$

and

$$S^- = \{\bar{x}^{(i)} | \bar{x}^{(i)} \notin L(G)\} \tag{9-2b}$$

The goal is to use H to learn a grammar, G_{learn}, where G_{learn} is, in some way, 'close' to G. One formulation of this goal is as follows:

- Develop a grammar, G_{learn}, where G_{learn} can generate[2] S^+, but not S^-.

A more ambitious and perhaps more useful goal might be to develop G_{learn} as above, but also require that G_{learn} reflect properties that might be ascribed to H, that is, if

$$S^+ = \{ab, \quad aabb, \quad aaabbb, \quad aaaabbbb\} \qquad (9-3a)$$

then one might 'extrapolate' this training data to infer that

$$L(G_{learn}) = \{a^n b^n | n \geq 1\} \qquad (9-3b)$$

and that G_{learn} is recursive with productions

$$S \rightarrow ab$$

$$S \rightarrow aSb \qquad (9-3c)$$

Finite Sample Size. Since $L(G)$ is seldom finite,[3] we should be concerned with the cardinality of S^+, since

$$S^+ \subseteq L(G) \qquad (9-4a)$$

and typically

$$|S^+| \ll |L(G)| \qquad (9-4b)$$

Similarly, denoting the complement of $L(G)$ as $\overline{L(G)}$, we observe

$$S^- \subseteq \overline{L(G)} \qquad (9-5a)$$

and typically,

$$|S^-| \ll |\overline{L(G)}| \qquad (9-5b)$$

Recall that there is not a unique 1:1 relationship between a language $L(G)$ and a grammar G, which generates $L(G)$. The finite size of S^+ introduces another concern, namely, *since a finite sample of a language does not uniquely define a language, a finite sample may be associated with an infinite number of languages.* Therefore, inferring a unique grammar from S^+ is impossible. These observations lead to a more modest and constrained formulation of grammatical inference objectives.

Structural Completeness of the Training Data. An important characteristic of S^+ is that it be *structurally complete*, that is, S^+ reflects every production in P. This makes intuitive sense, since we are trying to learn structure from examples. Formally, S^+ is said to be structurally complete if each production in P is used in at least one $x^{(i)} \in S^+$.

Certain limitations of grammatical inference are well known [Gold 1967], [Gold 1978]. For one, the problem of identifying an arbitrary grammar by using only S^+ is known to be undecidable. Surprisingly, this remains the case if we restrict our attention to regular grammars. Furthermore, even if S^- is available, the problem is NP hard

---

[2] As well as other x.

[3] Although we still may seek a compact (e.g., recursive) form to represent $L(G)$.

[Angluin 1978]. Lest we appear overly pessimistic, we note that SyntPR applications often suggest or allow appropriate heuristics such that computationally reasonable, problem-specific GI procedures may be developed [Garcia/Vidal 1990].

Using H for Partitioning of V_T^*. Any subset $L \subseteq V_T^*$ is a language. Recall previously that G constrains the production of strings in L, that is,

$$L(G) \subseteq L \qquad\qquad (9-6a)$$

and

$$|L(G)| \leq |L| \qquad\qquad (9-6b)$$

Thus, *G partitions L into the disjoint sets* $L(G)$ *and* $\overline{L(G)}$.

GRAMMATICAL INFERENCE (GI) APPROACHES

Grammatical Inference Objectives

- Constrain the grammar G_{learn} to be inferred from S^+ and S^-. This may involve choosing a 'standard' type (e.g., T_2 or T_3) or possibly developing other constraints that restrict the class of grammar to be learned. For example, requiring G_{learn} to be of *minimal complexity* is reasonable.
- Infer G_{learn} such that G_{learn} generates all strings in S^+ and does not generate any string in S^-. Also (this is difficult to quantify and predict), G_{learn} may generate other strings which are 'similar' to those in S^+.
- Carry out the inference procedure by using an algorithm of reasonable computational complexity. Because of the (usually enormous) number of possible choices or alternatives, this spawns the need for additional constraints or heuristics.

Intuitive Sample GI Procedure

As a prelude to more formal approaches, consider the following (skeletal) procedure, which relies heavily upon parsing.

Given: S^+, S^-

Assumed: $G^{(0)}$ (our zeroth 'guess' about G) $= \{V_T^{(0)}, V_N^{(0)}, P^{(0)}, S^{(0)}\}$ as well as P, V_N, V_T modification (or creation) procedures (see below).

Objective: Formulate $G^{(N)} = G_{learn}$ such that $L(G^{(N)})$ and $\overline{L(G^{(N)})}$ are consistent with S^+ and S^-, respectively.

Procedure:[4] Use elements of S^+ and S^- to iteratively refine $G^{(0)}$. For example:

Step 0: Set $k = 0$.

Step 1: Choose one $x^{(i)} \in S^+$. Using $G^{(k)}$, parse $x^{(i)}$. If parse is successful, continue. Otherwise modify $G^{(k)}$.

---

[4]Non-unique. Other variants are possible.

Step 2: Choose one $\bar{x}^{(i)} \in S^-$. Using $G^{(k)}$, parse $\bar{x}^{(i)}$. If parse is successful, modify $G^{(k)}$. Otherwise continue.

Step 3: If all elements of S^+ and S^- have been considered, STOP. Otherwise GOTO step 1.

Ramifications of the Sample Procedure.
1. The procedures for modification of P, V_N, and V_T are difficult to design.
2. The possible 'modifications' at each step lead to combinatorial explosion in producing possible $G^{(k+1)}$.

Thus, this skeletal procedure, while intuitively appealing, is of limited practical utility.

PROCEDURES TO GENERATE CONSTRAINED GRAMMARS

Using a Single String to Partially Infer G_{learn}

Suppose we restrict G_{learn} to a finite state (FS) or regular grammar and concentrate on developing elements of G_{learn} from a single string.[5]

EXAMPLE 1
Assume that we are given the string $x^{(i)}$, which is a labeled sample known to be an element of $L(G)$, where

$$x^{(i)} = caaab \qquad (9-7)$$

Immediately, we could infer that the minimum V_T is

$$V_T = \{a, b, c\} \qquad (9-8)$$

and

$$V_N = \{S, A_1, A_2\} \qquad (9-9)$$

Consider the following productions in G_{learn}, which successively generate $x^{(i)}$ from left to right, using a FS grammar:

$$S \rightarrow cA_1 \qquad (9-10)$$

$$A_1 \rightarrow aA_2 \qquad (9-11)$$

$$A_2 \rightarrow aA_3 \qquad (9-12)$$

$$A_3 \rightarrow aA_4 \qquad (9-13)$$

$$A_4 \rightarrow b \qquad (9-14)$$

Thus, the above choice of G_{learn} satisfies the requirement that G_{learn} be able to generate string x.

Notice from (9-11) through (9-13) that each A_i generated by considering terminals from left to right in $x^{(i)}$ is a *new* nonterminal symbol. For large sample sizes and long strings, this procedure may lead to generation of excessive numbers of nonterminals.

---

[5]Recall that this restricts productions to either $A_1 \rightarrow a$ or $A_1 \rightarrow aA_2$.

The procedure does, however, provide a starting or reference point in developing grammatical inference techniques.

Generation of Cannonical Definite Grammars

The above procedure may be formalized to generate a *cannonical, definite, finite-state grammar* (CDFSG), denoted G_c, from S^+.

LEMMA: Any finite set of strings can be exactly described by at least one definite FSG [Fu/Booth 1986].   ■

General Procedure to Generate CDFSG, (G_c)

Step 1:   For all $x^{(i)} \in S^+$, determine the set of distinct terminals. This yields V_T.

Step 2:   For each $x^{(i)} \in S^+$, define the corresponding set of productions by considering the string from left to right as in Example 1. Doing this $\forall x^{(i)} \in S^+$ defines V_N and P.

Using the above procedure yields $L(G_c) = S^+$. However, P, at this step, may contain significant redundancies. More importantly, $L(G_c)$ *is finite.* An additional step (step 3) may be used to merge productions and to produce a recursive grammar and a corresponding infinite language. This is shown below in Example 2.

EXAMPLE 2: Inferring a FS Grammar from Several Samples

Assume that we are given

$$S^+ = \{bbaab, \quad caab, \quad bbab, \quad cab, \quad bbb, \quad cb\} \qquad (9-15)$$

By introducing new nonterminals as necessary in the left–right consideration of each $x^{(i)}, i = 1, 2, \ldots 6$, the following productions result (the reader should verify this):

$$S \to bA_1 \qquad (9-16a)$$

$$S \to cA_4 \qquad (9-16b)$$

$$A_1 \to bA_2 \qquad (9-16c)$$

$$A_2 \to b \qquad (9-16d)$$

$$A_2 \to aA_3 \qquad (9-16e)$$

$$A_3 \to b \qquad (9-16f)$$

$$A_3 \to aA_{3\prime} \qquad (9-16f')$$

$$A_{3\prime} \to b \qquad (9-16f'')$$

$$A_4 \to b \qquad (9-16g)$$

$$A_4 \to aA_5 \qquad (9-16h)$$

$$A_5 \to aA_{5\prime} \qquad (9-16h')$$

$$A_5 \rightarrow b \tag{9-16i}$$

$$A_{5'} \rightarrow b \tag{9-16j}$$

An additional step (step 3 cited above) consists of merging (9-16a) through (9-16j) into

$$S \rightarrow bA_1 \tag{9-17a}$$

$$S \rightarrow cA_4 \tag{9-17b}$$

$$A_1 \rightarrow bA_2 \tag{9-17c}$$

$$A_2 \rightarrow b \tag{9-17d}$$

$$A_2 \rightarrow aA_2 \tag{9-17e}$$

$$A_4 \rightarrow b \tag{9-17f}$$

$$A_4 \rightarrow aA_4 \tag{9-17g}$$

Note that (9-17e) and (9-17g) are recursive productions resulting from the respective merging of (9-16e) through (9-16f''), as well as (9-16h) through (9-16j). An infinite language results.[6] Furthermore, notice that (9-17) still contains redundancy [e.g., the reader should note the similarity of (9-17d) and (9-17e) with (9-17f) and (9-17g)]. Removing this redundancy yields P of G_c as follows:

$$S \rightarrow bA_1 | cA_2 \tag{9-18a}$$

$$A_1 \rightarrow bA_2 \tag{9-18b}$$

$$A_2 \rightarrow b | aA_2 \tag{9-18c}$$

BIBLIOGRAPHICAL REMARKS

Grammatical inference (GI) is one of the most interesting and challenging aspects of SyntPR. In fact, the availability of grammatical inference algorithms that correspond to descriptively adequate grammar may limit the applicability of SyntPR. Some of the fundamental results concerning theoretical as well as computational limitations of GI are found in [Gold 1967], [Gold 1978], [Angluin 1978], [Angluin 1980], [Feldman 1972], and [Angluin/Smith 1983]. GI using regular (FS) grammars is addressed in [Garcia et al. 1987]. Good starting points for extended study are Chapter 6 in [Gonzalez/Thomason 1978], Chapter 10 in [Fu 1 1982], [Lu/Fu 1984], and [Fu/Booth 1986]. Sample applications of GI to specific PR problems are shown in [Itoga 1981], [Miclet 1980], and [Richetin/Vernadad 1984]. Learning methods for higher dimensional grammars, such as trees, have been developed [Levine 1981], [Brayer/Fu 1977]. Many of these techniques are generalizations of string-grammar based approaches. We note that other significant applications of GI are in areas of programming language design Aho/Ullman 1972] and artificial intelligence.

---

[6]Note, that if 5 were available, we might have some guidance on whether this merging is reasonable.

EXERCISES

9.1   Can a property analogous to structural (in)completeness for S^- be defined?

9.2   To show the non-uniqueness of grammars that generate a prespecified language, consider:
$$L = \{a^n b \,|\, n = 1, 2, \ldots\}$$

    (a) Develop a finite state grammar that generates L.

    (b) Repeat part (a), but develop a CFG.

9.3   Can a successful grammatical inference procedure be based exclusively on S^+? On S^-?

9.4   Suppose that in developing productions (9-11) to (9-13), we instead postulated a single production of the form:
$$A \to aA$$

Discuss the ramifications of this approach.

9.5   Repeat Exercise 9.4; however, consider the implications of

    (a) $S^+ = \{x^{(i)}\} = \{caaab\}$ and $S^- = \{\bar{x}^{(i)}\} = \{caaaab\}$.

    (b) Repeat part (a) with $S^- = \{\bar{x}^1, \bar{x}^2\} = \{caaaab, \ caab\}$.

9.6   Referring to Example 2, one might conclude from S^+ in (9-15) that
$$L(G) = \{bba^n b, \quad ca^n b \,|\, n \geq 0\}$$

Is this consistent with the language of the derived G_{learn}?

9.7   Referring to Exercise 9.6 and Example 2, suppose that we also had knowledge of S^-, e.g.,
$$S^- = \{caab\}$$

How would you modify the generation of G_{learn}? Show an example.

9.8   Verify the resultant productions in (9-16).

9.9   Verify that

    (a) The set of strings produced by (9-17e) contains those produced by (9-16e) and (9-16f).

    (b) The set of strings produced by (9-17g) contains those produced by (9-16h) to (9-16j).

Part 4

*Neural Pattern Recognition
(NeurPR)*

Introduction to Neural Networks 10

Creatures extremely low in the intellectual scale may have conception. All that is required is that they should recognize the same experience again.

The Principles of Psychology [1890]. Chapter 12
William James 1842–1910

NEURONS AND NEURAL NETS

Introduction

This chapter begins an extended look at (artificial) neural networks (ANNs) by examining the basic building blocks of ANNs. ANNs provide an emerging paradigm for pattern recognition implementation that involves large interconnected networks of relatively simple and typically nonlinear units (so-called neural nets). Although a number of artificial neural structures exist, and more continue to appear as research continues, many of these structures have common topological properties, unit characteristics, and training approaches.

ANN research has a rich history of approximately 40 years; however, it seems to be presently (1991) at an all-time peak. Basically, three entities characterize an ANN:

1. The network topology, or interconnection of neural 'units;'
2. The characteristics of individual units or artificial neurons; and
3. The strategy for pattern learning or training.

This chapter introduces some of the history of ANNs. Unit or neuron characteristics are developed, and the relationship to biological neural systems is shown. Not surprisingly, there are several popular and different ANN computational paradigms, each suited for a particular type of PR application. Chapter 11 introduces a special class of relatively simple pattern associators. Chapter 12 studies the feedforward-with-back-propagation learning structure, which is quite popular for pattern mapping, especially classification. Finally, Chapter 13 explores the concepts of a highly interconnected dynamic network of nonlinear elements, which is usually attributed to Hopfield, as well as several ANNs with unsupervised learning capabilities. The computational structures we develop may be implemented in a number of nonbiological ways, most typically through electronic elements. Therefore, the descriptor 'artificial' is hereafter omitted, except where significant.

History

Biological systems implement pattern recognition computations via interconnections of physical cells called neurons. This provides motivation to consider emulation of this computational mechanism for automated PR applications. Researchers from such diverse areas as neuroscience, mathematics, psychology, engineering, and computer science are attempting to relate underlying models for pattern recognition, the computation that is desired, the potential parallelism that emerges, and the operation of biological neural systems. In fact, a whole field of study, centered around the creation and study of intelligent systems by recreating the computational structures of the human (or animal) brain, has fully emerged in only the last decade. This movement is known by several names, including (Artificial) Neural Networks, Connectionist Modeling, Neuromorphic Modeling, and Parallel Distributed Processing (PDP).

The idea that computations underlying the emulation of intelligent behavior may be accomplished via interactions of large numbers of simple processing units is hardly new. For one, the neuron models of the behavior of brain cells provides biological inspiration and plausibility for ANNs. The adaptable, context-sensitive, error-tolerant, large memory capacity, and real-time capability of the human information processing system (mostly the brain) suggests an alternative architecture to emulate. The mere fact that the basic computing element of the human information processing system is relatively slow (in the millisecond range and therefore ridiculously slow vis-à-vis electronic devices), but the overall processing operation is achieved in a few hundred milliseconds, suggests that *the basis of the biological computation is a small number of serial steps, each massively parallel.* Furthermore, in this inherently parallel architecture, each of the processing elements is locally connected and relatively simple. Thus, connectionist or 'neural' computing is not new or revolutionary. It is, rather, evolutionary, with roots in a number of well-understood concepts, including biological pattern recognition, perceptrons and linear machines, adaptive networks, and fine-grained parallel computing paradigms.

Neural Networks as a Black Box Approach and 'Artificial' Neural Systems

To some extent, the NeurPR approach is a *nonalgorithmic, black box strategy*, which is trainable. We hope to 'train' the neural black-box to 'learn' the correct response or output (e.g., classification) for each of the training samples. This strategy is attractive to the PR system designer, since the required amount of a priori knowledge and detailed knowledge of the internal system operation is minimal. Furthermore, after training we hope that the internal (neural) structure of the artificial implementation will *self-organize* to enable extrapolation when faced with new, yet similar, patterns, on the basis of 'experience' with the training set.

As shown in Chapter 1, the key aspect of black box approaches is developing relationships between input and output. The adage 'garbage in–garbage out' holds for black box PR approaches. Thus, we expect, as in SyntPR and StatPR, the success of the NeurPR approach is likely to be strongly influenced by the quality of the training data and algorithm. Furthermore, existence of a training set and a training algorithm does not guarantee that a given network will 'train' for a specific application.

Black box neural approaches offer an alternative to the development and implementation of more traditional software, where program (software) development may be replaced with development of appropriate neural computing architectures and training algorithms that adapt the network performance to a specific problem.

Key Neural Network Concepts

Prior to a detailed analysis of neural network pattern recognition applications, the reader should note the following key aspects of neural computing:

- The overall computational model consists of a *variable interconnection of simple elements, or units.*
- Modifying patterns of interelement connectivity as a function of training data is the key learning approach. In other words, the system knowledge, experience, or training is stored in the form of network interconnections.
- To be useful, neural systems must be capable of storing information ('trainable'). Neural PR systems are trained with the hope that they will subsequently display correct 'associative' behavior, when presented with new patterns to recognize or classify. That is, the objective is for the network (somehow) in the training process to develop an internal structure that enables it to correctly identify or classify new similar patterns. We consider both supervised and unsupervised training paradigms.
- Neural networks are dynamic systems, whose state (e.g., unit outputs and interconnection strengths) changes over time, in response to external inputs or an initial (unstable) state.

Characteristics of Neural Computing Applications

Emulation of biological system computational structures yields superior computational paradigms for certain classes of problems. Among these problems are the following: the class of NP-hard problems, which includes labeling problems, scheduling problems, search problems, and other constraint satisfaction problems; the class of pattern/object recognition problems, notably in vision and speech understanding; and the class of problems dealing with flawed, missing, contradicting, fuzzy, or probabilistic data. These problems are characterized by these qualities:

1. A high-dimensional problem space,
2. Complex interactions between problem variables, and
3. A solution space that may be empty, contain a unique solution, or (most typically) contain a number of (almost equally) useful solutions.

The myriad of potential neural network applications for pattern recognition includes

1. Feature extraction from complex data sets (e.g., images and speech);
2. Character recognition and image processing applications; and
3. Direct and parallel implementation of matching and search algorithms.

'Connectionist' Models and Computing

The connectionist or neural approach to computing is based on the notion that many human computational processes are naturally carried out in a highly parallel fashion (which could, provided architectures exist, be emulated in machine intelligence). One interpretation is that the burden of the computational process must fall on the connection structure of the network [Feldman 1985]. Connectionist computing models may be shown to have a number of abstract properties relevant to their application in problems involving cognitive processes [Amari 1982]. More specifically, however, the number of computational units is large, their connectivity is severely restricted (usually to be very local), and their internal complexity is limited. Thus, neural nets, as described above, satisfy this requirement (as do other computational structures, e.g., systolic arrays).

The connectionist approach is, in some ways, a generalization of the neural network concept, where the individual unit or 'extended neuron' is slightly more complex than the neuron defined above.

NEURAL NETWORK STRUCTURES FOR PR APPLICATIONS

Neural Network Structure (How Should I Connect My Neurons?)

The connectivity of a neural network determines its *structure*. Groups of neurons could be locally interconnected to form 'clusters' that are only loosely, weakly, or indirectly connected to other clusters. Alternately, neurons could be organized in groups or *layers* that are (directionally) connected to other layers. Thus, neural implementation of PR approaches requires an initial assessment of neural network architectures. Possibilities include the following:

1. Designing an application-dependent network structure that performs some desired computation. An example is [Carp/Gross 1 1987].

2. Selecting a 'commonly used' preexisting structure for which training algorithms are available. Examples are the feedforward and Hopfield networks.

3. Adapting a structure in item 2 to suit a specific application. An example is [Jamison/Schalkoff 1989]. This includes using *semantics* or other information to give meaning to the behavior of units or groups of units.

Several different 'generic' neural network structures, indicated in item 2, are useful for a class of PR problems. Examples are

> *The Pattern Associator (PA)*. This neural implementation is exemplified by feedforward networks. A sample feedforward network is shown in Figure 1(a). In Chapter 12, this type of network structure is explored in detail. We consider its learning (or training) mechanism (the backpropagation approach and the generalized delta rule) and explore properties and nuances of the approach.
>
> *The Content-Addressable or Associative Memory Model (CAM or AM)*. This neural network structure, best exemplified by the Hopfield model and shown in Chapter 13, is another attempt to build a pattern recognition system with useful pattern association properties. A sample structure is shown in Figure 1(b).
>
> *Self-Organizing Networks*. These networks exemplify neural implementations of unsupervised learning in the sense that they typically cluster, or self-organize input patterns into classes or clusters based on some form of similarity. Two examples are considered in Chapter 13.

Although these network structures are only examples, they seem to be receiving the vast amount of attention. Figures 1(c) and 1(d) give a more 'generic' viewpoint of these structures.

Feedback Interconnections and Network Stability.   The feedback structure of a recurrent network shown in Figure 1(b) or 1(d) suggests that network *temporal dynamics*, that is change over time, should be considered. In many instances the resulting system, due to the nonlinear nature of unit activation-output characteristics and the weight adjustment strategies, is a highly nonlinear dynamic system. This raises concerns with overall network stability, including the possibility of network oscillation, instability, or lack of convergence to a stable state. The stability of nonlinear systems is often difficult to ascertain.

Learning in Neural Networks

Learning in NeurPR may be either supervised or unsupervised. An example of supervised learning in a feedforward network is the generalized delta rule, considered in Chapter 12. An example of supervised learning in a recurrent structure is the Hopfield (CAM) approach. Unsupervised learning in a feedforward (nonrecurrent) network is exemplified by the Kohonen self-organizing network, whereas the ART approach exemplifies unsupervised learning with a recurrent network structure (Chapter 13).

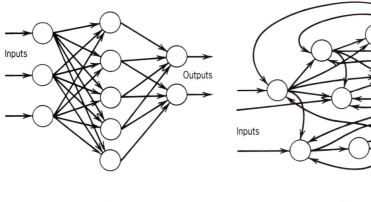

(a)

(b)

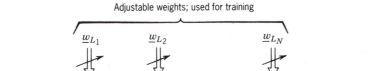

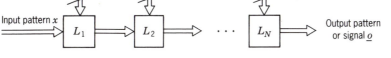

(c)

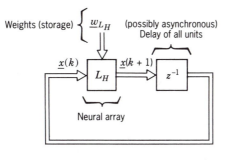

(d)

Figure 1:   Overview of neural network structures.
   (a) Sample feedforward neural network structure.
   (b) Sample Hopfield-like neural network structure.
   (c) 'Generic' or block diagram view of 1(a)—a multilayer
   network.
   (d) 'Generic' or block diagram view of 1(c)—a 'recurrent' or
   feedback network.

The Neural PR Application Design Phase

During the design of neural pattern classifiers, many questions occur, such as:

- Can the network be trained to perform the classification desired, or is there some inherent ambiguity in the problem that makes solution impossible?
- Assuming that the problem is solvable, what network structure is appropriate? How many layers and/or units are required?
- What kind of computing resources are available (time/memory/storage/processors) to train and implement the network?

These questions are the subjects of Chapters 11 to 13.

Why Is Neural Computation So Important?

We begin with a brief observation of the biological analogy. The brain is composed of approximately 20 billion (2×10^{10}) nerve cells termed *neurons*. Whereas each of these elements is relatively simple in design (and may easily and efficiently be replicated in silicon), *it is believed that the brain's computational power is derived from the interconnection, hierarchical organization, firing characteristics, and sheer number of these elements.* Thus, it appears that nature has provided a model for a computing paradigm that differs from the Von Neumann paradigm. The acknowledged shortcomings of the Von Neumann approach, particularly the processor–memory bottleneck, have prompted researchers to consider alternatives, thus spawning the field of parallel computing.

Reasons to Adopt a Neural Computational Architecture. Generally, the achievement of a computational paradigm based on a neural network is attractive for the following reasons:

1. The local computation, because of the local activation characteristic of the neural unit, is simple.
2. Computation proceeds *inherently in parallel*. The possibility of a delay time for network convergence must, however, be taken into account.
3. In many instances the structure of the problem is reflected directly in the structure of the network. This has been referred to as the *isomorphism hypothesis* [Rummelhart/McClelland 2 1986, Chapter 22] and is depicted in Figure 2. An example of the structural isomorphism is found in implementation of problems in syntactic pattern recognition, where the structure of word formation via productions is reflected in the structure of the neural network used for recognition.
4. The VLSI or optical implementation of neural networks (neglecting the difficulty of massive interconnections), owing to the simplicity and regularity of the network, is straightforward.
5. Emulation of the biological computing paradigm is probably desirable.
   - *Note that what is not simple is the mapping of an arbitrary PR problem into a neural network solution.*

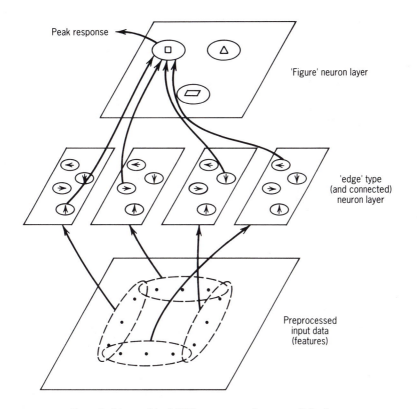

Figure 2:   Sample hierarchical NN structure that parallels data structure—
vision example.

PHYSICAL NEURAL NETWORKS

The Physical Neuron

There are more than 40 properties of biological neurons that influence their information processing capability. A biological neuron, as shown in Figure 3(a), is a nerve cell that is composed of three major parts: a soma, an axon, and dendrites. The connection of a neuron's axonic nerve fiber to the soma or dendrite of another neuron is called a *synapse*. There are usually between 1000 and 10,000 synapses on each neuron. The axon is the neuron's output channel and conveys the action potential of the neural cell (along nerve fibers) to synaptic connections with other neurons. The dendrites act as a neuron's input receptors for signals coming from other neurons and channel the postsynaptic or input potentials to the neuron's soma, which acts as an accumulator/amplifier. Figure 3(b) shows an electronic analog to the biological unit. The electronic representation of Figure 3(b) alludes to a much broader class of artificial unit models.

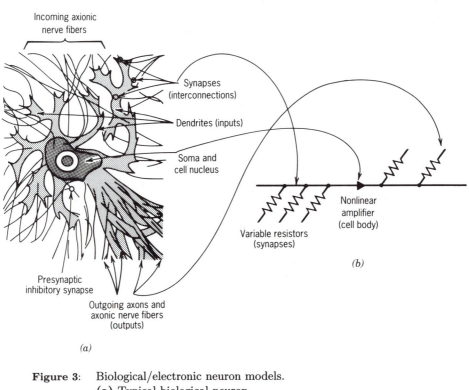

Figure 3: Biological/electronic neuron models.
(a) Typical biological neuron.
(b) Electronic analogy.

Dynamics of a Biological Neural System

The process of neural activation is a circular one. A neuron is activated by other activated neurons and, in turn, activates other neurons. Some neurons are stimulated by special-purpose nerve cells, called sensor neurons, or stimulate special-purpose nerve cells, called motor neurons. Sensor neurons act as interface cells between sensory energy stimulation (e.g., light, sound, touch) and the electrochemical neuronal system. An 'action' potential for an activated neuron is usually a spiked signal where the frequency is proportional to the potential of the soma. When and if the neuron's soma potential rises above some threshold value, the neuron begins 'firing.' An action potential, therefore, may cause changes in the potential of attached neurons. The average frequency of the action potential is known as the mean firing rate of the neuron. The mean soma potential with respect to the mean resting soma potential is known as the activation level of the neuron. Some neurotransmitters are excitatory, meaning that they cause an increase in the soma potential of the receiving neuron, and some are inhibitory, meaning that they either lower the receiving neuron's soma potential or prevent it from increasing. A special case of inhibition is presynaptic inhibition, caused by a synapse(s) appearing on the presynaptic nerve fiber or the synaptic knob.

This form of inhibition appears to result in a substantial reduction of the action potential magnitude at the synapse. The net result is a multiplicative effect on the transfer of activation.

Biological Memory Models.   Many different mechanisms have been proposed for the processing and memory capabilities of biological neural nets. Some researchers have proposed that individual neurons represent specific concepts (also known as the 'grandmother cell theory,' whereby, for example, a neuron fires whenever one's grandmother is seen or heard or thought about). Others believe that a more appropriate model is the mapping of patterns of activation across a large number of neurons to a given concept. This theory has the advantage of providing a more efficient coding scheme, in an information theoretic sense, and a higher tolerance for hard failures in the brain.

Biological Visual Systems.   The human visual system (HVS) is neurally based and is likely the most complex sensory system of the human body. There is no doubt that it is the significant component of the biological visual pattern-recognition system. The process of vision begins with the optical system of the eye, which converts energy from a 3-D scene into a two-dimensional array of intensities on the retina of the eye. The back surface of the retina contains a nonuniform array of sensory cells called photoreceptors, which sample and convert light intensity and wavelength information into the electrochemical signals used by the nervous system. Once converted, some preprocessing of the information takes place by special neural cells located in the retina. These cells then communicate, via their axons (collectively known as the optic nerve), to neurons in several areas of the brain.

THE ARTIFICIAL NEURAL NETWORK MODEL

In this section, we explore a set of general entities that characterize the design and application of a neural network and that make comparison of alternate approaches straightforward.

Artificial Neuron Activation and Output Characteristics

The individual neural unit activation (or 'firing') characteristic. Examples are shown in Figures 4 to 7. This activation characteristic may, for example, be simply a threshold test, thus emulating a relay characteristic. Conversely, the possibility of external (i.e., not the output of other neurons) inputs to the neural unit, inhibitory inputs (as in the perceptron [Minsky/Papert 1969]), and weighted and nonlinear combinations of inputs are also possible. The perceptron and other types of threshold logic were early attempts to employ single-layer, linear neurallike networks to classification problems in pattern recognition, as shown in Figure 6. In a more general sense, neural units may be thought of as programming objects. A number of characterizations of this concept are described in [Feldman/Ballard 1982]. Although there exist significant performance differences, we do not distinguish between analog and discrete firing characteristics.

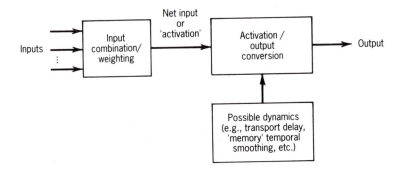

Figure 4: Abstract neuron I/O characteristic.

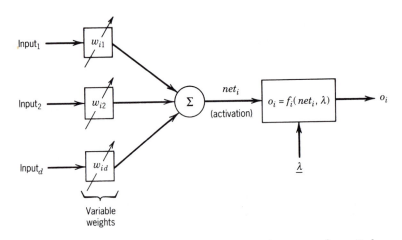

Figure 5: Specific artificial neuron computational structure (no unit dynamics).

Output Characteristics. As shown in Figure 7, a variety of *activation functions* that map neuron input activation into an output signal are possible. The simplest example is that of a linear unit, where

$$o_i = f(net_i) = net_i \qquad (10-1)$$

One particular functional structure that is often used is the *sigmoid characteristic*, where

$$o_i = f(net_i) = \frac{1}{1 + e^{-\lambda net_i}} \qquad (10-2a)$$

Equation (10-2a) yields $o_i \in [0, 1]$. Then λ is an adjustable gain parameter that controls the 'steepness' of the output transition, as shown in Figure 7(e). Typically, $\lambda = 1$,

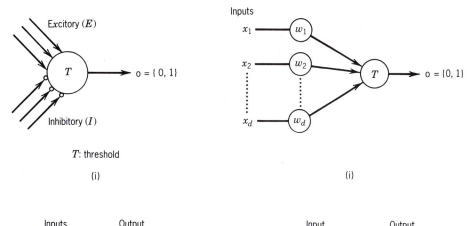

Inputs

Excitory (E)

T

$o = \{0, 1\}$

Inhibitory (I)

T: threshold

(i)

Inputs

$x_1 \longrightarrow w_1$

$x_2 \longrightarrow w_2$

$\vdots$

$x_d \longrightarrow w_d$

T

$o = \{0, 1\}$

(i)

Inputs	Output
$E \geq T;\quad I = 0$	1
$E \geq T;\quad I > 0$	0
$E < T;\quad I = 0$	0
$E < T;\quad I > 0$	0

(E: sum of activated excitory inputs
I: sum of activated inhibitory inputs)

(a)

Input	Output
$\displaystyle\sum_{k=1}^{d} x_i w_i < T$	0
$\displaystyle\sum_{k=1}^{d} x_i w_i \geq T$	1

(w_i may be positive or negative)

(ii)

(b)

Figure 6: Sample (individual) neural unit activation characteristics.
  (a) McCullouch-Pitts model.
    (i) Diagram
    (ii) Characteristics
  (b) Linear weighted threshold model.
    (i) Diagram
    (ii) Characteristics

and (10-2a) is often referred to in the literature as a *logistic function.* We assume this unless stated otherwise. A computational advantage of the activation function of (10-2a), which is useful in training, is that when $\lambda = 1$,

$$\frac{\partial o_i}{\partial net_i} = o_i \cdot (1 - o_i) \qquad (10-2b)$$

An interesting observation is that the average firing frequency of biological neurons, as a function of excitation, follows a sigmoidal characteristic.

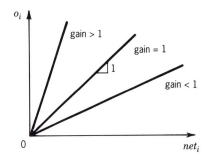

(a)

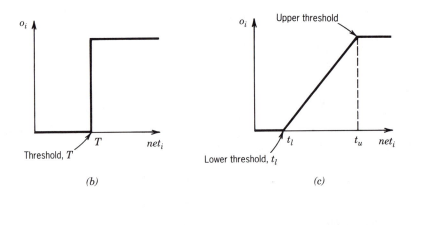

(b)   (c)

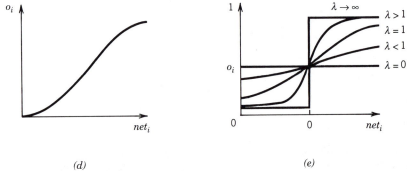

(d)   (e)

Figure 7:   Common output function/firing characteristics of artificial neurons.
(a) Linear, adjustable gain.
(b) (Relay) threshold characteristic.
(c) Linear threshold characteristic.
(d) General sigmoidal characteristic.
(e) Sigmoid function curves for different values of gain, λ.

Another particularly interesting class of activation functions are *bilevel* mappings or thresholding units. For example,

$$o_i = f(net_i) = \begin{cases} 1 & net_i \geq 0 \\ 0 & net_i < 0 \end{cases} \qquad (10-2c)$$

Figure 6(b) shows this unit characteristic using a general threshold, T. Alternately,

$$o_i = f(net_i) = \begin{cases} 1 & net_i \geq 0 \\ -1 & net_i < 0 \end{cases} \qquad (10-2d)$$

Thresholding units may be viewed as a limiting case of the sigmoidal unit characteristic of (10-2a). This is shown in Figure 7(e). In addition, thresholding units may be used to compute Boolean functions.

'Memory' or Individual Unit Activation Dynamics.   The characteristics of (10-2) suggest an instantaneous activation-to-output mapping. A more realistic model would involve delay or dynamics in the unit response. A model to incorporate dynamics might be

$$\frac{dnet_i(t)}{dt} = \frac{-1}{\alpha_i} net_i(t) + \frac{1}{\alpha_i} net_i^a(t) \qquad (10-3)$$

where $net_i(t)$ is the activation used in (10-2d), $net_i^a(t)$ is the actual input activation, and α_i is the time constant of the ith unit. Equation (10-3) constrains the time change of individual unit states and enables a local 'memory.' For a discrete time model, similar difference equations may be derived.

Bias Input.   Another neuron parameter is the (optional) bias or offset input into the unit. While this could be achieved simply by adding a constant input with an appropriate weight, often the bias is considered separately. Biases may be used, for example, to selectively inhibit the activity of certain neurons.

Neural Unit Interconnection Strengths (Weights)

As shown in Figure 5, each neuron input has an associated weight, indicating the strength of its connection with either an external input or another neuron output. Although the literature is somewhat inconsistent on this topic, we adopt the following convention. w_{ij} *represents the strength of the connection TO neuron unit i FROM (either) neuron unit j or input j.* Thus, a large, positive value of w_{ij} indicates a strongly excitory input, and as large a negative value would be considered highly inhibitory.

Vector-Matrix Formulation.   This convention facilitates the determination of individual unit activation via

$$net_i = \sum_j w_{ij} o_j \qquad (10-4)$$

In addition, defining an interconnection matrix W and a $d \times 1$ vector $\underline{o}$, where

$$W = [w_{ii}] \qquad (10-5)$$

and

$$\underline{o} = \begin{pmatrix} o_1 \\ o_2 \\ \vdots \\ o_d \end{pmatrix}$$

we may formulate the overall network activation in a vector form:

$$\underline{a} = W\underline{o} \qquad (10-6a)$$

where

$$\underline{a} = [net_i] \qquad (10-6b)$$

Geometric Analysis of Single-Unit I/O Characteristic.   The basis for forming the net unit activation in (10-4) is an inner product operation. Where the activation-output mapping is linear, for example, (10-1), we observe that the neuron of Figure 5 implements a linear discriminant function. Alternately, input space R^d is partitioned into two half-planes, determined by the unit weights (Appendix 6). Thresholding units, defined in (10-2c) and (10-2d), directly implement this partitioning. In a thresholding unit, the effect of weight w_{ij} is to stretch or contract the jth axis of the hyperspace. Thus, a single thresholding unit can directly implement the decision boundary to a linearly separable two class problem.

Inhibitory Inputs.   It is often desirable to have neuron unit inputs that serve to inhibit the unit's activation. An example of this utility is found in *competitive learning* (Chapter 13). This characteristic may be achieved in several ways. As shown in Figure 5, negative values of w_{ij} that are large in magnitude owing to the summation in (10-4), yield strong inhibitory characteristics. Alternately, a more severe form of inhibition may be achieved through a nonlinear activation-output model, as shown in Figure 6(a).

Other Neural Network Parameters

The Neural Unit Interconnection Strategy or Network Structure.   This may be as simple as allowing each neural output to be connected to all other neurons (perhaps with varying interconnection strength) or constraining the neural unit interconnection to be localized (e.g., the 'diameter-limited' perceptron). Conversely, the neural network interconnection strategy may be quite complex and reflect an n-dimensional and/or hierarchical structure. An example was shown in Figure 2. The latter may more accurately reflect the operation of biological systems.

The Goal or Desired Behavior of the Network.   This may be reflected in the choice of a numerical performance index, enumeration of a set of stable network states, or specification of a desired network output as a function of the network inputs and current state. We examine several of these later.

The Choice of Features Used as Input to the Network, as Well as Interpretation of the State of the Network (Output).   This aspect ranges considerably in neural network implementations, from situations where, for example, the states of individual neurons correspond to values of individual pixel intensities in an input image, to cases where groups of neurons are used to represent the values of certain features of an object. An example of the former is shown below in the character recognition example, and the latter is exemplified by the labeling problem.

The Training or Preprogramming of the Network.   It is not required that networks have a learning capability in all applications. In many cases, however, it is desirable to preprogram the network with information regarding preexisting stable states, for example, in the character recognition problem. Furthermore, it is often desirable to store new information in the network, as new inputs occur. This may be done in several ways, including adjustment of the interconnection network. For example, the Hopfield network uses minimization of a *performance index* via modification of the interconnection network to store additional states.

We note that the design of a neural net for a specific application involves consideration of the above aspects *in an interrelated manner.* For example, one may not independently choose the performance index, neural activation characteristic, and network interconnection for a given application. These design parameters are interrelated and, as shown below, often choice of two of the three constrains choice of the third.

Individual Unit Dynamics Versus Network Dynamics.   Care must be taken to distinguish the aforementioned *unit dynamics* from the dynamics of the neural network. In many cases (e.g., Hopfield nets) the overall network is a large, highly interconnected system of nonlinear elements with feedback. Putting aside stability concerns, such a network, when started in some state, will typically display time-varying behavior or dynamics. These may be described using either differential or difference equations. This is the case *even if the individual units are static input–output mappings, that is, they have no individual dynamical behavior.*

Network Implementations for Constraint Satisfaction and Matching Problems

Another potential utility of networks is in problems involving relational constraint satisfaction such as matching of attributed graphs. Many other symbolic constraint satisfaction problems involve the instantiation of values to variables in an observed relational structure (such as a relational graph) that are *consistent with an underlying constraint-based (relational) model* (such as a semantic net). The neural network may be a suitable structure for mapping into a PDP structure. Instantiation of constrained values to entities may be as direct as activating and inhibiting neuron states in a neural cluster representing the entity, as shown in Chapter 13.

Hardware Realizations of Neural Networks

The descriptor 'artificial' becomes less significant as specific neural network architectures (e.g., Hopfield, BAM, etc.) become available in hardware. An excellent overview is shown in [Roth 1990]. Currently, both electronic (principally analog) and optical implementations are receiving strong attention. A principal advantage of analog ANN implementations using VLSI (Very Large Scale Integrated Circuitry) is that the analog nature of neurons may be directly reflected by circuit elements. However, physical restrictions, such as on-chip unit interconnection densities, power consumption, and precision, continue to offer challenges. For this reason, holographic (optical) approaches are receiving increased attention. Examples of the former are [Mead 1989], [Mead/Mahowald 1988], [Jackel et al. 1987], and [Thakoor et al. 1987]. Optical implementations are explored in [Guest/TeKolste 1987], [Wagner/Psaltis 1987], [Farhat 1987], [Farhat et al. 1985], [White et al. 1988], and [Abu-Mostafa/Psaltis 1987].

The potential processing advantage of hardware achievement of such massively parallel computations is enormous. For the classes of PR problems where neural solutions are appropriate, computational capabilities well beyond that envisioned for digital supercomputers are likely.

BIBLIOGRAPHICAL REMARKS

Despite somewhat overstated early ambitions [Crick 1989], the credibility of neural networks as a research field continues to grow. Applications are beginning to emerge, and some progress in relating neural solutions or neural implementations to 'classical' or conventional solutions is being made. Comprehensive and generally readable references on general neural computing are [Rummelhart/McClelland 1 1986], [Khanna 1990], [Shriver 1988], [Feldman et al. 1988], and [Lippman 1987]. Descriptions of 27 artificial neural system paradigms and a brief history of the area are found in [Simpson 1990]. Biological ramifications are considered in [Rummelhart/McClelland 2 1986], [Rosenblatt 1959], and [Anderson/Rosenfeld 1988]. The flexibility and geometric complexity of decision boundaries resulting from individual unit characteristics and layering of units is shown in [Lippman 1987] and [Stevenson et al. 1990]. The use of neural networks as black box mechanisms for dimensionality reduction in PR is detailed in [Saund 1989]. Readers interested in dedicated hardware for ANN architectures should consult [Mead 1989] and [Roth 1990].

Introduction to Neural Pattern Associators and Matrix Approaches

11

Man errs as long as he strives.

Faust [1808–1832]. *The First Part. Prologue in Heaven*
Johann Wolfgang von Goethe 1749–1832

NEURAL NETWORK–BASED PATTERN ASSOCIATORS

Introduction

In this chapter and Chapter 12, we begin exploring neural approaches to developing *trainable mapping networks* for pattern association. In this chapter, our interest is restricted to linear unit characteristics, which give rise to linear network structures. This allows relating linear networks to linear discriminant functions in StatPR. Furthermore, the linear case allows us to use the tools of linear algebra to develop some insights into pattern storage and recall. In some cases, training or learning algorithms that relate to outer product or correlation-based weight formations result. This introduces the concept of *correlation* or *Hebbian learning* structures.

We also consider (or reconsider) the concepts of linear separability and network storage or association capacity. The limitations of linear networks with regard to both of these lead to and serve as a framework for the nonlinear formulations of Chapters 12 and 13.

Design Procedure

The design procedure for NN pattern classifiers/associators involves the following steps:

- Define suitable inputs/outputs and network structure.

- Choose training method and train network.
- Assess performance.
- Discover meaning/semantics of units (optional).

Different NN structures and input/output representations may yield different training convergence properties. Thus, different solution forms for the same problem exist. In some cases, training can be accelerated and noisy input patterns may be classified or completed by association.

'Black Box' Structure

We begin exploration of several different artificial neural network structures for PR by first considering networks and training algorithms that implement a 'black box' or pattern associator. The network, from a black box or I/O point of view, is shown in Figure 1. In many PR applications, availability of a comprehensive training set allows direct determination of an appropriate input–output mapping that approaches the inverse of the mappings shown in Chapter 1, Figure 1.

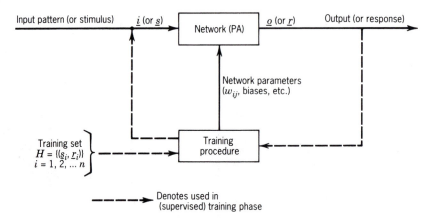

Figure 1:   General network formulation for pattern mapping ('black box' structure).

Inputs to the network are denoted as a vector $\underline{i}$, (or $\underline{s}$, for 'stimulus', or simply $\underline{x}$) and the corresponding desired output is denoted $\underline{o}$ (or $\underline{r}$, for 'response' or simply $\underline{y}$). Recall that the trainable black box approach does not require detailed knowledge of underlying statistical models or pattern structure, but merely a chosen 'internal' structure (which may be invisible to the user) and a training method. Choice of a 'black box' structure still requires several network design considerations involving parameters such as the following:

1. The topology, or structure, of the network;
2. The characteristics of the units;

3. The appropriate formulation of inputs and outputs. For example, as shown in Figure 2, several output structure choices are possible.

4. The design of training or learning procedures.

CAM and Other Neural Memory Structures

Autocorrelator Versus Heterocorrelator Structures.   All of the pattern associator structures in Figure 2 may be visualized as content addressable memories (CAM). These are discussed in Appendix 3. However, part 4 of Figure 2 is especially significant in certain applications. A distinction may be made between *autocorrelator* (or *autoassociative*) structures, where the black box or CAM simply stores (or 'memorizes') patterns, versus *heterocorrelator* (or *heteroassociative*) structures, wherein pattern *pairs* are stored.

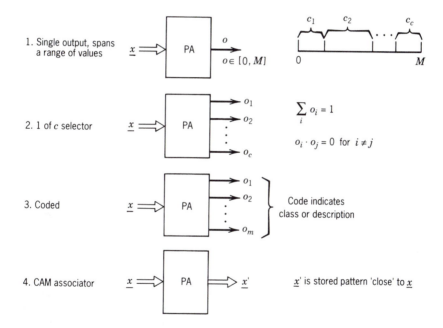

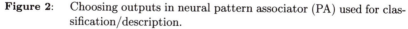

Figure 2:   Choosing outputs in neural pattern associator (PA) used for classification/description.

In autocorrelator structures, a set of d-dimensional patterns, $\underline{x}_k$, $k = 1, 2, \ldots n$, is encoded in the PA 'memory.' The autocorrelator, when presented with a pattern $\underline{x}_u$, is expected to return $\underline{x}_i$, where $\underline{x}_i$ is the stored pattern closest to $\underline{x}_u$. Thus, autoassociative structures are commonly used for pattern recollection, pattern correction, and pattern completion. In contrast, heteroassociative structures encode pattern pairs $(\underline{x}_k, \underline{y}_k)$, $k = 1, 2, \ldots n$, where $\underline{y}_k$ is the desired response for input $\underline{x}_k$. Since the desired response may be a pattern class, heteroassociative structures are commonly used for classification. We may unify the two structures by observing that a heteroassociative structure with pattern pairs $(\underline{x}_k, \underline{x}_k)$, $k = 1, 2, \ldots n$, implements an autoassociative structure.

Nearest Neighbor Versus Interpolative Recall. In both autoassociative and heteroassociative recall, a careful design and characterization of desired network pattern 'association' properties is important. Either structure should respond on the basis of stored patterns or stored pattern pairs. Given $\underline{x}_u$, *nearest neighbor (NN) recall* returns the stored pattern closest (using some measure of similarity) to $\underline{x}_u$. *Interpolative recall*, on the other hand, responds with an output that is based on interpolation over all stored patterns.

Desirable Pattern Associator (PA) Properties

Desirable characteristics of pattern associators include:

1. Ability to associate a reasonable number of pattern (stimulus/response) pairs.
2. Correct pattern response (in light of property 1, that is, correct discrimination ability with large stimulus/response set storage).
3. **(a)** Trainable, given H. (Supervised learning is possible.)
   (b) 'Self-organizing.' Given H_u, the network determines 'natural' data clusters.
4. Ability to associate or generate correct output(s) (response) when input pattern is a distorted or incomplete version of that used in training ('good' pattern association).

MATRIX APPROACHES (LINEAR ASSOCIATIVE MAPPINGS) AND EXAMPLES

The simplicity of linear classifiers and the vast tools available from linear algebra suggests the desirability of designing CAM (auto- or heteroassociative) structures by using matrix techniques. This is appropriate in some, but not all, applications. One of the problems that arises in attempting to apply matrix techniques in the design of pattern associators is the generality of the training data. We explore this in the approaches below.

An Elementary Linear Network Structure and Mathematical Representation

A Single-Layer Network. Referring to the general neuron model of Chapter 10, Figure 5, suppose that we choose the input–output characteristics of neuron i to be linear, and of the form

$$o_i = f_i(net_i) = net_i \qquad (11-1)$$

where the activation is determined by

$$net_i = \sum_j w_{ij}\bar{i}_j \tag{11-2}$$

where $\bar{i}_j$ is the activation source connected to neuron i through weight w_{ij}.[1] For a problem with c (output) units and d inputs, (11-1) and (11-2) may be cast as

$$o_i = <\underline{w}_i, \bar{\underline{i}}> \qquad i = 1, 2, \dots c \tag{11-3}$$

where $\underline{w}_i$ is a $d \times 1$ column vector with respective elements w_{ij}, and $\bar{\underline{i}}$ is a $d \times 1$ vector of inputs, the jth of which is denoted $\bar{i}_j$. This is shown in Figure 3(a). For c outputs, (11-3) may be formulated as

$$\underline{o} = W\bar{\underline{i}} \tag{11-4}$$

where $\underline{o}$ is $c \times 1$, $\bar{\underline{i}}$ is $d \times 1$, and W is a $c \times d$ matrix of the form:

$$W = [w_{ij}] = [\underline{w}_i] \tag{11-5}$$

This is shown in Figure 3(b). Keeping the unit output characteristic of (11-1), but adding a bias to each unit, yields

$$net_i = \sum_j w_{ij}\bar{i}_j + b_i \tag{11-6}$$

or the matrix formulation

$$\underline{o} = W\bar{\underline{i}} + \underline{b} \tag{11-7}$$

Multiple Layers (Linear Units).   Notice that (11-4) may be used to define a multilayer network where, in the two-layer case, the second layer input $\bar{\underline{i}}_2$ is the output of the first layer defined by (11-4), that is, $\bar{\underline{i}}_2 = \bar{\underline{o}}$, and the overall mapping is

$$\underline{o}_2 = W_2\bar{\underline{i}}_2 = W_2 W_1 \bar{\underline{i}} \tag{11-8}$$

Matrices W_1 and W_2 need not have the same dimension. In Chapter 12 multiple nonlinear layers that implement arbitrary mappings are considered.

Matrix Form for Networks with Recurrent Connections and Linear Elements.   Consider a network structure consisting of n^2 totally connected units. In such a network, every unit has a (possibly zero-valued) input connection from the output of every other unit (including itself, i.e., w_{ii} may be nonzero). Assuming, for simplicity, synchronized unit outputs, this linear network is represented by a discrete time difference equation of the form

$$\underline{o}(k+1) = W\underline{o}(k) \tag{11-9}$$

where $\underline{o}(k)$ is a vector of unit outputs at time k. The network therefore has a matrix representation corresponding to an unforced, linear time-invariant system. As a consequence, the network of (11-9) 'stores' information in both interconnections (W)

---

[1] In what follows we will be more specific about the origin of $\bar{i}$.

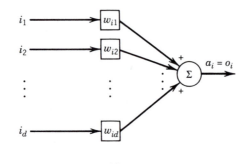

(a)

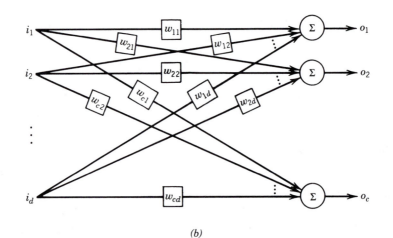

(b)

Figure 3: Single-layer linear networks as matrix computations.
  (a) Single linear unit characteristic corresponding to
    $o_i = \underline{w}_i^T \underline{i}$.
  (b) c-unit network corresponding to $\underline{o} = W\underline{i}$.

and previous states $[\underline{o}(k)]$. Furthermore, the network, over time, displays dynamic behavior.

In relating the above neural network structures to previous StatPR approaches, note that the structure of (11-4) may be visualized as a set of c linear discriminant functions. We now consider several possibilities.

Approach 1: A Linear CAM ('Hopfield') Network[2]

Suppose a simple pattern associator, which stores a d-dimensional pattern vector or stable state $\underline{o}^s$, achieves recall using (11-9) with the desired behavior:

---

[2]This type of network is discussed in detail in Chapter 13.

$$W\underline{o}^s = \underline{o}^s \qquad (11-10)$$

This network is an example of a linear network, with d^2 interconnection weights w_{ij} in W conveying the storage information. By analogy with Hopfield networks (considered in Chapter 13) we might constrain W as follows:

$$w_{ii} = 0 \qquad (11-11a)$$

$$w_{ji} = w_{ji} \quad \text{(symmetry)} \qquad (11-11b)$$

Note, from Appendix 1, that $\underline{o}^s$ in (11-10) corresponds to an e-vector of weight matrix W with corresponding e-value $\lambda = 1$. Unfortunately, the storage capacity of the linear structure of (11-10) is very limited.

Approach 2: Matched Filters/Adaptive Filters

Formulation.   Assume that the training set H consists of n stimulus–response pairs, each of the form $(\underline{s}^i, \underline{r}^i), \quad i = 1, 2, \dots n$. $\underline{s}^i$ is a d-dimensional vector. As a first attempt we could simply try to develop a network that recognizes each $\underline{s}^i$, as a prelude to forming the correct response $(\underline{r}^i)$. Note that the recognition of $\underline{s}^i$ by the network is the difficult part. This could be achieved by using a bank of n matched filters, each of the form

$$\underline{w}_i \underline{s}^i = p^i \qquad i = 1, 2, \dots n \qquad (11-12a)$$

where $\underline{w}_i$ is a $1 \times d$ row vector of weights corresponding to the ith filter and p^i denotes the filter response. Using this approach, $\max_i \{p^i\}$ is computed as a prelude to determining the network response. Equation 11-12a could be reformulated for the entire 'bank' of n filters as

$$W\underline{s} = \underline{p} \qquad (11-12b)$$

where $\underline{s}$ is a $d \times 1$ stimulus pattern (one of the n $\underline{s}^i$), and the ith row of $n \times d$ matrix W^s is $\underline{w}_i$. Thus, W^s 'stores' the n $\underline{s}_i$. In the formulation of (11-13), given a stimulus, $\underline{s}$, the ith element of $\underline{p}$ represents the output or response of the ith matched filter. By determining the largest element of $\underline{p}$, the stored stimulus closest to $\underline{s}$ is found, and the corresponding response $\underline{r}^i$ is generated in a second stage. Note that this structure is merely a neural implementation of a bank of linear discriminant functions (Chapter 2). More generally, the linear pattern associator computation could be shown as

$$W\underline{s} = \underline{r} \qquad (11-12c)$$

where W in (11-12c) is a $c \times d$ matrix that implements the pattern mapping.

Training.   Given H, numerous approaches to training the systems of (11-12a), (11-12b), or (11-12c) exist, including extensions of the iterative and batch techniques of Chapter 4 (linear classifiers). For example, a general formulation of (11-12c), using the n elements of H, yields

$$W[\underline{s}_1 \underline{s}_2 \dots \underline{s}_n] = [\underline{r}_1 \underline{r}_2 \dots \underline{r}_n] \qquad (11-13a)$$

or

$$WS = R \qquad (11-13b)$$

where W is $c \times d$, S is $d \times n$, and R is $c \times n$. Although a more direct formulation is considered in Approach 4, (11-13a) may be viewed as a set of n linear equations of the form

$$S\underline{w}_i = \underline{r}_i \qquad i = 1, 2, \ldots c \qquad (11-13c)$$

where $\underline{w}_i$ is the ith *row* of W. Each equation in (11-13c) yields a constraint on the values of $\underline{w}_i$ and may be solved independently for the corresponding row of W. Either iterative [that is, using the $(\underline{s}_k, \underline{r}_k)$ pairs individually and sequentially], or 'batch' (pseudoinverse) solution forms are possible. Furthermore, determination of $\underline{w}_i$ for each pattern pair may be done adaptively, as shown in Chapter 12. Appendix 4 shows a visualization of this process, which is continued and extended in Chapter 12 and in Approach 4 below.

Approach 3: Outer Product Formulations

Storage of a Single Pattern.   Given a single stimulus–response pair $(\underline{s}, \underline{r})$ with $d \times 1$ stimulus vector $\underline{s}$ normalized to unit length, that is, $\| \underline{s} \| = \sqrt{\underline{s}^T \underline{s}} = 1$, consider the formation of

$$W = \underline{r}\,\underline{s}^T \qquad (11-14)$$

Recall that $\underline{r}$ is $c \times 1$, so W is a $c \times d$ rank 1 matrix formed via the outer product operation of (11-14). Note that W is not necessarily square. The ijth element of W is the product $r_i s_j$. For an arbitrary stimulus vector, (11-12c) is used to find the network response. In the case $\underline{s}$ is the vector used to train the system in (11-14), forming the matrix product

$$W\underline{s} = \underline{r}\underline{s}^T \underline{s} = \| \underline{s} \|^2 \underline{r} = \underline{r} \qquad (11-15)$$

the correct response $\underline{r}$ is generated. If a stimulus vector $\underline{s}'$ is a distorted version of $\underline{s}$, the linear network response is

$$W\underline{s}' = \underline{r}\underline{s}^T \underline{s}' = (\underline{s}^T \underline{s}')\underline{r} \qquad (11-16)$$

where the term $\underline{s}^T \underline{s}'$ represents a weight that causes the network output to be a scaled version of the trained response. For normalized $\underline{s}$ and $\underline{s}'$, the reader should verify from the cosine inequality (Appendix 5) that

$$\underline{s}^T \underline{s}' < \| \underline{s} \|^2 \qquad (11-17a)$$

and therefore the weight or scaling of response $\underline{r}$ using (11-15) is

$$\underline{s}^T \underline{s}' < 1 \qquad (11-17b)$$

Storage of Multiple Patterns.   It is desirable to be able to use (11-14) and (11-15) to store several $(\underline{s}^i, \underline{r}^i)$ pairs, $i = 1, 2, \ldots n$. Consider forming W for the n-pair storage case by superposition of the single-pair case of (11-14), that is,

$$W = \sum_{i=1}^{n} \underline{r}^i (\underline{s}^i)^T \qquad (11-18)$$

Given an input stimulus, denoted $\underline{s}_u$, the response is computed from

$$W\underline{s}_u = \sum_{i=1}^{n} \underline{r}^i (\underline{s}^i)^T \underline{s}_u = \sum_{i=1}^{n} [(\underline{s}^i)^T \underline{s}_u] \underline{r}^i \qquad (11-19)$$

Notice that n terms contribute to the output in (11-19). Suppose the desired response to input $\underline{s}_u$ is $\underline{r}^p$, that is, $\underline{s}_u$ corresponds to $\underline{s}^p$ in 'stored' association $(\underline{s}^p, \underline{r}^p)$. A desirable characteristic in (11-19) would be

$$< \underline{s}^i, \underline{s}^p > = \delta_{ip} = \begin{cases} 1 & \text{for } i = p \\ 0 & \text{elsewhere} \end{cases} \qquad (11-20)$$

where δ is the Kroneker delta. Equation 11-20 defines $S = [\underline{s}^i]$ as a set of n orthonormal vectors, which could be achieved by using the Gram–Schmidt orthogonalization process. Unfortunately, since the $\underline{s}^i$ are input patterns or stimuli (and therefore not always controllable by the PR system designer), this desirable orthogonality is difficult to obtain in a general problem.

Approach 4: Generalized Inverse Applications

Generalized Inverses.   Given a general matrix equation

$$\underline{y} = A\underline{x} \qquad (11-21)$$

the concept of a generalized inverse, or pseudoinverse for A has been long studied [Penrose 1955]. If we denote the pseudoinverse of A as $A^\dagger$, $A^\dagger$ has the following characterizations:

$$AA^\dagger A = A \qquad (11-22a)$$

$$A^\dagger = A^{-1} \quad \text{if } A \text{ is square and nonsingular} \qquad (11-22b)$$

$$A^\dagger A = I \quad \text{(denoted the left inverse)} \qquad (11-22c)$$

$$AA^\dagger = I \quad \text{(denoted the right inverse)} \qquad (11-22d)$$

$$(A^\dagger)^\dagger = A \qquad (11-22e)$$

An especially important property is that *if A has full column rank,*

$$A^\dagger = (A^T A)^{-1} A^T \qquad (11-23)$$

This formulation of the pseudoinverse is most commonly associated with least squares solutions (Appendix 1).

Heteroassociators Directly from Generalized Inverses.   Suppose that the linear heteroassociative network structure is formulated by using (11-12c)

$$W\underline{s}_k = \underline{r}_k \qquad k = 1, 2, \ldots n \qquad (11-24)$$

where $\underline{r}_k$ is the $c \times 1$ response vector, $\underline{s}_k$ is a $d \times 1$ stimulus vector, and W is the $c \times d$ matrix that represents the linear network interconnection structure. The problem is determining W, especially when the training set $H = \{(\underline{s}_k, \underline{r}_k)\}$ is arbitrary. Using H, the formulation of (11-13b) yields:

$$WS = R \qquad (11-25)$$

Assuming S has full column rank, (11-25) is postmultiplied by $S^\dagger$, and (11-22d) yields

$$RS^\dagger = WSS^\dagger = W \qquad (11-26)$$

or

$$W = R(S^T S)^{-1} S^T \qquad (11-27)$$

When the $d \times n$ stimulus matrix S in (11-13b) or (11-25) does not have full column rank, there are not n linearly independent columns in S, and the procedure of (11-27) breaks down. One way to overcome this problem is to use *dummy augmentation* [Wang et al. 1990] on each of the $d \times 1$ stimulus vectors, $\underline{s}_i$. Additional components $(d + 1, d + 2, \text{etc.})$ are added to each vector to achieve a set of higher dimensional vectors that are linearly independent in the higher dimensional vector space.

Simplification for Orthogonal S.   Equation 11-27 is simplified considerably when S (the matrix of columns that are the stimulus vectors) is orthogonal.[3] In this case,

$$S^\dagger = S^{-1} = S^T \qquad (11-28)$$

so that

$$W = RS^T \qquad (11-29)$$

Expanding (11-29) yields

$$W = [\underline{r}_1 \, \underline{r}_2 \, \cdots \, \underline{r}_n] \begin{pmatrix} \underline{s}_1^T \\ \underline{s}_2^T \\ \vdots \\ \underline{s}_n^T \end{pmatrix} \qquad (11-30)$$

$$= \sum_{i=1}^{n} \underline{r}_i \underline{s}_i^T \qquad (11-31)$$

This reduces to an outer product formulation, and should be compared with (11-18) in Approach 3.

---

[3] Actually, it is considerably simplified when S is just invertable.

Extended Example: Heteroassociative Memory Design

Determining W.   Consider the following $n = 3$ training set, consisting of $d = 3$ S–R pairs $(\underline{s}_i, \underline{r}_i)$ where

$$\underline{s}_1 = \begin{pmatrix} 4 \\ 1 \\ 1 \end{pmatrix} \qquad \underline{r}_1 = \begin{pmatrix} 1 \\ 0 \\ 0 \end{pmatrix} \qquad (11-32a)$$

$$\underline{s}_2 = \begin{pmatrix} 4 \\ 1 \\ 0 \end{pmatrix} \qquad \underline{r}_2 = \begin{pmatrix} 0 \\ 1 \\ 0 \end{pmatrix} \qquad (11-32b)$$

$$\underline{s}_3 = \begin{pmatrix} 2 \\ 0 \\ 1 \end{pmatrix} \qquad \underline{r}_3 = \begin{pmatrix} 0 \\ 0 \\ 1 \end{pmatrix} \qquad (11-32c)$$

Clearly, the form of the desired output of the PA is a 1-of-3 selector, where in this $c = 3$ class example, element $r_i = 1$ corresponds to the (binary) classification of stimulus $\underline{s}_k$ to class w_i. In this example, (11-25) becomes

$$R = \overset{3 \times 3}{I} \qquad (11-33)$$

and

$$S = (\underline{s}_1 \ \underline{s}_2 \ \underline{s}_3) = \begin{pmatrix} 4 & 4 & 2 \\ 1 & 1 & 0 \\ 1 & 0 & 1 \end{pmatrix} \qquad (11-34)$$

Since S has full column rank and is of dimension 3×3, S is invertible (the reader should verify this), and by using (11-22b) and (11-28) W becomes

$$W = S^{-1} = \begin{pmatrix} -\frac{1}{2} & 2 & 1 \\ \frac{1}{2} & -1 & -1 \\ \frac{1}{2} & -2 & 0 \end{pmatrix} \qquad (11-35)$$

Verification of Recall Properties.   The reader should verify that, for the S–R pairs given in (11-32), the trained interconnection matrix of (11-35) yields

$$W\underline{s}_i = \underline{r}_i \qquad i = 1, 2, 3 \qquad (11-36)$$

It is interesting to consider the response of the network for both the training set and perturbed stimulus patterns. For example, given a perturbed version of $\underline{s}_1$, denoted $\underline{s}_p$, where

$$\underline{s}_p = \begin{pmatrix} 4 \\ 1 \\ 2 \end{pmatrix} \qquad (11-37a)$$

the response is

$$\underline{r}_p = W \underline{s}_p = \begin{pmatrix} 2 \\ -1 \\ 0 \end{pmatrix} \qquad (11-37b)$$

Clearly the network displays an interpolative form of response. This example is continued in the exercises. ∎

Hebbian or Correlation-Based Learning

A number of learning or training paradigms are used in neural systems. All, to some extent, involve learning or training as a change in 'memory.' Several of the previous approaches have relied on outer product or correlation techniques for weight determination. For example, consider the following ternary valued stimulus–response pair $(\underline{s}, \underline{r})$ where

$$\underline{s} = \begin{pmatrix} 1 \\ 1 \\ 1 \end{pmatrix} = \begin{pmatrix} s_1 \\ s_2 \\ s_3 \end{pmatrix} \qquad (11-38a)$$

and

$$\underline{r} = \begin{pmatrix} 1 \\ 0 \\ -1 \end{pmatrix} = \begin{pmatrix} r_1 \\ r_2 \\ r_3 \end{pmatrix} \qquad (11-38b)$$

For this pattern pair, the network weights, using (11-14) or (11-30), are

$$W = [w_{ij}] = \underline{r}\,\underline{s}^T = \begin{pmatrix} 1 & 1 & 1 \\ 0 & 0 & 0 \\ -1 & -1 & -1 \end{pmatrix} \qquad (11-38c)$$

In (11-38c), interconnection w_{11} is positive, indicating a (desired) positive correlation between s_1 and r_1. Conversely, w_{31} is negative, indicating a negative correlation, or relationship, between s_1 and r_3. From (11-18), the overall network weight set is determined by summation of the individual weights. Thus, each weight component of the form

$$\triangle w_{ij} = s_j \cdot r_i \qquad (11-39)$$

where s_j and r_i are the jth and ith components of $\underline{s}$ and $\underline{r}$, respectively, represents an incremental portion of the overall network weight w_{ij}. The overall weight is $w_{ij} = \sum_n \triangle w_{ij}$. Training set pattern pairs where s_j and r_i are positive increase or reinforce w_{ij}. If many such patterns appear in H, then as w_{ij} is developed sequentially processing H, the connection strength w_{ij} 'builds up' or becomes large and positive. This is an example of *Hebbian learning*. A similar remark holds for a negative correlation between s_j and r_j.

BIBLIOGRAPHICAL REMARKS

Hebbian, or correlation-based learning seems to have originated with [Hebb 1949]. Excellent sources for extensions and related work are [Kohonen 1972], [Kohonen 1984], and [Barto et al. 1981]. An especially good modern introduction to the concept of a generalized inverse is [Strang 1976]. A related strategy that achieves heteroassociative memory using a recurrent network of nonlinear (bipolar) elements is Bidirectional Associative Memory (BAM) [Kosko 1987], [Kosko 1988], and [Wang et al. 1990]. The basis of the BAM structure is Hebbian or correlation-based learning.

EXERCISES

11.1   Using (11-19), determine the response of the pattern associator to a distorted version of $\underline{s}$. Consider normalized vectors and both orthogonal and nonorthogonal cases.

11.2   Verify that (11-29) reduces to (11-31).

11.3   Verify (11-36).

11.4   Consider the response of the PA developed in (11-33) to (11-35) to the following perturbed inputs:

$$\underline{s}_{1p} = \begin{pmatrix} 2 \\ 1 \\ 1 \end{pmatrix} \qquad \underline{s}_{2p} = \begin{pmatrix} 4 \\ 0 \\ 1 \end{pmatrix} \qquad \underline{s}_{3p} = \begin{pmatrix} 2 \\ 0 \\ 0 \end{pmatrix}$$

How does the 'perturbation' of each of the above vectors (when compared with the training set) affect or perturb the response? (Again, with respect to the given $\underline{r}_i$.)

11.5   Consider an extension of a PA design example with inputs previously specified by (11-33) as follows:

$$\underline{s}_1 = \begin{pmatrix} 4 \\ 1 \\ 1 \end{pmatrix} \quad \underline{r}_1 = \begin{pmatrix} 1 \\ 0 \\ 0 \\ 0 \\ 0 \end{pmatrix} \quad \underline{s}_2 = \begin{pmatrix} 4 \\ 1 \\ 0 \end{pmatrix} \quad \underline{r}_2 = \begin{pmatrix} 0 \\ 1 \\ 0 \\ 0 \\ 0 \end{pmatrix}$$

$$\underline{s}_3 = \begin{pmatrix} 2 \\ 0 \\ 1 \end{pmatrix} \quad \underline{r}_3 = \begin{pmatrix} 0 \\ 0 \\ 1 \\ 0 \\ 0 \end{pmatrix} \quad \underline{s}_4 = \begin{pmatrix} 2 \\ 0 \\ 0 \end{pmatrix} \quad \underline{r}_4 = \begin{pmatrix} 0 \\ 0 \\ 0 \\ 0 \\ 1 \end{pmatrix}$$

(Note that this corresponds to the example of Chapter 12, Figure 3.)

(a) Formulate S and R.

(b) Consider forming the pseudoinverse of S. You will immediately note that S cannot have full column rank, and therefore the formulation of (11-23) is not applicable. Is this a consequence of the network having 'more outputs than features'? Does this suggest a problem with PA 'memory capacity'?

(c) Develop a PA for this case, using an alternative procedure.

11.6 [This problem explores the type of recall or association provided by a pseudoinverse-based PA. The results of (11-33) to (11-35) may be useful for verification.] Suppose a perturbed input pattern is a linear combination of the n stored patterns (denoted $\underline{s}_i$), i.e.,

$$\underline{s}_p = \sum_{i=1}^{n} k_i \underline{s}_i \qquad (P.6-1)$$

Is the PA response to $\underline{s}_p$ denoted $\underline{r}_p$ formed in the following manner?

$$\underline{r}_p = \sum_{i=1}^{n} k_i \underline{r}_i \qquad (P.6-2)$$

11.7 Referring to Table P.1, corresponding to Chapter 4, Exercise 4.6, develop a pseudoinverse-based PA for the training data shown.

11.8 Repeat Exercise 11.7 for the training data of Chapter 3, Figure P.5.

11.9 In this problem we investigate the rationale behind and influence of *repeated pattern pairs* in H. For example, suppose H contains two or more occurrences of a redundant pattern pair $(\underline{s}^{red}, \underline{r}^{red})$.

(a) Suppose $\underline{r}^{red}$ is a classification decision for stimulus pattern $\underline{s}^{red}$. If H accurately reflects patterns the PR system is likely to encounter, does the frequency of occurrence of $(\underline{s}^{red}, \underline{r}^{red})$ suggest anything concerning the a priori probability $P(w_r)$ where decision $\underline{r}^{red}$ corresponds to class w_r?

(b) What is the effect of this repeated pattern in developing weights using (11-18)? (Relate to Hebbian learning.)

(c) What is the effect of this repeated pattern in attempting to use the pseudoinverse training procedure?

(d) Discuss the circumstances under which the redundant patterns should be retained versus eliminated from H.

Feedforward Networks and Training by Backpropagation

12

Science repulses the indefinite.

Introduction à l'Étude de la Médecine Expérimentale [1865]
Claude Bernard 1813–1878

MULTILAYER, FEEDFORWARD NETWORK STRUCTURE

Introduction

In this chapter a neural network with a layered, feedforward structure and error gradient–based training algorithm is developed. Although a single-layer network of this type, known as the 'perceptron,' has existed since the late '50s [Minsky/Papert 1969], it did not see widespread application owing to its limited classification ability and the lack of a training algorithm for the multilayer case. Furthermore, the training procedure evolved from the early work of Widrow [Widrow/Hoff 1960] in single-element, nonlinear adaptive systems such as ADALINE.

Overall Feedforward Structure

The *feedforward network* is composed of a hierarchy of processing units, organized in a series of two or more mutually exclusive sets of neurons or layers. The first, or input, layer serves as a holding site for the values applied to the network. The last, or output, layer is the point at which the final state of the network is read. Between these two extremes lie zero or more layers of hidden units. Links, or weights, connect each unit in one layer to only those in the next-higher layer. There is an implied directionality in these connections, in that the output of a unit, scaled by the value of a connecting weight, is fed forward to provide a portion of the activation for the units in the next-higher layer. Figure 1 illustrates the typical feedforward network. The network as shown consists of a layer of d input units (L_i), a layer of c output units (L_o), and a variable number (5 in this example) of internal or 'hidden' layers (L_{h_i}) of units. Observe the *feedforward* structure, where the inputs are directly connected to only units in L_i, and the outputs of layer L_k units are connected only to units in layer L_{k+1}.[1]

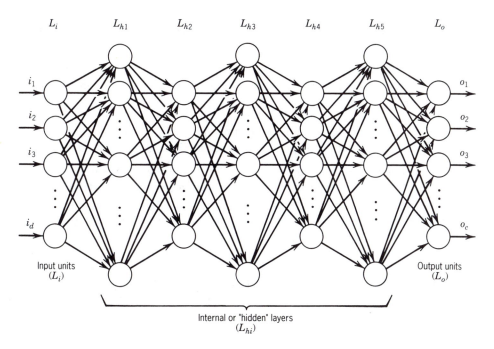

Figure 1:   Structure of a multiple-layer feedforward network.

The role of the input layer is somewhat fictitious, in that input layer units are used only to 'hold' input values and distribute these values to all units in the next layer. Thus, the input layer units do not implement a separate mapping or conversion of the input data, and their weights are insignificant. The feedforward network must have the ability to learn pattern mappings. The network may be made to function as a pattern associator through training. Training is accomplished by presenting the patterns to be classified to the network and determining its output. The actual output of the network is compared with a 'target' and an error measure is calculated. The error measure is then propagated backward through the network and used to determine weight changes within the network. This process is repeated until the network reaches a desired state of response. Although this is an idealized description of training, this does not imply that an arbitrary network will converge to the desired response.

---

[1]Or are outputs, if $L_k = L_o$.

The Role of Internal/Hidden Layers (What's 'Hidden'?)

There are several interesting and related interpretations that may be attached to the units in the internal layers (the internal units). They are the following:

1. The internal layers *remap* the inputs and results of other (previous) internal layers to achieve a more separable[2] or 'classifiable' representation of the data. In fact, in this case suitable external preprocessing (or remapping) of the inputs can have the same effect.

2. The internal layers may allow attachment of semantics to certain combinations of layer inputs.

How Many Hidden Layers Are Needed?   This is possibly one of the most interesting and difficult questions related to multilayer, feedforward networks. A corollary is

'How many units should be in a (the) hidden layer?'

To answer these questions, we show a nonconstructive existence proof by Kolmogorov in 1957 [Sprecher 1965], and popularized by [Hecht-Nielsen 2 1987].

Kolmogorov's Mapping Neural Network Existence Theorem.   Given any continuous function $\phi : I^d \rightarrow R^c$, $\phi(x) = y$, where I is the closed unit interval $[0, 1]$ (and therefore I^d is the d-dimensional unit cube), ϕ can be implemented exactly by a three-layer neural network having d processing elements in the input layer, $(2d + 1)$ processing elements in the (single) hidden layer, and c processing elements in the output layer. As noted above, the input layer serves merely to 'hold' or freeze the input and distribute each input to the hidden layer.

The processing elements in the hidden layer implement the mapping function

$$z_k = \sum_{j=1}^{d} \lambda^k \psi(x_j + \epsilon k) + k \tag{12-1}$$

where x_i are the network inputs and the real constant λ as well as the continuous real monotonic increasing function ψ are independent of ϕ (although they do depend on d). The constant ϵ is a rational number $0 < \epsilon \leq \delta$, where δ is an arbitrarily chosen positive constant. Further, it can be shown that ψ can be chosen to satisfy a Lipschitz condition $|\psi(x) - \psi(y)| \leq c|x - y|^\alpha$ for any $0 < \alpha \leq 1$.

The output layer elements implement the following mapping

$$y_i = \sum_{k=1}^{2d+1} g_i(z_k) \tag{12-2}$$

where the functions g_i, $i = 1, 2, \ldots, c$ are real and continuous (and depend on ϕ and ϵ).

The utility of this result is somewhat limited since no indication of how to construct the ψ and g_i functions is given. For example, it is not known whether the commonly used sigmoidal characteristics even approximate these functions.

---

[2]Linearly separable.

The concept of layered machines and input remapping is explored further in the exercises.

Training Considerations

Once an appropriate network structure is chosen, much of the effort in designing a neural network for PR concerns the design of a reasonable training strategy. Often, for example, while observing a particular training experiment, the designer will notice the weight adjustment strategy 'favoring' particular S–R patterns, becoming 'painfully' slow (perhaps while stuck in a local minimum), becoming unstable, or oscillating between solutions. This necessitates engineering judgment in considering the following training parameters:

- Training by pattern or epoch;
- Use of momentum and corresponding weight;
- Learning weight and weight changes over time;
- Sequential vs. random ordering of training vectors;
- Determining whether the training algorithm is 'stuck' at a local energy minimum;
- Choosing 'suitable' unit biases (if applicable);
- Designing appropriate initial conditions on biases, weights, and so on.

As shown in what follows, training the network structure of Figure 1 with the 'GDR' algorithm is akin to developing a data-dependent filter.

Adding (an Optional) Bias to the Artificial Neuron Model.   In many applications, it is advantageous to consider modifying the neural unit characteristic to include a *bias*. For example, recalling the sigmoidal activation function

$$f(net_j) = \frac{1}{1 + e^{-net_j}} \qquad (12-3)$$

we observe that

$$0 \le f(net_j) \le 1 \qquad (12-4)$$

and with no activation, that is,

$$net_i = 0 \qquad (12-5a)$$

$$f(0) = \frac{1}{2} \qquad (12-5b)$$

We may wish to bias this unit such that $f(0)$ is another value. As we show later, this bias may also be adjusted as part of the network training. A simple model for the unit with bias is to modify net_j; such that

$$net_j = \sum_i w_{ji} o_i + bias_j \qquad (12-6)$$

TRAINING THE FEEDFORWARD NETWORK: THE DELTA RULE (DR) AND GENERALIZED DELTA RULE (GDR)

Overview

The GDR is a *product learning rule* for a feedforward, multiple-layer structured neural network that uses gradient descent to achieve training or *learning by error correction*. Network weights are adjusted to minimize an error based on a measure of the difference between desired and actual feedforward network output. Desired input–output behavior is given by the training set. The GDR is one instance of a training algorithm for a NN-based pattern associator with the structure shown in Figure 2.

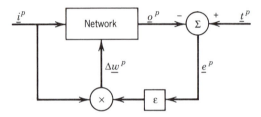

Note: $\otimes$ denotes product indicated in (12–8)

Figure 2: Structure of iterative training strategy using pth element of H.

Basic Operation of the Generalized Delta Rule (GDR).

- Apply input (stimulus) vector to network.
- 'Feed forward' or propagate input pattern to determine all unit outputs.
- Compare unit outputs in output layer with desired pattern response.
- Compute and propagate error measure backward (starting at output layer) through network.
- Minimize error at each stage through unit weight adjustments.

Terminology. The following are defined:

$\underline{i}$: input pattern (vector),

$\underline{o}$: corresponding output pattern or response (vector),

$\underline{w}$: network weights (vector),

$\underline{t}$: desired (or target) system output (vector).

To begin with, we consider a 2-layer network (that is, a structure with no 'hidden' units). Thus, $\underline{i}$ denotes the state of the input layer, and $\underline{o}$ denotes the state of the output layer. Recall that weight w_{ji} denotes the strength of interconnection FROM unit i (or network input i) TO unit j.[3] Using this structure, we develop the delta rule (DR). We

---

[3]Although the notation may bother some readers, we consider w_{ji} (as opposed to w_{ij}) in order to develop a notation that is consistent with most (not all) of the literature, as well as Chapters 10, 11, and 13.

later extend this formulation to the multilayer case, to develop the generalized delta rule (GDR).

Gradient Descent Approaches for Training

The basis of the algorithms derived below is gradient descent (Appendix 1, 4). Specifically, to adjust network weights we compute (or estimate) a mapping error E, and the gradient $\partial E / \partial w_{ji}$. The weight adjustment $\triangle w_{ji}$, is then set proportional to $-\partial E / \partial w_{ji}$.

The training set for this type of network consists of ordered pairs of vectors and is denoted

$$H = \{(\underline{i}^k, \underline{t}^k)\} \qquad k = 1, 2, \ldots, n \qquad (12-7)$$

where, for the pth input–output pair $i_i^p \in \underline{i}^p$ is the ith input element (also denoted i_{pi} in the literature). Similarly, o_j^p (also denoted o_{pj} in the literature) and t_j^p (or t_{pj}) are the jth elements of $\underline{o}^p$ and $\underline{t}^p$, respectively, where $\underline{o}^p$ is the actual network output resulting from input $\underline{i}^p$ and the current set of network weights $\underline{w}$. Given a preselected network structure, the goal is to develop a learning or training algorithm that uses $\underline{i}^p$, $\underline{o}^p$, and $\underline{t}^p$ to adjust the network weights.

An Initial Weight Adjustment Strategy. We initially postulate a form for individual weight correction, or update, based on the difference between $\underline{t}^p$ and $\underline{o}^p$, for a pre-specified $\underline{i}^p$, as

$$\triangle^p w_{ji} = \epsilon(t_j^p - o_j^p)i_i^p = \epsilon(e_j^p)i_i^p \qquad (12-8)$$

where ϵ is an adjustment or scaling parameter and the error of the jth output unit is defined

$$e_j^p \equiv t_j^p - o_j^p \qquad (12-9)$$

The superscript p on $\triangle^p w_{ji}$ indicates that the weight correction is based upon the pth input–output pair of H. This is thus a pattern-based training strategy.

Intuitive Assessment of the Correction Procedure. The training or learning procedure of (12-8) is intuitively appealing. For nonzero and positive i_i^p, if the desired output of the jth unit is less than that actually obtained, (o_j^p), the interconnection between input unit i and output unit j is strengthened, by increasing w_{ji}. We should note, however, that we have not considered the effect of this change on the network response to other pattern pairs in the training process. Furthermore, $i_j^p = 0$ does not result in a correction, even for nonzero e_j^p. For the pth training sample this scheme has the overall structure shown in Figure 2. *This is typical of a product-based weight correction or adjustment rule.* Notice that this also is a specific case of the training strategy shown in Chapter 11, Figure 1.

Training by Sample or Training by Epoch

We could correct the network weights for the pth training pair using (12-8) for all i and j as indicated above and thus implement *training by sample*. An alternative is training by epoch, where we form

$$\triangle \bar{w}_{ji} = \sum_p \triangle^p w_{ji} \qquad (12-10)$$

This represents an overall or accumulated correction to the weight set after each sweep of all pattern pairs in the training set, or training 'epoch.' Of course, intermediate or hybrid training methods are also possible. This parallels our concern for adjustment of the weights in developing linear discriminant functions for StatPR in Chapter 4.

Derivation of the DR

We have shown intuitively, and somewhat imprecisely, that the previous weight correction scheme makes sense. We now formalize the analysis. We define an output error *vector* for the pth pattern pair as

$$\underline{e}^p = \underline{t}^p - \underline{o}^p \qquad (12-11)$$

A scalar measure of the output error based on the pth training sample is denoted E_p and defined as

$$E_p = \frac{1}{2}(\underline{e}^p)^T \underline{e}^p = \frac{1}{2} \parallel \underline{e}^p \parallel^2 \qquad (12-12)$$

Quick Review of the Chain Rule. To rigorously derive the DR algorithm, we need to consider the *chain rule* and composite functions. E_p is an example of a composite function. Without proof, we observe the following:

- A differentiable function of a differentiable function is itself differentiable.
- If $\varsigma = \phi(x, y, \ldots)$, $\eta = \psi(x, y, \ldots)$, $\ldots$ are differentiable functions of $x, y, \ldots$, and $f(\varsigma, \eta, \ldots)$ is a differentiable function of $\varsigma, \eta, \ldots$, then $f[\phi(x, y, \ldots), \psi(x, y, \ldots), \ldots]$ is a differentiable function of $x, y, \ldots$,[4] with partial derivatives given by

$$\frac{\partial f}{\partial x} = \frac{\partial f}{\partial \phi}\frac{\partial \phi}{\partial x} + \frac{\partial f}{\partial \psi}\frac{\partial \psi}{\partial x} + \ldots \qquad (12-13a)$$

$$\frac{\partial f}{\partial y} = \frac{\partial f}{\partial \phi}\frac{\partial \phi}{\partial y} + \frac{\partial f}{\partial \psi}\frac{\partial \psi}{\partial y} + \ldots \qquad (12-13b)$$

$$\vdots$$

This result is independent of the number of independent variables $x, y, \ldots$

A General Assessment of Error Sensitivity

The chain rule is used in various ways to formally develop the DR and GDR training algorithms. For example, consider the formulation

---

[4]Specification of the region R over which this holds true is also necessary.

$$\frac{\partial E_p}{\partial w_{ji}} = \frac{\partial E_p}{\partial o_j^p} \frac{\partial o_j^p}{\partial net_j^p} \frac{\partial net_j^p}{\partial w_{ji}} \qquad (12-14)$$

where, from (12-11) and (12-12),

$$E_p = \frac{1}{2} \parallel \underline{t}^p - \underline{o}^p \parallel^2 \qquad (12-15)$$

or

$$E_p = \frac{1}{2} \sum_j (t_j^p - o_j^p)^2 \qquad (12-16)$$

We could also develop an alternative formulation by considering the total epoch error

$$E = \sum_p E_p \qquad (12-17)$$

Therefore, $2E$ and $2E_p$ are sums of squared errors.

Assume an activation function for the jth output unit of the general form:

$$o_j^p = f_j(w_{ji}, \underline{i}^p) \qquad (12-18)$$

where f_j is a *nondecreasing* and *differentiable* function with respect to each of its arguments.[5] Typically, f_j is the same, that is, all units have the same activation function. Recall that our weight convention for the artificial neuron activation for unit j is formed from the weighted linear sum of the inputs to unit j:

$$net_j = \sum_i w_{ji} i_i \qquad (12-19)$$

or, in the case where a bias input is included

$$net_j = \sum_i w_{ji} i_i + bias_j \qquad (12-20)$$

Note that (12-20) shows a model of a neural unit where the bias is added directly to net_j. The training of the bias input is considered in a later section entitled 'Training the Unit Bias Inputs.' The exercises explore additional alternatives for modeling and training unit biases.

Recall that i_i is the ith input to unit j and f is chosen to be a sigmoid function, that is,

$$f(net_j) = \frac{1}{1 + e^{-net_j}} \qquad (12-21)$$

Consider

$$\frac{\partial E_p}{\partial w_{ji}} = \frac{\partial E_p}{\partial o_j^p} \frac{\partial o_j^p}{\partial w_{ji}} \qquad (12-22)$$

---

[5]Unless this holds true, the derivatives we compute are meaningless. Thus, linear threshold units (relay-like characteristics) may not be handled without modification. Strictly linear output functions $[f(net_j) = k \times net_j$, for example], are acceptable but yield other shortcomings.

which represents the incremental change in E_p due to incremental change in network weight w_{ji}. The first term, $\partial E_p/\partial o_j^p$, is the effect on E_p due to the jth output, whereas the second term, $\partial o_j^p/\partial w_{ji}$, measures the change on o_j^p as a function of ∂w_{ji}. From (12-16), $\partial E_p/\partial o_j^p$ is easy to form for units in the output layer

$$\frac{\partial E_p}{\partial o_j^p} = -(t_j^p - o_j^p) = -e_j^p \tag{12-23}$$

from the definition in (12-9). The second term in (12-22) requires closer examination.

The Case of Linear Units.   For illustration, assume that we have linear units, where $f(net_j)$ is the identity function $[f(net_j) = net_j]$. Therefore, from (12-18) through (12-20)

$$o_j^p = \sum_i w_{ji} i_i^p \tag{12-24}$$

so that

$$\frac{\partial o_j^p}{\partial w_{ji}} = i_i^p \tag{12-25}$$

Therefore, (12-22) becomes

$$\frac{\partial E_p}{\partial w_{ji}} = (-e_j^p)(i_i^p) \tag{12-26}$$

which is the product form postulated in (12-8). From this, a gradient descent approach may be developed. To verify that this strategy minimizes the epoch error E, note from (12-17) that

$$\frac{\partial E}{\partial w_{ji}} = \sum_p \frac{\partial E_p}{\partial w_{ji}} \tag{12-27}$$

The case of hidden units requires an extension of the previous derivation.

Application to Semilinear Activation Functions.   A *semilinear activation function* f_j for the jth neuron

$$o_j^p = f_j(net_j^p) \tag{12-28}$$

is one where f_j is nondecreasing and differentiable. Recall that if $f_j(net_j^p) = k \times net_j^p$, we revert to a linear activation function. The correction procedure developed above, though an important step, must be modified for the case where the units are not linear, but semilinear. Therefore, we revise our formulation of (12-22) as follows:

$$\frac{\partial E_p}{\partial w_{ji}} = \frac{\partial E_p}{\partial net_j^p} \frac{\partial net_j^p}{\partial w_{ji}} \tag{12-29}$$

where

$$net_j^p = \sum_i w_{ji} \tilde{o}_i^p \tag{12-30a}$$

In order to generalize our results to hidden units, we model the ith input to neuron j, denoted $\tilde{o}_i^p$, as

$$\tilde{o}_i^p = \begin{cases} o_i^p & \text{if input is the output of a neuron in a previous layer} \\ & \text{(true for unit inputs in hidden and output layers)} \\ \\ i_i & \text{if this input is a direct input to the network (from the} \\ & \text{input layer)} \end{cases} \qquad (12-30b)$$

From (12-30),

$$\frac{\partial net_j^p}{\partial w_{ji}} = \tilde{o}_i^p \qquad (12-31)$$

Defining the sensitivity of the pattern error on the net activation of the jth unit as

$$\delta_j^p = -\frac{\partial E_p}{\partial net_j^p} \qquad (12-32)$$

(12-29) may be written

$$\frac{\partial E_p}{\partial w_{ji}} = -(\delta_j^p)\tilde{o}_i^p \qquad (12-33)$$

Therefore, by analogy with the previous case, a reasonable iterative weight correction procedure using the pth training sample is to use

$$\triangle^p w_{ji} = -\epsilon \left(\frac{\partial E_p}{\partial w_{ji}} \right) \qquad (12-34a)$$

where ϵ is a positive constant, referred to as the *learning rate.*

Learning Rate.   The learning rate determines what portion of the calculated weight change will be used for correction. The 'best' value of the learning rate depends on the characteristics of the error surface, that is, the plot of E vs. w_{ij}. If the surface changes rapidly, the gradient calculated only on local information will give poor indication of the true 'right path.' In this case, a smaller rate is desirable. On the other hand, if the surface is relatively smooth, then a larger learning rate will speed convergence.[6] A rate that is too large may cause the system to oscillate, and thereby to slow or prevent the network's convergence. Appendix 4 considers this further.

To move in a direction opposite the gradient, the weight correction is therefore

$$\triangle^p w_{ji} = \epsilon \delta_j^p \tilde{o}_i^p \qquad (12-34b)$$

This is still a product correction rule. Unfortunately, we need to compute (or estimate) δ_j^p. Notice that for the jth unit

$$\frac{\partial E_p}{\partial net_j^p} = \frac{\partial E_p}{\partial o_j^p} \frac{\partial o_j^p}{\partial net_j^p} \qquad (12-35)$$

and, from (12-28)

---

[6]This is based on the shape of the error surface, which is rarely known. Some indication may be given by calculation of E at each iteration and observation of the impact of previous weight corrections. A general rule might be to use the largest learning rate that works and does not cause oscillation.

$$\frac{\partial o_j^p}{\partial net_j^p} = f_j'(net_j^p) \qquad (12-36)$$

Recall that choice of certain activation functions (e.g., sigmoid) makes computation of (12-36) easier. For example, if a sigmoidal characteristic is chosen, where

$$o_j = f(net_j) = \frac{1}{1 + e^{-net_j}} \qquad (12-37a)$$

the derivative computation required by (12-36) is quite simple, that is,

$$f'(net_j) = o_j(1 - o_j) \qquad (12-37b)$$

Handling Output Units.   For an output unit, using the error definition in (12-16)

$$\frac{\partial E_p}{\partial o_j^p} = -(t_j^p - o_j^p) \qquad (12-38)$$

Therefore, *in the case of output units*, using (12-32), (12-35) becomes

$$\delta_j^p = (t_j^p - o_j^p)f_j'(net_j^p) \qquad (12-39)$$

and the sample-based weight correction from (12-34a) becomes

$$\triangle^p w_{ji} = \epsilon(t_j^p - o_j^p)f_j'(net_j^p)\tilde{o}_i^p \qquad (12-40)$$

This weight correction technique is still a product correction strategy.

EXTENSION OF THE DR FOR UNITS IN THE HIDDEN LAYERS [THE GENERALIZED DELTA RULE (GDR)]

Layers other than input and output are denoted *hidden layers* and contain so-called *hidden units*. These are shown in Figure 1. The formulation for training hidden units requires at least two modifications:

1. A revised method of computing the weight derivatives or changes must be developed. This is owing to the 'indirect' effect of hidden units on E_p.
2. Since hidden units yield an error surface that may not be concave upward, there is a possibility of convergence to a local minimum in E.

We first address concern 1.

A Revised Procedure.   For units that are not output units, we need a method for computing $\triangle w_{ji}$. Consequently, an estimate of $\partial E_p/\partial w_{ji}$ for these weights is desired. Recall that E_p is based on comparing the outputs of *output units* with desired or target values. For a 3-layer (input, hidden, output) network with hidden unit u_k, first consider how the weights for u_k affect E_p:

1. The output of u_k feeds (activates) neurons in the output layer; and

2. The output of u_k is a function of its inputs, weights, and activation function.[7]
On this basis, we reformulate our approach for hidden unit u_k by considering its influence on the output units by again resorting to the chain rule as follows:

$$\frac{\partial E_p}{\partial o_k^p} = \sum_{n=1}^{c} \frac{\partial E_p}{\partial net_n^p} \frac{\partial net_n^p}{\partial o_k^p} = \sum_{n=1}^{c} (-\delta_n^p w_{nk}) \qquad (12-41)$$

The result in (12-41) incorporates (12-32) and differentiation of (12-30a). Therefore, (12-32), (12-35), and (12-36) yield

$$\delta_k^p = -\frac{\partial E_p}{\partial o_k^p} f_k'(net_k^p) \qquad (12-42)$$

This, combined with (12-41) yields the *recursive formulation* for update of the hidden layer weights:

$$\delta_k^p = f_k'(net_k^p) \sum_n \delta_n^p w_{nk} \qquad (12-43)$$

where δ_n^p is obtained from the output layer.

Symmetry of Hidden Unit Weight Adjustment.   The hidden layer weight correction of (12-43) obscures several important practical difficulties in minimizing E_p. For example, if the learning phase of the network is started with all weights equal, the correction to the weights of each hidden unit from the same input unit are identical. This yields an evolving 'symmetry' of weights in the network, which may not correspond to the optimal weight solution. Typically, the network weights are initially chosen randomly to avoid this problem. The symmetry effect is illustrated by Case 4 of Example 2.

Back Propagation — Summary of the Multistep Procedure

Beginning with an initial (possibly random) weight assignment for a 3-layer feedforward network, proceed as follows:

Step 1:   Present $\underline{i}^p$, form outputs o_i, of all units in network.

Step 2:   Use (12-40) to update w_{ji} for output layer.

Step 3:   Use (12-34b) and (12-43) to update w_{ji} for hidden layer(s).

Step 4:   Stop if updates are insignificant or error is below a preselected threshold, otherwise proceed to Step 1.

This leads to an adjustment scheme based on *back propagation*. This is shown in Figure 3.

Adding *Momentum* to the Training Procedure

Examination of the change in E_p as a function of $\triangle w_{ji}$ at each iteration suggests that care must be taken in choosing the learning parameter ϵ. Often in gradient approaches

---

[7]These are the prespecified inputs, $\underline{i}^p$, in a 3-layer network. In n-layer ($n > 3$) networks, these may be the outputs of units in other (hidden) layers.

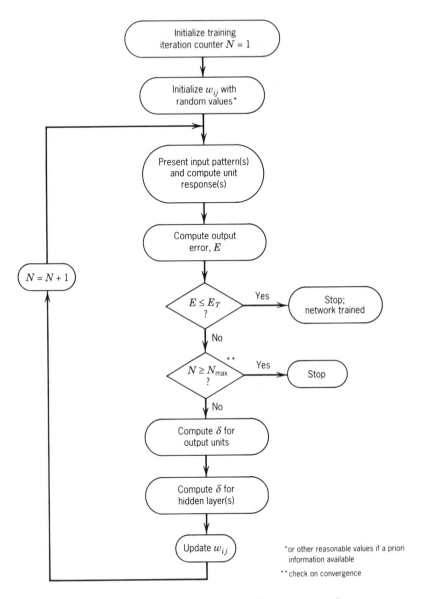

Figure 3: Summary of the back-propagation learning procedure.

this scaling parameter is adjusted as a function of the iteration, for instance, $\epsilon(n) = \epsilon_o/n$. This type of adjustment allows for large initial corrections, yet avoids weight oscillations around the minimum when near the solution. To add *momentum* to the weight update at the $(n + 1)$st iteration, the correction $\triangle^p w_{ji}$ is modified:

$$\triangle^p w_{ji}(n+1) = \underbrace{\epsilon \delta_j^p \tilde{o}_i^p}_{\text{as before}} + \alpha \triangle^p w_{ji}(n) \qquad (12-44)$$

The second term in (12-44), for positive α, yields a correction at step $n+1$ that is somewhat larger than would be the case if (12-34b) alone were used. This additional correction is in the same direction as that at step n; hence, the 'momentum' characterization. Analogous formulations for epoch-based corrections $\triangle \bar{w}_{ji}$ are possible.

The momentum term may prevent oscillations in the system and may help the system escape local minima of the error function in the training process. The momentum term is much like the learning rate in that it is peculiar to specific error surface contours. The momentum term, if it overwhelms the learning rate, can make the system less sensitive to local changes. Also, if the system enters a local minima that is steep on one side, and less so on another, the momentum 'built-up' during entry into the minima may be enough to push it back out.

Training the Unit Bias Inputs

Equation 12-20 showed an example of a unit that included an (assumed) adjustable bias term, $bias_j$. In this instance, we extend the training procedure to include an algorithm for bias adjustment. We could extend the previous derivations to compute $\partial E_p / \partial bias_j$ and form a bias adjustment strategy for unit u_j. However, a simpler alternative, using the unit bias structure of (12-20), is to note that an equivalent formulation is that of an additional input to u_j. This extra input is only connected to u_j and is denoted i_b, with corresponding weight w_{jb}. If we *assume i_b is the output of a unit that is always ON*, that is, 1.0, $bias_j$ may be adjusted through changes in w_{jb}. Therefore, the previous weight adjustment (training) procedure is directly applicable.

Table 12.1:   Summary of the GDR Equations for Training Using Backpropagation

(pattern) error measure	$E_p = \frac{1}{2}\sum_j (t_j^p - o_j^p)^2$	(12-16)
(pattern) weight correction	$\triangle^p w_{ji} = \epsilon \delta_j^p \tilde{o}_i^p$	(12-34b)
(output units)	$\delta_j^p = (t_j^p - o_j^p) f_j'(net_j^p)$	(12-39)
(internal units)*	$\delta_j^p = f_j'(net_j^p)\sum_n \delta_n^p w_{nj}$	(12-43)
output derivative (assumes sigmoidal characteristic)	$f_j'(net_j^p) = o_j^p(1 - o_j^p)$	(12-37b)

* Where δ_n^p are from the next (lower-numbered) layer.

EXAMPLE 1: 'Handworked' Training of a Single Unit Using the GDR

Consider the development of a single-unit single-layer PA, as shown in Figure 4. (Input units, which merely 'hold' the input are not shown.) The objective is for the unit to 'learn' a single input pattern, specifically for

$$\underline{i} = \begin{pmatrix} 1 \\ 4 \end{pmatrix} = \begin{pmatrix} i_1 \\ i_2 \end{pmatrix} \tag{12 - 45}$$

The desired output is $o_1 = 1$. Initially, assume $w_{11} = w_{12} = 0$.[8] The unit has a sigmoidal output function. The learning rate $\epsilon = 1.0$; no momentum is used.

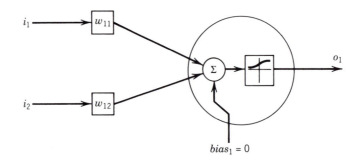

Figure 4: Network configuration for Example 1: Training single-layer/ single-unit.

Step 1. Applying $\underline{i}^p$ to the network produces $net_1 = 0$; therefore, $o_1^p = \frac{1}{2}$. Therefore, the pattern sum of squares error, $2E_p = (1 - \frac{1}{2})^2 = 0.25$. From (12-45), (12-37b) and (12-40) for output units,

$$\triangle^p w_{1i} = \left(1 - \frac{1}{2}\right)\left[\frac{1}{2}\left(1 - \frac{1}{2}\right)\right] i_i^p \tag{12 - 46}$$

or

$$\triangle^p w_{11} = 0.125 i_1^p = 0.125$$

$$\triangle^p w_{12} = 0.125 i_2^p = 0.5$$

Thus, the weights become $w_{11} = 0.125$ and $w_{12} = 0.5$.

Step 2. Applying $\underline{i}^p$ with the corrected weights yields $net_1 = 2.125$; thus $o_1 = (1 + e^{-2.125})^{-1} = 0.893$. Consequently, $2E_p = (1 - 0.893)^2 = 0.0114$. (Note that the error has decreased.) The weight corrections are therefore

$$\triangle^p w_{1i} = (0.107)\left[0.893(1 - 0.893)\right] i_i^p = 0.0853 i_i$$

or, using the inputs given in (12-45),

---

[8]Note that since this is the output layer, a problem with 'symmetry breaking' does not occur.

$$\triangle^P w_{11} = 0.0853$$

$$\triangle w_{12} = 0.341$$

This yields the new weights $w_{11} = 0.210$; $w_{12} = 0.841$.

Step 3 and Beyond. The reader should verify that the next iteration yields $net_1 = 3.57$; $o_1 = 0.973$; $2E_p = 0.00073$ and that the ratio w_{12}/w_{11} is asymptotically approaching 4.0. Since

$$\lim_{n \to \infty} \frac{w_{11}}{w_{12}} \to \frac{1}{4.0} \qquad (12-47)$$

the unit behaves as a *matched filter* (Appendix 5) for the single training pattern. Furthermore, notice that the converged weight vector and $\underline{i}_p$ have the same direction. ∎

Extended Example 2: Pattern Associator For Character Classification

Consider the 4-class classification problem shown in Figure 5. A variety of pattern associators will be developed for this example.

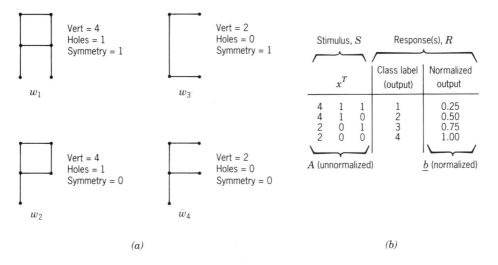

(a)   (b)

Figure 5:   Extended character recognition example.
(a) Basic patterns and extracted features.
(b) Stimulus–response characteristic for Case 1 (first) classification example. Note stimulus (A) is unnormalized.

Chosen Features

For this example, we (somewhat arbitrarily) choose a feature vector as follows:
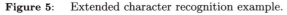

$$\underline{x} = \begin{pmatrix} x_1 \\ x_2 \\ x_3 \end{pmatrix} = \begin{pmatrix} \textit{No. of vertices} \\ \textit{No. of 'holes'} \\ \textit{symmetry measure} \end{pmatrix} = \begin{pmatrix} \textit{vert} \\ \textit{holes} \\ \textit{symmetry} \end{pmatrix} \qquad (12-48)$$

where the variables *vert* and *holes* correspond to the number of vertices (horizontal and vertical segment intersections) and holes (regions completely bounded by segments), respectively. The binary $(0, 1)$ variable symmetry is '1' if the character displays symmetry about a horizontal or vertical axis; otherwise it is zero.

Case 1: Single 4-Valued Output, Pseudoinverse Solution

Formulation. As shown in Figure 5(b), S–R specifications for a classifier, implemented as a pattern associator of the Type 1 form shown in Figure 2 of Chapter 11, may be developed. In order to compare this case with the neural solution, a normalized input and output are used.

We seek a solution using a linear formulation as follows:

$$A\underline{w} = \underline{b} \qquad (12-49)$$

where A and $\underline{b}$ are shown in Figure 5(b) and $\underline{w} = (w_1\ w_2\ w_3)^T$ is a set of weights to be determined. The solution, following normalization[9] of A, using Q-R decomposition to compute

$$\hat{\underline{w}} = A^+ \underline{b} \qquad (12-50)$$

is

$$\hat{\underline{w}} = \begin{pmatrix} 2.0 \\ -6.0 \\ -1.0 \end{pmatrix} \qquad (12-51)$$

Analysis of the Solution. The numerical results indicate:

1. Very small residuals (the reader should compute these).
2. A linear classification strategy based on strongest weighting of the second feature (x_2), followed by x_1. Apparently, x_3 provides (relatively) insignificant class discrimination information.

The resulting network structure is shown in Figure 6(a), with numerical results (including Q, R, and residuals) in Figure 6(b).

Case 2: Single 4-Valued Output, 2-Layer Neural Network Solution

Here we use a network structure with an input layer, consisting of 3 units to 'hold' x_1, x_2, and x_3, respectively. The output is a single neuron with a sigmoid characteristic. To keep all unit outputs in the $[0, 1]$ range, we normalize the inputs as follows:

---

[9]There are several ways to do this. In this example, we simply scale A such that the largest element is 1.0.

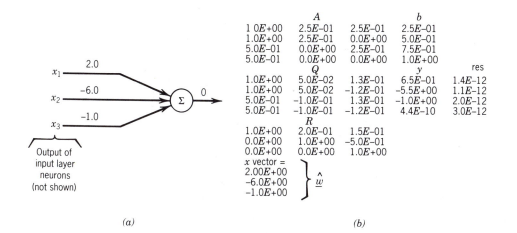

(a)   *(b)*

Figure 6:   Network for Case 1.
(a) Solution to Case 1 (weight values shown above input).
(b) Numerical results using Q-R decomposition.

Case 2 Training Data.

		Input Pattern (Normalized) ($\underline{x}^T$)			**Output Desired**
p_1	(w_1)	1.0	0.25	0.25	0.25
p_2	(w_2)	1.0	0.25	0	0.50
p_3	(w_3)	0.5	0	0.25	0.75
p_4	(w_4)	0.5	0	0	1.00

Results are shown in Figure 7.

Case 3: 4-Output ('One-of') 2-Layer Neural Network Solution

We design a 1 of 4 output neural net, of the Type 2 form of Figure 2, Chapter 11. Outputs o_1 through o_4 correspond to classes w_1 through w_4, respectively. S–R (training) data are shown below. Note that the S–R data have been scaled by 100.0 for display.

Cases 3, 4, Training Data

Pattern	**Input, $\underline{x}^T$**			**Output, $\underline{o}^T$**			
p_1	100	25	25	100	0	0	0
p_2	100	25	0	0	100	0	0
p_3	50	0	25	0	0	100	0
p_4	50	0	0	0	0	0	100

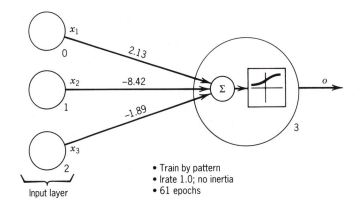

Figure 7: The results for Case 2.

Case 3: Summary of Results

$2E = 4.0$ initially (The reader should verify this.)

$2E = 0.1$ after training (80 epochs)

Pattern-by-Pattern Evaluation of Trained Network Response.   Note that p_i^d represents the ith *desired* pattern, whereas p_i^a represents the *actual network response* after training.

	p_1		p_2		p_3		p_4	
Output unit (i)	t_i	o_i	t_i	o_i	t_i	o_i	t_i	o_i
3	100	74	0	17	0	23	0	2
4	0	7	100	85	0	0	0	18
5	0	6	0	0	100	88	0	7
6	0	0	0	12	0	10	100	77

Resulting weights are shown in Figure 8.

Case 4: 4-Output, 3-Layer (Hidden) Neural Network Solution

The network of Case 3 is extended to include a 3-unit hidden layer. To illustrate the symmetry problem and the impact of initial network weight and bias choices of the training procedure, two cases are shown. The training set was identical to that used for Case 3, shown in the preceding table.

Case 4a: Random Initial Weights and Biases.   In Case 4a, the initial network weights and unit biases were 'randomly' chosen. These are shown in Figure 9(a). Following 69 training epochs, $2E \equiv 0.09$ and the resulting network weights are shown in Figure 9(b).

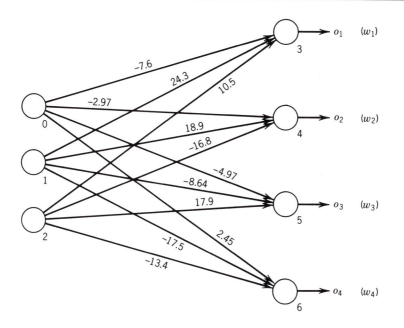

Figure 8: The network for Case 3, following training.

Case 4a: Pattern-by-Pattern Assessment of Network Response

	p_1		p_2		p_3		p_4	
Output unit (i)	t_i	o_i	t_i	o_i	t_i	o_i	t_i	o_i
6	100	88	0	10	0	5	0	0
7	0	6	100	90	0	0	0	5
8	0	9	0	0	100	89	0	8
9	0	0	0	7	0	8	100	89

Case 4b: Nonrandom, Symmetric Initialization of Network. In this case, initial network weights and biases were set to zero. Following 300 training epochs, $2E = 0.27$. Resulting weights and biases are shown in Figure 9(c). A pattern-by-pattern assessment of network performance is shown in the next table.

Case 4b: Pattern-By-Pattern Assessment of Network Response.

	p_1		p_2		p_3		p_4	
Output unit (i)	t_i	o_i	t_i	o_i	t_i	o_i	t_i	o_i
6	100	91	0	8	0	0	0	0
7	0	49	100	44	0	9	0	6
8	0	9	0	11	100	41	0	48
9	0	0	0	0	0	10	100	90

Clearly, according to the above tables, Case 4b performance is inferior to that of Case 4a. Furthermore, the weight symmetries developed are apparent from Figure 9(c). ∎

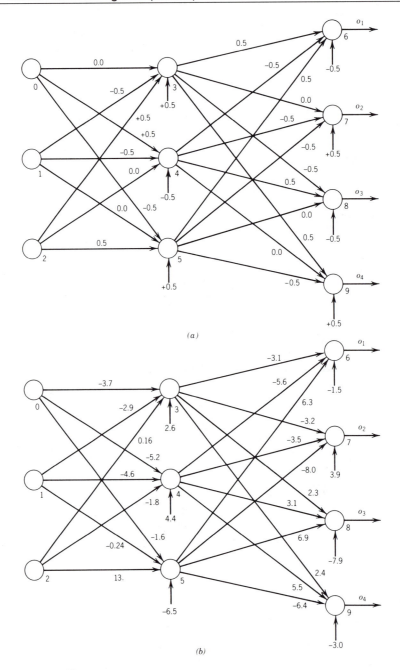

Figure 9:   Case 4.

(a) Case 4a: 'Random' initial weights and biases.

(b) Case 4a: Network structure and resulting weights/biases [from 'random' network initialization of (a)].

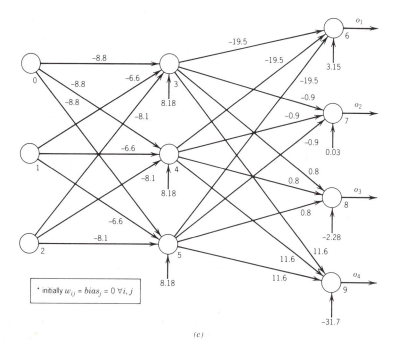

(c)

Figure 9 (cont.):   **(c)** Case 4b: Network structure and resulting weights/
biases from nonrandom network initialization.
* Note symmetry.
* Initially $w_{ij} = bias_j = 0$ $\forall i, j$.

Other Ramifications of Hidden Units

Training Time and Mapping Accuracy.   The choice of the number of hidden units in
a feedforward structure design is problem dependent and often involves considerable
engineering judgment. Often, trade-offs between training time and mapping accuracy
lead to iterative adjustment of the network using simulation. For a given problem, the
design of an appropriately sized hidden layer is often nonobvious. Intuition suggests
that 'the more the better' could be used to guide sizing of the hidden layer, since
the number of hidden units controls the flexibility of decision boundaries. However,
excessively large numbers of hidden units may be counterproductive. For one, the
network training time is influenced by the size of the hidden layer, as shown in the
example of Figure 10 [Gaborski 1990]. Notice that an application-dependent minimum training time exists, corresponding to a hidden layer of approximately 33 units.
Increasing the number of hidden units greatly beyond this number increases training
time substantially, with little gain in overall recognition (mapping) accuracy. Furthermore, excessively large numbers of hidden units lead to an undesirable 'grandmothering' effect, which results in overly complex and perhaps overly localized decision
regions. The latter is explored in the exercises.

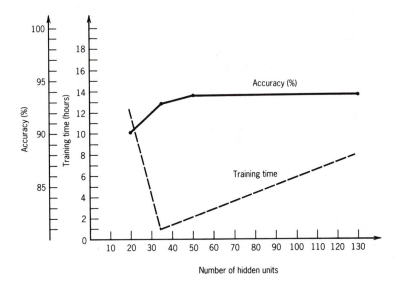

Figure 10:   Comparison of the number of hidden units, training time, and recognition accuracy for a specific problem. From [Gaborski 1990].

Semantics of the Hidden Layer.   It is often illustrative to examine the structure of the internal layer remapping that evolves from training. For example, in investigating edge classification [Cox/Schal 1990], it was observed that hidden units behaved like 'feature detectors,' each implementing a portion of a matched filter. 'Grandmothering,' as described above, may be an extreme case of this behavior.

BIBLIOGRAPHICAL AND HISTORICAL REMARKS

The history of feedforward ANNs is partially rooted in attempts to extend the use and training of linear discriminant functions (considered in Chapter 4). Initial perceptron research is generally credited to [Rosenblatt 1959]. The general feedforward structure is also an extension of the work of [Minsky/Papert 1969] and the early work of [Nilsson 1965], on the transformations enabled by layered machines, as well as the effort of [Widrow/Hoff 1960] in adaptive systems. A comparison of standard and neural classification approaches is found in [Huang/Lippmann 1987]. A geometrical analysis of ANN classification capabilities is shown in [Wieland/Leighton 1987]. An important consideration in neural implementations with limited precision analog or digital circuits is the network sensitivity to weight errors. An excellent examination of this effect is [Stevenson et al. 1990].

EXERCISES

12.1   This exercise considers development of a feedforward-structure neural network pattern associator to implement a security system. Consider the following hierarchy of security levels, often used by the U.S. government:

$$security\_levels = \{top\_secret, secret, confidential, unclassified\}$$

and

$$top\_secret \quad > \quad secret \quad > \quad confidential \quad > \quad unclassified$$

A system is denoted an *object*, with an associated security level denoted its *classification*, and a potential user is denoted a *subject*, with an associated security level denoted his/her *clearance*. If clearance $\geq$ classification, the user is allowed access.

Denote the 8 inputs to the network as

$$i^S_{top\_secret}, \quad i^S_{secret}, \quad i^S_{confidential}, \quad i^S_{unclassified}$$

$$i^O_{top-secret}, \quad i^O_{secret}, \quad i^O_{confidential}, \quad i^O_{unclassified}$$

where $i^S_{security\_levels}$ denotes the levels of the subject and $i^O_{security\_levels}$ denotes the levels of the object. The single output is denoted o_{access} and is 1 when access is allowed, 0 otherwise.

(a) Formulate a suitable network. Consider both cases with and without a hidden layer.

(b) Develop a suitable training set.

(c) Train the network.

(d) Analyze your results, including the possibility of attaching semantics to unit operation.

12.2   Repeat Exercise 12.1, except consider *encoded inputs* and a 1-of-2 output, i.e., there are two inputs for i^S and two for i^O, and the binary representation of i^S and i^O denotes the security level. Output $o_1 = 1$, $o_2 = 0$ denotes access allowed, whereas $o_1 = 0$, $o_2 = 1$ denotes access denied.

12.3   Using a bias input of the form

$$net_j = \sum_i w_{ji} o_i + bias_j$$

and a sigmoidal activation function, what $bias_j$ is necessary for $f(0) = 0$? Is this reasonable? Are there alternatives?

12.4   Consider several other mechanisms to implement a unit bias. Discuss ramifications with respect to

(a) Differentiation of $f(net_j)$,

(b) Training or adjusting the bias.

12.5   (This exercise makes an excellent long-term project and illustrates many practical aspects of 'blindly' applying neural networks. Students should not be surprised at the complexity and lack of 'ideal' results.) Consider the development of a feedforward network that determines whether a 2-D pattern is a member of the class of connected patterns or not. A connected binary pattern is one in which each location p_i, which is 'ON' (contains a '1') has at least one neighbor in a 3×3 region, centered at p_i, which is also ON. Consider a 5×5 array of points as the space of possible patterns, each represented by a 5×5 binary matrix. Form the network input vector by column concatenation to yield a 25×1 vector.

(a) Develop a suitable structure [especially the hidden layer(s)].

(b) Develop a suitable training set.

(c) Train the network and show sample results.

12.6   Repeat the example of Case 1 using only features x_1 and x_2. Analyze your results.

12.7   Repeat the example of Case 2, but add a $c + 1$st (5th) output class, denoted 'none of the above.' Choose several characters not in w_1 through w_4, and develop a suitable training set.

12.8   Repeat the examples of Cases 1 through 3, but with the following alternative feature set choice:

(a) Number of right angles,

(b) Number of horizontal and vertical segments,

(c) Longest closed path.

12.9   Repeat the design of Case 3 *using linear units*. Solve for the network weights by extending the approach of (12-50).

12.10   A more general activation function is of the form

$$o_j = f(net_j) = \frac{1}{1 + e^{-\{\frac{(net_j - \theta_j)}{\theta_o}\}}} \qquad (P.10-1)$$

(a) Show how the parameter θ_j serves as a threshold and 'positions' f.

(b) Show how θ_o determines the abruptness of the transition of f.

(c) Suggest applications for each of the parameters in (a) and (b).

12.11   For $f(net_j)$ as given by (P.10-1),

(a) Compute and plot $f'(net_j)$ for $\theta_j = 0; \theta_o = 1$.

(b) Repeat for $\theta_j = 0; \theta_o = 10$ and $\theta_o = 0.1$.

12.12   Suppose the training set H has two S–R pairs $\{(\underline{s}_1, \underline{r}_1), (\underline{s}_2, \underline{r}_2)\}$ that are related to an error or pattern ambiguity as follows:

$$\underline{s}_1 = \underline{s}_2 \qquad (P.12-1a)$$

but

$$\underline{r}_1 \neq \underline{r}_2 \qquad (P.12-1b)$$

(a) Discuss how the presence of this pair in H causes potential concerns in training.

(b) Is it possible that a cycle in the training process may occur?

(c) Is it possible that the GDR will 'average' or otherwise 'smooth' the effect of different targets for the same input pair?

(d) Show examples to support your answers to (a) to (c). Consider both training-by-sample and training-by-epoch.

12.13   **(a)** Show that the weight correction strategy of (12-40) is still a product rule.

   (b) In the case of a single layer of linear units, does (12-40) reduce to (12-8)?

12.14   **(a)** Prove that if

$$o_j = f(net_j) = \frac{1}{1 - e^{net_j}} \qquad (P.14-1)$$

then

$$\frac{\partial f(net_j)}{\partial net_j} = f'(net_j) = o_j(1 - o_j) \qquad (P.14-2)$$

   (b) Since (P.14-2) is used in a product correction rule (12-40), do values of net_j exist that cause $f'(net_j) = 0$?

   (c) Does the result of (P.14-2) hold for the more 'general' sigmoid function of (P.10-1)?

(Exercises 12.15 and 12.16 form the basis for interesting long-term projects/simulations.)

12.15   Design feedforward networks that given binary inputs A and B, implement:

   (a) The logical AND function;

   (b) The logical OR function;

   (c) The logical function $\bar{A}\bar{B} + AB$. (This function is useful in matching binary patterns.)

12.16   Design a feedforward network that implements a 4-bit digital-to-analog (D/A) converter. Use a single output $o_1 \in [0, 1]$ and consider the input bit pattern $i_1\ i_2\ i_3\ i_4$ to be a binary number with i_1 the MSB.

12.17   The 'XOR problem' is one of the most common examples of the use of a multilayer network for input remapping. Given the specifications for an XOR PA as follows:

Input $(i_1\ i_2)$	Output (o_1)	
00	0	
01	1	
11	0	
10	1	(P.17-1)

   (a) Show that the XOR function is not linearly separable.

   (b) Show that an elliptical decision boundary may be used to separate input regions where $o_1 = 0$ from $o_1 = 1$.

   (c) Consider expanding the input space to 3-D, i.e., using inputs i'_1, i'_2, and i'_3 that are derived from i_1 and i_2.

   (i)   For example, show that the following formulation is linearly separable:

extended input pattern $(i'_1\ i'_2\ i'_3)$	output (o_1)	
000	0	
010	1	
111	0	
100	1	(P.17-2)

       (ii)   How are i'_1 i'_2 and i'_3 related to i_1 and i_2 in part (i)?

   (d)   Design and train a NN with a single hidden layer to implement this function. Compare the operation of the hidden layer with the remapping results of part (c).

12.18   Using (12-27) and (12-17), show how the computation of $\triangle w_{ji}$ (the epoch-based weight adjustment) is easily obtained from $\triangle^p w_{ji}$.

12.19   This exercise encourages exploration of training alternatives using the GDR. Discuss (and implement if possible) each of the following alternatives:

   (a)   Consider the case where a 'representative' initial partition of H is used to refine initial weights into more suitable, albeit 'coarse weight,' estimates. This partition could consist, for example, of 10% of the samples of H and lead to significant overall computational savings. Following this, H could then be used to refine the coarse weights in a more exhaustive training step. Hopefully, the cost of the initial computations is more than offset by savings in the second step. In other words, the network weights converge much more quickly.

   (b)   Cite instances where training-by-sample is preferable to training-by-epoch and vice versa. Include such variables as contour of the error function and the ordering by class, of samples in H.

   (c)   [This extends part (b)]. Consider two alternative formulations for H in a $c = 2$ class case with $n = 200$:

       (i)   The first $n_1 = 100$ samples in H are representative of w_1 and the following $n_2 = 100$ are examples of w_2 pattern associations.

       (ii)   The samples in H are randomly ordered so that it is equally likely that the next training sample comes from w_1 or w_2.

       Which case, and for what reasons, might be preferable? Does it matter if the training is epoch-based or sample-based?

12.20   (This is an extension of Exercise 11.9, Chapter 11.) Consider, as quantitatively as possible, the effect of one or more redundant pattern pairs, denoted $(\underline{i}^r, \underline{o}^r)$, in H on the training of a feedforward network using the GDR.

12.21   Suppose we are designing a NN to determine if an input pattern (of varying length) corresponds to the binary representation of an (unsigned) even or odd number. For our purposes, consider the input pattern to be fixed length, with '0's in the higher order bit positions, e.g.,

$000101_2 = 3_{10}$ is in class *odd*.

$010000_2 = 16_{10}$ is in class *even*.

Choose a NN structure and develop a training set. Determine the NN weights. After training, does your NN place as much significance on the least significant bit as a human would?

12.22   The design of an appropriately sized hidden layer, for a given problem, often presents an interesting design challenge. Develop and discuss the merits and effects of hidden layer sizing strategies based on iteratively 'shrinking' or 'expanding' the hidden layer.

12.23   Consider a $c = 2$ class problem with overlapping class features, i.e., perfect classification is not possible. Show how a large internal layer may lead to overly complicated decision boundaries, which yield no better classification performance than the simple boundary that results from a small (or nonexistent) internal layer.

12.24 This problem tests your ability to implement the GDR training procedure. The network shown in Figure 9(a) is initialized for GDR training with weights (and biases) as shown. Units have a sigmoid output characteristic. For a learning rate, $\epsilon = 1.0$, and the following single-pattern training set:

$$H = \left\{ \left((1, 0.25, 0.25)^T, (1, 0, 0, 0)^T \right) \right\} = \left\{ (\underline{i}^1, \underline{t}^1) \right\}$$

(a) Determine the output of all units and $2E$, using $\underline{i}^1$ as input.

(b) For *the first iteration*, determine weight adjustments $\triangle^p w_{63}$ and $\triangle^p w_{30}$, where $p = 1$. Use the generalized delta rule (GDR).

Content Addressable Memory Approaches and Unsupervised Learning in NeurPR

13

The effort really to see and really to represent is no idle business in face of the constant force that makes for muddlement.

Prefaces [1907–1909]. What Maisie Knew
Henry James 1843-1916

INTRODUCTION

In this chapter, several alternative forms of neural networks suitable for PR applications are considered. First, a nonlinear, totally interconnected, and recurrent symmetric network is developed that forms an autoassociative memory. Stored patterns correspond to the stable states of a nonlinear system. This device is able to recall as well as *complete* partially specified patterns. The network is trained via a *storage prescription* that forces stable states to correspond to (local) minima of a network 'energy' function. The memory capacity, or allowable number of stored patterns, is shown to be related to the network size. Several examples are shown. The reader should note (as shown in the examples that follow) that alternative activation characteristics, interconnection strength computations, and energy functions are allowable. This approach thus serves as a *framework* or exemplar for other related neural network design paradigms.

In addition, several structures for unsupervised learning are considered. This includes adaptive-resonant structures and self-organizing feature maps.

THE HOPFIELD APPROACH TO NEURAL COMPUTING

Hopfield [Hopfield 1 1982], [Hopfield 2 1984], [Hopfield/Tank 1985], [Hopfield/Tank 1986] characterized a neural computational paradigm for using a neural net as an autoassociative memory.

Network Parameters

The following variables are defined:

o_i : the output state of the ith neuron

α_i : the activation threshold of the ith neuron

w_{ij}: the interconnection weight, that is, the strength of the connection FROM the output of neuron j TO neuron i. Thus, $\Sigma_j w_{ij} o_j$ is the total input or activation (net_i) to neuron i. We assume $w_{ij} \in R$, although other possibilities (e.g., binary interconnections) are possible. With the constraints developed below, for a d-unit network there are $d(d-1)/2$ possibly nonzero and unique weights.

In the Hopfield network, every neuron is allowed to be connected to all other neurons, although the value of w_{ij} varies (it may also be 0 to indicate no unit interconnection). To avoid false reinforcement of a neuron state, the constraint $w_{ii} = 0$ is also employed. The w_{ij} values, therefore, play a fundamental role in the structure of the network. In general, a Hopfield network has significant interconnection (i.e., practical networks seldom have sparse W matrices, where $W = [w_{ij}]$).

Network Dynamics

Sample Firing Characteristic. A simple form for Hopfield neuron firing characteristics is the nonlinear threshold device

$$o_i = \begin{cases} 1 & \text{if } \sum_{j;\ j \neq i} w_{ij} o_j > \alpha_i \\ 0 & \text{otherwise} \end{cases} \qquad (13-1)$$

Notice from (13-1) that the neuron activation characteristic is nonlinear. Commonly, the threshold $\alpha_i = 0$.[1] Notice from (13-1) where $\alpha_i = 0 \quad \forall i$, that there is no impetus for the system to move from the state $\underline{o}(t_k) = \underline{0}$.

State Propagation. Viewing the state of a d-neuron Hopfield network at time (or iteration) t_k as a $d \times 1$ vector, $\underline{o}(t_k)$, the state of the system at time t_{k+1} (or iteration $k+1$ in the discrete case) may be described by the nonlinear state transformation

$$W\underline{o}(t_k) \stackrel{*}{\Rightarrow} \underline{o}(t_{k+1}) \qquad (13-2a)$$

---

[1]As shown in Example 2, sometimes this firing characteristic requires careful interpretation, since the network behavior may be different when $\alpha_i = 0^-$ vs. $\alpha_i = 0^+$.

where the $\overset{*}{\Rightarrow}$ operator indicates the element-by-element state transition characteristic from (13-1) that is used to form $\underline{o}(t_{k+1})$. Note that the matrixlike formulation above uses matrix multiplication for the formation of the LHS of (13-2a). This represents a vector of activations, $\underline{net}(t_k)$, whose ith element is $net_i(t_k)$. The $\overset{*}{\Rightarrow}$ in (13-2a) does not imply equality or assignment, however, unless the units have a linear input–output characteristic. It is merely a convenient notational shorthand and allows an interpretation of stable network states in a manner analogous to a linear systems formulation. It is important to note that the basis of the computation is a network-wide nonlinear characteristic of interconnected elements.

Equation 13-2a may be generalized for each unit to accommodate an additional vector of unit bias inputs, that is,

$$[(W\underline{o}(t_k) + \underline{i}] \overset{*}{\Rightarrow} \underline{o}(t_{k+1}) \qquad (13-2b)$$

For example, based on the output characteristic of (13-1), (13-2b) may be written for each unit as

$$o_i(t_{k+1}) = \mu_s \left[\sum_j w_{ij} o_j(t_k) + i_i \right] \qquad (13-2c)$$

where i_i is the external or bias input to unit i and μ_s is the unit step function,

$$\mu_s(x) = \begin{cases} 1 & x > 0 \\ 0 & x \leq 0 \end{cases} \qquad (13-2d)$$

Network Updating Strategies.   The network state propagation given by (13-2) suggests that the unit transitions are synchronous, that is, each unit, in lockstep fashion with all other units, computes its net activation and subsequent output. Although this is achievable in (serial) simulations, it is not necessary. Also, empirical results have shown that it is not even necessary to update all units at each iteration. Surprisingly, network convergence is relatively insensitive to the fraction of units (15–100%) updated at each step. This is explored further in the exercises.

Energy Function and Storage Prescription.   For the case of $\alpha_i = 0$, stable (stored) states correspond to minima of the following energy function:

$$E = -\left(\frac{1}{2}\right) \sum_{i \neq j} \sum w_{ij} o_i o_j \qquad (13-3)$$

This leads to the rule for determination of w_{ij} from (13-3) and (13-1) and a set of desired stable states $\underline{o}^s, s = 1, 2, ...n$, that is, the training set (stored states) $H = \{\underline{o}^1, \underline{o}^2, \ldots, \underline{o}^n\}$, as

$$w_{ij} = \sum_{s=1}^{n} (2o_i^s - 1)(2o_j^s - 1) \qquad i \neq j \qquad (13-4)$$

(with the previous constraint $w_{ii} = 0$). One is encouraged to verify the consistency of (13-1), (13-3), and (13-4) for achieving a minimum in E. The reader should also compare the structure of the weight determination procedure of (13-4) with the Hebbian, correlation, or outer product–based weight formulations for linear networks in Chapter 12.

Symmetry of the Hopfield Learning Prescription. The storage prescription of (13-4) yields a network with considerable interconnection symmetry, since

$$w_{ji} = \sum_s (2o_j^s - 1)(2o_i^s - 1) = w_{ij} \qquad (13-5)$$

Comparison with Linear Dynamic Systems. The determination of neural network state evolution in the formulation of (13-2) parallels that of the unforced discrete *linear* time invariant system:

$$\underline{x}(t_{k+1}) = A\underline{x}(t_k) \qquad (13-6)$$

For example, given A, (13-6) may be used to determine states such that as $k \to \infty$,

$$\underline{x}(t_{k+1}) = \underline{x}(t_k) \qquad (13-7)$$

These are analogous to the stable states of the nonlinear system of (13-2). It is well known that these states are given by the eigenvectors of the A matrix that correspond to e-values of unity.

When employing the network in certain constraint satisfaction problems, the energy of a state can be interpreted [Hinton 1981] as the extent to which a combination of hypotheses or instantiations fit the underlying neural-formulated model. Thus, low energy values indicate a good level of constraint satisfaction.

One of the most interesting aspects of the Hopfield network is that stable states other than those prescribed by (13-4) may arise because of the nonlinear nature of the network. Thus, the user of the network may, in the course of storing a set of desired stable states $\underline{o}^s, s = 1, 2, \dots n$, introduce other local minima in E.

Hamming Distance and Its Significance in CAM

It is common to use the Hopfield (CAM) network for storing binary-valued feature vectors. Many approaches may be used to determine the similarity of binary-valued feature vectors. One particularly important measure in neural network applications is the *Hamming distance (HD)*. A $d \times 1$ binary vector $\underline{x}$ may be viewed as a vertex of a d-dimensional cube. The HD between two vectors $\underline{x}_1$ and $\underline{x}_2$ is the minimum number of element transitions that must occur to make the vector equal. Equivalently, the HD is the number of edges that must be traversed to get from the vertex represented by $\underline{x}_1$ to that represented by $\underline{x}_2$.

EXAMPLE 1: Hamming Distances Between Stored States

Consider the following vectors:

$$\underline{x}_1 = \begin{pmatrix} 0 \\ 1 \\ 0 \\ 1 \\ 0 \end{pmatrix} \quad \underline{x}_2 = \begin{pmatrix} 1 \\ 1 \\ 0 \\ 1 \\ 0 \end{pmatrix} \quad \underline{x}_3 = \begin{pmatrix} 0 \\ 1 \\ 0 \\ 1 \\ 1 \end{pmatrix} \quad \underline{x}_4 = \begin{pmatrix} 1 \\ 1 \\ 1 \\ 1 \\ 1 \end{pmatrix}$$

The reader should verify:

$HD\,(\underline{x}_1, \underline{x}_2) = 1$

$HD\,(\underline{x}_1, \underline{x}_3) = 1$

$HD\,(\underline{x}_1, \underline{x}_4) = 3$

$HD\,(\underline{x}_2, \underline{x}_3) = 2$

$HD\,(\underline{x}_2, \underline{x}_4) = 2$

$HD\,(\underline{x}_3, \underline{x}_4) = 2$ ■

Classification Using the HD. Given binary-valued vectors, a pattern classifier based on the HD between the class exemplar (e.g., $\underline{\mu}_i$) and a feature vector $\underline{x}$ could operate as follows.

Assign $\underline{x}$ to class w_m iff $HD\,(\underline{x}, \underline{\mu}_m) < HD\,(\underline{x}, \underline{\mu}_i)$ for all $i = 1, 2, \ldots c$ and $i \neq m$

The HD also serves as a measure of the separability of stable states in a Hopfield network. In the binary case, for d-dimensional vectors with elements $\{-1, 1\}$, the HD may easily be computed from

$$2 \cdot HD(\underline{x}_1, \underline{x}_2) = d - <\underline{x}_1, \underline{x}_2> \tag{13 - 8}$$

where $<\,>$ denotes the inner product.

Network Capacity. The convergence of the network to a stable state involves the Hamming distance between the initial state and the desired stable state. Different stable states that are close in Hamming distance are undesirable, since convergence to an incorrect stable state may result. [Hopfield 1982] suggests that an n-neuron network allows approximately $0.15n$ stable states; other researchers have proposed more conservative bounds [Abu-Mostafa/St. Jacques 1985].

EXAMPLE 2: Design of a Simple Hopfield Network—Storing and Accessing Stable States

We show in detail the design of a Hopfield network. Assume the neuron threshold $\alpha_i = 0$ and a binary, that is, $\{0, 1\}$ output. The network is required to store the following stable state:

$$\underline{o}^s = \begin{pmatrix} 1 \\ 0 \\ 1 \\ 0 \end{pmatrix} \qquad\qquad (13-9)$$

First we determine the unit interconnections and verify that $\underline{o}_s$ is a stable state.

Solution.   For a $d = 4$-neuron network, there are $16 - 4 = 12$ possible nonzero network weights or coefficients. Because of the symmetry of the network, 6 are unique. From the storage prescription of (13-5), given the number of stable states $n = 1$, weights are

$$w_{ij} = (2o_i^s - 1)(2o_j^s - 1) \qquad\qquad (13-10)$$

where

$$\underline{o}^s = \begin{pmatrix} o_1^s \\ o_2^s \\ o_3^s \\ o_4^s \end{pmatrix} = \begin{pmatrix} 1 \\ 0 \\ 1 \\ 0 \end{pmatrix} \qquad\qquad (13-11)$$

Therefore, $w_{12} = (2o_1^s - 1)(2o_2^s - 1) = (2 - 1)(-1) = -1$ and similarly

$$w_{13} = (2 - 1)(2 - 1) = +1 = w_{31}$$
$$w_{14} = (2 - 1)(-1) = -1 = w_{41}$$
$$w_{23} = (-1)(2 - 1) = -1 = w_{32} \qquad\qquad (13\text{-}12)$$
$$w_{24} = (-1)(-1) = +1 = w_{42}$$
$$w_{34} = (2 - 1)(-1) = -1 = w_{43}$$

Recall also the constraint $w_{11} = w_{22} = w_{33} = w_{44} = 0$. Therefore, the network state is propagated using (13-2):

$$\begin{pmatrix} 0 & -1 & 1 & -1 \\ -1 & 0 & -1 & 1 \\ 1 & -1 & 0 & -1 \\ -1 & 1 & -1 & 0 \end{pmatrix} \underline{o}(t_k) \overset{*}{\Rightarrow} \underline{o}(t_{k+1}) \qquad\qquad (13-13)$$

where $\overset{*}{\Rightarrow}$ denotes the nonlinear activation to output mapping from (13-1) that results from the specified neuron characteristic.

Checking for a Stable State.   Notice that for $\underline{o}(t_k) = \underline{o}^s$;

$$W\underline{o}^s = \begin{pmatrix} 1 \\ -2 \\ 1 \\ -2 \end{pmatrix} \qquad\qquad (13-14)$$

Therefore $\underline{o}(t_{k+1}) = \underline{o}^s$. Thus, $\underline{o}^s$ is indeed a stable state, and any trajectory that includes $\underline{o}^s$ converges to $\underline{o}^s$.

Assessment of Network Behavior for Initial States.   If the network is started in other initial states, denoted ϱ^1, ϱ^2, and ϱ^3, where

$$\varrho^1(t_o) = \begin{pmatrix} 1 \\ 0 \\ 0 \\ 1 \end{pmatrix} \qquad \varrho^2(t_o) = \begin{pmatrix} 1 \\ 0 \\ 0 \\ 0 \end{pmatrix} \qquad \varrho^3(t_o) = \begin{pmatrix} 0 \\ 0 \\ 0 \\ 1 \end{pmatrix}$$

it is interesting to explore $\varrho(t_k)$ for $k > 0$.

Given $\varrho^1(t_o)$, $\varrho^1(t_1)$ is found from

$$W\varrho^1(t_o) = \begin{pmatrix} -1 \\ 0 \\ 0 \\ -1 \end{pmatrix} \overset{*}{\Rightarrow} \begin{pmatrix} 0 \\ 0 \\ 0 \\ 0 \end{pmatrix} = \varrho^1(t_1)$$

Furthermore, at t_2

$$W\varrho^1(t_1) = \begin{pmatrix} 0 \\ 0 \\ 0 \\ 0 \end{pmatrix} \overset{*}{\Rightarrow} \varrho^1(t_2) = \varrho^1(t_1)$$

and the network is in a stable state, but not one that was explicitly stored. Thus, $\varrho(t_k) = \underline{0}$ is another stable state.

For $\varrho^2(t_k)$, consider

$$W\varrho^2(t_o) = \begin{pmatrix} 0 \\ -1 \\ 1 \\ -1 \end{pmatrix} \overset{*}{\Rightarrow} \begin{pmatrix} 1 \\ 0 \\ 1 \\ 0 \end{pmatrix} = \varrho^2(t_1) = \varrho^s$$

The network therefore converges from initial state $\varrho^2(t_o)$ to ϱ^s after one iteration.

For $\varrho^3(t_k)$, a very interesting case occurs.

$$W\varrho^3(t_o) = \begin{pmatrix} -1 \\ 1 \\ -1 \\ 0 \end{pmatrix} \overset{*}{\Rightarrow} \begin{pmatrix} 0 \\ 1 \\ 0 \\ 0 \end{pmatrix} = \varrho^3(t_1)$$

$$W\varrho^3(t_1) = \begin{pmatrix} -1 \\ 0 \\ -1 \\ 1 \end{pmatrix} \overset{*}{\Rightarrow} \begin{pmatrix} 0 \\ 0 \\ 0 \\ 1 \end{pmatrix} = \varrho^3(t_2) = \varrho^3(t_0)$$

The system is therefore in a *cycle*. In the next section we explore the 'energies' associated with network states to help explain this dynamic behavior. ∎

Why the Hopfield Strategy Should Work

Network Stability.   A Hopfield net is a nonlinear dynamic network. Systems theory is well equipped to handle stability concerns for linear dynamic networks; however, the nonlinear case is generally difficult. The Russian mathematician Liapunov devised a stability test based on energylike (or Liapunov) functions [Brogan 1985], denoted $E(\underline{o})$. Determining suitable Liapunov functions in general is difficult. Fortunately, many problems allow the use of constrained quadratic forms. *Local minima* of the energy function correspond to *locally stable* system or network states.

Energy Analysis Simplified Hopfield Networks.   For the case of $\alpha_i = 0$ in (13-1), an energy function is defined using the quadratic form:

$$E(\underline{o}) = -\frac{1}{2}\underline{o}^T W \underline{o} \qquad (13-15a)$$

where network interconnection matrix $W = [w_{ij}]$ is symmetric with $w_{ii} = 0$. E is a nonlinear function of the four variables o_1, o_2, o_3, and o_4, and contains no terms of the form o_i^2. Alternately, (13-15a) may be rewritten as

$$E(\underline{o}) = -\frac{1}{2}\sum_{i\neq j}\sum w_{ij}o_i o_j \qquad (13-15b)$$

Computing $\partial E(\underline{o})/\partial \underline{o}$ yields (Appendix 1)

$$\frac{\partial E(\underline{o})}{\partial \underline{o}} = -W\underline{o} \qquad (13-16a)$$

or

$$\frac{\triangle E(\underline{o})}{\triangle o_i} = -\sum_{i\neq j} w_{ij}o_j \qquad (13-16b)$$

Relating the result of (13-16b) with (13-1) is quite interesting. If the right-hand side of (13-16b) is negative, then it must be that

$$\sum_{i\neq j} w_{ij}o_j > 0 \qquad (13-17)$$

From the neural unit activation characteristic of (13-1), (13-17) requires either $\triangle o_i > 0$ (if o_i were initially 0) or $\triangle o_i = 0$ (if o_i were already 1). Thus, $\triangle o_i$ in (13-16b) cannot be negative, and consequently any change in energy function E *cannot be positive* in this network. From (13-15a), since each o_i is bounded, that is, $o_i \in [0, 1]$, E is bounded. Therefore, the network state $\underline{o}(t_k)$, as $k \to \infty$, must converge to a value that represents a local minimum in E. Unfortunately, there may be more than one local minimum (or stable state, as shown in Example 2), and it is not possible to ascertain which local minima the network state will converge toward. Clearly, 'separation' of stable states that correspond to local minima is desirable. This is related to the issue of memory capacity.

This brief convergence analysis yields some insight into the dynamics of the Hopfield network structure. The reader should verify that for the system of Example 2,

$$E[\underline{o}^s] = -1$$

$$E[\underline{o}^1(t_o)] = +1; \quad E[\underline{o}^1(t_1)] = 0$$

$$E[\underline{o}^2(t_o)] = 0; \quad E[\underline{o}^2(t_1)] = E[\underline{o}^s] = -1$$

and, most interestingly, for the cycle of trajectory $\underline{o}^3(t_k)$

$$E[\underline{o}^3(t_o)] = E[\underline{o}^3(t_1)] = E[\underline{o}^3(t_2)] = -0$$

It is also quite illustrative to relate the system state changes (trajectory) to the HD between the given initial state and the stored states. This is left as an exercise for the reader.

Hopfield Network Unit Updating Strategies. In an analog implementation of a Hopfield network, each unit adjusts its output according to (13-1), with the actual network dynamics due to inter-unit propagation delays (and unit dynamics, if present). The unit updating is therefore highly asynchronous.

In discrete simulations, it is interesting to consider alternative unit update strategies, especially considering the highly interconnected nature of the network. Examples are

1. Randomly updating units;
2. Sequential updating using (13-2), starting at a particular unit; and
3. (A variation of 2) updating units using as inputs the most current values of previously computed unit outputs.

Unfortunately, it is difficult to formulate general conclusions regarding the applicability of these different strategies.

ADDITIONAL EXAMPLES OF CAM APPLICATIONS IN PR

EXAMPLE 3: Character Recognition

As an example of pattern recognition, suppose it is desired to recognize characters in a spatially discretized array of binary intensities [Schalkoff 1989]. Figure 1 is used to illustrate the application. One approach is the following strategy:

1. Map an $n \times n$ binary intensity array into an n^2-neuron network. In other words, interpret the state of an $n^2 \times 1$ neural array as a 2-D binary character. Note that this does not fully utilize the 2-D nature of the problem features.
2. Store each character to be recognized as a stable state using (13-4). The state of each neuron in a stable state therefore corresponds to its binary value in a stored character.
3. Given an unknown input character, make the neural representation of this character the initial state of the neural network and hope the network converges to a stored character that is close to the input.

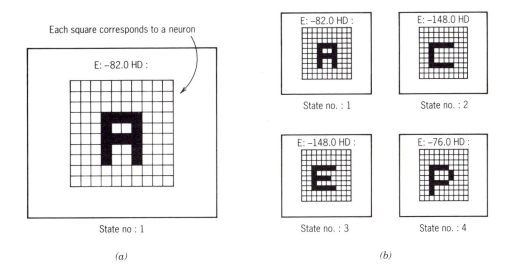

Figure 1:   Neural network as CAM for character recognition (adapted from [Schalkoff 1989]).

(a) Neural network mapping to 2-D binary image (10×10 pixels; 100 neurons).

(b) Stored stable states (block versions of uppercase A, C, E, P).

For illustration, we use a 10×10 array as a character box. The underlying neural network is therefore modeled as a 100×1 neuron unit state vector, and W is a 100×100 interconnection matrix. Figure 2 shows network behavior for the case of 4 stored stable states [which, as shown in part (b), are in some cases close in Hamming distance]. The desirable convergence properties of the network for a range of distorted input patterns is shown.

This application of a neural computing approach, while illustrative, is a relatively obvious example of neural network CAM capability. Other similar examples are possible [Fukushima 1982]. The direct mapping of (binary) pixel intensity to neuron state is conceptually obvious and somewhat successful in that the network behaves as a CAM. An alternative neural network implementation, based on a Hamming network [Lippmann 1987], is possible. In this case the neural network behaves essentially as a binary correlator.   ■

EXAMPLE 4: Relational Constraint Satisfaction (Coloring)

This example is from [Ball 1986] and typifies neural implementation of relational constraint satisfaction solutions. Consider the problem of labeling four regions with the possible (color) labels shown in Figure 3. In this case, consider the relation 'adjacent_to.' Each region may be labeled with the colors shown, but no adjacent regions may have the same color. To map this problem to a neural network, consider the following approach:

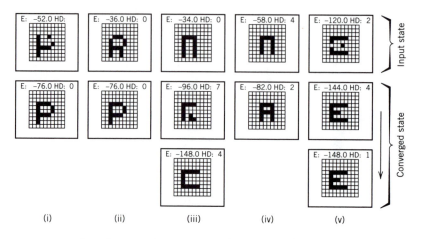

Figure 2: Sample network recognition (convergence) properties (5 cases).

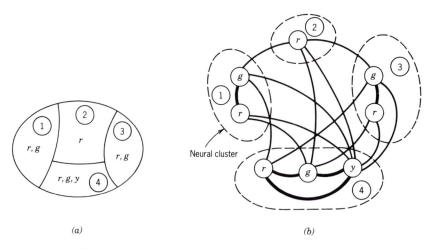

Figure 3: Coloring problem example.
(a) Four-region map with possible colorings red (r), green (g), and yellow (y) for different regions. (Adjacent regions may not have same color.)
(b) Map coloring problem cast in network formalism. Bold-face links denote negative weights; other links denote positive weights.

1. The allowable colors of each region are assigned to neural units. Thus, for a region such as region 4, with three allowable colors, a three-neuron 'cluster' represents the allowable labelings, as shown in Figure 3(b). Active (ON) neurons in each region indicate that their corresponding color is a valid value of the color label for that region. For example, if the converged network solu-

tion for region 4 indicates that the output of the color red neuron is active, the region is said to be labeled red.

2. Adjacent regions may not have the same color. Furthermore, each region must have only one color label; therefore, we allow only one neuron to be active in each neuron cluster.

3. Based on the observations in 1 and 2, we map the above constraints into interconnection values between neurons. Inhibitory interconnections within a region cluster (values of w_{ij} that are negative) with weight -3 are used to enforce the constraint that a region must have a single label. Thus, intraregion unit clusters have a 'competitive' interconnection structure. The compatibility of colors on adjacent regions is embedded into the network via excitory (positive) w_{ij} weights of $+1$. This is shown in Figure 3(b).

4. Note that up to this point we have not determined a neural firing characteristic or energy function, but instead have determined w_{ij} that satisfy the given relational constraints. To establish the required firing characteristic of the neurons, consider the energy function in (13-3). By computing the gradient of E with respect to o_i, we observe that a sequential gradient descent procedure is:

$$o_i(t_{k+1}) = \begin{cases} 1 & \text{if } \sum_{j \neq i} w_{ij} o_i(t_k) > 0 \\ 0 & \text{otherwise} \end{cases} \qquad (13-18)$$

The interesting result of this formulation is that (13-18) is precisely the firing characteristic of (13-1). The reader may verify that stable states of the network, as formulated, correspond to minima of E and yield allowable labelings.

An Extension—Interactive Activation and Competition (IAC) Network. The neural solution to this relational constraint satisfaction exhibits the interesting interconnection structure characteristic of selective intercluster activation and intracluster inhibition. This is typical of the class of interactive activation and competition (IAC) networks. ∎

EXAMPLE 5: Symbolic Constraint Satisfaction (Labeling)

As suggested above, one of the principal utilities of neural networks is in problems involving constraint satisfaction. The mapping of symbolic information into a neural network in a manner that facilitates feature extraction and high-level recognition (in the form of unification of observed data, i.e, low-level inputs) with a high-level (semantic) model recognition is desirable. This is shown in detail in [Schalkoff 1989, Chapter 8]. ∎

UNSUPERVISED LEARNING IN NeurPR: SELF-ORGANIZING NETWORKS

Introduction

The multilayer feedforward and the CAM (Hopfield) neural networks both exemplify supervised learning. In this section, neural-based examples of unsupervised learning are shown. Specifically, networks that are used to determine natural clusters or feature similarity from unlabeled samples are explored. The 'cluster discovery' capability of such networks leads to the descriptor *self-organizing*. Recalling from Chapter 5 the c-means and ISODATA clustering approaches for StatPR unsupervised learning, we may view several of the neural approaches as parallel or related formulations. Note also that the structures and learning procedures of unsupervised learning networks are different from, but related to, those neural networks considered previously. Also, biological implications, extensions, and modifications of these approaches are significant; however, we consider only the elementary concepts here.

Fundamentally, unsupervised learning algorithms (or 'laws') may be characterized by first-order differential equations [Kosko 1990]. These equations describe how the network weights evolve or adjust over time (or iterate, in the discrete case). Often, some measure of pattern *associativity* or similarity is used to guide the learning process, which usually leads to some form of network correlation, clustering, or competitive behavior.

Adaptive Resonance Architectures

Overall Structure.   Neural self-organizing architectures based on 'adaptive resonance theory' (ART) [Carp/Gross 1 1987], [Carp/Gross 2 1987] consist principally of a pair of interacting neural subsystems, shown somewhat generically in Figure 4. Neural unit interconnections are both intra- and intersystem. The concepts of competitive learning and interactive activation are 'fused' in this approach, in a manner that leads to a stable[2] learning algorithm. The intersystem feedback structure is apparent from Figure 4. The 'control' signals shown are used to regulate the system operational 'mode,' as described subsequently, and distinguish this system from a simple Hopfield network.

Neural Layer Structure Details.   Figure 5 shows an expanded view of the neural subsystems of Figure 4. Note that the FA and FB layers are totally interconnected, that is, the activation of each FA unit is fed to all FB units and vice versa. This interlayer feedback structure is used to facilitate 'resonance' when a match between an encoded pattern and an input pattern occurs. This typifies an ART1 architecture. The FA subsystem may be viewed as the 'bottom' layer that both 'holds' the input pattern and, through the bottom-up weights b_{ij} (the interconnection strength from FA unit j to FB unit i), forms the FB layer excitation.

The FB layer is composed of 'grandmother' cells, each representing a pattern class. FB unit activations are fed back to the FA layer units via the interlayer t_{ij} interconnections. These may be viewed as long-term memory (pattern storage) interconnections. Most importantly, the FB layer units employ a self-exciting, competitive, neighbor-inhibiting interconnection structure, whereby each FB unit reinforces its own output through a positive interconnection between its output and one of its inputs, while maintaining a negative (inhibitory) connection to every other FB layer unit. A sample

---

[2]In the sense that unit activation convergence is achieved.

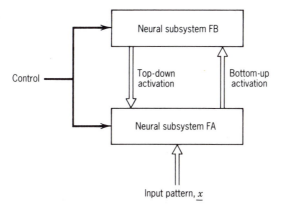

Figure 4:   Overall structure of adaptive resonance network.

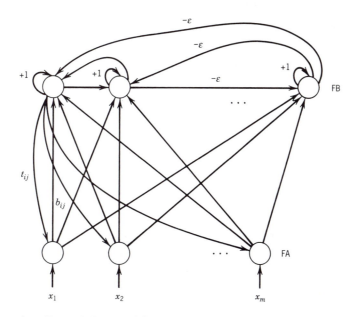

Figure 5:   Expanded view of ART network subsystems.

implementation of this structure and resulting action is as follows. Interconnection weights w_{ij}, for units totally within layer FB, are determined by

$$w_{ij} = \begin{cases} 1 & i = j \\ -\epsilon & \text{if } i \neq j \text{ and } i \text{ and } j \text{ correspond to units in FB} \end{cases} \qquad (13-19)$$

This corresponds to an 'on-center, off-surround' interconnection strategy. Inter-layer interconnection weight values t_{ij}, where i corresponds to units in the FA layer, are described later. The competition or inhibition parameter ϵ is a design parameter, with the constraint:

$$\epsilon < \frac{1}{N_{FB}} \qquad (13-20)$$

where N_{FB} is the number of units in layer FB. Competition dynamics in layer FB are modeled via

$$o_i(N+1) = f_i\big[o_i(N) - \epsilon \sum_{i \neq k} o_k(N)\big] \qquad i = 1, 2, \ldots N_{FB} \qquad (13-21)$$

where $o_i = f_i(net_i)$ and $f_i(\ )$ is a unit activation-output mapping function that must be monotonically nondecreasing for positive net_i and zero for negative net_i, and is a fundamental part of the MAXNET [Lippman 1987] structure. Thus, only one pattern class is designed to 'win' if the overall network converges for a given input pattern. The reader will note some similarity of this local competition or inhibition-based structure with the Kohonen structure discussed subsequently. The overall ART1 architecture, then, is a cooperative–competitive feedback (recurrent) structure.

Network Dynamics.   The previous static network architecture description only partially characterizes the operation of the network. Because of the feedback structure, temporal dynamics are an important component of both recognition (recall) and learning (encoding). These actions are governed by the additional control signals shown in Figure 4 and enable two phases of operation. An *attentional phase* engages FA units only when an input pattern is presented. An *orienting phase* successively 'thins' units in FB, until a 'winner,' or pattern class is found. If it is not possible to determine a winner, an uncommitted FB unit is used to represent this new pattern class, thus facilitating learning.

When presented with an input pattern, the ART network implements a combined recognition/learning paradigm. If the input pattern is one that is the same as, or close to, one previously 'memorized,' desired network behavior is that of *recognition*, with possible reinforcement of the FB layer on the basis of this 'experience.' The recognition phase is a cyclic process of bottom-up adaptive filtering (adaptive since the weights b_{ij} are changeable at each iteration) from FA to FB, selection of a stored pattern class in FB (the 'competition'), and mapping of this result back to FA, until a consistent result at FA is achieved. The top-down feedback of the competition 'winner' output from FB to form FA activations that may be viewed as encoded or 'learned expectations.' This is then the network state of 'resonance' and represents a search through the 'encoded' or memorized patterns in the overall network structure. If the input pattern is not 'recallable,' desired behavior is for the FB layer to adapt or 'learn' this class, by building or assigning a new node henceforth representing this pattern class.

Algorithm Specifics and Equations.   An algorithm that accommodates binary ($\{-1, 1\}$) input features is as follows:

1. Select ϵ, ρ and initialize the interlayer connections as follows:

$$t_{ij}^{\circ} = 1 \qquad \forall i, j \tag{13-22a}$$

$$b_{ij}^{\circ} = \frac{1}{1+n} \tag{13-22b}$$

Equations 13-22a and 13-22b are specific cases of more general constraints [Carp/Gross 1987] that must be placed on the initial values of t_{ij} and b_{ij}. Equation 13-22a satisfies the so-called *template learning inequality*, whereas (13-22b) satisfies the *direct access inequality*.

2. Present d-dimensional binary pattern $\underline{x} = (x_1, x_2, \ldots x_d)^T$ to the FA layer.

3. Using b_{ij}, determine the activations of the FB layer units, that is, each unit has activation

$$net_i^{FB} = \sum_j b_{ij} x_j \tag{13-23a}$$

4. Use the competition-based procedure of (13-21) to determine a 'winner' or unit with maximum activation (and therefore output) in FB.[3] Each unit in FB therefore 'competes' with all others in FB, until iteration within FB yields only one active unit. Denote the output [activation $f_i(\ )$ is the identity function] of the winning unit as $o_j^{FB_{WIN}}$, that is

$$o_j^{FB_{WIN}} = \max_{o_k \in FB} \{o_k^{FB}\} \tag{13-23b}$$

Related to 'the winner' unit in (13-23b) is function $m(j)$, used for weight updates and shown in (13-26c).

5. The top-down verification phase begins. Using the 'winner' unit found in step 4, this result is then fed back to FA via the top-down or t_{ij} interconnections, using

$$net_i^{FA} = t_{ij} o_j^{FB_{WIN}} \tag{13-24}$$

for each unit in FA. The fed-back FA unit activations (or outputs) are then compared with the given input pattern. This is an attempted confirmation of the 'winning' unit class found in step 4. Numerous comparisons are possible, with the overall objective of determining whether the top-down and input activations are sufficiently close. For example, since the inputs are binary, the comparison

$$\sum_i net_i^{FA} > \rho \parallel \underline{x} \parallel \tag{13-25}$$

may be used. In ART1, $\parallel \underline{x} \parallel = \sum_i |x_i|$. Here ρ is a design parameter representing 'vigilance' of the test, that is, how critically the match should be evaluated.

---

[3]Other procedures are allowable; for example, the Shunting Grossberg form [Simpson 1990] may be used.

6. If (13-25) is true, that is, the test succeeds, the b_{ij} and t_{ij} interconnections are updated to accommodate the results of input $\underline{x}$ using discrete versions of the slow learning dynamics equations:

$$\dot{t}_{ij} = \alpha_1 m(j)[-\beta_1 t_{ij} + f_i(x_i)] \qquad (13 - 26a)$$

where we recall that t_{ij} is the strength of interconnection FROM unit j in FB TO unit i in FA. α_1 is a positive parameter that controls the learning rate, and β_1 is a positive constant that allows gradual 'forgetting' or decay. $f_i(x_i)$ is the output of FA unit i using input x_i as activation, and $m(j)$ is described more fully below and in (13-26c). Note that the competitive interconnections *within* FB defined in (13-19) are not adjusted through (13-26a); only the top-down interlayer weights t_{ij} are modified. Similarly, the bottom-up weights are adjusted by

$$\dot{b}_{ji} = \alpha_2 m(j)[-\beta_2 b_{ji} + f_i(x_i)] \qquad (13 - 26b)$$

where we recall that b_{ji} is the strength of the interconnection FROM unit i in layer FA TO unit j in layer FB. Similarly, α_2 and β_2 are analogous to those in (13-26a). Function $m(j)$ is used to restrict the updating of weights to those involving only the winning class $o_j^{FB_{WIN}}$ as defined in (13-23b), using

$$m(j) = \begin{cases} 1 & \text{if } o_j = o_j^{FB_{WIN}} \\ 0 & \text{otherwise} \end{cases} \qquad (13 - 26c)$$

If the test of (13-25) fails, this unit is ruled out and step 4 is repeated until a winner can be found or there are no remaining candidates.

Equation 13-26 represents one example of a learning strategy in the ART approach. In [Carp/Gross 1 1987] and [Carp/Gross 2 1987] separate 'slow' and 'fast' learning procedures are considered. Parameters α_1 and α_2 control the rate at which the system learns or adapts and must be chosen carefully. Learning rates that are too slow, yield systems that are rigid (or nonadaptive in the extreme case). Conversely, learning rates that are too fast cause the system to display chaotic (or what is termed 'plastic') behavior. In the extreme case, the system tries to learn every input pattern as a new class. Thus, a trade-off exists between system insensitivity to novelty (truly new patterns) and an overly plastic behavior. Simplified versions of these updating strategies are shown in [Pao 1989].

Sample Results and Related Network Structures. Results of the ART1 system are shown in Figure 6. A neural network structure that is somewhat simpler, but related to the ART, is the Hamming Net [Lippman 1987]. This is a two-layer nonrecurrent (feedforward) structure, usually used with supervised training, that classifies binary patterns on the basis of Hamming distance. The similarity is chiefly in the competitive interaction of the upper layer, used to find a maximum match to stored exemplars.

Self-Organizing Feature Maps (Kohonen)

Introduction. Kohonen ([Kohonen 1984], [Kohonen 1 1982], [Kohonen 2 1982], [Kohonen 1987], [Kangas et al. 1990]) has shown an alternative neural learning structure

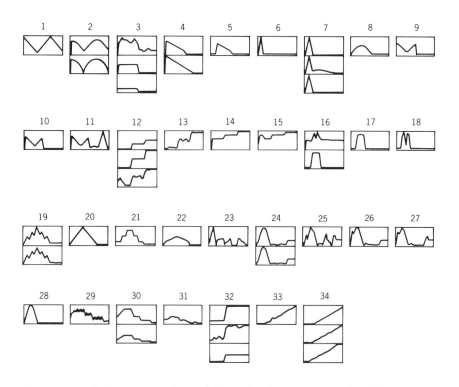

Figure 6: Category groupings of 50 analog input patterns into 34 recognition categories. Each input pattern I is depicted as a function of $i(i = 1 \ldots M)$, with successive I_i values connected by straight lines. The category structure established on one complete presentation of the 50 inputs remains stable thereafter if the same inputs are presented again. From [Carp/Gross 2 1987].

involving networks that perform dimensionality reduction through conversion of feature space to yield *topologically ordered* similarity graphs or maps or clustering diagrams (with potential statistical interpretations). In addition, a lateral unit interaction function is used to implement a form of local competitive learning.

Unit Topologies.   Figure 7 shows possible 1-D and 2-D configurations of units to form feature or pattern dimensionality reducing maps. For example, a 2-D topology yields a planar map, indexed by a 2-D coordinate system. Of course, 3-D and higher dimensional maps are possible. Notice that each unit, regardless of the topology, receives the input pattern $\underline{x} = (x_1, x_2, \ldots x_d)^T$ in parallel. Considering the topological arrangement of the chosen units, the d-D feature space is mapped into 1-D, 2-D, 3-D, and so on. The coordinate axes used to index the unit topology, however, have no explicit meaning or relation to feature space. They may, nevertheless, reflect a similarity relationship between units in the reduced dimensional space, where topological distance is proportional to dissimilarity.

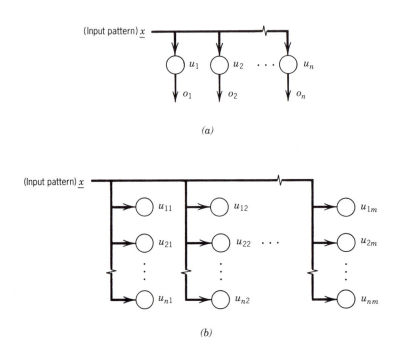

(a)

(b)

Figure 7:   Examples of topological map configurations.
(**a**) 1-D topology.
(**b**) 2-D topology.

Choosing the dimension of the feature map involves engineering judgment. Some PR applications naturally lead to a certain dimension; for example, a 2-D map may be developed for speech recognition applications, where 2-D unit clusters represent phonemes. The dimensions of the chosen topological map may also influence the training time of the network. It is noteworthy, however, that powerful results have been obtained by just using 1- and 2-dimensional topologies.

Defining Topological Neighborhoods ('Bubbles').   Once a topological dimension is chosen, the concept of an equivalent dimension neighborhood (or cell or bubble) around each neuron may be introduced. An example for a 2-D map is shown in Figure 8. This neighborhood, denoted N_c, is centered at neuron u_c, and the cell or neighborhood size (characterized by its radius in 2-D, for example) may vary with time (typically in the training phase). For example, initially N_c may start as the entire 2-D network, and the radius of N_c shrinks as iteration (described subsequently) proceeds. As a practical matter, the discrete nature of the 2-D net allows the neighborhood of a neuron to be defined in terms of nearest neighbors; for example, with a square array the 4 nearest neighbors of u_c are its N, S, E, and W neighbors; the 8 nearest neighbors would include the 'corners.'[4] In 1-D, a simple distance measure may be used.

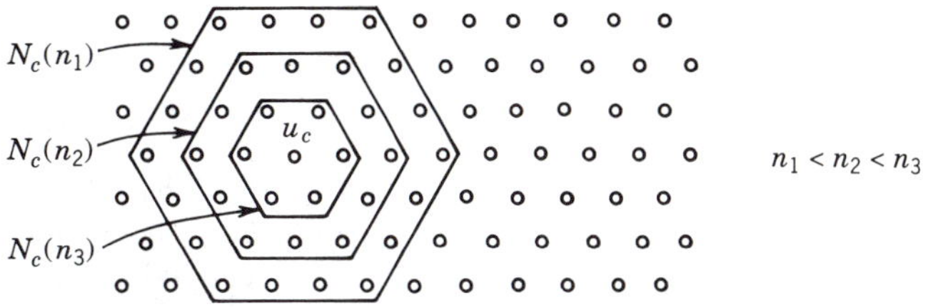

Figure 8:   Example of topological neighborhood N_c of unit u_c, showing shrinking with training iteration n_i. Adapted from [Kangas et al. 1990].

Network Learning Algorithm.   Each unit u_i in the network has the same number of weights as the dimension of the input vector and receives the input pattern $\underline{x} = (x_1, x_2, \ldots x_d)^T$ in parallel. The goal of the self-organizing network, given a large, unlabeled training set, is to have individual neural clusters self-organize to reflect input pattern similarity. Defining a weight vector for neural unit u_i as $\underline{m}_i = (w_{i1}, w_{i2}, \ldots w_{id})^T$, the overall structure may be viewed as *an array of matched filters, which competitively adjust unit input weights on the basis of the current weights and goodness of match.*[5] A useful viewpoint is that each unit tries to become a matched filter, in competition with other units. This learning concept is now more fully quantified.

Assume that the network is initialized with the weights of all units chosen randomly. Thereafter, at each training iteration, denoted k for an input pattern $\underline{x}(k)$, a distance measure $d(\underline{x}, \underline{m}_i)$ between $\underline{x}$ and $\underline{m}_i$ $\forall i$ in the network is computed. This may be an inner product measure (correlation), Euclidean distance, or another suitable measure. For simplicity, we proceed by using the Euclidean distance. For pattern $\underline{x}(k)$, a *matching phase* is used to define a 'winner' unit u_c, with weight vector $\underline{m}_c$, using

$$\| \underline{x}(k) - \underline{m}_c(k) \| = \overset{min}{i} \left\{ \| \underline{x}(k) - \underline{m}_i(k) \| \right\} \qquad (13-27)$$

Thus, at iteration k, given $\underline{x}$, c is the index of the best matching unit. This affects all units in the currently defined cell, bubble or cluster surrounding u_c, $N_c(k)$ through the global network *updating phase* as follows:

$$\underline{m}_i(k+1) = \begin{cases} \underline{m}_i(k) + \alpha(k)[\underline{x}(k) - \underline{m}_i(k)] & i \in N_c(k) \\ \\ \underline{m}_i(k) & i \notin N_c(k) \end{cases} \qquad (13-28)$$

---

[4]The reader may observe that a hexagonal array makes the nearest neighbors of u_c equidistant.

[5]The use of $\underline{m}_i$, as opposed to w_{ij}, allows easier visualization of the network behavior, and is consistent with the literature.

The updating strategy in (13-28) is particularly interesting and bears a strong similarity to the LVQ algorithm presented in Chapter 5 [(5-17)]. Furthermore, (13-28) corresponds to a discretized version of the differential adaptation law:

$$\frac{d\underline{m}_i}{dt} = \alpha(t)[\underline{x}(t) - \underline{m}_i(t)] \qquad i \in N_c(t) \tag{13 - 29a}$$

$$\frac{d\underline{m}_i}{dt} = 0 \qquad i \notin N_c(t) \tag{13 - 29b}$$

Clearly, (13-29a) shows that $d(\underline{x}, \underline{m}_i)$ is decreased for units inside N_c, by moving $\underline{m}_i$ in the direction $(\underline{x} - \underline{m}_i)$. Therefore, after the adjustment, the weight vectors in N_c are closer to input pattern $\underline{x}$. Weight vectors for units outside N_c are left unchanged. The competitive nature of the algorithm is evident since after the training iteration, units outside N_c are *relatively* further from $\underline{x}$. That is, there is an opportunity cost of not being adjusted. Again, α is a possibly iteration-dependent design parameter.

Discussion of Algorithm Properties. The resulting accuracy of the mapping depends on the choices of N_c, $\alpha(k)$, and the number of iterations. Kohonen cites the use of 10,000–100,000 iterations as typical. Furthermore, $\alpha(k)$ should start with a value close to 1.0, and gradually decrease with k. Similarly, the neighborhood size $N_c(k)$ deserves careful consideration in algorithm design. Too small a choice of $N_c(0)$ may lead to maps without topological ordering. Therefore, it is reasonable to let $N_c(0)$ be fairly large (Kohonen suggests $\frac{1}{2}$ the diameter of the map) shrinking $N_c(k)$ (perhaps linearly) with k to the fine-adjustment phase, where N_c consists only of the nearest neighbors of unit u_c. Of course, a limiting case is where $N_c(k)$ becomes one unit. Additional details of the self-organizing algorithm are summarized in the cited references.

Sample Results. Figure 9 shows sample results for a 5-D feature vector case. Figure 9(a) shows the unlabeled training set samples H_u; Figure 9(b) shows the self-organized map resulting from the algorithm. As evidenced by Figure 9(b), 2-D clustering of the different dimensionality-reduced input patterns occurs. As in other learning examples, vectors were chosen randomly from H_u at each iteration. $\alpha(k)$ decreased linearly with k from 0.5 $[= \alpha(0)]$ to 0.04 for $k \leq 10,000$. Similarly, for this simulation the 2-D map was chosen [see Figure 9(b)] to be of hexagonal structure with 7×10 units. For $k \leq 1000$, the radius of N_c decreased from 6 (almost all of the network) to 1 (u_c and its six nearest neighbors).[6]

SUMMARY

Many questions regarding neural computing, and its application to PR problems, exist. Furthermore, the mapping of a PR problem into the neural domain, that is, the design of a problem-specific neural architecture, is a challenge that requires considerable

---

[6]Recall that in hexagonal sampling, the number of nearest neighbors is 6, not 4 or 8 as in square lattices.

```
    Item
    A B C D E F G H I J K L M N O P Q R S T U V W X Y Z 1 2 3 4 5 6
Attribute
  a1  1 2 3 4 5 3 3 3 3 3 3 3 3 3 3 3 3 3 3 3 3 3 3 3 3 3 3 3 3 3 3 3
  a2  0 0 0 0 0 1 2 3 4 5 3 3 3 3 3 3 3 3 3 3 3 3 3 3 3 3 3 3 3 3 3 3
  a3  0 0 0 0 0 0 0 0 0 1 2 3 4 5 6 7 8 3 3 3 3 6 6 6 6 6 6 6 6 6 6 6
  a4  0 0 0 0 0 0 0 0 0 0 0 0 0 0 0 0 0 1 2 3 4 1 2 3 4 2 2 2 2 2 2 2
  a5  0 0 0 0 0 0 0 0 0 0 0 0 0 0 0 0 0 0 0 0 0 0 0 0 0 1 2 3 4 5 6
```

```
┌─────────────────────────┐
│ B  C  D  E  ·  Q  R  ·  Y  Z │
│ A  ·  ·  ·  P  ·  ·  X  ·  │
│ ·  F  ·  N  O  ·  W  ·  ·  1 │
│ ·  G  ·  M  ·  ·  ·  ·  2  · │
│ H  K  L  ·  T  U  ·  3  ·  · │
│ ·  I  ·  ·  ·  ·  ·  ·  4  · │
│ ·  J  ·  S  ·  ·  V  ·  5  6 │
└─────────────────────────┘
```

(a)   (b)

Figure 9:   Sample results for self-organized feature mapping (2-D case).
From [Kohonen 1988].
(a) Unlabeled 5-D pattern data (patterns indexed by A-6).
(b) Self-organized map of the data matrix of (a).

engineering judgment. A fundamental problem is selection of the network parameters cited previously, as well as the selection of critical and representable problem features.

Research is needed to further explore the application of neural networks to PR problems involving:

- Feature extraction and recognition with incomplete feature information.
- Recognition with features with varying geometric distortions.
- Encoding of relational information via neural networks.
- Problems with significant hierarchical structures and corresponding network structures.

In addition, theoretical topics related to CAM neural network applications, such as state convergence, Hamming distance between stable states, calculation of the neural network system energy as a function of state, the use of nonzero thresholds in the neural model, and the resolution/size of the network, are noteworthy. Other open issues include:

- The formal/mathematical design of artificial neural networks (ANNs), so as to replicate capabilities and structural properties of organic brains.
- The implementation of NN designs in high-efficiency dedicated hardware, taking full advantage of the potential for massively parallel analog circuits, using VLSI and/or optical hardware.

BIBLIOGRAPHICAL REMARKS

The characteristics and PR applications of the neural networks considered in this chapter continue to be an active area of research. Especially significant is the dynamics of the resulting network and related concepts such as convergence and stability [Carp/Gross 1986]. The Hopfield network structure is introduced in [Hopfield 1982] and [Hopfield 1985]. Applications include solutions of optimization problems, such as the traveling salesman problem [Hopfield/Tank 1985], and constraint satisfaction problems, such as image labeling [Jamison/Schalkoff 1988]. An excellent overview of unsupervised learning in the neural network domain and a unification of many approaches is [Kosko 1990]. The unsupervised learning approaches using ART are documented in [Carp/Gross 1 1987] and [Carp/Gross 2 1987]. Mathematical foundations for such structures are found in [Cohen/Grossberg 1983] and [Carpenter 1989]. Additional details regarding Kohonen's self-organizing nets are found in [Kohonen 1984], [Kohonen 1 1982], [Kohonen 2 1982], [Kohonen 1987] and [Kangas et al. 1990]. One of the major difficulties in relating NeurPR results to the more conventional syntactic and statistical solutions is the lack of a good set of 'benchmark' problems.

EXERCISES

13.1   Draw the resulting network corresponding to Example 2 (13-12).

13.2   Repeat Example 2, but update only alternate (e.g., even or odd) units at each iteration. Compare the convergence of the network with this procedure with that of a global update, and assess relative computational costs.

13.3   This exercise makes an excellent project and is an extension/alternative formulation of Exercise 12.5 in Chapter 12. In this case, we desire a neural network that connects patterns that are not connected. (Connectivity is defined in Exercise 12.5 of Chapter 12.) By using an $n \times n$ array to represent the pattern, develop a Hopfield network that ideally takes fragments of a connected curve that have been disconnected and 'connects' these fragments to form a connected curve. Determine a suitable n in order that a reasonable number of sample connected patterns may be stored, yet the number of weights is not excessive.[7] Train the network and show sample responses to fragmented patterns.

13.4   Referring to Chapter 12, Exercise 12.10, show that the Hopfield relay characteristic of (13-1) is approached as a limiting case of the generalized sigmoid function given in equation P.10-1.

13.5   Explore the relationship between the formation of w_{ij} in (13-4) with the correlation or Hebbian approach of Chapter 11. (Recall that $o_i \in \{0, 1\}$ in the Hopfield network.)

(Exercises 13.6, 13.7, and 13.8 concern the design and use of software simulators for Hopfield or Hopfield-derived networks and serve as the basis for extended projects.)

13.6   The purpose of this exercise is to design a simulator for a neural network pattern recognizer, using the approach of Hopfield. The application is for optical character recognition (OCR).

    (a)   Design a neural network in software, where the neuron characteristics are given by (13-1) and stable states are stored using (13-4). Choose a 25-neuron model, where characters are discretized using a 5×5 sampling grid and therefore generate a 25×1 binary feature vector.

---

[7]Recall that the earlier problem used $n = 5$.

(b) Show the response of your network to discretized versions of the 4 characters: 'A,' 'C,' 'E,' 'P.' Specifically, show the convergence of the network as a function of the size, orientation, position, and shape (due to discretization) of input characters. In addition, show the response of the network with incomplete (i.e., missing parts) character input. Quantify, as much as possible, convergence in terms of Hamming distance of states.

13.7   [Hopfield 1982] suggests that alternative networks with modified or 'clipped' weights perform acceptably.

(a) For example, consider the replacement of w_{ij} with the algebraic sign of w_{ij}, yielding a network with weights of either -1 or $+1$. Repeat the simulation of Exercise 13.5 with this case.

(b) Repeat part (a) where the weights are quantized into ternary values $-1, 0, +1$ and compare the results with part (a).

13.8   Repeat the simulation of Exercise 13.6 for 'diameter limited' neural interconnections. Specifically, set

$$w_{ij} = \begin{cases} w_{ij} & \text{if } |i-j| \le D \\ 0 & \text{otherwise ('diameter limited')} \end{cases} \qquad (P.8-1)$$

13.9   In biological networks, the 'updating' of neuron activity is highly asynchronous. In (13-2) a highly synchronous version of the updating is shown. This exercise is intended to explore the alternatives available for such nets in simulation. Discuss ramifications (and implement them in simulations, if possible) of the following:

(a) At each iteration, (13-2) is used. Notice that if the units are updated serially, some activations using 'old' o_i values are used.

(b) In contrast with (a), at each iteration the current activation and consequent output of the unit is computed using the latest available o_i values.

(c) The unit updating is random. At each iteration, only a certain percentage of the units is updated.

13.10 What if the initial weights $\underline{m}_i(0)$ in (13-28) are not different? Consider two different cases: (a) They are nonrandom but all unique; and (b) they are random but some values are the same.

13.11 Kohonen states that if the input patterns $\underline{x}$ are characterized by a density $p(\underline{x})$, the point density function of the resulting weight vectors $\underline{m}_i$ approximates $p(\underline{x})$. Discuss intuitively and using (13-28), why this makes sense.

13.12 The Kohonen self-organizing or adaptation law of (13-29a), for each element of $\underline{m}_i$ and $\underline{x}$, may be rearranged as

$$\frac{dw_{ij}(t)}{dt} = \alpha[x_j - w_{ij}(t)] \qquad (P.12-1)$$

which is a specific case of the more general adaptation equation [Kohonen 1984]

$$\frac{dw_{ij}(t)}{dt} = \alpha(t)\{u_i(t)x_i(t) - \gamma u_i(t)w_{ij}(t)\} \qquad (P.12-2)$$

where $u_i(t)$ is taken to be unity.

    (a) Show that (P.12-2) represents a form of Hebbian or correlation learning with a 'forgetting' term.

    (b) What conditions are necessary to simplify (P.12-2) into (P.12-1)?

13.13 Show why the updating strategy of (13-26) is reasonable. Cite a simple example to support your reasoning.

Appendix 1
Linear Algebra Review

INTRODUCTION

This appendix reviews a number of topics from linear algebra and estimation theory that will prove useful in developing pattern recognition algorithms.

DIFFERENTIATION OF MATRICES AND VECTORS

Differentiation of a Scalar Function with Respect to a Vector

Let $f(\underline{x})$ be a scalar-valued function of n variables x_i, written as an $n \times 1$ vector $\underline{x}$. The derivative of $f(\underline{x})$ with respect to $\underline{x}$ is an $n \times 1$ vector defined as

$$\frac{df(\underline{x})}{d\underline{x}} = \begin{pmatrix} \frac{\partial f(\underline{x})}{\partial x_1} \\ \frac{\partial f(\underline{x})}{\partial x_2} \\ \vdots \\ \frac{\partial f(\underline{x})}{\partial x_n} \end{pmatrix} \qquad (A.1-1)$$

This quantity is often referred to as the gradient vector of f, denoted as $\nabla_x \underline{f}$ or $grad_x \underline{f}$. It defines the direction of maximum increase of the function.

Differentiation of a Vector Function with Respect to a Vector

The differentiation of a vector function, that is, $\underline{f}(\underline{x})$ where $\underline{f}$ is $m \times 1$ and $\underline{x}$ is $n \times 1$, results in an $m \times n$ matrix of the form

$$\frac{d\underline{f}(\underline{x})}{d\underline{x}} = \begin{pmatrix} \frac{\partial f_1}{\partial x_1} & \cdots & \frac{\partial f_1}{\partial x_n} \\ & \ddots & \\ \frac{\partial f_m}{\partial x_1} & \cdots & \frac{\partial f_m}{\partial x_n} \end{pmatrix} \qquad (A.1-2)$$

where the ijth element of this matrix is $\partial f_i / \partial x_j$ and f_i is the ith element of $\underline{f}$ and x_j is the jth element of $\underline{x}$. This matrix is also referred to as the Jacobian of $\underline{f}(\underline{x})$, denoted $J_{\underline{x}}$.

Differentiation of a Matrix with Respect to a Vector

The differentiation of a matrix with respect to a vector requires a 3-D array representation, and this generally employs tensor notation.

Vector-Matrix Differentiation Formulae

Examples of properties using the above definitions may be easily derived and are summarized in the discussion that follows. For a matrix A and vectors $\underline{x}$ and $\underline{y}$

$$\frac{d}{d\underline{x}}(A\underline{x}) = A$$

$$\frac{d}{d\underline{x}}(\underline{y}^T A\underline{x}) = A^T \underline{y}$$

$$\frac{d}{d\underline{x}}(\underline{x}^T A\underline{x}) = (A + A^T)\underline{x} \qquad (A.1-3)$$

MULTIDIMENSIONAL TAYLOR SERIES EXPANSIONS

The Taylor series expansion for a scalar function of a vector variable $f(\underline{x})$ about point $\underline{x}_o$ is written, using the results of the previous section, as

$$f(\underline{x}) = f(\underline{x}_o) + \left[\frac{df(\underline{x}_o)}{d\underline{x}}\right]^T (\underline{x} - \underline{x}_o) + \frac{1}{2}(\underline{x} - \underline{x}_o)^T \left[\frac{d^2 f(\underline{x}_o)}{d\underline{x}^2}\right](\underline{x} - \underline{x}_o)$$

$$+ \text{ higher order terms} \qquad (A.1-4)$$

Similarly, a vector function expansion is

$$\underline{f}(\underline{x}) = \underline{f}(\underline{x}_o) + \left[\frac{d\underline{f}(\underline{x}_o)}{d\underline{x}}\right](\underline{x} - \underline{x}_o) + \text{ higher order terms} \qquad (A.1-5)$$

VECTOR INNER AND OUTER PRODUCTS

If $\underline{x}$ and $\underline{y}$ are real $n \times 1$ vectors, their vector inner product is the scalar given by $<\underline{x}, \underline{y}> = (\underline{x})^T \underline{y} = \underline{y}^T \underline{x}$. If $<\underline{x}, \underline{y}> = 0$ the vectors are said to be orthogonal. The outer product of $\underline{x}$ and $\underline{y}$, denoted $> \underline{x}, \underline{y} <$, is the $n \times n$ rank 1 matrix $\underline{x}\,\underline{y}^T$.

LEAST SQUARES TECHNIQUES (DETERMINISTIC)

The Formulation of a Pseudoinverse of a Matrix

The problem of forming an inverse of a rectangular matrix A with specified properties has been studied for some time [Rao 1971]. The pseudoinverse of an $m \times n$ real matrix A is an $n \times m$ matrix denoted by $A^\dagger$. Examples of desirable properties are

$$AA^\dagger A = A$$

$$A^\dagger AA^\dagger = A^\dagger$$

$$(AA^\dagger)^T = AA^\dagger \qquad (A.1-6)$$

If A has full column rank, one inverse of considerable interest is the so-called least squares inverse, denoted by

$$A^\dagger = (A^T A)^{-1} A^T \qquad (A.1-7)$$

The properties of this solution are considered extensively in references on least squares estimation, interpolation, and the like. One important note is that the formulation of this pseudoinverse requires the inversion of an $M \times M$ nonsingular matrix (or conversely, the solution of the so-called normal equations, which are also of order M). Numerous successful algorithms for the solution of this problem are available.

Basic Formulation

Suppose we are given an overdetermined linear equation of the form:

$$\underline{b} = A\underline{x} \qquad (A.1-8)$$

where $\underline{b}$ is $m \times 1$, $\underline{x}$ is $n \times 1$, $m > n$ and A is $m \times n$ with rank n. There is no way to exactly satisfy this equation for arbitrary $\underline{b}$. We define an $m \times 1$ error function vector corresponding to some approximate solution, $\hat{\underline{x}}$:

$$\underline{e} = \underline{b} - A\hat{\underline{x}} \qquad (A.1-9)$$

and then determine a procedure to minimize some function of this error. Often, in unweighted least squares, this function, denoted J, is chosen to be

$$J = \underline{e}^T \underline{e} \qquad (A.1-10)$$

To find the minimum of this function, we set

$$\frac{dJ}{d\underline{x}} = \underline{0} \qquad (A.1-11)$$

and use (A.1-3) to develop the so-called normal equations, that is,

$$A^T A \hat{\underline{x}} = A^T \underline{b} \qquad (A.1-12)$$

from which $\underline{b}$ may be determined. Note that in theory $A^T A$ may be inverted to yield $\hat{\underline{x}}$.

The Modern Approach

The modern approach proceeds from a geometrical view of vector-matrix relationships in m- and n-dimensional spaces. For example, $A\underline{x} = \underline{b}$ may be thought of as a way to map the n-dimensional vector $\underline{x}$ into the m-dimensional vector $\underline{b}$. The problem concerns inverting this mapping.

In the overdetermined case, $\underline{b}$ does not lie in the column space of A, denoted as the *range of* A, or $R(A)$. Thus, we desire a solution $\hat{\underline{x}}$ such that the orthogonal distance between $A\hat{\underline{x}}$ and $\underline{b}$ is minimum. As in the previous approach, we characterize this distance as the length of the error vector $\underline{e}$, defined in (A.1-9).

The geometrical approach notes that the length of $\underline{e}$ is minimum when $\underline{e}$ lies in a vector space orthogonal to $R(A)$. This space is known as the *null space of* A^T, denoted $N(A^T)$. Any vector $\underline{y}$ in this space is characterized by

$$A^T \underline{y} = \underline{0} \qquad (A.1-13)$$

Therefore, the modern or geometrical approach stipulates that $\underline{e}$ must satisfy

$$A^T \underline{e} = \underline{0} \qquad (A.1-14)$$

from which the so-called normal equations, identical to the previous solution given by (A.1-12), arise.

The geometrical solution may also be characterized as finding the *projection* of $\underline{b}$ onto $R(A)$ (call this $\underline{b}^P$) and then finding the vector $\hat{\underline{x}}$ that exactly satisfies $A\hat{\underline{x}} = \underline{b}^P$. This approach also yields the normal equations, as shown previously.

Once the normal equations have been formed, if $(A^T A)$ is invertible, we may form the solution for $\hat{\underline{x}}$ as

$$\hat{\underline{x}} = (A^T A)^{-1} A^T \underline{b} \qquad (A.1-15)$$

The quantity $(A^T A)^{-1} A^T \underline{b}$ is known as the pseudoinverse of A.

Probabilistic Interpretation of Least Squares Estimators

An extension to $(A.1-8)$ is

$$\underline{b} = A\underline{x} + \underline{\eta} \qquad (A.1-16)$$

where $\underline{b}$ is an $m \times 1$ process 'output' vector; A is an $m \times n$ known, measurable, or calculable matrix; $\underline{x}$ is an $n \times 1$ parameter vector to be estimated (denote this estimate by $\hat{\underline{x}}$); and $\underline{\eta}$ is an $m \times 1$ 'noise' vector. It is desired to estimate $\underline{x}$, with the following constraints on estimate $\hat{\underline{x}}$:

Table A.1-1:   Desired Estimator Properties

(1)	$\hat{\underline{x}} = M\underline{b}$	(linearity)	(A.1-17a)
(2)	$E\{\hat{\underline{x}}\} = \underline{x}$	(unbiasedness)	(A.1-17b)
(3)	$cov\{\hat{\underline{x}}\} = \hat{\Sigma}$	'small' or perhaps minimal in some sense	(A.1-17c)

It may be shown that the estimate that minimizes a loss function of the type $|\underline{b} - A\hat{\underline{x}}|_R$ in accordance with property (1) of Table A.1-1 is of the form:

$$\hat{\underline{x}} = M\underline{b} \qquad (A.1-18)$$

where

$$M = A_R^{\dagger} = (A^T R A)^{-1} A^T R \qquad (A.1-19)$$

M equals the pseudoinverse of A, based on an R norm, denoted by $A_R^{\dagger}$. Often $R = I$ is chosen. Assuming that A and $\underline{\eta}$ are statistically independent, property (2) of Table A.1-1 may be satisfied, since

$$E\{\hat{\underline{x}}\} = E\{(A^T R A)^{-1} A^T R A \underline{x}\} + E\{(A^T R A)^{-1} A^T R \underline{\eta}\}$$

$$= \underline{x} + E\{(A^T R A)^{-1} A^T R\} E\{\underline{\eta}\}$$

if either

$$E(\underline{\eta}) = \underline{0} \qquad (A.1-20)$$

or

$$E\{(A^T R A)^{-1} A^T R\} = [0] \qquad (A.1-21)$$

It is possible to show $cov[\hat{\underline{x}}] = \Sigma_{\hat{\underline{x}}} = E\{[MA\underline{x}+M\underline{\eta}-\underline{x}][MA\underline{x}+M\underline{\eta}-\underline{x}]^T\}$. Defining $cov[\underline{\eta}] \triangleq N$, this becomes $cov[\hat{\underline{x}}] = (A^T R A)^{-1} A^T R N R A (A^T R A)^{-1}$. Property (3) of Table A.1-1 may be satisfied by choosing $R = N^{-1}$, yielding

$$cov\{\hat{\underline{x}}\} = (A^T N^{-1} A)^{-1} \qquad (A.1-22)$$

which can be shown to be *minimum variance, hence efficient.*

PRACTICAL CONCERNS REGARDING LEAST SQUARES SOLUTIONS

QR Decomposition

Although, in theory, the quantity $(A^T A)^{-1}$ exists, significant numerical difficulties may occur in computing this inverse in instances where $A^T A$ is nearly singular.[1] In

---

[1]Since we required the rank of $A = n$.

addition, the process of forming $A^T A$, for large A, is computationally expensive. The numerical errors incurred in forming $A^T A$, and then forming the inverse, spawn a need for alternate approaches that are not plagued by numerical sensitivities. One solution is to avoid forming the normal equations explicitly, but still to follow the geometrical approach. This solution is known as QR decomposition. QR (or generally orthogonalization) methods are based on decomposition of the $m \times n$ matrix A (with rank n) into

$$A = QR \qquad\qquad (A.1-23)$$

where Q is $m \times m$ and satisfies

$$Q^T Q = D \qquad\qquad (A.1-24)$$

D is a diagonal matrix with nonzero diagonal elements. R is an $n \times n$ upper triangular matrix with diagonal entries $r_{kk} = 1$; therefore, R^{-1} exists. Given $(A.1 - 8)$ and $(A.1 - 23)$, we may reformulate the least squares solution as

$$R^T Q^T (\underline{b} - A\hat{\underline{x}}) = \underline{0} \qquad\qquad (A.1-25)$$

Since

$$Q^T A = Q^T QR = DR \qquad\qquad (A.1-26)$$

(A.1-25) may be rewritten as

$$R^T (Q^T \underline{b} - DR\hat{\underline{x}}) = \underline{0} \qquad\qquad (A.1-27)$$

Thus, we arrive at

$$DR\hat{\underline{x}} = Q^T \underline{b}$$

or

$$R\hat{\underline{x}} = D^{-1}Q^T \underline{b} \qquad\qquad (A.1-28)$$

Using (A.1-28), we could solve for $\hat{\underline{x}}$ via back-substitution. The problem of computing Q, R, and the above quantities is addressed via a modified Gram-Schmidt procedure.

EIGENVALUE/EIGENVECTOR PROBLEMS

Eigenvalue/eigenvector formulations are very useful in StatPR and NeurPR for:

1. Predicting the behavior of some types of linear pattern associators;
2. Determining key features that are, in some sense, 'most important'; and
3. Transforming probabilistic models for easier visualization.

Basic Theory

Consider an $n \times n$ (square) matrix A. It is useful to explore if a scalar λ and a vector $\hat{\underline{x}}$ exist[2] such that

$$A\hat{\underline{x}} = \lambda\hat{\underline{x}} \qquad\qquad (A.1-29)$$

---

[2]Readers should not confuse this $\hat{\underline{x}}$ with the least squares estimator considered previously.

In other words, $A\hat{x}$ has the same direction in R^n as $\hat{x}$, and is scaled by a factor of λ. Obviously, $\hat{x} = \underline{0}$ is a trivial solution. Equation A.1-29 may be rewritten

$$(A - \lambda I)\hat{x} = \underline{0} \qquad (A.1 - 30)$$

Recall that $(A - \lambda I)^{-1}$ exists only if $|A - \lambda I| \neq 0$; therefore, if $|A - \lambda I| \neq 0$, $\hat{x} = (A - \lambda I)^{-1}\underline{0} = \underline{0}$. For 'interesting' (nontrivial) solutions for $\hat{x}$, we require $|A - \lambda I| = 0$. For an $n \times n$ matrix, this yields a scalar polynomial in λ of order n of the form:

$$|A - \lambda I| = \lambda^n + a_1\lambda^{n-1} + \ldots + a_{n-1}\lambda + a_n = 0 \qquad (A.1 - 31)$$

Equation (A.1-31) is called the *characteristic equation* or *characteristic polynomial of the matrix A*, often denoted as $P(\lambda)$. Thus, we see that there are n solutions for the λ constrained by (A.1-31) (although not all necessarily unique and possibly complex). These n solutions for λ are termed the *eigenvalues* or e-values of A and the corresponding vectors $\hat{x}$ are the *eigenvectors* or e-vectors. If any characteristic value of A is zero, we get $P(0) = a_n = 0 = |+A|$, and therefore A is singular. Furthermore, note from (A.1-31) that if A is specified in either upper or lower triangular (or diagonal) form, the diagonal elements are the e-values. Unfortunately, only under certain conditions do we get n linearly independent eigenvectors. Note also that only the *direction* of this vector is specified. Because (A.1-30) is homogeneous, any solution vector of nonzero length satisfies the equation.

The Modal Matrix

The matrix formed by the column vectors $\hat{x}_i$ (the e-vectors of A) is called the *modal* matrix, often denoted by M.

$$M = [\hat{x}_i] \quad i = 1, 2, \ldots n \qquad (A.1 - 32)$$

For the case of nonrepeated λ_i's [roots of $P(\lambda)$], the matrix will have n *linearly independent* eigenvectors.[3] Thus, any matrix with *distinct e-values* yields a modal matrix M that is invertible. Recall that M is not unique, because of a possible scaling of the $\hat{x}_i$. Given n solutions for λ_i and $\hat{x}_i$ in the equation $A\hat{x}_i = \lambda_i\hat{x}_i$, these equations may be written as

$$AM = M\Lambda \qquad (A.1 - 33)$$

where

$$\Lambda = \begin{pmatrix} \lambda_1 & 0 & \ldots & 0 & 0 \\ 0 & \lambda_2 & \ldots & 0 & 0 \\ & & \ddots & & \\ 0 & 0 & \ldots & 0 & \lambda_n \end{pmatrix} \qquad (A.1 - 34)$$

Since M is invertible,

$$A = M\Lambda M^{-1} \qquad (A.1 - 35)$$

---

[3]Note that matrices with repeated e-values also may have a linearly independent set of e-vectors, but this is not guaranteed. The identity matrix I is a good example.

or

$$\Lambda = M^{-1}AM \qquad (A.1-36)$$

Equations A.1-35 and A.1-36 provide a means for diagonalization of the matrix A or the representation of A with respect to its eigenvectors. This is a *coordinate transformation*.

Application to Symmetric Matrices

Concerns from the previous section regarding the uniqueness of the λ_i and the existence of a set of linearly independent e-vectors are minimized in the case of (real) symmetric matrices. Symmetric matrices are of special concern, since the covariance matrix of a vector random variable is symmetric. It is straightforward to show that a matrix satisfying $A = A^T$ has the following properties:

1. The matrix has real e-values.
2. The e-vectors comprise a set of *orthogonal* vectors. Thus, by normalizing each of the e-vectors such that they are orthonormal (have unity length),

$$M^{-1} = M^T \qquad (A.1-37)$$

3. Equation (A.1-37) yields a diagonal Λ.

Deterministic and Probabilistic Applications of Diagonalization

The deterministic applications of eigenvalue–eigenvector formulations are well known in systems theory. For example, the use of linear transformations on state vectors leads to conclusions regarding state coupling, system stability, and so on. Probabilistic applications are of equal importance. Two areas of immediate interest are based on the diagonalization of the covariance matrix of a random vector, leading to (i) a method for statistically removing signal redundancy, often referred to as the Karhounen-Loeve transform; and (ii) an efficient approach to extract, classify, and visualize the underlying characteristics of features.

The basis for both of these approaches is the linear transformation of a random vector. The technique is briefly shown below.

A linear transformation of a r. v. yields another r. v. of the form:

$$\underline{Y} = A^T \underline{X} \qquad (A.1-38)$$

Assuming A is orthogonal, the inverse of this transformation is

$$\underline{X} = A\underline{Y} \qquad (A.1-39)$$

We assume hereafter that $\underline{X}$ is zero mean, that is, $E(\underline{X}) = \underline{m}_X = \underline{0}$. From the definition of covariance in Appendix 2, we may compute the covariance matrix of $\underline{Y}$ as

$$\Sigma_Y = E(\underline{Y}\underline{Y}^T) = A^T \Sigma_{\underline{X}} A \qquad (A.1-40)$$

Recall from (A.1-36) and (A.1-37) that if A is chosen to be the modal matrix of $\Sigma_{\underline{X}}$, then $\Sigma_{\underline{Y}}$ will be diagonal. More specifically, since $\Sigma_{\underline{X}}$ is symmetric, the analysis of the previous section indicates that real e-values exist, and in addition, the e-vectors form an orthogonal set. Thus, the choice of the modal matrix (derived from the co-variance matrix) to achieve the linear transformation yields a transformed r. v. whose components are uncorrelated.

Digital Computation of e-Values and e-Vectors

Rarely does the computer implementation of the e-value–e-vector determination procedure shown above emulate the hand computations. In addition, the derivation of a general procedure to handle cases of repeated e-values and nonsymmetric matrices (yielding cases wherein a full set of e-vectors may not exist) is quite challenging.

Techniques for numerical linear algebra applied to real, symmetric matrices are well known [Dahlquist 1974]. Most of the modern techniques are based on a series of similarity transformations, perhaps the most popular of which is the QR decomposition described above. The reader is referred to numerical methods handbooks [Wilkenson 1971], [Dahlquist 1974] for detailed descriptions of algorithms.

MATRIX NORMS

Various matrix norms exist [Dahlquist 1974]. One of the most useful is the matrix-bound norm

$$\| A \| = \max_{\underline{x} \neq \underline{0}} \frac{\| A\underline{x} \|}{\| \underline{x} \|} \qquad (A.1-41)$$

which has the property

$$\| A\underline{x} \| \leq \| A \| \| \underline{x} \| \qquad (A.1-42)$$

where $\| \underline{x} \|$ is a vector norm.

Appendix 2
Probability and Random
Variables/Vectors

PROBABILITY

Intuitive Development

Probability may be developed from the viewpoint of relative frequency of occurrence. For example, the probability of event A could be defined as

$$P(A) = \lim_{n \to \infty} \frac{N(A)}{n} \qquad (A.2 - 1a)$$

where $N(A)$ is the number of times A occurred in n trials. The intuitive approach is conceptually appealing; however, numerous shortcomings lead us to search for more precise and versatile alternatives.

Probability (Geometric and Set-Based)

Defining

Ω: Sample space; contains all possible outcomes of an experiment. Ω can be *discrete* (in which case the number of elements is either finite or countably infinite) or *continuous* (with an uncountable number of elements).

w: A single outcome; $w \in \Omega$

A: Specific event of interest or *set of outcomes* $A \subset \Omega$. An event A is said to *occur* if the observed outcome w is an element of A, that is, $w \in A$. Associated with these definitions is a *probability space*. For example,

$$A_1 \subset A_2 \Rightarrow P(A_1) \leq P(A_2) \qquad (A.2 - 1b)$$

where $P(A)$ is a probability function that assigns a real, scalar-valued function to each set A, with the constraints:

1. $P(A) \geq 0 \quad \forall \quad A \in \Omega$ $(A.2-2a)$
2. $P(\Omega) = 1$ $(A.2-2b)$
3. If sets or experiment outcomes $A_1, A_2, \ldots A_n$ are mutually exclusive, that is, $A_i \cap A_j = \emptyset, \quad \forall i, j$, then $P(\bigcup_{i=1}^{n} A_i) = \sum_{i=1}^{n} p(A_i)$ $(A.2-2c)$

   Given the set of all outcomes, $A_i, \ i = 1, 2, \ldots n$, which constitute a partition of Ω,

$$\sum_i P(A_i) = 1 \qquad (A.2-2d)$$

4. $P(\emptyset) = 0$ $(A.2-2e)$

The probability of the joint occurrence of *independent* events A, B, C is given by

$$P(ABC) = P(A)P(B)P(C) \qquad (A.2-3)$$

One of the most significant (and useful) concepts is that of *conditional probability*, where the probability of occurrence of outcome A is conditioned on occurrence of outcome B, that is,

$$P(A|B) = \frac{P(AB)}{P(B)} \qquad (A.2-4a)$$

Bayes theorem is an important extension to (A.2-4a), which provides a means to convert a priori probabilities to a posteriori probabilities, that is,

$$P(A|B)P(B) = P(B|A)P(A) \qquad (A.2-4b)$$

If events $A_i, \ i = 1, 2, \ldots c$, represent a partitioning of Ω (note from Appendix 3 that this requires they be mutually exclusive), then

$$P(B) = \sum_{i=1}^{c} P(A_i \cap B) \qquad (A.2-4c)$$

The *Total Probability Theorem* [Papoulis 1984], which involves an event conditioned on a r.v., $\underline{X}$, is useful in StatPR error analysis:

$$P(A) = \int_{-\infty}^{\infty} P(A|\underline{X} = \underline{x})p(\underline{x})d\underline{x} \qquad (A.2-5)$$

RANDOM VARIABLES

A (scalar) random variable (r.v.), denoted X, is a *function* that maps the outcome of a random event into real scalar values. As shown in Figures A.2-1(a) and (b), the notions of sets, probability and random variables may be unified by considering set

$A = \{w | X(w) < \varsigma\} \subset \Omega$ where $\varsigma \in R^1$. A cumulative probability distribution function (cdf) for X is defined as[1]

$$F_X(x) = P(X \leq x) \qquad (A.2-6)$$

This concept leads to the *probability density function*

$$p_X(x) = \frac{dF_X(x)}{dx} \qquad (A.2-7)$$

where $p_X(x)$ may be viewed as the probability that the random variable X takes on values in the infinitesimal interval around x. Thus, $p_X(x)$ has 'histogram-like' characteristics. Although the definition in (A.2-7) is convenient, it is crucial to note that $p_X(x)$ *does not always exist*. If $F_X(x)$ is absolutely continuous, the density function will exist.[2]

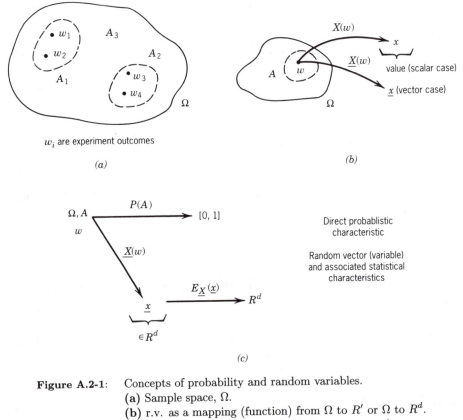

w_i are experiment outcomes

(a)

(b)

(c)

Figure A.2-1: Concepts of probability and random variables.
(a) Sample space, Ω.
(b) r.v. as a mapping (function) from Ω to R' or Ω to R^d.
(c) Overall view of mappings (includes vector r.v.s).

---

[1] Often simply referred to as the distribution of X. We hereafter drop the designation $X(w)$.
[2] The number of points where it is not differentiable is countable.

From the preceding two equations:

$$\int_{-\infty}^{\infty} p_X(x)dx = 1.0 \qquad (A.2-8)$$

Often we need to simultaneously consider more than one random variable. This leads to joint probability distribution and density functions:

$$F_{XY}(x,y) = P(X \le x \bigcap Y \le y) \qquad (A.2-9)$$

and

$$p_{XY}(x,y) = \frac{\partial^2 F_{XY}(x,y)}{\partial x \partial y} \qquad (A.2-10)$$

If X and Y are independent r.v.s,

$$F_{XY}(x,y) = F_X(x)F_Y(y) \qquad (A.2-11)$$

and

$$p_{XY}(x,y) = p_X(x)p_Y(y) \qquad (A.2-12)$$

Note that often, for notational simplicity, the subscript X on F and p is omitted. This is acceptable when it is clear *which* r.v. is meant and that X is a r.v. and x is a value that X may assume.

The conditional probability density of two r.v.s may be characterized by analogy with (A.2-4a), yielding

$$p_{X|Y}(x|y) = \frac{p_{XY}(x,y)}{p_Y(y)} \qquad (A.2-13)$$

The Discrete Case

Numerous instances exist, however, wherein X is a discrete r.v. That is, X may only take on discrete values. Examples are where X is constrained to be an integer or where X is binary valued. Given that X may assume only one of m discrete values, $x_1, x_2, \ldots x_m$, integrals of the form of (A.2-8) are replaced by sums of the form:

$$\sum_x P_X(x) = 1.0 \qquad (A.2-14)$$

Sample Distributions

Uniform.   A r.v., X, that is uniformly distributed between x_1 and x_2 has density function

$$p_X(x) = \begin{cases} \dfrac{1}{x_2 - x_1} & x_1 \le x \le x_2 \\ 0 & \text{elsewhere} \end{cases} \qquad (A.2-15)$$

Binomial.   The binomial distribution is a useful tool for exploring nonparametric training in SyntPR. A random variable X, which takes on integer values in the interval $[0, n]$, has a *binomial distribution of order n* if

$$P(X = k) = \binom{n}{k} p^k (1 - p)^{n-k} \qquad (A.2 - 16a)$$

This leads to a staircase-shaped cdf of the form

$$F_X(x) = \sum_{k=0}^{m} \binom{n}{k} p^k (1 - p)^{n-k} \qquad (A.2 - 16b)$$

where $m \le x < m + 1$. An interesting fact is that if n is large, $F_X(x)$ approximates a normal distribution with $\mu_X = np$ and $\sigma_X^2 = np(1 - p)$.

The all-important Gaussian, or 'normal' distribution is covered later.

STATISTICAL CHARACTERIZATIONS

In order to characterize a random variable, the cdf or pdf would be sufficient. However, these are often neither convenient nor achievable characterizations, and therefore several statistical measures are often employed. The most popular is the measure of *expectation*:

$$E(X) = \int_{-\infty}^{\infty} x p_X(x) dx \qquad (A.2 - 17a)$$

often referred to as the *mean* or first moment of X, and

$$E(X^2) = \int_{-\infty}^{\infty} x^2 p_X(x) dx \qquad (A.2 - 17b)$$

referred to as the *second moment* of X. The latter quantity may be normalized by the mean to yield a measure of the *variance* or *scatter* of X, that is,

$$\mathrm{Var}(X) = E\{[X - E(X)]^2\} = \int_{-\infty}^{\infty} (x - E[X])^2 p_X(x) dx$$

$$= E[X^2] - (E[X])^2 \qquad (A.2 - 17c)$$

Note that expectation is a linear operator. As noted in the previous section, summation-based analogies for these operators exist for the discrete case. The *covariance* of two scalar r.v.s X and Y is given by

$$E\{[X - E(X)][Y - E(Y)]\} = \int_{-\infty}^{\infty} \int_{-\infty}^{\infty} [x - E(X)][y - E(Y)] p_{XY}(x, y) dx dy$$

$$= E[XY] - E[X]E[Y] \qquad (A.2 - 18)$$

where the quantity $E[XY]$ represents the *correlation* of X and Y. If $X = Y$ in the above formulation, $E[XY] = E[X^2]$ is the *mean squared value* of X.

Table A.2-1 and Figure A.2-1(c) summarize these concepts.

Table A.2-1:   Summary of Random Variables

Concept	Discrete case	Continuous case
$P(X \leq x)$	$F_X(x) = \sum_{k=0}^{i} {}^{(1)} p_x(x_k)$	$F_X(x) = \int_{-\infty}^{x} p_X(\varsigma) d\varsigma$
$P(X = x)$	$p_X(x)$	$0^{(2)}$
$P(X = x \mid Y = y)$	$p_{X\mid Y}(x, y)$	$0^{(2)}$
$P(X \leq x \mid Y = y)$	$\sum_{k=0}^{i} {}^{(1)} p_{X\mid Y}(x_k \mid y)$	$\int_{-\infty}^{x} p_{X\mid Y}(\varsigma \mid y) d\varsigma$
$P_{X\mid Y}(x, y)$	$\dfrac{p_{XY}(x, y)}{p_Y(y)}^{(3)}$	$\dfrac{p_{XY}(x, y)}{p_Y(y)}^{(3)}$
$p_X(x)^{(4)}$	$p_X(x) = \sum_{y_i} p_{XY}(x, y_i)$	$p_X(x) = \int_{-\infty}^{\infty} p_{XY}(x, \varsigma) d\varsigma$
$p_X(x)$	$P(X = x)$	$\dfrac{\partial}{\partial x} F_X(x)^{(5)}$

Notes:
^{1} Where i is the largest integer such that $x_i \leq x$.
^{2} Unless F_X is discontinuous.
^{3} $p_Y(y) > 0$.
^{4} Associated with a joint density p_{XY}.
^{5} In cases where the derivative exists; (F_X is absolutely continuous.)

EXTENSION TO VECTOR RANDOM VARIABLES

Vector random variables find application in numerous modeling situations and are direct extensions of the scalar case. A vector random variable, denoted $\underline{X}$, is a vector whose components X_i are themselves random variables, that is,

$$\underset{\underline{X}}{d \times 1} = \begin{pmatrix} X_1 \\ X_2 \\ \vdots \\ X_n \end{pmatrix} \qquad (A.2 - 19)$$

Vector random variables give rise to multivariate probability distribution and density functions (where they exist). The cumulative distribution function of the d-dimensional vector r.v. $\underline{X}$ (also referred to herein as simply a *random vector*) is a *scalar* function defined by

$$F_{\underline{X}}(\underline{x}) = P(X_1 \leq x_1 \cap \underline{X}_d \leq x_2 \cdots \cap X_d \leq x_d) \qquad (A.2 - 20)$$

Therefore, $F_{\underline{X}}(\underline{x})$ is a monotonically nondecreasing function of any component of $\underline{x}$. $F_{\underline{X}}(\underline{x})$ is sometimes referred to as the joint probability distribution function of $x_1, x_2, \ldots x_d$.

A scalar function $p_{\underline{X}}(\underline{x})$, which satisfies

$$F_{\underline{X}}(\underline{x}) = \int_{-\infty}^{x_1} \int_{-\infty}^{x_2} \cdots \int_{-\infty}^{x_d} p_{\underline{X}}(\xi_1, \xi_2, \ldots \xi_n) d\xi_1 d\xi_2 \ldots d\xi_d \qquad (A.2 - 21)$$

or

$$F_{\underline{X}}(\underline{x}) = \int_{-\infty}^{\underline{x}} p_{\underline{X}}(\underline{\xi}) d\underline{\xi} \qquad (A.2 - 22)$$

is called the probability density function of $\underline{X}$. The Fundamental Theorem of Calculus yields

$$p_{\underline{X}}(\underline{x}) = \frac{\partial^n}{\partial x_1 \partial x_2 \ldots \partial x_d} F_{\underline{X}}(\underline{x}) \qquad (A.2 - 23)$$

Mass or Density Interpretations.   In StatPR, identification of class-specific cdfs or pdfs is often fundamental. In the d-dimensional case, a limiting argument shows the probability that X lies in an (infinitesmal) hypercube[3] of volume $d\underline{\varsigma}$, located at $\underline{\varsigma}$ is $P\big(w : \underline{x}(w) \in [\underline{\varsigma}, \underline{\varsigma} + d\underline{\varsigma}]\big) = p_X(\underline{\varsigma}) d\underline{\varsigma}$.

Conditional probabilities and corresponding distributions and densities may be developed for random vectors. The vectors need not have the same dimension. For example, considering

$$P(\underline{X} = \underline{x} | \underline{Y} = \underline{y}) = \frac{P(\underline{X} = \underline{x} \cap \underline{Y} = \underline{y})}{P(\underline{Y} = \underline{y})} \qquad (A.2 - 24a)$$

leads to

$$p_{\underline{X}|\underline{Y}}(\underline{x}|\underline{y}) = \frac{p_{\underline{XY}}(\underline{x}, \underline{y})}{p_{\underline{y}}(\underline{y})} \qquad (A.2 - 24b)$$

Equation (A.2-24b) may be used to develop a Bayesian formulation analogous to (A.2-4).

Independence, Functional Dependence, and Mutual Exclusivity.   The independence of events A and B implies that knowledge of $P(A)$ yields no information about $P(B)$ and vice versa. If r.v.s X and Y are independent and the appropriate densities exist,

$$p_{\underline{XY}}(\underline{x}, \underline{y}) = p_{\underline{X}}(\underline{x}) p_{\underline{Y}}(\underline{y}) \qquad (A.2 - 25a)$$

Independent events should not be confused with mutually exclusive events. If $A \cap B = \emptyset$, then A and B are *mutually exclusive* and $P(A) + P(B) = P(A \cup B)$.

An extreme case of dependence is *functional or deterministic dependence*. For example, if f is a deterministic function of r.v.s X_1 and X_2 that yields r.v X_3

$$X_3 = f(X_1, X_2) \qquad (A.2 - 25b)$$

---

[3]'Interval' in the case $d = 1$.

then the conditional pdf

$$p_{X_3|X_1X_2}(x_3|x_1x_2) = \delta[x_3 - f(x_1, x_2)] \qquad (A.2-25c)$$

Similarly, the joint pdf of X_1X_2 and X_3, that is,

$$p_{X_1X_2X_3}(x_1, x_2, x_3) = p_{X_1X_2}(x_1, x_2)p_{X_3|X_1X_2}(x_3|x_1, x_2) \qquad (A.2-25d)$$

will reflect this impulse, from (A.2-25c). Another characterization of the situation in (A.2-25d) is that the distribution of a corresponding r.v. $\underline{X} = (X_1\ X_2\ X_3)^T$ 'collapses' from R^3 to R^2.

The expectation of a random vector is defined in a manner similar to that of its scalar counterpart, that is,

$$E(\underline{X}) = \int_{-\infty}^{\infty} \underline{x}p_X(\underline{x})d\underline{x} \qquad (A.2-26)$$

$$= \begin{pmatrix} E(X_1) \\ E(X_2) \\ \vdots \\ E(X_d) \end{pmatrix}$$

$$= \begin{pmatrix} \int_{-\infty}^{-\infty}\int_{-\infty}^{\infty}\cdots\int_{-\infty}^{\infty} x_1p_{\underline{X}}(\underline{x})dx_1, dx_2, \ldots dx_d \\ \int_{-\infty}^{\infty}\int_{-\infty}^{\infty}\cdots\int_{-\infty}^{\infty} x_2p_{\underline{X}}(\underline{x})dx_1, dx_2 \ldots dx_d \\ \vdots \\ \int_{-\infty}^{\infty}\int_{-\infty}^{\infty}\cdots\int_{-\infty}^{\infty} x_dp_{\underline{X}}(\underline{x})dx_1, dx_2 \ldots dx_d \end{pmatrix}$$

$$= \underline{\mu}_X$$

The *covariance matrix* of X is defined as

$$\Sigma_X = E\{(\underline{X} - \underline{\mu}_X)(\underline{X} - \underline{\mu}_X)^T\}$$

$$= E\{\underline{X}\,\underline{X}^T\} - \underline{\mu}_X\underline{\mu}_X^T \qquad (A.2-27)$$

Finally, we note that a multitude of estimators for the mean and covariance of a random vector exist. Given v sample vectors $\underline{x}_k, k = 1, 2, \ldots v$, two unbiased estimators are given by

$$\underline{\mu}_X = \frac{1}{v}\sum_{k=1}^{v}\underline{x}_k \qquad (A.2-28)$$

and

$$\Sigma_{\underline{X}} = \frac{1}{v-1}\sum_{k=1}^{v}(\underline{x}_k - \underline{\mu}_X)(\underline{x}_k - \underline{\mu}_X)^T \qquad (A.2-29)$$

THE MULTIDIMENSIONAL GAUSSIAN PROBABILITY DENSITY FUNCTION

Perhaps the most popular multivariate pdf, owing to its suitability and mathematical tractability, is the multivariate Gaussian, or Normal, pdf. For a $d \times 1$ vector $\underline{X}$, the pdf is given by:

$$p(\underline{x}) = \frac{\exp[-\frac{1}{2}(\underline{x} - \underline{\mu})^T \Sigma^{-1}(\underline{x} - \underline{\mu})]}{(2\pi)^{d/2}|\Sigma|^{1/2}} \qquad (A.2 - 30)$$

where the $d \times 1$ mean vector $\underline{\mu}$ and the $d \times d$ covariance matrix Σ uniquely determine the pdf. The previous section indicated how to obtain estimates of these quantities. The contours of constant density in R^d are, in general, hyperellipsoids along which the quantity $r^2 = \| \underline{x} - \underline{\mu} \|^2 \Sigma_{-1}$ is constant. The r is often referred to as the *Mahalanobis distance* from $\underline{x}$ to $\underline{\mu}$. In the scalar case, (A.2-30) reduces to the familiar $p(x) = \left(1/\sqrt{2\pi\sigma^2}\right) \exp\left[-\frac{1}{2}((x - u)/\sigma)^2\right].$

TRANSFORMATIONS OF RANDOM VARIABLES

The Karhunen–Loeve (K-L) Transformation

This transformation is also referred to as the principal component or Hotelling transform. The K-L transformation facilitates feature extraction and classification as well as analysis of PR models. The transformation is based on diagonalization, via an e-value–e-vector-based coordinate transformation, of the covariance matrix of the vector random variable.

A Linear Transformation.   Suppose a $d \times 1$ vector random variable $\underline{X}$, with covariance matrix $\Sigma_{\underline{X}}$, is used to represent feature data. Furthermore, consider a transformation of this r.v., using a $d \times d$ nonsingular real matrix A, of the form:

$$\underline{Y} = A^T \underline{X} = \sum_{i=1}^{d} \underline{a}_i^T X_i \qquad (A.2 - 31)$$

where $\underline{a}_i^T$ is the ith column of the matrix A^T, and X_i is the ith component of the r.v. $\underline{X}$. Note that $\underline{Y}$ is also a r.v. Assuming that A is an orthogonal matrix, that is, $A^T = A^{-1}$, (A.2-31) yields

$$\underline{X} = A\underline{Y} = \sum_{i=1}^{d} \underline{a}_i Y_i \qquad (A.2 - 32)$$

where $\underline{a}_i$ is the ith column of A and Y_i is the ith component of $\underline{Y}$. In equations (A.2-31) and (A.2-32) note that:

1. Each element of $\underline{X}$, that is, X_i, contributes to the representation of $\underline{Y}$ by weighting the appropriate column vector of A^T; and

2. Each element of $\underline{Y}$, that is, Y_i contributes to the representation of $\underline{X}$, again by weighting the corresponding column vector of A.

In what follows, we assume for simplicity that the r.v. $\underline{X}$ is *zero mean*. This does not restrict the approach to zero mean vectors, since a random vector $\underline{X}'$, with mean vector

$$E_{\underline{X}'}(\underline{X}') = \underline{\mu}_{\underline{X}'} \neq \underline{0} \qquad (A.2-33)$$

may easily be converted to a zero-mean random vector by the transformation:

$$\underline{X} = \underline{X}' - \mu_{\underline{X}'} \qquad (A.2-34)$$

If $\underline{X}$ in (A.2-32) is a zero-mean r.v., $\underline{Y}$ is also.

Diagonalization.   Given the covariance matrix Σ_X of $\underline{X}$, the covariance matrix of $\underline{Y}$ is given by

$$\Sigma_{\underline{Y}} = E\{\underline{Y}\underline{Y}^T\} = E\{A^T \underline{X}\underline{X}^T A\} = A^T \Sigma_{\underline{X}} A \qquad (A.2-35)$$

The matrix A is chosen to be the modal matrix of $\Sigma_{\underline{X}}$ (that is, the columns of A, denoted $\underline{a}_i$, are the e-vectors of the covariance matrix of Σ_X). This involves solving

$$\Sigma_{\underline{X}}\underline{a}_i = \lambda_i \underline{a}_i \qquad (A.2-36)$$

for d values of λ_i and $\underline{a}_i$. The consequences of this transformation in this case are twofold:

1. $\Sigma_{\underline{Y}}$ is a diagonal matrix with the diagonal entries σ_{ii}^2, the corresponding variances of the components Y_i of $\underline{Y}$. Note that $\sigma_{ii}^2 > 0$.
2. Since $\Sigma_{\underline{X}}$ is a symmetric matrix, the matrix A (see Appendix 1) consists of a set of orthogonal and normalized e-vectors, that is, the inverse of this matrix is given by:

$$A^{-T} = A^T \qquad (A.2-37)$$

Utility.   The transformation of (A.2-31), with A chosen as the modal matrix, serves as a mechanism to determine *directions of variance* in the feature vector $\underline{X}$. This is useful in choosing features in *measurement-limited systems*. By using the above analysis, we now consider the ramifications of representing feature vector $\underline{X}$ using $k < d$ components of $\underline{Y}$, choosing A as above. Since $\underline{X}$ and $\underline{Y}$ are random vectors, we consider representation error in the probabilistic sense, in particular by using a mean squared measure. To show the error incurred in this formulation, we make the following definitions:

$$A = [A_k : A_d] \qquad (A.2-38)$$

where A_k is a $d \times k$ matrix consisting of the first k columns of A (the first k e-vectors of $\Sigma_{\underline{X}}$) and A_d consists of the remaining $(d-k)$ deleted columns of A, corresponding to the $d-k$ terms not used to represent the vector $\underline{X}$. Thus, (A.2-31) may be written as

$$\underline{X} = [A_k \vdots A_d] \begin{pmatrix} \underline{Y}_k \\ \underline{Y}_{d-k} \end{pmatrix} \qquad (A.2-39)$$

where $\underline{Y}_k$ is the vector consisting of the k components of $\underline{Y}$ used to represent $\underline{X}$; $\underline{Y}_{d-k}$ consists of $d - k$ components not used. The representation of $\underline{X}$, denoted $\underline{X}_R$, resulting from using only k elements of $\underline{Y}$, may be written as

$$\underline{X}_R = A_k \underline{Y}_k \qquad (A.2 - 40)$$

where $\underline{X}_R$ is $d \times 1$ and A_k is $d \times k$. Therefore, the representation error is given by the $d \times 1$ vector, $\underline{\varepsilon}$, where

$$\underline{\varepsilon} = \underline{X} - \underline{X}_R = A_d \underline{Y}_{d-k} = \sum_{i=k+1}^{d} \underline{a}_i Y_i \qquad (A.2 - 41)$$

and the norm squared value of $\underline{\varepsilon}$ is given by

$$\| \varepsilon \|^2 = <\underline{\varepsilon}, \underline{\varepsilon}> = \underline{Y}_{d-k}^T A_d^T A_d \underline{Y}_{d-k} = \| \underline{Y}_{d-k} \|^2 \qquad (A.2 - 42)$$

because of the orthogonality of the columns of A_d (the e-vectors). Therefore, from (A.2-41)

$$\| \varepsilon \|^2 = \sum_{i=k+1}^{d} Y_i^2 \qquad (A.2 - 43)$$

and the representation error is given by the expected value of this quantity, that is,

$$E\{\| \varepsilon \|^2\} = \sum_{i=k+1}^{d} E\{Y_i^2\} \qquad (A.2 - 44)$$

which may be rewritten, using rows of (A.2-31) as

$$E\{\| \varepsilon \|^2\} = \sum_{i=k+1}^{d} E\{(\underline{a}_i^T \underline{X})(\underline{a}_i^T \underline{X})\} = \sum_{i=k+1}^{d} \underline{a}_i^T E\{\underline{X}\underline{X}^T\}\underline{a}_i = \sum_{i=k+1}^{d} \underline{a}_i^T \Sigma_{\underline{X}} \underline{a}_i$$
$$(A.2 - 45)$$

The scalars in the summation of (A.2-45) are given by (A.2-36) and are therefore the respective e-values of $\underline{X}$ (denoted λ_i). Thus, the result:

$$E\{\| \varepsilon \|^2\} = \sum_{i=k+1}^{d} \lambda_i \qquad (A.2 - 46)$$

Notice that, since the λ_i represent variances, $\lambda_i > 0$. Therefore, in representing a d-dimension vector $\underline{X}$ via the transformation above, with fewer than d components, the M.S. error will be given by the sum of the e-values of the covariance matrix corresponding to the e-vectors of the transformation (that is, the columns of A_d) *which are not used.*

General Functions of Random Variables

Basic Objective. If $\underline{X}$ and $\underline{Y}$ are Gaussian r.v.s with parameters $\underline{\mu}_{\underline{X}}$ and $\Sigma_{\underline{X}}$ and $\underline{\mu}_{\underline{Y}}$ and $\Sigma_{\underline{Y}}$ respectively, and

$$Z = A\underline{X} + B\underline{Y} \qquad (A.2-47a)$$

we seek to determine the pdf of r.v. $\underline{Z}$. Two immediate questions are the following:

1. Is $\underline{Z}$ still Gaussian?

2. If so, what are $\underline{\mu}_{\underline{Z}}$ and $\Sigma_{\underline{Z}}$?

We begin with the following intermediate result:

Given a Gaussian r.v. $\underline{X}$ and constant (nonrandom) matrix A with

$$\underline{Y} = A\underline{X} \qquad (A.2-47b)$$

with $\underline{\mu}_{\underline{X}} = E(\underline{X})$ and $\Sigma_{\underline{X}} = E(\underline{X} - \underline{\mu}_{\underline{X}})(\underline{X} - \underline{\mu}_{\underline{X}})^T$, then:

(i) $\underline{Y}$ is Gaussian (this is the hard part); and

(ii) The parameters of $\underline{X}$ and $\underline{Y}$ are related by:

$$E(\underline{Y}) = \underline{\mu}_{\underline{Y}} = A\underline{\mu}_{\underline{X}} \quad \text{and} \quad \text{Cov}(\underline{Y}) = \Sigma_{\underline{Y}} = A\Sigma_{\underline{X}}A^T \qquad (A.2-48)$$

Result (ii) follows from the definition and linearity[4] of expectation. Part (i) is more subtle. We now prove this result.

First we show for

$$\underline{Y} = A\underline{X} \qquad (A.2-49)$$

with $\underline{X} \sim N(\underline{\mu}_{\underline{X}}, \Sigma_{\underline{X}})$ that

$$\underline{Y} \sim N(\underline{\mu}_{\underline{Y}}, \Sigma_{\underline{Y}}) \qquad (A.2-50)$$

$$\underline{Y} \sim N(A\underline{\mu}_{\underline{X}}, A\Sigma_{\underline{X}}A^T) \qquad (A.2-51)$$

An easy way is to assume that A is invertible, and put $A^{-1}\underline{Y}$ in the pdf for $p_{\underline{X}}(\underline{x})$. However, we use characteristic functions.

Characteristic Functions. For a r.v. $\underline{X}$, the characteristic function $\phi_{\underline{X}}(\cdot)$ of $\underline{X}$ is defined as

$$\phi_{\underline{X}}(\underline{\mu}) = E_{\underline{X}}[e^{j\underline{\mu}^T\underline{X}}] = \int e^{j\underline{\mu}^T\underline{\varsigma}}p_{\underline{X}}(\underline{\varsigma})d\underline{\varsigma} \qquad (A.2-52)$$

Notice that *the characteristic function is the inverse Fourier transform of the pdf*, that is,

$$\mathcal{F}\{\phi_{\underline{X}}(\underline{\mu})\} = p_{\underline{X}}(\underline{x}) \qquad (A.2-53)$$

Although useful for generation of moments of r.v.s, characteristic functions are important in determining the pdfs of functions of r.v.s.

Application to Functions of r.v.s. If $\underline{X} \sim N(\underline{\mu}_{\underline{X}}, \Sigma_{\underline{X}})$, then

$$p_{\underline{X}}(\underline{x}) = \frac{1}{(2\pi)^{d/2}|\Sigma_{\underline{X}}|^{1/2}}e^{-\frac{1}{2}\|\underline{x} - \underline{\mu}_{\underline{X}}\|^2_{\Sigma_{\underline{X}}^{-1}}} \qquad (A.2-54)$$

---

[4]Due to linearity, $E(A\underline{X}) = AE(\underline{X})$.

with a corresponding characteristic function[5]:

$$\phi_{\underline{X}}(\underline{\mu}) = e^{j\underline{\mu}^T\underline{\mu}_{\underline{X}} - \frac{1}{2}\underline{\mu}^T\Sigma_{\underline{X}}\underline{\mu}} \qquad (A.2-55)$$

Note that in this formulation $\phi_{\underline{X}}$ does not require $\Sigma_{\underline{X}}$ to be invertible. Using this result, we now return to the form:

$$\underline{Y} = A\underline{X} \qquad (A.2-56)$$

The characteristic function for $\underline{Y}$ is

$$\phi_{\underline{Y}}(\underline{\mu}) = E\{e^{j\underline{\mu}^T\underline{Y}}\} = E\{e^{j\underline{\mu}^T A\underline{X}}\} = E\{e^{j(A^T\underline{\mu})^T\underline{X}}\} = \phi_{\underline{X}}(A^T\underline{\mu}) \qquad (A.2-57)$$

where the last result follows from the definition of the characteristic function. Since $\underline{X}$ is Gaussian

$$\phi_{\underline{X}}(A^T\underline{\mu}) = \exp\{j(A^T\underline{\mu})^T\underline{\mu}_{\underline{X}} - \frac{1}{2}(A^T\underline{\mu})^T\Sigma_{\underline{X}}(A^T\underline{\mu})\}$$

$$= \exp\{j(\underline{\mu}^T A\underline{\mu}_{\underline{X}}) - \frac{1}{2}\underline{\mu}^T A\Sigma_{\underline{X}}A^T\underline{\mu}\}$$

thus,

$$\phi_{\underline{Y}}(\underline{\mu}) = \exp\{j\underline{\mu}^T(A\underline{\mu}_{\underline{X}}) - \frac{1}{2}\underline{\mu}^T(A\Sigma_{\underline{X}}A^T)\underline{\mu}\} \qquad (A.2-58)$$

which means, by comparison with (A.2-55),

$$\underline{Y} \sim N(A\underline{\mu}_{\underline{X}}, A\Sigma_{\underline{X}}A^T) \qquad (A.2-59)$$

Sums of Gaussian r.v.s. Continuing on toward our larger objective, we now consider

$$\underline{Z} = \underline{X} + \underline{Y} \qquad (A.2-60)$$

Given $p_{\underline{X}}(\underline{x})$ and $p_{\underline{Y}}(\underline{y})$, we ask about $p_{\underline{Z}}(\underline{z})$. It is straightforward to show that

$$p_{\underline{Z}}(\underline{z}) = \int p_{\underline{Y}}(\underline{z} - \underline{\varsigma})p_{\underline{X}}(\underline{\varsigma})d\underline{\varsigma} \qquad (A.2-61)$$

This yields a *convolution integral*. However,

$$\phi_{\underline{Z}}(\underline{\mu}) = E[e^{j\underline{\mu}^T\underline{\varsigma}}] = \int e^{j\underline{\mu}^T\underline{\varsigma}}p_{\underline{Z}}(\underline{\varsigma})d\underline{\varsigma} = \ldots = \phi_{\underline{X}}(\underline{\mu})\phi_{\underline{Y}}(\underline{\mu}) \qquad (A.2-62)$$

Equation A.2-62, in the Gaussian case, yields $\phi_{\underline{Z}}$ as the product of two exponentials, which results in a summation of their arguments. Therefore, $\phi_{\underline{Z}}(\underline{\mu})$ yields the characteristic function of a Gaussian r.v.

Extended (Overall) Result. Using the above results we can easily show for $\underline{Z} = A\underline{X} + B\underline{Y}$ that

---

[5]This is a non-trivial integration. See [Maybeck 1979] p. 105.

$$\underline{\mu}_Z = A\underline{\mu}_X + B\underline{\mu}_Y$$

$$\Sigma_{\underline{Z}} = A\Sigma_{\underline{X}}A^T + A\Sigma_{\underline{XY}}B^T + B\Sigma_{\underline{YX}}A^T + B\Sigma_{\underline{Y}}B^T \qquad (A.2-63)$$

The Univariate (1-D) Case and Application to Supervised Learning. Given a pdf, $p(x|H)$, for a r.v. X where

$$X \sim N(\mu_n, \sigma^2 + \sigma_n^2) \qquad (A.2-64)$$

one model for the generation of r.v. X is as the *sum* of two independent r.v.s, X_1 and X_2:[6]

$$X = X_1 + X_2 \qquad (A.2-65)$$

where

$$X_1 \sim N(0, \sigma^2) \qquad (A.2-66a)$$

and

$$X_2 \sim N(\mu_n, \sigma_n^2) \qquad (A.2-66b)$$

GENERATING RANDOM VARIABLES WITH DESIRED CHARACTERISTICS

Scalar Case

General Approach. Assume the availability of a uniformly distributed random number generator in the inverval [0, 1] whose output is designated by the r.v. R.[7] A specific value of R is denoted r. A random variable, X, with a *specified distribution function* $F_X(x)$ is desired. The solution for x in

$$F_X(x) = r \qquad (A.2-67a)$$

or alternately[8]

$$F_X(x) = 1 - r \qquad (A.2-67b)$$

yields a random variable with the desired distribution.

Proof. Refer to Figure A.2-2. $F_X(x)$ is assumed to be a *nondecreasing* continuous function of x. Therefore

$$P(X \le x) = P[F_X(X) \le F_X(x)] = P[R \le F_X(x)]$$

which, from Figure A.2-2, becomes

$$= P(R \le r) = r \qquad (A.2-68)$$

Thus, $P(X \le x) = F_X(x)$ as desired. Note that even if $F_X(x)$ is not easily invertible, we may either tabulate $x - r$ pairs or use alternative approaches, as shown below.

---

[6]An alternate proof ([Maybeck 1979], p. 112) is to just form a r.v. $\underline{w} = [x/y]$.
[7]There are lots of hardware-dependent numerical techniques available to achieve this.
[8]Proof of this is left to the reader. It is almost trivial.

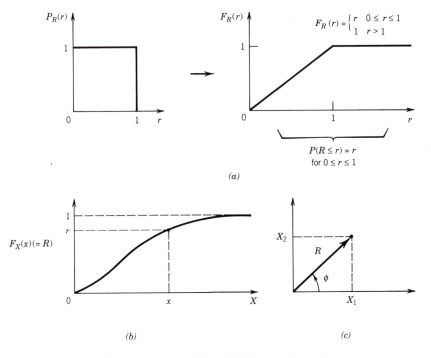

Figure A.2-2: Geometric view of Box–Muller transformation.
(a) Example.
(b) General case.
(c) Generating X_1 and X_2 from R.

Example: Achieving an Exponentially Distributed r.v.

Consider the *exponential* distribution function

$$F_X(x) = 1 - e^{\lambda x} \qquad\qquad (A.2-69)$$

where (the reader should verify this)

$$\mu_X = \frac{1}{\lambda} \qquad\qquad (A.2-70)$$

Given uniformly distributed r.v. R we use (A.2-67b) to form

$$1 - e^{-\lambda x} = 1 - r$$

or

$$r = e^{-\lambda x}$$

which has the solution

$$x = -\lambda^{-1} \ln(r) \qquad\qquad (A.2-71)$$

with the desired (exponential) distribution.

Generating Gaussian r.v.s

Direct application of (A.2-67a) for the case of a Gaussian distribution function is difficult. (The reader should verify this.) As an alternative, we consider the following procedure known as *Box–Muller's transformation*.

Strategy. Given two independent, uniformly distributed random variables R_1 and R_2 in the inverval [0, 1] with values r_1 and r_2, respectively, suppose we transform these r.v.s as follows:

$$X_1 = (-2 \ln R_1)^{1/2} \cos(2\pi R_2)$$

$$X_2 = (-2 \ln R_1)^{1/2} \sin(2\pi R_2) \qquad (A.2 - 72)$$

As shown below, X_1 and X_2 are independent Gaussian r.v.s with zero mean and unity variance, that is, if

$$\underline{X} = \begin{pmatrix} X_1 \\ X_2 \end{pmatrix}$$

then $\underline{\mu}_{\underline{X}} = \underline{0}$ and $\Sigma_{\underline{X}} = I$.

Given $X_i \sim N(0,1)$, $i = 1, 2$, we can obtain Gaussian random variables with parameters (μ, σ^2) by forming

$$X = \sigma X_i + \mu \qquad (A.2 - 73)$$

In the multidimensional $(d \geq 2)$ case, we use similarity transforms of the form of (A.2-48) to achieve the desired covariance matrix.

Justification. Notice that a graphical interpretation in polar (r, ϕ) coordinates of (A.2-72) yields the mapping

$$R^2 = X_1^2 + X_2^2 = -2 \ln R_1 \qquad (A.2 - 74)$$

$$\phi = 2\pi R_2$$

This is shown in Figure A.2-2. Therefore, R^2 is, from (A.2-71), exponentially distributed with $\mu_{R^2} = 2$. We state, without proof, that the sum of the squares of two independently distributed Gaussian r.v.s with zero mean and unity variance will have this distribution. Notice, since R_2 is independent of R_1, that the angle ϕ, in (A.2-74), is uniformly distributed and independent of R^2.

The reader should compare the computational effort in generating Gaussian r.v.s via (A.2-72) with that of simply averaging large numbers of samples with unknown distribution and invoking the Central Limit Theorem [Papoulis 1984].

Appendix 3
Discrete Mathematics Review

Useful and comprehensive discrete mathematics references include [Johnsonbaugh 1986], [Kolman/Busby 1984], and [Wiitala 1987].

SETS

Basic Concepts

Sets provide a rich and powerful framework in which to study many aspects of PR; however, they are somewhat difficult to define formally and rigorously. The following summary is adequate for our purposes:

- A *set* is a collection of objects or *elements*, which are members of the set.
- The *empty set* is a set with nothing in it. It may be denoted $\{\}$ or $\emptyset$.
- Membership of an element a of a set A is denoted $a \in A$.
- Two sets are *equal* if they contain exactly the same elements. For two sets A and B, this is denoted $A = B$.
- Two sets A and B are *disjoint* if they have no elements in common.
- A is a *subset* of B if every element in A is also in B. This is denoted[1] $A \subset B$. If $A = B$, then $A \subset B$ and $B \subset A$. A set with n elements has 2^n subsets.
- The *cardinal number* or *cardinality* of a finite set is a nonnegative integer representing the number of elements in the set. This is denoted $|A|$.
- If $A \subset B$ and $A \neq B$, A is a *proper subset* of B.
- The set of all subsets of A, denoted $P(A)$, is the *power set* of A.

---

[1]Some books use the notation $\subseteq$ to denote general subsets and reserve the notation $\subset$ for proper subsets.

- The complement, $\bar{A}$, of a set A is the set of all elements (of a special set S, the *space or universe*) that are not elements of A.

Operations on Sets

Intersection.

$$A \cap B = \{x | (x \in A) \cap (x \in B)\} \qquad (A.3 - 1)$$

Union.

$$A \cup B = \{x | (x \in A) \cup (x \in B)\} \qquad (A.3 - 2)$$

Intersection and union are commutative and associative.

Two sets A and B are *mutually exclusive* or *disjoint* if they have no members in common, that is, $A \cap B = \emptyset$.

Partitions. A *partition* P of a set A is a collection of mutually exclusive subsets A_i that satisfy:

$$A_i \cap A_j = \emptyset \qquad \text{unless } i = j$$

and

$$\bigcup_i A_i = A$$

Partitions of sets are an extremely useful concept in clustering and grammatical inference.

RELATIONS

Relations are based on the notion of set mappings and provide a mathematical formalism for the representation of structure.

DEFINITION: Relation

If A and B are sets, a relation from A to B is a subset of $A \times B$. $\qquad (A.3 - 3)$

Here $A \times B$ denotes the Cartesian product of the sets A and B. Given a set

$$A = \{a, b, c, d, \ldots\}$$

and

$$B = \{x, y, z, \ldots\}$$

a relation from A to B, namely R, satisfies $R \subset A \times B$.

This definition is mathematically precise and somewhat esoteric. Equation A.3-3 defines a *binary relation*, since it involves only two sets and provides a way of 'connecting' or relating members of the sets. Specifically, how the sets are connected, and the properties of this connection, or relation, are of interest.

For example, consider the ordered pair of numbers (x, y). The set of all possible values of x is the *domain* and the set of all possible y values is the *range*. This relation may be enumerated as a set of ordered pairs, for example, relation $R1$ may be defined as

$$R1 = \{(1,2),(2,3),(3,4),(4,5)\}$$

Relations between entities in structural representations often involve *positional* and *temporal attributes*. For example, suppose we have been given a preprocessed image with several extracted regions, as shown in Figure A.3-1(a). The regions are given symbol labels that are elements of the set

$$L = \{a,b,c,d\}$$

We proceed to develop a relationship between these labels (a subset of $L \times L$) that connotes 'contained inside of' or 'enclosed within.' This is shown in Figure A.3-1(b) using a directed graph.

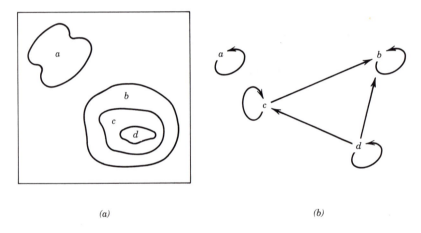

(a)   (b)

Figure A.3-1:   Simple example of a relation using processed image data.
(a) Image data (regions).
(b) Relation 'contained in,' for regions depicted in (a), shown as digraph.

Alternately, another relation $R2$, based on members of sets that contain symbolic entities, might be:

$$R2 = \{(floor, foundation),(rug, floor),(chair, rug),(person, chair)\}$$

where the set A consists of entities that lie on others. Relation $R2$ therefore denotes 'lies on,' or perhaps 'is supported by.' From the enumeration of $R2$, for example, we may represent the fact that a chair 'is supported by' a floor, and so on.

RELATION PROPERTIES

In representing relations as sets of ordered pairs, note that *the order in which an entity appears in the pair is significant*. For example, referring to the relation 'contained in,' '*a* is contained in b' does not signify, in general, that 'b is contained in a.' Thus, *relations have a 'direction' or ordering*, as the graphical representation shows.

The inherent directionality or ordering of relations gives rise to a number of relation properties. Three properties of prime importance are

1. *Reflexive*: R is reflexive if, $\forall a \in A, (a, a) \in R$. $(A.3 - 4a)$
2. *Symmetric*: R is symmetric if, $\forall (a, b) \in R, (b, a) \in R$. $(A.3 - 4b)$
3. *Transitive*: R is transitive if, $\forall (a, b) \in R$ and $(b, c) \in R, (a, c) \in R$. $(A.3 - 4c)$

DEFINITION: Equivalence Relation

A relation that satisfies all three properties (i.e., it is reflexive, symmetric, and transitive) is termed an equivalence relation. $(A.3 - 4d)$

Relations and Properties

The concept of an entity possessing a property or attribute is important in modeling. Properties may include color, age, function, application, and the like. For example, we may wish to represent the fact that a 'computer has chips.' In terms of the previously defined *relation*, we could merely note that the relation 'has' or, more specifically, 'has_attribute' includes the *ordered* pair (computer, chips). This representation, while correct, is somewhat cumbersome. Instead, we often loosely speak of chips as one value of a *property* ('has') attributed to a computer. Furthermore, this type of property representation may loosely be called a *unary relation*, although it does not fit the previous definition.

Relations as Functions

Most scientists and engineers are familiar with a subset of relations called *functions*. Functions are not restricted to numerical quantities. A *function* from A to B is a relation (denoted by the symbol f) such that for every $a \in A, \exists$ one and only one $b \in B s.t. (a, b) \in f$. Usually we show this relation as

$$f : A \Rightarrow B \qquad (A.3 - 5)$$

where A is the domain of function f and B is the range. For a particular member of f, that is, $(a, b) \in f$, we say that b is the *value* of f at a. In other words,

$$b = f(a) \qquad (A.3 - 6)$$

Another way to view a *function* is a special relation in which each $a_i \in A$ belongs to only one ordered pair in the relation. Thus, given one element of R, that is, (a_i, b_i), no other element of the form (a_i, c_i) belongs to R unless $b_i = c_i$. From (A.3-6), this is written as $b_i = f(a_i)$ to denote the function mapping.

Notice that the previous definition allows f to contain pairs (a_i, b_i) and (d_i, b_i). If this occurs, the function is not 1:1, and

$$f(a_i) = f(d_i) \xrightarrow{not} a_i = d_i \qquad (A.3 - 7)$$

GRAPHS AND DIGRAPHS

Graphs

Graph theory is a fundamental area of discrete mathematics. A *graph* G is an ordered pair

$$G = \{N, R\} \qquad (A.3 - 8)$$

where N is a set of nodes (or vertices) and R is a subset of $N \times N$, or ordered pairs of nodes. Elements of R represent arcs (or edges) that connect nodes in G. N is denoted the *node set*, and R is denoted the *edge set*.

Subgraphs

A *subgraph* of G is itself a graph, $G_s = \{N_s, R_s\}$ where $N_s \subset N$ and R_s consists of arcs in R that connect only nodes in N_s. A less formal definition is that a G_s is a graph that has some of the nodes and some of the arcs of G.

Directed Graphs (Digraphs)

Often, there is significance attached to the direction of an arc, in the sense that an arc emanates *from* a node and is incident on another node. Therefore, $(a, b) \in R$ means there is an arc *from* node a *to* node b. This directional significance characterizes a *digraph*. It is *not the case* that $(a, b) \in R$ implies $(b, a) \in R$ in a digraph.

Undirected Graphs

When the direction of edges in a graph is not important, that is, specification of either (a, b) or $(b, a) \in R$ is acceptable, an *undirected graph* results.

Directed Graphs and Intraset Relations

A relationship may be represented graphically by using an arrow to show each element of R. In this way, the 'connection' between members of the sets is displayed graphically. When $R \subseteq A X A$, a *directed graph* or *digraph* is a convenient tool to represent the relationship between elements of a set.

Suppose that

$$A = \{a, b, c, d\} \qquad (A.3 - 9)$$

Then

$$A \times A = \{(a, a), (a, b), (a, c), (a, d), (b, a), (b, b), \ldots\} \qquad (A.3 - 10)$$

If we assume, for example, that a relation R is defined as

$$R = \{(a, b), (b, c), (b, d), (b, a), (c, c), (d, a)\} \qquad (A.3 - 11)$$

then we may graphically represent R where *the elements of A are nodes in the graph and the elemental relationships are indicated by arrows from the element in the domain to the corresponding element in the range.* Often we refer to these arrows as *edges*. The use of arrows in the digraph reinforces the notion of a direction to the relation.

Uniqueness of Relation Digraphs and Isomorphism

The digraph for a specific relation is not unique, since two digraphs may be isomorphic. This is a consequence of the arbitrary choice of nodes to represent specific elements of set A. The *structure* of the graphs resulting from any choice of nodes (or 'vertices') will be the same, however. The isomorphism of graphs $G1$ and $G2$ implies there is a 1:1 (onto function), denoted $v(\ )$, from the vertices of $G1$ to the vertices of $G2$, as well as a 1:1 (onto function), denoted $e(\ )$, from the edges of $G1$ to the edges of $G2$. For an edge e_1, connecting vertices v_1 and w_1 in $G1$, an edge $e_2 = e(e_1)$ exists in $G2$ and connects nodes $v_2 = v(v_1)$ and $w_2 = v(w_1)$, if $G1$ and $G2$ are isomorphic.

Ternary (and Higher Order) Relations and Constraints

Ternary and quarternary (and higher order) relations may be shown to be defined via straightforward extension of the set-based derivation for the binary case. Furthermore, ternary and quarternary (and higher order) relations may be cast in terms of ordered n-tuples, which in turn may be viewed as ordered pairs [each pair consisting of an $(n-1)$-tuple and a single element], and therefore may be studied within the framework of binary relations.

A ternary relation among objects of three sets A, B, and C is defined as a subset of the Cartesian product of the two sets $(A \times B) \times C$ and is described by ordered triples of the form $[(a,b),c]$. Note that each element of the relation may be viewed as an ordered pair where the first term itself is an ordered pair. Similarly, a quarternary relation among four sets A, B, C, and D is defined as a subset of $(((A \times B) \times C) \times D)$, and described by ordered quadruples of the form $(((a,b),c),d)$. Again, we may view the description of this relation in terms of ordered pairs, the first element being $((a,b),c)$ and the second d.

SEMANTIC NETS

From Digraph to Semantic Net

The use of graphical constructs to enumerate both numerical and symbolic relations among sets of entities is fundamental to many structural representation approaches. In fact, the careful structuring of this construct (e.g., such that it may be efficiently decomposed into tightly coupled subgraphs) is fundamental to many efficient schemes for knowledge manipulation.

DEFINITION: Semantic Net

A semantic network, or simply semantic net, is a labeled digraph used to describe relations (including properties) of objects, concepts, situations, or actions. $(A.3 - 12)$

Unfortunately, for most reasonable structural representations, the overall semantic net is usually a large and highly interconnected entity. This causes major difficulty in the *matching* or unifying of observed features or entities and their properties, with the structure indicated by the semantic net. If one considers the possible numbers of matches for each node, it is easy to see how combinatorial explosion may occur.

Semantic Net Examples

A semantic net represents *objects as nodes* (shown as circles) and *relations as labeled arcs* (or edges). For 'real-world' entities, they are usually quite complicated. A relatively simple semantic net for a 'blocks-world' problem is shown in Figure A.3-2.

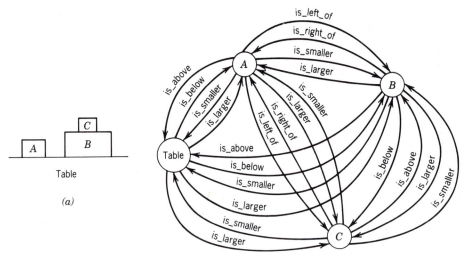

(a)

(b)

Figure A.3-2:   Semantic net representation of 'blocks-world.'
(a) System.
(b) Semantic net.

TREES

Digraphs and 'Degree'

In the digraph representation of a relation R recall that a node exists for every $a \in A$ where $(a, b) \in R$. Furthermore, a (directed) arc from node a to node b appears in the digraph.

The number of b, such that $(a, b) \in R$, or the number of arcs *emanating from node a* in the digraph representation is called the *out-degree of node a*. Similarly, the number of arcs in the digraph *terminating at node b* is the *in-degree* of node b.   ($A.3 - 13$)

DEFINITION: Tree

A tree is a data structure that is a finite acyclic (containing no closed loops or paths or cycles) digraph. One node, called the root, has in-degree = 0, and every other node has out-degree $\geq$ 1, except leaf-nodes, which have out-degree = 0. There exists exactly one path between any two (distinct) nodes. The set of leaf nodes is often referred to as the **frontier** *of the tree.*   ($A.3 - 14$)

Trees are useful in SyntPR for a number of tasks. First, they serve as potentially useful data structures for the representation of structure. This is the basis for tree grammars (Chapter 7). In addition, trees provide a mechanism to 'catalog' the generation and parsing of structures. The fact that they are acyclic and may be derived from a general digraph makes trees suitable for studying the search complexities of structural matching.

Special Types of Trees.   An n-ary tree is one where each vertex (or node) has out-degree n or less. A common instance of this is the 2-ary or binary tree, where every node has either 0 or 2 descendents.

As shown in Chapter 7, it is often convenient to label the nodes of a tree, as a prelude to tree description. Suppose we are given a tree description using a node-labeling alphabet V, with root node labeled v_o. This tree is denoted $T(v_o)$ and the set of labeled nodes is denoted $T^s(v_o)$. $T^s(v_o)$ consists of the labels of v_o and all its descendants. If $T(v_o)$ contains a node v, a *subtree* $T(v)$ is generated with node label set $T^s(v) \subseteq T^s(v_o)$, with the restriction that the labels of v *and all its descendants* must be in $T^s(v)$.

COMPUTER MEMORY MODEL(S)

'Standard' Memory Model

The memory model for the 'memory' of a typical computer (for either read or write) may be simply shown in Figure A.3-3(a). We may view memory as a (large) lookup table or 1-D array that is indexed by an address. Elementary computer operations using this model are simply the reading (fetching) and writing (storing) of data.

Associative/Content-Addressable Memory

Another useful memory structure or model (which may be implemented in hardware and/or software) is that of an *associative* or *content-addressable* (AM or CAM, respectively) memory. CAM has the structure shown in Figure A.3-3(b). Note that the CAM model in Figure A.3-3(b), loosely speaking, is a kind of 'inverse' of the conventional model of Figure A.3-3(a). In traditional computer design, CAM finds application in

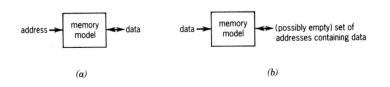

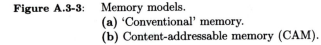

Figure A.3-3:   Memory models.
   (a) 'Conventional' memory.
   (b) Content-addressable memory (CAM).

the design of memory management schemes. More importantly, *CAM may be used to facilitate search through a data structure, and for pattern association*. When used for pattern association, associative memory may be viewed as a mapping from data to (associated) data.

Appendix 4
Descent Procedures: Examples and Error Function Contours

BASIC FORMULATION

Gradient approaches are used extensively in optimization procedures in both StatPR and NeurPR. It is important to become comfortable with the underlying concept. In this section we show simple examples and compare with 'batch' (noniterative) procedures.

Steepest (Ascent) Descent Procedures

Since $\nabla_x f$ defines the direction of maximum increase in the function, we may maximize (or minimize) a scalar function $f(\underline{x})$ by recursively calculating $\nabla_x f$ and adjusting $\underline{x}$ until we reach a minimum (or maximum). This algorithm for minimization of a function, termed steepest descent, is

(a) Choose initial guess, $\underline{x}^0$

(b) Compute $\nabla_x f$, that is,

$$\frac{df(\underline{x}^0)}{d\underline{x}}$$

(c) Adjust $\underline{x}^0$ to get $\underline{x}^1$ by moving in a direction *opposite* to the gradient, that is,

$$\underline{x}^1 = \underline{x}^0 - K\left[\frac{df(\underline{x}^0)}{d\underline{x}}\right] \qquad (A.4-1)$$

(d) Stop when $\underline{x}^{n+1} - \underline{x}^n$ is sufficiently small.

Linear Applications

Consider the equation:

$$A\underline{x} = \underline{b} \qquad (A.4-2a)$$

where A is a $n \times n$ matrix and $\underline{x}$ and $\underline{b}$ are $n \times 1$ vectors. In this formulation, consider A and $\underline{b}$ as given, with $\underline{x}$ unknown. (A.4-1) may be thought of as

1. A matrix equation;
2. A set of n linear constraints of the form

$$\underline{a}_i^T \underline{x} = b_i \qquad (A.4-2b)$$

where $\underline{a}_i^T$ is the ith row of A; or

3. A set of I/O specifications for a linear classifier (or 'neural net'), where row i of A and element b_i of $\underline{b}$ are the desired input and output patterns, respectively, and $\underline{x}$ is a set of weights to be determined (Chapter 11).

'Batch' Solution (Matrix Inversion).   Clearly, an easy solution to (A.4-2a) is to (attempt) to compute the 'batch' solution

$$\underline{x} = A^{-1}\underline{b} \qquad (A.4-3)$$

However, we instead explore the ramifications of more general and extendable formulations. Temporarily, let us assume that there is *at least* one solution to (A.4-2a). Defining

$$\underline{e} = A\underline{x} - \underline{b} \qquad (A.4-4)$$

we note that $\underline{e} = \underline{0}$ when a solution to (A.4-2a) is found.

Error Measures.   Instead of dealing with $\underline{e}$, consider

$$E = \| \underline{e} \|^2 = e_1^2 + e_2^2 + \ldots + e_n^2 \qquad (A.4-5)$$

where $e_i, \; i = 1, 2, \ldots n$, is an element of vector $\underline{e}$. With this choice of *solution metric* or *error function*, when $E = 0$ a solution is found, and $E \geq 0$ everywhere else. $E = 0$ is therefore the minimum error. From (A.4-4)

$$E = \| \underline{e} \|^2 = <\underline{e}, \underline{e}> = \underline{e}^T \underline{e} = (A\underline{x} - \underline{b})^T (A\underline{x} - \underline{b}) = (\underline{x}^T A^T - \underline{b}^T)(A\underline{x} - \underline{b})$$

$$= \underline{x}^T A^T A\underline{x} - \underline{x}^T A^T \underline{b} - \underline{b}^T A\underline{x} + \underline{b}^T \underline{b} \qquad (A.4-6)$$

From (A.4-6), we see that E is a function of $\underline{x}$. Our objective is to explore the minimization of $E(\underline{x})$.

Gradient Descent.   Computing the gradient of $E(\underline{x})$ with respect to $\underline{x}$ (see Appendix 1), that is,

$$\nabla_{\underline{x}} E(\underline{x}) = \frac{dE(\underline{x})}{d\underline{x}} = \begin{pmatrix} \dfrac{\partial E(\underline{x})}{\partial x_1} \\[1.2em] \dfrac{\partial E(\underline{x})}{\partial x_2} \\[0.6em] \ddots \\[0.6em] \dfrac{\partial E(\underline{x})}{\partial x_n} \end{pmatrix} \qquad (A.4-7)$$

yields:

$$\nabla_{\underline{x}} E(\underline{x}) = 2(A^T A)\underline{x} - 2A^T \underline{b} \qquad (A.4-8)$$

Since the gradient of E defines the direction of *maximum increase in E*, (A.4-8) is used to form an iterative minimization procedure. Consider a procedure to find $\hat{\underline{x}}$, that is, the solution vector that minimizes (A.4-6), of the form:

$$\hat{\underline{x}}^{n+1} = \hat{\underline{x}}^n - \mu(n)\nabla_{\underline{x}} E(\hat{\underline{x}}^n) \qquad (A.4-9)$$

We show this via a simple 2-D example.

Extended Example

Consider a specific example of (A.4 - 1) for $n = 2$, that is,

$$\begin{pmatrix} 1 & -1 \\ 2 & 1 \end{pmatrix} \begin{pmatrix} x_1 \\ x_2 \end{pmatrix} = \begin{pmatrix} -1 \\ 4 \end{pmatrix} \qquad (A.4-10)$$

The 'batch' (inverse) solution yields

$$\begin{pmatrix} x_1 \\ x_2 \end{pmatrix} = \begin{pmatrix} 1 \\ 2 \end{pmatrix}$$

Formulating the error measure of (A.4-6) with

$$A^T A = \begin{pmatrix} 1 & 2 \\ -1 & 1 \end{pmatrix} \begin{pmatrix} 1 & -1 \\ 2 & 1 \end{pmatrix} = \begin{pmatrix} 5 & 1 \\ 1 & 2 \end{pmatrix}$$

$$\underline{b}^T A = (-1 \quad 4) \begin{pmatrix} 1 & -1 \\ 2 & 1 \end{pmatrix} = (7 \quad 5)$$

$$\underline{b}^T \underline{b} = \| \underline{b} \|^2 = 17$$

yields

$$E(\underline{x}) = (x_1 \quad x_2) \begin{pmatrix} 5 & 1 \\ 1 & 2 \end{pmatrix} \begin{pmatrix} x_1 \\ x_2 \end{pmatrix} + (-14 \quad -10) \begin{pmatrix} x_1 \\ x_2 \end{pmatrix} + 17$$

or

$$E(\underline{x}) = 5x_1^2 + 2x_1x_2 + 2x_2^2 - 14x_1 - 10x_2 + 17$$

Therefore, $E(\underline{x})$ is quadratic in x_1 and x_2. This is shown in Figure A.4-1. Loci of constant E are

$$5x_1^2 + 2x_1x_2 + 2x_2^2 - 14x_1 - 10x_2 = k$$

Other gradient descent problems are considered in Chapter 4.

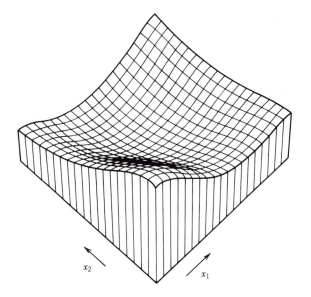

Figure A.4-1:   Error function.

Traversing the Error Function Contours

Choice of Starting Point.   In steepest descent procedures, the initial solution 'guess' or starting point may influence the rate of convergence (as well as possibility of convergence) to the minimum error solution. This is shown in Figure A.4-2, for different starting points A and A'.

Trajectories Near a Minima.   Another aspect of descent procedures is the behavior of the solution near a minima. We wish to avoid the solution trajectory from straddling a minimum of E by alternately climbing the 'hill' on either side and thereby oscillating between two locations. This behavior is a consequence of the shape of the error function and the amount of correction allowed at each step.

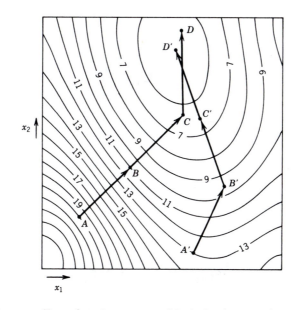

Figure A.4-2:   Error function topographical plot (contours).

Appendix 5
Similarity Measures, Matching Techniques, and Scale-Space Approaches

MATCHING FOR CLASSIFICATION AND RECOGNITION

Introduction

Measures of similarity (or dissimilarity) are fundamental in classification and recognition tasks. We restrict our attention to scalar measures.

Measures of Similarity in Vector Space

Distance is one measure of vector similarity. The Euclidean distance between $d \times 1$ vectors $\underline{x}$ and $\underline{y}$ is given by

$$d(\underline{x}, \underline{y}) = \parallel \underline{x} - \underline{y} \parallel = \sqrt{(\underline{x} - \underline{y})^T (\underline{x} - \underline{y})}$$

$$= +\sqrt{\sum_{i=1}^{d} (x_i - y_i)^2} \qquad (A.5 - 1a)$$

Note that $\underline{x}$ and $\underline{y}$ must be the same dimension for (A.5-1a) to make sense. A related and more general metric is

$$d_p(\underline{x}, \underline{y}) = \left(\sum_{i=1}^{d} |x_i - y_i|^p \right)^{1/p} \qquad (A.5 - 1b)$$

Notice that (A.5-1b) reduces to (A.5-1a) for $p = 2$.

Commonly, weighted distance measures are used. An example is

$$d_w^2(\underline{x}, \underline{y}) = (\underline{x} - \underline{y})^T R(\underline{x} - \underline{y}) = \parallel \underline{x} - \underline{y} \parallel_R^2 \qquad (A.5 - 1c)$$

Equation A.5-1c implements on a *weighted inner product* or weighted R-norm. The matrix R is often required to be positive definite and symmetric. In this case, R may be factored. The reader may verify that (A.5-1c) merely represents the transformation of a vector space, that is, the linear transformations

$$\tilde{\underline{x}} = T\underline{x} \qquad (A.5-1d)$$

$$\tilde{\underline{y}} = T\underline{y} \qquad (A.5-1e)$$

yield

$$d^2(\tilde{\underline{x}}, \tilde{\underline{y}}) = (T\underline{x} - T\underline{y})^T (T\underline{x} - T\underline{y}) \qquad (A.5-1f)$$

$$= (\underline{x} - \underline{y})^T T^T T (\underline{x} - \underline{y})$$

$$= d_w^2(\underline{x}, \underline{y})$$

When $\underline{x}$ and $\underline{y}$ are binary, measures such as the Hamming distance (Chapter 13) are useful.

In exploring vector similarity measures, the following properties are important:

$$|<\underline{x}, \underline{y}>| \leq \| \underline{x} \| \quad \| \underline{y} \| \qquad \text{(Schwartz)} \qquad (A.5-1g)$$

$$\| \underline{x} + \underline{y} \| \leq \| \underline{x} \| + \| \underline{y} \| \qquad \text{(triangle)} \qquad (A.5-1h)$$

If

$$\underline{x}_1 = \frac{\underline{x}}{\| \underline{x} \|} \qquad (A.5-1i)$$

then

$$<\underline{x}, \underline{y}> = \| \underline{x} \| <\underline{y}, \underline{x}_1> \qquad (A.5-1j)$$

where $<\underline{y}, \underline{x}_1>$ is the projection of $\underline{y}$ onto a unit length vector with direction $\underline{x}_1$.

Similarity Measures for Strings and Sets

Measures for string and set similarity are equally important in PR. In some instances it is possible to relate string and set similarity measures to each other as well as to the vector similarity measures described above.

Set Similarity.   Given sets A and B, intuitively a measure of similarity might be the cardinality of the set $A \cap B$.[1] However, this does not account for the possibility that sets A and B have unequal cardinalities, that is, $A \subset B$ or $B \subset A$ is possible. Therefore, some normalization is necessary. An example might be

$$d(A, B) = \frac{|A \cap B|}{|A \cup B|} \qquad (A.5-1k)$$

Expanding (A.5-1k)

---

[1]The reader may wish to refer to Appendix 3 for a review of sets.

$$d(A, B) = \frac{|A \cap B|}{|A| + |B| - |A \cap B|} \qquad (A.5 - 1l)$$

into a more useful form also indicates a similarity with normalized correlation (see A.5-4). Another related measure is the *Levenshtien distance*, computed via

$$d_L(A, B) = \max\{|A|, |B|\} - |A \cap B| \qquad (A.5 - 1m)$$

String Similarity.   Given strings u and v, with possibly different lengths, the comparison of u and v may take a variety of forms. Unlike sets, however, the *ordering* of elements is important. When the strings are composed of binary-valued elements and are of equal lengths, a simple element-by-element comparison and computation of a Hamming distance (see Chapter 13 and Appendix 6) may be used. Otherwise, more general similarity measures must be developed, which could be based on the following:

1. *Inclusion*, that is, does string u contain v (or vice versa)?
2. *Overlap*, that is, finding the size of the largest substring in both u and v.
3. *Variational similarity*, that is, determining similarity on the basis of the minimum cost of 'converting' one string into another. This is discussed at length in Chapter 8, in the matching of attributed relational descriptions.

Correlation and Template Matching

Correlation is a simple and extremely popular matching approach that is applicable to signals, vectors, strings, and sets. A set of reference patterns, denoted *templates*, is used together with an unknown pattern. Often, the template may be contained within the unknown pattern and therefore the problem may also involve determining the relative position of the template and pattern match. Correlation of the template with the unknown pattern is achieved by shifting the template over all possible relative locations and, using a suitable matching metric, computing a *correlation function*. This leads to more generalized approaches, including matched filtering. A visual example of correlation matching using image data is shown in Figure A.5-1.

Defining

g: The (input) pattern. For example, this may be simply a $d \times 1$ vector $\underline{g}$.

f: The reference pattern or template for a particular class. For example, this may be a $d \times 1$ mean vector, $\underline{f} = \underline{\mu}_i$ corresponding to class w_i.

R: The extent of g over which the match occurs. This extent, in some PR applications, is all of g, for instance, all d components of vector $\underline{g}$. However, it may also be over a smaller extent, an example being finding a subpattern in a larger pattern.

Consider the discrete formulation of the following two candidate metrics indicating *mismatch* (indices are omitted for simplicity):

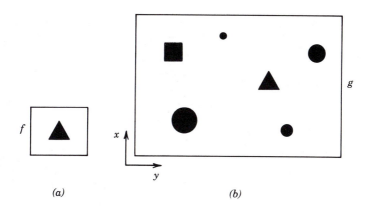

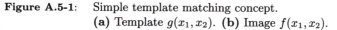

$$(a) \qquad\qquad\qquad\qquad (b)$$

Figure A.5-1:   Simple template matching concept.
(a) Template $g(x_1, x_2)$. (b) Image $f(x_1, x_2)$.

$$m_1 = \sum_R |f - g| \qquad\qquad (A.5 - 2a)$$

$$m_2 = \sum_R (f - g)^2 \qquad\qquad (A.5 - 2b)$$

Intuitively, m_1 and m_2 will be small (ideally zero) when f and g are identical, and large when they are significantly different. Whereas the first metric is easy to compute, a closer examination of (A.5-2b) leads us to some interesting results. Expanding the second-order term in (A.5-2b) yields

$$m_2 = \sum f^2 - 2 \sum fg + \sum g^2 \qquad\qquad (A.5 - 2c)$$

We observe several things concerning this expansion:

1. f and g *individually* contribute to m_2, through the $\sum f^2$ and $\sum g^2$ terms. In the case that f and g are vectors, these factors are the squares of the respective vector lengths. For a given input pattern, $\sum g^2$ is insignificant, since it is constant throughout the matching process.

2. The *combined* or *joint effect* of these intensities reflected in the $\sum fg$ term is of fundamental interest. Again, in the vector example, where

$$\sum fg = < \underline{f}, \underline{g} > \qquad\qquad (A.5 - 2d)$$

We denote this quantity as c_{un}, where

$$c_{un} = \sum_R fg \qquad\qquad (A.5 - 3a)$$

Since the coefficient of this term in (A.5-2c) is negative, when this term is large, measure m_2 will be small. Therefore, m_2 provides a good measure of *mismatch*, and $\sum fg$ provides a reasonable measure of match. This operation is denoted the *unnormalized correlation* of f and g (over R), and amounts to an element-by-element multiplication followed by a summation. The unnormalized matching operation in the vector case is equivalent to the inner product. Furthermore, if we assume that the magnitudes of the two vectors are fixed, unnormalized matching will yield a maximum when $\underline{f}$ and $\underline{g}$ have the same direction, that is, when

$$\underline{g} = k_1 \underline{f}, \qquad (A.5 - 3b)$$

where

$$k_1 \neq 0 \qquad (A.5 - 3c)$$

Unnormalized correlation has several shortcomings. For example, note that *zero intensity value elements in either $\underline{f}$ or $\underline{g}$ contribute nothing to the unnormalized measure of match in (A.5-3a).* This is a potentially serious shortcoming of the unnormalized approach, since if $\underline{f}$ and $\underline{g}$ have significant numbers of corresponding zero elements, c_{un} does not reflect this (correct) match or correspondence.[2] This effect would be most pronounced in applying c_{un} to binary patterns, where only '1's would contribute to the matching metric $< \underline{f}, \underline{g} >$. Corresponding zero-valued elements in f and g should also affect the overall similarity measure.

Equation A.5-3a may be revised to form a *normalized matching* or *correlation metric*

$$c_n = \left(\frac{1}{E}\right) \sum_R fg \qquad (A.5 - 4)$$

where

$$E = \sum_R f^{1/2} \sum_R g^{1/2} = \| \underline{f} \| \cdot \| \underline{g} \| \qquad (A.5 - 5)$$

SCALE SPACE APPROACHES AND HIERARCHICAL (PYRAMIDAL) OR MULTILEVEL PATTERN ANALYSIS

Introduction

A hierarchical pattern processing approach is thought to parallel the operation of human sensory functions, including vision. Basically, processing proceeds from a coarse pattern description level to levels of increasing detail or information. Such processing approaches are applicable to the tasks of feature extraction, description, and matching. One resolution-mapping kernel with particularly important properties for scale-space filtering is the Gaussian kernel.

An Example of Multiresolution Correlation for Pattern Matching

Multiresolution Correlation for Pattern Matching.   The multiple resolution approach to correlation embodies the above principle. The features in this case could be simply

---

[2]Which it is important to note constitutes a significant amount of match that would be accounted for by metrics m_1 and m_2 above.

input signal intensities at varying (increasing) resolution levels. The matching process consists of simple correlation of these features. For computational efficiency, we probably would choose these extracted features such that they were easy to extract as well as to match. In addition, we could then continue our search by eliminating pattern 'regions' whose extracted features (at this processing level) differ (via some test) from those of the reference pattern, and thus concentrate processing effort only on the remaining 'promising' regions of the input pattern. Note that one risk in this approach is that a particular pattern region (which corresponds to the sought entity) may be excluded from further processing at a low level, thus 'missing' the overall pattern matching objective for the sake of computational efficiency. For illustration, we show a simple 1-D example using an array of intensities as the 'input pattern.'

A Simple (Numerical) Example.   Consider the following 'template,' whose existence and (if so) location we wish to find in the corresponding array:

Template Pattern (T_f).

> 1   2   3   4

Input Pattern (P_f).

> 7   6   3   4   1   2   4   3   1   2   3   4   5   6   5   4

There are (considering edge effects) 13 possible match locations. Assuming that the computational expense of matching is primarily due to the multiplication incurred as part of correlation, each of these potential matches costs four computations, resulting in a computational expense of 13(4) or 52 operations to fully explore the full resolution pattern array for matches.

Lower resolution arrays are formed by simple one-neighbor averaging. Thus the template and pattern arrays become:

Reduced Template Pattern (T_{r_1})

> $\frac{3}{2}$ $\frac{7}{2}$

Reduced Input Pattern Array (P_{r_1})

> $\frac{13}{2}$ $\frac{7}{2}$ $\frac{3}{2}$ $\frac{7}{2}$ $\frac{3}{2}$ $\frac{7}{2}$ $\frac{11}{2}$ $\frac{9}{2}$

We note that the matching process now involves 7 candidate locations, each with a computational expense of 2; therefore the total computational cost at this level is 14. Further reducing by continued averaging yields:

Further Reduced Template Pattern (T_{r_2})

> $\frac{10}{2}$

Further Reduced Pattern Array (P_{r_2})

> $\frac{20}{2}$ $\frac{10}{2}$ $\frac{10}{2}$ $\frac{20}{2}$

We observe that the matching process now involves 4 candidate locations, each with a cost of one computation, thus yielding a total computational cost at this level of 4.

The hierarchical matching process starts at the lowest resolution level, where there are 2 candidate locations. Assume that the locations are candidates for further investigation if the measure of match is above a threshold. Matching T_{r_2} against P_{r_2} yields 2 promising match locations, shown as (b) and (c) below.

Pattern Array (P_{r_2})

    (a)   (b)   (c)   (d)

   $\frac{20}{2}$ $\frac{10}{2}$ $\frac{10}{2}$ $\frac{20}{2}$

The preliminary matching process cost 4 match operations and yielded 2 regions of further interest. Proceeding to the next higher resolution level, the matching process is continued but *restricted to these regions*, thereby excluding regions (a) and (d) from any further processing. The increased resolution (T_{r_1} and P_{r_1}) arrays, from above, are

Template

   $\frac{3}{2}$ $\frac{7}{2}$

Pattern Array

(a)		(b)		(c)		(d)	
$\frac{13}{2}$	$\frac{7}{2}$	$\frac{3}{2}$	$\frac{7}{2}$	$\frac{3}{2}$	$\frac{7}{2}$	$\frac{11}{2}$	$\frac{9}{2}$
XXXXXXXXXX						XXXXXXXXXX	

where the XXXX indicates that a region has been excluded from further consideration. Again, the matching process indicates that expanded regions (b) and (c) warrant further investigation. The reader is encouraged to conclude this example.

GENERAL SCALE-SPACE PATTERN FILTERING AND THE GAUSSIAN KERNEL

Introduction

Varying resolution or scale-space pattern representations should be (in some sense) consistent. An important ramification of consistency is the ability to relate features or descriptors at different pattern resolutions. One important constraint is that as the resolution of the pattern is increased, significant features should not appear and disappear at random.

- *A scale-space representation of a pattern may be formed by convolving the highest resolution pattern with a kernel containing a scale parameter. This generates a family of different-resolution signals, each corresponding to a particular scale parameter value.*

Scale-Space Filtering

An averaging approach, as shown in the above example, meets the requirement for generating a scale-dependent family of patterns. The scale parameter in this case could be the extent of the pattern region being averaged. Consider the input pattern to be a signal. As the scale parameter varies, one may examine the effect of derivatives and singular points in the signal. For simplicity, the theory is shown for a 1-D signal, $f(x)$, but may be extended to multidimensional signals [Baubaud et al. 1986].

Denote the smoothing or scale-reduction parameter y and the respective smoothing kernel function as $g(x, y)$. The scale parameter y is positive, and we adopt the convention that an increase in y denotes increased smoothing or scale reduction.[3]

The output signal, or surface, is formed by convolution of f and g and is denoted $\phi(x, y)$. Since $y > 0$, this surface is defined over only the xy half-plane. Denoting the convolution operation by $*$:

$$\phi(x, y) = f(x) * g(x, y) = \int_{-\infty}^{\infty} f(x)g(x - u, y)du \qquad (A.5 - 6)$$

(A.5-6) produces an ensemble of signals as a function of the scale parameter y. Furthermore, as y increases, the range of representational values of x decreases. A desirable property of (A.5-6) is that as $y \to 0$ (there is no smoothing), $\phi(x, y) \to f(x)$. This requires the smoothing kernel $g(x, y)$ to approach an impulse as $y \to 0$.

Assume that the significant features to be preserved in scale-space versions of $f(x)$ are extrema, specifically the zero crossings of $L(f)$, where $L()$ is a linear differential operator. By using a second derivative operator, these extrema are found where

$$\phi_{xx}(x, y) = \frac{\partial^2 f}{\partial x^2} = 0 \qquad (A.5 - 7)$$

and correspond to zero crossings of $f_x(x, y)$. Since the differential operator is linear, we may examine the behavior of the scale-reduction operator via the second partial derivative of $\phi(x, y)$ with respect to x. This leads to consideration of the behavior of solutions to

$$\phi_{xx}(x, y) = 0 \qquad (A.5 - 8)$$

as y varies. If $g(x, y)$ preserves the presence of extrema as resolution is increased (moving from large values of y to smaller values), new zero crossings appear, but existing ones never disappear. The plot of $\phi_{xx}(x, y)$ is three dimensional, but only (x,y) locations where $\phi_{xx}(x, y) = 0$ are significant. The preceding consistency constraint requires that the plot of the contours of $\phi_{xx}(x, y) = 0$ versus x and y be closed above, but never below. These are shown in Figure A.5-2.

The constraints on $g(x, y)$ that lead to the type of consistent hierarchy of extrema illustrated by Figure A.5-2 are summarized below. The inverse of the scale parameter y is denoted $\hat{y}$ and sometimes is referred to as a bandwidth parameter. A kernel function $g(x, \hat{y})$ must satisfy the following:

---

[3]The literature sometimes refers to this kernel in terms of a *bandwidth parameter,* which is inversely related to the scale parameter.

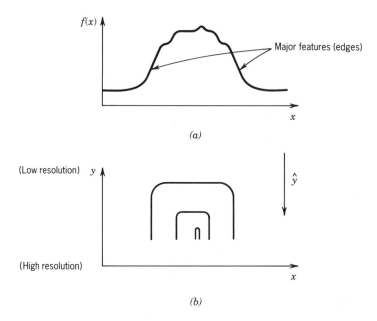

Figure A.5-2: Extrema consistency constraint for scale-space filtering.
(a) Sample function (note 'major' and 'minor' edges).
(b) Required behavior of contours $\phi_{xx} = 0$, as function of x and $\hat{y}$.

$$g(x, \hat{y}) = \hat{y}h(x\hat{y}) \qquad (A.5-9)$$

$$g(-x, \hat{y}) = g(x, \hat{y}) \qquad (A.5-10)$$

Equation (A.5-10) requires g to be symmetric. Furthermore,

$$\int_{-\infty}^{-\infty} g(x, \hat{y})dx = 1 \qquad (A.5-11)$$

As shown in [Baubaud et al. 1986], a function that satisfies the above requirements is the Gaussian kernel,

$$g(x, \hat{y}) = (\frac{1}{\sqrt{2\pi}})\hat{y} \exp\left[-\left(\frac{1}{2}\right)(x\hat{y})^2\right] \qquad (A.5-12)$$

Note that most of the popular scale-reduction methodologies, such as averaging, do not satisfy the requirements above; however, they may be viewed as approximations to the ideal kernel function. Examples using image data are shown in [Schalkoff 1989] and [Tan/Martin 1986].

Appendix 6
Geometry for Classification
and State-Space Visualization

In this section we present several results that are useful for analyzing decision regions and visualizing feature vectors R^d.

PLANES

3-D Case; Through Origin

In 3-D or (x_1, x_2, x_3) space, *a plane through the origin*[1] is determined by three parameters (w_1, w_2, w_3) via:

$$(w_1 \ w_2 \ w_3) \begin{pmatrix} x_1 \\ x_2 \\ x_3 \end{pmatrix} = 0 \qquad (A.6-1a)$$

or simply

$$\underline{w}^T \underline{x} = 0 \qquad (A.6-1b)$$

If $\underline{x}$ represents the position vector of a point X in the plane measured with respect to the (assumed Cartesian) coordinate system origin, then (A.6-1b) indicates that the plane parameter vector $\underline{w}$ and $\underline{x}$ are *orthogonal*. Parameter vector $\underline{w}$ is therefore the normal to the plane, but since (A.6-1) is homogeneous, only the direction of $\underline{w}$ is constrained.

---

[1]Or which contains the origin.

General Case; Not Necessarily Through Origin

A plane through any other point X_d, represented by position vector $\underline{x}_d$, may be written as

$$\underline{w}^T(\underline{x} - \underline{x}_d) = 0 \qquad (A.6 - 2a)$$

or

$$\underline{w}^T\underline{x} - d = 0 \qquad (A.6 - 2b)$$

where $d = \underline{w}^T\underline{x}_d$. This is shown in Figure A.6-1 for a reduced dimension (2-D) case. This reformulation of (A.6-1) is equivalent to a coordinate system transformation, where we shift the origin to $\underline{x}_d$, and therefore measure vectors $\underline{x}' = \underline{x} - \underline{x}_d$, where $\underline{x}'$ and $\underline{x}$ are the shifted and unshifted coordinate locations, respectively. Notice from (A.6-2a) that $\underline{w}$ is orthogonal to any vector, for instance, $\underline{x}_1 - \underline{x}_d$, lying in the plane. The plane determined by (A.6-2) is denoted H in Figure A.6-1. Interestingly, (A.6-2b) may be used to determine the 'distance' of H from the origin; and for a given $\underline{x}$, the 'side' of H in R^d that $\underline{x}$ is on and the distance of $\underline{x}$ from H. We explore both of these ramifications.

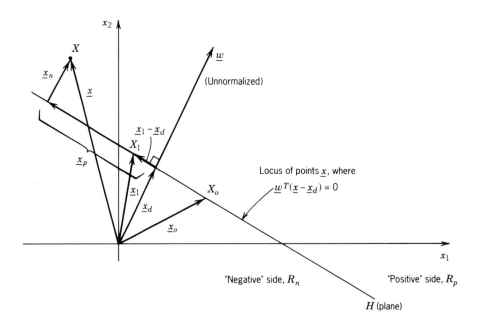

Figure A.6-1:   'Plane' representation in 2-D.

We normalize $\underline{w}$ to unit length by forming $\underline{w}' = \underline{w}/\|\underline{w}\|$. In considering perpendicular distance, vector $\underline{x}_d$ in Figure A.6-1 may be written as

$$\underline{x}_d = \alpha\underline{w}' \qquad (A.6 - 3)$$

where $\| \underline{x}_d \| = |\alpha|$. If we use (A.6-2b), since $\underline{x}_d$ represents a point on H,

$$\underline{w}^T \underline{x}_d - d = 0 \qquad (A.6-4)$$

or

$$\alpha \frac{\underline{w}^T \underline{w}}{\| \underline{w} \|} - d = 0$$

yielding

$$\alpha \| \underline{w} \| = d$$

or

$$\alpha = \frac{d}{\| \underline{w} \|} \qquad (A.6-5)$$

Therefore, the distance from the origin to H is given by $|\alpha| = \| \underline{x}_d \| = |d|/\| \underline{w} \| = |\underline{w}^T \underline{x}_d|/\| \underline{w} \|$. Clearly, if $\underline{x}_d = \underline{0}$, the plane includes the origin and $\alpha = 0$.

In addition, the location of any point X, represented by vector $\underline{x}$, may be considered relative to H. Defining $\underline{x}_p$ as the projection[2] of $\underline{x}$ onto H and (shown in Figure A.6-1) $\underline{x}_n$ as the component orthogonal to H, we may decompose[3] $\underline{x}$ as

$$\underline{x} = \underline{x}_d + \underline{x}_p + \underline{x}_n \qquad (A.6-6)$$

where $\underline{x}_d$ is defined in (A.6-3) and $k = \| \underline{x}_n \|$ so

$$\underline{x}_n = k \frac{\underline{w}}{\| \underline{w} \|} \qquad (A.6-7)$$

Therefore,

$$\underline{w}^T \underline{x} = \underline{w}^T(\underline{x}_d + \underline{x}_p + \underline{x}_n) = \underline{w}^T \underline{x}_n + \underline{w}^T \underline{x}_d = k \| \underline{w} \| + \alpha \| \underline{w} \| \qquad (A.6-8)$$

For simplicity, assume $\alpha = 0$, that is, the plane is through the origin. Then since $\underline{x}_n = k\underline{w}'$, the quantity $\underline{w}^T \underline{x} = k \| \underline{w} \|$ tells which side of H $\underline{x}$ is on. If $\underline{w}^T \underline{x} > 0$, $k > 0$ and, from Figure A.6-1, $\underline{x}$ is on the 'positive' side of H. Similarly, if $\underline{w}^T \underline{x} < 0$, $\underline{x}$ is on the 'negative' side, and if $\underline{w}^T \underline{x} = 0$, $\underline{x}$ is in H.

Extension to Linear Decision Region Boundaries and Discriminant Functions

Notice that plane H, characterized by (A.6-2a) *partitions* R^2 (in general R^d, as described below) into two mutually exclusive regions, denoted R_p and R_n in Figure A.6-1. The assignment of vector $\underline{x}$ to either the 'positive' side, 'negative' side, or along H can be implemented by

---

[2]This causes $\underline{w}^T \underline{x}_p = 0$ from our remarks above.

[3]Other decompositions are possible.

$$
\underline{w}^T \underline{x} - d \begin{cases} > 0 & \text{if } \underline{x} \in R_p \\ = 0 & \text{if } \underline{x} \in H \\ < 0 & \text{if } \underline{x} \in R_n \end{cases} \qquad (A.6-9)
$$

This suggests a *linear discriminant function* $g(\underline{x})$ to implement the classification of (A.6-9) as

$$
g(\underline{x}) = \underline{w}^T \underline{x} - d \qquad (A.6-10)
$$

Examination of (A.6-10) and Figure A.6-1 indicates that the linear discriminant function that yields H and is used to partition R^d into two regions has the following characteristics:

1. The *orientation* of H is determined by $\underline{w}$.
2. The *location* of H is determined by d.

Extension to R^d

Although we have only considered R^3 (and R^2) in the previous analysis, the results are easily extendable to R^d simply by choosing $d > 3$. This allows linear classification of d-dimensional feature vectors $\underline{x}$. Visualization, however, is more difficult. The surface H in this context is referred to as a *hyperplane*.

QUADRIC DECISION BOUNDARIES (AND ASSOCIATED DISCRIMINANT FUNCTIONS)

In R^d, with $\underline{x} = (x_1, x_2, \ldots, x_d)^T$, consider the equation[4]

$$
\sum_{i=1}^{d} w_{ii} x_i^2 + \sum_{i=1}^{d-1} \sum_{j=i+1}^{d} w_{ij} x_i x_j + \sum_{i=1}^{d} w_i x_i + w_o = 0 \qquad (A.6-11)
$$

Equation A.6-11 defines a *quadric surface*, defined by *quadric discriminant functions*. Notice that when $d = 2$, (A.6-11) reduces to $\underline{x} = (x_1 \; x_2)^T$ and

$$
w_{11} x_1^2 + w_{22} x_2^2 + w_{12} x_1 x_2 + w_1 x_1 + w_2 x_2 + w_o = 0 \qquad (A.6-12)
$$

For illustration, consider several special cases of (A.6-12). When $w_{11} = w_{22} = w_{12} = 0$, (A.6-12) defines a line. If $w_{11} = w_{22} = 1$ and $w_{12} = w_1 = w_2 = 0$, a circle, whose center is at the origin, results. When $w_{11} = w_{22} = 0$, a *bilinear constraint* between x_1 and x_2 results. When $w_{11} = w_{12} = w_2 = 0$, a parabola with a specific orientation results. When $w_{11} \neq 0$, $w_{22} \neq 0$, $w_{11} \neq w_{22}$, $w_{12} = w_1 = w_2 = 0$, a simple ellipse results. The reader is encouraged to consider other conic sections.

---

[4]Which is ideally viewed as a constraint in R^d.

Extrapolation from the $d = 2$ case in (A.6-12) suggests that (A.6-11) defines another family of 'hyper' surfaces in R^d. Before considering these forms, we recast (A.6-11) in a more compact and tractable form. There are $(d+1)(d+2)/2$ parameters in (A.6-11), which may be organized as the $d \times d$ matrix W:

$$W = [\bar{w}_{ij}] \qquad (A.6-13)$$

where

$$\bar{w}_{ij} = \begin{cases} w_{ii} & \text{if } i = j \\ \frac{1}{2} w_{ij} & \text{if } i \neq j \end{cases} \qquad (A.6-14a)$$

and the vector $\underline{w}$:

$$\underline{w} = \begin{pmatrix} w_1 \\ w_2 \\ \vdots \\ w_d \end{pmatrix} \qquad (A.6-14b)$$

which yields the equivalent representation

$$\underline{x}^T W \underline{x} + \underline{w}^T \underline{x} + w_o = 0 \qquad (A.6-15)$$

Analysis of the Quadratic Term

In (A.6-15) the analysis of *quadratic* term $\underline{x}^T W \underline{x}$ is particularly useful. An interesting observation is that only the symmetric part of W contributes to the value of the quadratic. If $\underline{x}^T W \underline{x} > 0 \; \forall \underline{x} \neq \underline{0}$, then the matrix W is said to be *positive definite*. An e-vector–based transformation of coordinates (Appendix 1) thus requires all e-values of W to be positive. Similarly, if $\underline{x}^T W \underline{x} \geq 0 \; \forall \underline{x} \neq \underline{0}$, then all e-values of W are required to be nonnegative. In this case we refer to W as *positive semidefinite*.

Types of Quadric Surfaces from (A.6-15)

1. If W is positive definite, (A.6-15) defines a hyperellipsoid surface, whose axes are in the directions of the e-vectors of W.
2. If $W = kI$ where $k > 0$, (A.6-15) defines a *hypersphere*.
3. If W is positive semidefinite, (A.6-15) defines a *hyperellipsoidal cylinder*.
4. If none of the above cases hold true, (A.6-15) defines surface referred to as a *hyperhyperboloid*.

Implementation of Quadric Discrimination Functions Using Linear Machines

Direct implementation of (A.6-15) is possible. In addition, linear transformations of $\underline{x}$ that make (A.6-15) somewhat more direct are useful. However, a third alternative, which is useful in both StatPR and NeurPR, is illustrated. Suppose we are given a 2-D surface

$$g(\underline{x}) = x_2 - x_1^2 - 3x_1 + 6 = 0 \qquad (A.6-16)$$

Instead of implementing (A.6-16) directly, consider the following alternative:

$$x_3 = x_1^2 \qquad (A.6-17a)$$

$$g(\underline{x}) = x_2 - x_3 - 3x_1 + 6 = 0 = [-3 \ 1 \ -1]^T \underline{x} + 6 = \underline{w}^T \underline{x} + w_o \qquad (A.6-17b)$$

where $\underline{x}$ in (A.6-17b) is $\underline{x} = (x_1 \ x_2 \ x_3)^T$.

Thus, the strategy of (A.6-17) is based on the following:

1. Defining a new feature, x_{i+1} by *preprocessing* $\underline{x}$ in (A.6-17a).

2. Increasing the dimensionality of $\underline{x}$, to achieve a linear machine[5] in (A.6-17b).

Generalizations of this strategy are possible.

VISUALIZING BINARY-VALUED FEATURE VECTORS IN I^d

Suppose that

$$\underline{x} = \begin{pmatrix} x_1 \\ x_2 \\ \vdots \\ x_d \end{pmatrix} \qquad (A.6-18)$$

where $x_i \in \{0, 1\}$. For example, vector $\underline{x}$ could represent the state of a neural network. A convenient visualization of this vector in I^d is as the 'corner' or vertex of a d-dimensional cube. Other vectors that differ from $\underline{x}$ by a Hamming distance of 1 are directly connected to $\underline{x}$ via a vertex, whereas those that differ from $\underline{x}$ by HD > 1 require a traversal in I^d of at least one other vertex.

In developing classifiers for patterns in R^d, whether by conventional (Chapter 4) or neural (Chapters 12–13) means, the distribution of input training vectors in R^d must be considered. One measure of the 'dispersion' of this set is a histogram of Hamming distances between vectors. An example is shown in Figure A.6-2. In this example, notice that the vast majority of the vectors are well separated ($HD \approx 8$).

---

[5]This strategy is used in other applications, for example, computer graphics. The concept of homogeneous and superhomogeneous coordinates is treated in [Schalkoff 1989].

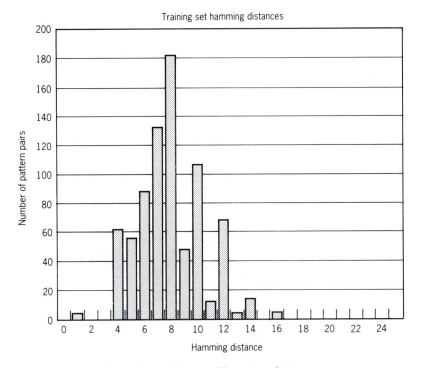

Figure A.6-2:   A sample training set Hamming distances.

References

[Abu-Mostafa/Psaltis 1987] ABU-MOSTAFA, Y.S., AND D. PSALTIS, 'Optical Neural Computers,' *Scientific American*, Vol. 256, No. 3, 1987, pp. 88–95.

[Abu-Mostafa/St. Jacques 1985] ABU-MOSTAFA, YASER S., AND JEANNINE-MARIE ST. JACQUES, 'Information Capacity of the Hopfield Model,' *IEEE Trans. on Information Theory*, IT-31, No. 4, 1985, pp. 461–464.

[Agarwala 1977] AGARWALA, A.K., (ed.), *Machine Recognition of Patterns*, IEEE Press, 1977.

[Agin 1981] AGIN, G.J., 'Hierarchical Representation of Three-Dimensional Objects Using Verbal Models,' *IEEE Transactions on Pattern Analysis and Machine Intelligence*, Vol. PAMI-3, No. 2, March 1981, pp. 197–204.

[Agin/Binford 1976] AGIN, G.J., AND T.O. BINFORD, 'Computer Description of Curved Objects,' *IEEE Transactions on Computers*, Vol. 25, 1976, pp. 439–440.

[Aho/Ullman 1972] AHO, A.V., AND J.D. ULLMAN, *The Theory of Parsing, Translation and Compiling, Vol. 1: Parsing*, Prentice-Hall, Englewood Cliffs, N.J., 1972.

[Allen 1987] ALLEN J., *Natural Language Understanding*, Benjamin Cummings, Reading, Mass., 1987.

[Amari 1982] AMARI, S., AND M.A. ARBIB, (eds.), *Competition and Cooperation in Neural Nets*, Springer-Verlag, Berlin, 1982.

[Anderberg 1973] ANDERBERG, M.R., *Cluster Analysis for Applications*, Academic Press, New York, 1973.

[Anderson/Rosenfeld 1988] ANDERSON, J.A., AND E. ROSENFELD (eds.), *Neurocomputing: Foundations of Research*, MIT Press, Cambridge, Mass., 1988.

[Angluin 1978] ANGLUIN, D., 'On the Complexity of Minimum Inference of Regular Sets,' *Information and Control*, Vol. 39, 1978, pp. 337–350.

[Angluin 1980] ANGLUIN, D., 'Inductive Inference of Formal Languages from Positive Data,' *Information and Control*, Vol. 45, 1980, pp. 117–135.

[Angluin/Smith 1983] ANGLUIN, D., AND C.H. SMITH, 'Inductive Inference: Theory and Methods,' *Computing Surveys*, Vol. 15, No. 3, 1983, pp. 237–269.

[Ball 1986] BALLARD, D.H., 'Parallel Logical Inference and Energy Minimization,' Tech Report TR 142, March 1986, Computer Science Dept., University of Rochester, Rochester, N.Y.

[Barto et al. 1981] BARTO, A., R. SUTTON, AND P. BROWER, 'Associative Search Network: A Reinforcement Learning Associative Memory,' *Biological Cybernetics*, Vol. 40, 1981, pp. 201–211.

[Batchelor/Wilkins 1969] BATCHELOR, B.G., AND B.R. WILKINS, 'Method for Location of Clusters of Patterns to Initialize a Learning Machine,' *Electronics Letters*, Vol. 5, No. 20, Oct. 1969, pp. 481–483.

[Baubaud et al. 1986] BAUBAUD, J., A. WITKIN, M. BAUDIN, AND R.O. DUDA, 'Uniqueness of the Gaussian Kernel for Scale-Space Filtering,' *IEEE Transactions on Pattern Analysis and Machine Intelligence*, Vol. PAMI-8, No. 1, Jan. 1986, pp. 26–33.

[Biederman 1985] BIEDERMAN, I., 'Human Image Understanding: Recent Research and a Theory,' *Computer Vision, Graphics and Image Processing*, Vol. 32, 1985, pp. 29–73.

[Blashfield et al. 1982] BLASHFIELD, R.K., M.S. ALDENDERFER, AND L.C. MOREY, 'Cluster Analysis Software,' in *Handbook of Statistics*, Vol. 2, P. R. Krishniah and L. N. Kanal (eds.), North Holland, Amsterdam, The Netherlands, 1982, pp. 245–266.

[Bolc 1984] BOLC, LEONARD (ed.), *Natural Language Communication with Pictorial Information Systems*, Springer-Verlag, New York, 1984.

[Bolles 1979] BOLLES, ROBERT, *Learning Theory*, Holt, Rinehart and Winston, New York, 1979.

[Boorman/Olivier 1973] BOORMAN, S.A., AND D.C. OLIVIER, 'Metrics on Spaces of Finite Trees,' *Journal of Mathematical Psychology*, Vol. 10, 1973, pp. 26–59.

[Booth/Thompson 1973] BOOTH, T.L., AND R.A. THOMPSON, 'Applying Probability Measures to Abstract Languages,' *IEEE Transactions on Computers*, Vol. c-22, No. 5, May 1973, pp. 442–450.

[Bow 1984] BOW, S.T., *Pattern Recognition*, Marcel Dekker, New York, 1984.

[Brayer/Fu 1977] BRAYER, J.M., AND K.S. FU, 'A Note on the k-tail Method of Tree Grammar Inference,' *IEEE Transactions on Systems, Man and Cybernetics*, Vol. SMC-7, April 1977, pp. 293–300.

[Brogan 1985] BROGAN, W.L., *Modern Control Theory* (2nd edition), Prentice-Hall, Englewood Cliffs, N.J., 1985.

[Brooks 1981] BROOKS, R. A., 'Symbolic Reasoning Among 3-D Models and 2-D Images,' *Artificial Intelligence*, Vol. 17, 1981, pp. 285–348.

[Bryant 1979] BRYANT, J., 'On the Clustering of Multidimensional Pictorial Data,' *Pattern Recognition*, Vol. 11, 1979, pp. 115–125.

[Bundy et al. 1985] BUNDY, A., B. SILVER, AND D. PLUMMER, 'An Analytical Comparison of Some Rule-Learning Programs,' *Artificial Intelligence,* Vol. 27, 1985, pp. 137–181.

[Bunke 1982] BUNKE, H., 'Attributed Programmed Graph Grammars and Their Application to Schematic Diagram Interpretation,' *IEEE Transactions on Pattern Analysis and Machine Intelligence*, Vol. PAMI-4, No. 6, Nov. 1982, pp. 574–582.

[Carbonell/Hayes 1987] CARBONELL, J.G., AND P.J. HAYES, 'Natural Language Understanding,' in S.C. Shapiro (ed.), *Encyclopedia of Artificial Intelligence*, John Wiley & Sons, New York, 1987, pp. 660–677.

[Carpenter 1989] CARPENTER, G., 'Neural Network Models for Pattern Recognition and Associative Memory,' *Neural Networks*, Vol. 2, 1989, pp. 243–257.

[Carp/Gross 1986] CARPENTER G., AND S. GROSSBERG, 'Associative Learning, Adaptive Pattern Recognition and Cooperative Decision Making by Neural Networks,' *Proceedings of the SPIE*, Vol. 634, 1986, pp. 218–247.

[Carp/Gross 1 1987] CARPENTER, G.A., AND S. GROSSBERG, 'A Massively Parallel Architecture for a Self-Organizing Neural Pattern Recognition Machine,' *Computer Vision, Graphics and Image Processing*, Vol. 37, 1987, pp. 54–115.

[Carp/Gross 2 1987] CARPENTER, G.A., AND S. GROSSBERG, 'ART 2: Self-organization of Stable Category Recognition Codes for Analog Input Patterns,' *Applied Optics*, Vol. 26, No. 3, Dec. 1987, pp. 4919–4930.

[Casasent 1976] CASASENT, D., 'Position, Rotation and Scale Invariant Optical Correlation,' *Applied Optics*, Vol. 15, No. 7, July 1976, pp. 1795–1799.

[Casasent/Psaltis 1977] CASASENT, D., AND D. PSALTIS, 'New Optical Transforms for Pattern Recognition,' *Proceedings of the IEEE*, Vol. 65, No. 1, Jan. 1977, pp. 77–84.

[Casey/Nagy 1984] CASEY, R.G., AND G. NAGY, 'Decision Tree Design Using a Probabilistic Model, *IEEE Transactions on Information Theory*, Vol. 30, 1984, pp. 93–99.

[Cendrowska 1987] CENDROWSKA, J., 'PRISM. An Algorithm for Inducing Modular Rules,'*International Journal of Man-Machine Studies*, Vol. 27, 1987, pp. 249–310.

[Chen 1973] CHEN, C.H., *Statistical Pattern Recognition*, Hayden, Washington, D.C., 1973

[Cheng/Huang 1981] CHENG, J.K., AND T.S. HUANG, 'A Subgraph Isomorphism Algorithm Using Resolution,' *Pattern Recognition*, Vol. 13, No. 5, 1981, pp. 371–379.

[Chiang/Fu 1984] CHIANG, Y.T., AND K.S. FU, 'Parallel Parsing Algorithms and VLSI Implementations for Syntactic Pattern Recognition,' *IEEE Transactions on Pattern Analysis and Machine Intelligence*, Vol. PAMI-6, No. 3, May 1984, pp. 302–313.

[Chien 1978] CHIEN, Y.T., *Interactive Pattern Recognition*, Marcel Dekker, New York, 1978.

[Chomsky 1957] CHOMSKY, N., *Syntactic Structures*, Mouton, The Hague, Netherlands, 1957.

[Cohen/Grossberg 1983] COHEN, M.A., AND S. GROSSBERG, 'Absolute Stability of Global Pattern Formation and Parallel Memory Storage by Competitive Neural Networks,' *IEEE Transactions on Systems, Man, and Cybernetics*, Vol. SMC-13, 1983, pp. 815–826.

[Coleman/Andrews 1979] COLEMAN, G.B., AND H.C. ANDREWS, 'Image Segmentation by Clustering,' *Proceedings of the IEEE*, Vol. 67, May 1979, pp. 773–785.

[Cover 1965] COVER, T.M., 'Geometrical and Statistical Properties of Systems of Linear Inequalities with Applications in Pattern Recognition,' *IEEE Transactions on Electronic Computing*, Vol. EC-14, June 1965, pp. 326–334.

[Cover/Hart 1967] COVER, T.M., AND P.E. HART, 'Nearest Neighbor Pattern Classification,' *IEEE Transactions on Information Theory*, Vol. IT-13, No. 1, Jan. 1967, pp. 21–27.

[Cox/Schal 1990] COX, C.E., AND R.J. SCHALKOFF, 'Application of Artificial Feedforward Neural Networks to Binary Image Edge Classification and Motion Estimation,' in press.

[Crespi-Reghizzi et al. 1973] CRESPI-REGHIZZI, S., M.A. MELKANOFF, AND L. LICHTEN, 'The Use of Grammatical Inference for Designing Programming Languages,' *Communications of the Association for Computing Machinery*, Vol. 16, Feb. 1973, pp. 83–90.

[Crick 1989] CRICK, F., 'The Recent Excitement about Neural Networks,' *Nature*, Vol. 337, Jan. 1989, pp. 129–132.

[Dahlquist et al. 1974] DAHLQUIST, G., A. BJORK, AND N. ANDERSON, *Numerical Methods*, Prentice-Hall, Englewood Cliffs, N.J., 1974.

[Derouault/Merialdo 1986] DEROUAULT, A.M., AND B. MERIALDO, 'Natural Language Modeling for Phenome-to-Text Transcription,' *IEEE Transactions on Pattern Analysis and Machine Intelligence*, Vol. PAMI-8, No. 6, Nov. 1986, pp. 742–749.

[Devijver/Kittler 1982] DEVIJVER, P., AND J. KITTLER, *Pattern Recognition: A Statistical Approach*, Prentice-Hall, Englewood Cliffs, N.J., 1982.

[Don/Fu 1985] DON, H.S., AND K.S. FU, 'A Syntactic Method for Image Segmentation and Object Recognition,' *Pattern Recognition*, Vol. 18, No. 1, 1985, pp. 73–87.

[Dubes/Jain 1976] DUBES, R.C., AND A.K. JAIN, 'Clustering Techniques: The User's Dilemma,' *Pattern Recognition*, Vol. 8, 1976, pp. 247–260.

[Dubes/Jain 1980] DUBES, R.C., AND A.K. JAIN, 'Clustering Methodologies in Exploratory Data Analysis,' in *Advances in Computers*, Vol. 19, M. Yovits (ed.), Academic Press, New York, 1980, pp. 113–228.

[Duda/Hart 1973] DUDA, R.O., AND P. E. HART, *Pattern Classification and Scene Analysis*, John Wiley & Sons, New York, 1973.

[Evans 1971] EVANS, T.G., 'Grammatical Inference Techniques in Pattern Analysis' in *Software Engineering*, J. Ton (ed.), Academic Press, New York, 1971.

[Everitt 1977] EVERITT, B., *Cluster Analysis*, Heinemann Educational Books, 1977.

[Farhat 1987] FARHAT, N.H., 'Optoelectronic Analogs of Self-Programming Neural Nets: Architecture and Methodologies for Implementing Fast Stochastic Learning by Simulated Annealing,' *Applied Optics*, Vol. 26, No. 23, Dec. 1987, pp. 5093–5103.

[Farhat et al. 1985] FARHAT, N.H., D. PSALTIS, A. PRATA, AND E. PEAK, 'Optical Implementation of the Hopfield Model,' *Applied Optics*, Vol. 24, 1985, pp. 1469–1475.

[Feiv 1983] FEIVSON, A. H., 'Classification by Thresholding,' *IEEE Transactions on Pattern Analysis and Machine Intelligence*, Vol. PAMI-5, No. 1, Jan. 1983, pp. 48–54.

[Fekete 1981] FEKETE, G., J.O. EKLUNDH, AND A. ROSENFELD, 'Relaxation: Evaluation and Applications,' *IEEE Transactions Pattern Analysis and Machine Intelligence*, Vol. PAMI-3, No. 4, July 1981, pp. 459–469.

[Feldman 1972] FELDMAN, J., 'Some Decidability Results on Grammatical Inference and Complexity,' *Information and Control*, Vol. 20, 1972, pp. 244–262.

[Feldman 1985] FELDMAN, J.A., 'Connectionist Models and Parallelism in High-Level Vision,' *Computer Vision, Graphics and Image Processing*, Vol. 31, 1985, pp. 178–200.

[Feldman/Ballard 1982] FELDMAN, J.A., AND D.H. BALLARD, 'Connectionist Models and Their Properties,' *Cognitive Science*, Vol. 6, 1982, pp. 205–254.

[Feldman et al. 1988] FELDMAN, J.A., M.A. FANTY, N.H. GODDARD, AND K.J. LYNNE, 'Computing with Structured Connectionist Networks,' *Communications of the Association for Computing Machinery*, Vol. 31, No. 2, Feb. 1988, pp. 170–187.

[Findler/Leeuwen 1979] FINDLER, N.V., AND J.V. LEEUWEN, 'A Family of Similarity Measures Between Two Strings,' *IEEE Transactions on Pattern Analysis and Machine Intelligence*, Vol. PAMI-1, No. 1, Jan. 1979, pp. 116–118.

[Fisch/Elsch 1973] FISCHLER, M.A., AND R. A. ELSCHLAGER, 'The Representation and Matching of Pictorial Structures,' *IEEE Transactions on Computers*, Vol. C-22, No. 1, Jan 1973, pp. 67–92.

[Fisher 1936] FISHER, R.A., 'The Use of Multiple Measurements in Taxonomic Problems,' (reprinted in) *Contributions to Mathematical Statistics*, John Wiley & Sons, New York, 1950.

[Forgy 1965] FORGY, E.W., 'Cluster Analysis of Multivariate Data: Efficiency vs. Interpretability of Classifications,' *Biometrics*, Vol. 21, abstract, 1965, p. 768.

[Friedman 1977] FRIEDMAN, J.H., 'A Recursive Partitioning Decision Rule for Non-parametric Classification,' *IEEE Transactions on Computers*, Vol. C-26, April 1977, pp. 404–408.

[Friedman et al. 1975] FRIEDMAN, J.H., F. BASHETT, AND L. J. SHUSTEK, 'An Algorithm for Finding Nearest Neighbors,' *IEEE Transactions on Computers*, Vol. C-24, Oct. 1975, pp. 1000–1006.

[Fu 1968] FU, K.S., *Sequential Methods in Pattern Recognition and Machine Learning*, Academic Press, New York, 1968.

[Fu 1974] FU, K.S., *Syntactic Methods in Pattern Recognition*, Academic Press, New York, 1974.

[Fu 1980] FU, K.S., 'Recent Developments in Pattern Recognition,' *IEEE Transactions on Computers*, Vol. C-29, No. 10, Oct. 1980, pp. 845–857.

[Fu 1 1982] FU, K.S., *Syntactic Pattern Recognition and Applications*, Prentice-Hall, Englewood Cliffs, N.J., 1982.

[Fu 2 1982] FU, K.S. (ed), *Application of Pattern Recognition*, CRC Press, Cleveland, OH, 1982.

[Fu 1985] FU, K.S., 'Modeling Rule-Based Systems by Stochastic Programmed Production Systems,' *Information Science*, Vol. 36, Sept. 1985, p. 207.

[Fu 1986] FU, K.S., 'A Step Towards Unification of Syntactic and Statistical Pattern Recognition,' *IEEE Transactions on Pattern Analysis and Machine Intelligence*, Vol. PAMI-8, No. 3, May 1986, pp. 398–404.

[Fu/Bhargava 1973] FU, K.S., AND B.K. BHARGAVA, 'Tree Systems for Syntactic Pattern Recognition,' *IEEE Transactions on Computers*, Vol. C-22, No. 12, Dec. 1973, pp. 1087–1099.

[Fu/Booth 1986] FU, K.S., AND T.L. BOOTH, 'Grammatical Inference: Introduction and Survey-Part I,' *IEEE Transactions on Pattern Analysis and Machine Intelligence*, Vol. PAMI-8, No. 3, May 1986, pp. 343–375.

[Fu/Young 1985] FU, K.S., AND T.Y. YOUNG (eds.), *Handbook of Pattern Recognition and Image Processing*, Academic Press, New York, 1985.

[Fukunaga 1972] FUKUNAGA, K., *Introduction to Statistical Pattern Recognition*, Academic Press, New York, 1972.

[Fukunaga/Olsen 1970] FUKUNAGA, K., AND D.R. OLSEN, 'Piecewise Linear Discriminant Functions and Classification Errors for Multiclass Problems,' *IEEE Transactions on Information Theory*, Vol. IT-16, 1970, pp. 99–100.

[Fukushima/Miyake 1982] FUKUSHIMA, K., AND S. MIYAKE, 'Neocognitron: A New Algorithm for Pattern Recognition Tolerant of Deformations and Shifts in Position,' *Pattern Recognition*, Vol. 15, No. 6, 1982, pp. 455–469.

[Gaborski 1990] GABORSKI, R., 'An Intelligent Character Recognition System Based on Neural Networks,' *Research Magazine*, Eastman Kodak Company, Rochester, N.Y., Spring 1990.

[Garcia et al. 1987] GARCIA, P., E. VIDAL, AND F. CASACUBERTA, 'Local Languages, the Successor Method and a Step Towards a General Methodology for the Inference of Regular Grammars,' *IEEE Transactions on Pattern Analysis and Machine Intelligence*, Vol. PAMI-9, No. 6, Nov. 1987, pp. 841–845.

[Garcia/Vidal 1990] GARCIA, P., AND E. VIDAL, 'Inference of k-Testable Languages in the Strict Sense and Application to Syntactic Pattern Recognition,' *IEEE Transactions on Pattern Analysis and Machine Intelligence,* Vol. 12, No. 9, Sept. 1990, pp. 920–925.

[Giles/Maxwell 1987] GILES C.L., AND T. MAXWELL, 'Learning, Invariance, and Generalization in High-Order Neural Networks,' *Applied Optics*, Vol. 26, 1987, pp. 4972–4978.

[Gloroiso/Colon-Osorio 1980] GLOROISO, R.M., AND F.C. COLON-OSORIO, *Engineering Intelligent Systems—Concepts, Theory and Applications*, Digital Press, Bedford, Mass., 1980.

[Gold 1967] GOLD, E.M., 'Language Identification in the Limit,' *Information and Control*, Vol. 10, 1967, pp. 447–474.

[Gold 1978] GOLD, E.M.,'Complexity of Automaton Identification from Given Data,' *Information and Control*, Vol. 37, 1978, pp. 302–320.

[Gonzalez/Thomason 1978] GONZALEZ, R.C., AND M.G. THOMASON, *Syntactic Pattern Recognition*, Addison-Wesley, Reading, Mass., 1978.

[Goodman/Smyth 1990] GOODMAN, R.M., AND P. SMYTH, 'Decision Tree Design Using Information Theory,' *Knowledge Acquisition*, Vol. 2, No. 1, 1990, pp. 1–19.

[Gray/Karnin 1982] GRAY, R.M., AND E.D. KARNIN, 'Multiple Local Optima in Vector Quantizers,' *IEEE Transactions on Information Theory*, Vol. IT-28, No. 2, March 1982, pp. 256–261.

[Griffiths/Petrick 1965] GRIFFITHS, T.V., AND S.R. PETRICK, 'On the Relative Efficiencies of Context-Free Grammar Recognizers,' *Communications of the Association for Computing Machinery*, Vol. 8, 1965, pp. 289–299.

[Guest/Te Kolste 1987] GUEST, C.C., AND R. TE KOLSTE, 'Designs and Devices for Optical Bidirectional Associative Memories,' *Applied Optics*, Vol. 26, No. 23, Dec. 1987, pp. 5055–5060.

[Haralick 1978] HARALICK, R.M., 'Structural Pattern Recognition, Homomorphisms, and Arrangements,' *Pattern Recognition*, Vol. 10, 1978, pp. 223–236.

[Haralick 1979] HARALICK, R. M., 'Statistical and Structural Approaches to Texture,' *Proceedings of the IEEE*, Vol. 67, No. 5, May 1979, p. 786–804.

[Haralick 1980] HARALICK, R.M., AND G.L. ELLIOTT, 'Increasing Tree Search Efficiency for Constraint Satisfaction Problems,' *Artificial Intelligence*, Vol. 14, 1980, pp. 263–313.

[Hartigan 1975] HARTIGAN, J.A., *Clustering Algorithms*, John Wiley & Sons, New York, 1975.

[Hebb 1949] HEBB, D., *Organization of Behavior*, John Wiley & Sons, N.Y., 1949.

[Hecht-Nielsen 1 1987] HECHT-NIELSEN, R., 'Nearest Matched Filter Classification of Spatiotemporal Patterns,' *Applied Optics*, Vol. 26, No. 10, May 15, 1987, pp. 1892–1899.

[Hecht-Nielsen 2 1987] HECHT-NIELSEN, R., 'Kolmogorov's Mapping Neural Network Existence Theorem,' *Proc. IEEE 1st International Conference on Neural Networks*, June 1987, San Diego, Calif., pp. III-11–III-14.

[Henderson 1984] HENDERSON, T.C., 'A Note on Discrete Relaxation,' *Computer Vision, Graphics and Image Processing*, No. 28, 1984, pp. 384–388.

[Henrichon/Fu 1969] HENRICHON, E.G., AND K.S. FU, 'A Nonparametric Partitioning Procedure for Pattern Classification,' *IEEE Transactions on Computers*, Vol. C-18, July 1969, pp. 614–624.

[Hinton 1981] HINTON, G.E., AND J.A. ANDERSON (eds.), *Parallel Models of Associative Memory*, Lawrence Erlbaum and Associates, Hillside, N.J., 1981.

[Ho/Kashyap 1965] HO, Y.C., AND R.L. KASHYAP, 'An Algorithm for Linear Inequalities and Its Application,' *IEEE Transactions on Electronic Computing*, Vol. EC-14, October 1965, pp. 683–688 (reprinted in [Sklansky 1973]).

[Holtzman 1981] HOLTZMAN, S., 'Using Generative Grammars for Music Composition,' *Computer Music Journal*, Vol. 5, No. 1, 1981, pp. 51–64.

[Hopcroft/Ullman 1969] HOPCROFT, J.E., AND J.D. ULLMAN, *Formal Languages and Their Relation to Automata*, Addison-Wesley, Reading, Mass., 1969.

[Hopfield 1982] HOPFIELD, J.J., 'Neural Networks and Physical Systems with Emergent Collective Computational Abilities,' *Proceedings of the National Academy of Sciences*, Vol. 79 (Biophysics), April 1982, pp. 2554–2558.

[Hopfield 1984] HOPFIELD, J.J., 'Neurons with Graded Response Have Collective Computational Properties Like Those of Two-state Neurons,' *Proceedings of the National Academy of Sciences*, Vol. 81 (Biophysics), May 1984, pp. 3088–3092.

[Hopfield/Tank 1985] HOPFIELD, J.J., AND D.W. TANK, 'Neural Computation of Decisions in Optimization Problems,' *Biological Cybernetics*, Vol. 52, 1985, pp. 141–152.

[Hopfield/Tank 1986] HOPFIELD, J.J., AND D.W. TANK, 'Computing with Neural Circuits: A Model,' *Science*, Vol. 233, Aug. 1986, pp. 625–633.

[Hu 1961] HU, M.K., 'Pattern Recognition by Moment Invariants,' *Proceedings of the Institute of Radio Engineers*, Vol. 49, 1961, p. 1428.

[Huang/Lippmann 1987] HUANG, W.Y., AND R.P. LIPPMANN, 'Comparison Between Neural Net and Conventional Classifiers,' *Proceedings of the IEEE International Conference on Neural Networks*, San Diego, June 1987, Vol. IV, pp. 485–493.

[Hummel/Zucker 1983] HUMMEL, R.A., AND S.W. ZUCKER, 'On the Foundations of Relaxation Labelling Processes,' *IEEE Transactions on Pattern Analysis and Machine Intelligence*, Vol. PAMI-5, May 1983, pp. 267–287.

[Hwang et al. 1986] HWANG, V.S., L.S. DAVIS, AND T. MATUSUYAMA, 'Hypothesis Integration in Image Understanding Systems,' *Computer Vision, Graphics and Image Processing*, Vol. 36, 1986, pp. 321–371.

[Itoga 1981] ITOGA, S.Y., 'A New Heuristic for Inferring Regular Grammars,' *IEEE Transactions on Pattern Analysis and Machine Intelligence*, Vol. PAMI-3, No. 2, 1981, pp. 191–197.

[Jackel et al. 1987] JACKEL, L.D., H.P. GRAF, AND R.E. HOWARD, 'Electronic Neural-Network Chips,' *Applied Optics*, Vol. 26, No. 23, December 1987, pp. 5077–5080.

[Jain/Dubes 1988] JAIN, A.K., AND R. DUBES, *Algorithms for Clustering Data*, Prentice-Hall, Englewood Cliffs, N.J., 1988.

[Jamison/Schalkoff 1988] JAMISON, T.A., AND R.J. SCHALKOFF, 'Image Labelling Via a Neural Network Approach and a Comparison with Existing Alternatives,' *Image and Vision Computing*, Vol. 6, No. 4, Nov. 1988, pp. 203–214.

[Jamison/Schalkoff 1989] JAMISON, T.A., AND R.J. SCHALKOFF, 'Feature Extraction and Shape Classification of 2-D Polygons Using a Neural Network,' *Proceedings of the IEEE Southeastcon '89*, Columbia, S.C., April 1989, p. 953.

[Johnsonbaugh 1986] JOHNSONBAUGH, R., *Discrete Mathematics*, Macmillan Publishing, New York, 1986.

[Kanal 1979] KANAL, L.N., 'Problem-solving Models and Search Strategies for Pattern Recognition,' *IEEE Transactions on Pattern Analysis and Machine Intelligence*, Vol. PAMI-1, April 1979, pp. 194–201.

[Kangas et al. 1990] KANGAS, J.A., T.K. KOHONEN, AND J.T. LAAKSONEN, 'Variants of Self-Organizing Maps,' *IEEE Transactions on Neural Networks*, Vol. 1, No. 1, March 1990, pp. 93–99.

[Khanna 1990] KHANNA, T., *Foundations of Neural Networks*, Addison-Wesley, Reading, Mass., 1990.

[Kitchen 1980] KITCHEN, L., 'Relaxation Applied to Matching Quantitative Relational Structures,' *IEEE Transactions on Systems, Man and Cybernetics*, Vol. 10, No. 2, Feb. 1980, pp. 96–101.

[Knuth 1968] KNUTH, D.E., 'Semantics of Context-Free Languages,' *Mathematical Systems Theory*, Vol. 2, No. 2, pp. 127–146.

[Kohonen 1972] KOHONEN, T., 'Correlation Associative Memories,' *IEEE Transactions on Computers*, Vol. C-21, No. 4, April 1972, pp. 353–357.

[Kohonen 1 1982] KOHONEN, T., 'Self-Organized Formation of Topologically Correct Feature Maps,' *Biological Cybernetics*, Vol. 43, 1982, pp. 59–69.

[Kohonen 2 1982] KOHONEN, T., 'Analysis of a Simple Self-Organizing Process,' *Biological Cybernetics*, Vol. 44, 1982, pp. 135–140.

[Kohonen 1984] KOHONEN, T., *Self-Organization and Associative Memory*, Springer-Verlag, Berlin, 1984.

[Kohonen 1987] KOHONEN, T., 'Adaptive, Associative and Self-Organizing Functions in Neural Computing,' *Applied Optics*, Vol. 26, No. 3, Dec. 1987, pp. 4910–4918.

[Kohonen 1988] KOHONEN, T., 'Self-Organizing Feature Maps,' tutorial course notes from 1988 Conference on Neural Networks, San Diego, Calif., 1988. (Accompanying videotape available from the Institute of Electrical and Electronics Engineers, Inc., 345 E. 47th St., New York, 10017.)

[Kolman/Busby 1984] KOLMAN, B., AND R.C. BUSBY, *Discrete Mathematical Structures for Computer Science*, Prentice-Hall, Englewood Cliffs, N.J., 1984.

[Kosko 1987] KOSKO, B., 'Adaptive Bidirectional Associative Memories,' *Applied Optics*, Vol. 26, No. 23, Dec. 1987, pp. 4947–4960.

[Kosko 1988] KOSKO, B., 'Bidirectional Associative Memories,' *IEEE Transactions on Systems, Man and Cybernetics*, Vol. SMC-18, 1988, pp. 42–60.

[Kosko 1990] KOSKO, B., 'Unsupervised Learning in Noise,' *IEEE Transactions on Neural Networks*, Vol. 1, No. 1, March 1990, pp. 44–57.

[Land 1981] LANDGREBE, D.A., 'Analysis Technology for Land Remote Sensing,' *Proceedings of the IEEE*, Vol. 69, No. 5, May 1981, pp. 628–642.

[Levine 1981] LEVINE, B., 'Derivatives of Tree Sets with Applications to Grammatical Inference,' *IEEE Transactions on Pattern Analysis and Machine Intelligence*, Vol. PAMI-3, No. 3, May 1981, pp. 285–293.

[Lin/Fu 1984] LIN, W.C., AND K.S. FU, 'A Syntactic Approach to 3-D Object Representation,' *IEEE Transactions on Pattern Analysis and Machine Intelligence*, Vol. PAMI-6, No. 3, May 1984, pp. 351–364.

[Linde et al. 1980] LINDE, Y., A. BUZO, AND R.M. GRAY, 'An Algorithm for Vector Quantizer Design,' *IEEE Transactions on Communications* Vol. COM-28, No. 1, Jan. 1980, pp. 84–95.

[Lippmann 1987] LIPPMANN, R.P., 'An Introduction to Computing with Neural Nets,' *IEEE ASSP Magazine*, Vol. 4, April 1987, pp. 4–22.

[Lowe 1987] LOWE, D.G., 'Three-Dimensional Object Recognition from Single Two-Dimensional Images,' *Artificial Intelligence*, Vol. 31, 1987, pp. 335–395.

[Lu 1979] LU, S.Y., 'A Tree to Tree Distance and Its Application to Cluster Analysis,' *IEEE Transactions on Pattern Analysis and Machine Intelligence*, Vol. 1, No. 2, 1979, pp. 219–229.

[Lu/Fu 1984] LU, H.R., AND K.S. FU, 'A General Approach to Inference of Context-Free Programmed Grammars,' *IEEE Transactions on Systems, Man and Cybernetics*, Vol. SMC-14, No. 2, March/April 1984, pp. 191–202.

[Mackworth 1977] MACKWORTH, A. K., 'Consistency in Networks of Relations,' *Artificial Intelligence*, Vol. 8, 1977, p. 99–118.

[Makhoul et al. 1985] MAKHOUL, J., S. ROUCOS, AND H. GISH, 'Vector Quantization in Speech Coding,' *Proceedings of the IEEE*, Vol. 73, No. 11, Nov. 1985, pp. 1551–1588.

[Maybeck 1979] MAYBECK, P., *Stochastic Models, Estimation and Control, Vol. 1*, Academic Press, New York, 1979.

[Mead 1989] MEAD, C., *Analog VLSI and Neural Systems*, Addison-Wesley, Reading, Mass., 1989.

[Mead/Mahowald 1988] MEAD, C.A., AND M.A. MAHOWALD, 'A Silicon Model for Early Visual Processing,' *Neural Networks*, Vol. 1, 1988, pp. 91–97.

[Michalski et al. 1986] MICHALSKI, R.S., J. G. CARBONELL, AND T.M. MITCHELL (eds.), *Machine Learning: An Artificial Intelligence Approach*, Vol. II, Morgan Kaufman Publishers, Los Altos, Calif., 1986.

[Miclet 1980] MICLET, L., 'Regular Inference with a Tail-Clustering Method,' *IEEE Transactions on Systems, Man and Cybernetics.*, Vol. SMC-10, 1980, pp. 737–747.

[Miclet 1986] MICLET, L., *Structural Methods in Pattern Recognition*, Springer-Verlag, New York, 1986.

[Minsky/Papert 1969] MINSKY, M., AND S. PAPERT, *Perceptrons—An Introduction to Computational Geometry*, MIT Press, Cambridge, Mass., 1969.

[Moll et al. 1988] MOLL, ROBERT N., M.A. ARBIB, AND A.J. KFOURY (eds.), *An Introduction to Formal Language Theory*, Springer-Verlag, New York, 1988.

[Mousavi/Schalkoff 1990] MOUSAVI, M., AND R.J. SCHALKOFF, 'A Neural Network Approach for Stereo Vision,' *Proceedings of the IEEE Southeastcon '90*, New Orleans, La., April 1990

[Mulder/Mackworth 1988] MULDER, J.A., AND A. MACKWORTH,'Knowledge Structuring and Constraint Satisfaction: the Mapsee Approach,' *IEEE Transactions on Pattern Analysis and Machine Intelligence*, Vol. 10, No. 6, Nov. 1988, pp. 866–867.

[NASA 1990] 'Analog Delta Back Propagation Neural Network Circuitry,' NASA Tech Briefs (and Support Package), Vol. 14, No. 6, Item # 159, June 1990. (Invention report NPO - 17564/7069.)

[Nev 1982] NEVATIA, R., *Machine Perception*, Prentice-Hall, Englewood Cliffs, N.J., 1982.

[Ni/Jain 1985] NI, L.M., AND A.K. JAIN, 'A VLSI Systolic Architecture for Pattern Clustering,' *IEEE Transactions on Pattern Analysis and Machine Intelligence*, Vol. PAMI-7, No. 1, Jan. 1985, pp. 80–89.

[Nilsson 1965] NILSSON, N.J., *Learning Machines*, McGraw-Hill, New York, 1965. (This has been revised as *Mathematical Foundations of Learning Machines*, Morgan-Kaufmann, San Mateo, Calif., 1989.)

[Ota 1975] OTA, P.A., 'Mosaic Grammars,' *Pattern Recognition*, Vol. 7, 1975, pp. 61–65.

[Pao 1988] PAO, Y.H., 'Autonomous Machine Learning of Effective Control Strategies with Connectionist-Net,' *Journal of Intelligent and Robotic Systems*, Vol. 1, No. 1, Kluwer Academic Publishers, Boston, MA, 1988, pp. 35–53.

[Pao 1989] PAO, Y.H., *Adaptive Pattern Recognition and Neural Networks*, Addison-Wesley, Reading, Mass., 1989.

[Papoulis 1984] PAPOULIS, A., *Probability, Random Variables, and Stochastic Processes* (2nd edition), McGraw-Hill, New York, 1984.

[Patrick 1972] PATRICK, E.A., *Fundamentals of Pattern Recognition*, Prentice-Hall, Englewood Cliffs, N.J., 1972.

[Patrick/Fattu 1986] PATRICK, E.A., AND J.M. FATTU, *Artificial Intelligence with Statistical Pattern Recognition*, Prentice-Hall, Englewood Cliffs, N.J., 1986.

[Pavlidis 1977] PAVLIDIS, T., *Structural Pattern Recognition*, Springer-Verlag, New York, 1977.

[Peleg 1980] PELEG, S., 'A New Probabilistic Relaxation Scheme,' *IEEE Transactions on Pattern Analysis and Machine Intelligence*, Vol. PAMI-2, No. 4, 1980, pp. 362–369.

[Peleg/Ros 1978] PELEG, S., AND A. ROSENFELD, 'Determining Compatability Coefficients for Curve Enhancement Relaxation Processes,' *IEEE Transactions on Systems, Man and Cybernetics*, Vol. 7, 1978, pp. 548–555.

[Penrose 1955] PENROSE, R., 'A Generalized Inverse for Matrices,' *Proceedings of the Cambridge Philosophical Society*, Vol. 51, 1955, pp. 406–413.

[Pineda 1987] PINEDA, F. J., 'Generalization of Back Propagation to Recurrent Networks,' *Physics Review Letters*, Vol. 59, No. 19, Nov. 1987, pp. 2229–2232.

[Rao 1971] RAO, C., AND S. MITRA, *Generalized Inverse of Matrices and Its Applications*, John Wiley & Sons, New York, 1971.

[Read/Corneil 1977] READ, R.C., AND D.G. CORNEIL, 'The Graph Isomorphism Disease,' *Journal of Graph Theory*, 1977, pp. 339–363.

[Richetin/Vernadad 1984] RICHETIN, M., AND F. VERNADAD, 'Efficient Regular Grammatical Inference for Pattern Recognition,' *Pattern Recognition*, Vol. 17, No. 2, 1984, pp. 245–250.

[Riesenfeld 1981] RIESENFELD, R., 'Homogeneous Coordinates and Projective Planes in Computer Graphs,' *IEEE on Computer Graphics and Applications*, Vol. 1, 1981, pp. 50–55.

[Roads 1979] ROADS, CURTIS, 'Grammars as Representations for Music,' *Computer Music Journal*, Vol. 3, No. 1, 1979, pp. 48–55.

[Roads/Strawn 1985] ROADS, C., AND J. STRAWN (eds.), *Foundations of Computer Music*, MIT Press, Cambridge, Mass., 1985.

[Rosenblatt 1959] ROSENBLATT, R., *Principles of Neurodynamics*, Spartan Books, New York, 1959.

[Rosenfeld 1973] ROSENFELD, A., 'Array Grammar Normal Forms,' *Information and Control*, Vol. 23, No. 2, 1973, pp. 173–182.

[Rosenfeld 1979] ROSENFELD, A., *Picture Languages*, Academic Press, New York, 1979.

[Roth 1990] ROTH, M.W., 'Survey of Neural Network Technology for Automatic Target Recognition,' *IEEE Transactions on Neural Networks*, Vol. 1, No. 1, March 1990, p. 43.

[Rummelhart et al. 1986] RUMMELHART, D.E., P. SMOLENSKY, J. McCLELLAND, AND G.E. HINTON, 'Schemata and Sequential Thought Processes in PDP Models,' *Parallel Distributed Processing*, Vol. 2, pp. 7–57.

[Rummelhart/McClelland 1 1986] RUMMELHART, D.E., AND J.L. McCLELLAND, *Parallel Distributed Processing—Explorations in the Microstructure of Cognition, Volume 1: Foundations*, MIT Press, Cambridge, Mass., 1986.

[Rummelhart/McClelland 2 1986] RUMMELHART, D.E., AND J.L. McCLELLAND, *Parallel Distributed Processing—Explorations in the Microstructure of Cognition, Volume 2: Psychological and Biological Models*, MIT Press, Cambridge, Mass., 1986.

[Rutkow et al. 1981] RUTKOWSKI, W.S., S. PELEG, AND A. ROSENFELD, 'Shape Segmentation Using Relaxation,' *IEEE Transactions on Pattern Analysis and Machine Intelligence*, Vol. PAMI-3, No. 4, July 1981, pp. 368–375.

[Sanfeliu/Fu 1983] SANFELIU, A., AND K.S. FU, 'A Distance Measure Between Attributed Relational Graphs for Pattern Recognition,' *IEEE Transactions on Systems, Man and Cybernetics*, Vol. SMC-13, No. 3, May-June 1983, pp. 353–362.

[Saund 1989] SAUND, E.,'Dimensionality Reduction Using Connectionist Networks,' *IEEE Transactions on Pattern Analysis and Machine Intelligence*, Vol. 11, No. 3, March 1989, pp. 304–314.

[Schalkoff 1989] SCHALKOFF, R. J., *Digital Image Processing and Computer Vision*, John Wiley & Sons, New York, 1989.

[Schalkoff 1990] SCHALKOFF, R. J., *Artificial Intelligence: An Engineering Approach*, McGraw-Hill, New York, 1990.

[Sebesta 1989] SEBESTA, R.W., *Concepts of Programming Languages*, Benjamin Cummings, Redwood City, Calif., 1989.

[Selkow 1977] SELKOW, S.M., 'The Tree-to-Tree Editing Problem,' *Information Processing Letters*, Vol. 6, No. 6, 1977, pp. 184–186.

[Sethi 1981] SETHI, I.K., 'A Fast Algorithm for Recognizing Nearest Neighbors,' *IEEE Transactions on Systems, Man and Cybernetics*, Vol. SMC-11, No. 3, March 1981, pp. 245–248.

[Sethi/Sarvarayudu 1982] SETHI, I.K., AND G.P.R. SARVARAYUDU, 'Hierarchical Classifier Design Using Mutual Information,' *IEEE Transactions on Pattern Analysis and Machine Intelligence*, Vol. 4, 1982, pp. 441–445.

[Shapiro/Haralick 1985] SHAPIRO, L.G., AND R.M. HARALICK, 'A Metric for Comparing Relational Descriptions,' *IEEE Transactions on Pattern Analysis and Machine Intelligence*, Vol. PAMI-7, Jan. 1985, pp. 90–94.

[Shaw 1969] SHAW, A.C., 'A Formal Picture Description Scheme as a Basis for Picture Processing Systems,' *Information and Control*, Vol. 14, 1969, pp. 9–51.

[Shaw 1970] SHAW, A.C., 'Parsing of Graph-Representable Pictures,' *Journal of the Association for Computing Machinery*, Vol. 17, No. 3, 1970, pp. 453–481.

[Shriver 1988] SHRIVER, B.D., 'Artificial Neural Systems,' *IEEE Computer*, Vol. 21, No. 3, March 1988.

[Silverman 1986] SILVERMAN, B.W., *Density Estimation*, Chapman and Hall, London, England, 1986.

[Simpson 1990] SIMPSON, P.K., *Artificial Neural Systems*, Pergamon Press, Elmsford, New York, 1990.

[Singh 1966] SINGH, J., *Great Ideas in Information Theory, Language and Cybernetics*, Dover Publications, New York, 1966.

[Sklansky 1973] SKLANSKY, J. (ed.), *Pattern Recognition: Introduction and Foundations*, Dowden, Hutchinson and Ross, Stroudsburg, Pa., 1973.

[Sowa 1984] SOWA, J.F., *Conceptual Structures: Information Processing in Mind and Machine*, Addison-Wesley, Reading, Mass., 1984.

[Sprecher 1965] SPRECHER, D.A., 'On the Structure of Continuous Functions of Several Variables,' *Transactions of the American Mathematical Society*, 115, March 1965, pp. 340–355.

[Stevenson et al. 1990] STEVENSON, M., R. WINTER, AND B. WIDROW, 'Sensitivity of Feedforward Neural Networks to Weight Errors,' *IEEE Transactions on Neural Networks*, Vol. 1, No. 1, March 1990, pp. 71–80.

[Strang 1976] STRANG, G., *Linear Algebra and Its Applications*, Academic Press, New York, 1976.

[Swain et al. 1980] SWAIN, P.H., SIEGEL, H. J., AND SMITH, B.W., 'Contextual Classification of Multispectral Remote Sensing Data Using a Multiprocessor System,' *IEEE Transactions on Geoscience and Remote Sensing*, Vol. GE-18, No. 2, April 1980, pp. 197–203.

[Tan/Martin 1986] TAN, C.L., AND W.N. MARTIN, 'A Distributed System for Analyzing Time-Varying Multiresolution Imagery,' *Computer Vision, Graphics and Image Processing*, Vol. 36, 1986, pp. 162–174.

[Tenen et al. 1981] TENENBAUM, J.M., M.A. FISCHLER, AND H.G. BARROW, 'Scene Modeling: A Structural Basis for Image Description,' *Image Modeling*, A. Rosenfeld, ed., Academic Press, New York, 1981.

[Thakoor et al. 1987] THAKOOR, A.P., A. MOOPENN, J. LAMBE, AND S.K. KHANNA, 'Electronic Hardware Implementations of Neural Networks,' *Applied Optics*, Vol. 26, No. 23, Dec. 1987, pp. 5085–5092.

[Therrien 1989] THERRIEN, C. W., *Decision Estimation and Classification: An Introduction to Pattern Recognition and Related Topics*, John Wiley & Sons, New York, 1989.

[Topa/Schalkoff 1987] TOPA, L. C., AND R. J. SCHALKOFF, 'A Rule Based Expert System for the Determination of Object Structure and Motion Information from a Sequence of Digital Images,' submitted to *Computer Vision, Graphics and Image Processing*. (Also available as L. C. Topa, PhD Thesis, Electrical and Computer Engineering Dept., Clemson University, December 1987.)

[Tou/Gonzalez 1974] TOU, J., AND R. GONZALEZ, *Pattern Recognition Principles*, Addison Wesley, Reading, Mass., 1974.

[Trahanias/Skordalakis 1990] TRAHANIAS, P., AND E. SKORDALAKIS, 'Syntactic Pattern Recognition of the ECG,' *IEEE Transactions on Pattern Analysis and Machine Intelligence*, Vol. 12, No. 7, July 1990, pp. 648–657.

[Tremblay/Sorenson 1985] TREMBLAY, J.P., AND P.G. SORENSON, *The Theory and Practice of Compiler Writing*, McGraw-Hill, New York, 1985.

[Tsai/Fu 1980] TSAI, W.H., AND K.S. FU, 'Attributed Grammar—A Tool for Combining Syntactic and Statistical Approaches to Pattern Recognition,' *IEEE Transactions on Systems, Man and Cybernetics*, Vol. SMC-10, No. 12, 1980, pp. 873–885.

[Tsai/Fu 1983] TSAI, W.H., AND K.S. FU, 'Subgraph Error-Correcting Isomorphisms for Syntactic Pattern Recognition,' *IEEE Transactions on Systems, Man and Cybernetics*, Vol. SMC-13, No. 1, Jan. 1983, pp. 48–62.

[Ullman 1976] ULLMAN, J.R., 'An Algorithm for Subgraph Isomorphism,' *Journal of the Association for Computing Machinery*, Vol. 23, Jan. 1976, pp. 31–42.

[VanTrees 1968] VANTREES, H., *Detection Estimation and Modulation Theory*, John Wiley & Sons, New York, 1968.

[Wagner/Psaltis 1987] WAGNER, K., AND D. PSALTIS, 'Multilayer Optical Learning Networks,' *Applied Optics*, Vol. 26, No. 23, Dec. 1987, pp. 5061–5076.

[Wang 1980] WANG, P.S., 'Some New Results on Isotonic Array Grammars,' *Information Processing Letters*, Vol. 10, No. 3, April 1980, pp. 129–131.

[Wang et al. 1990] WANG, Y.F., J.B. CRUZ, AND J.H. MULLIGAN, 'Two Coding Strategies for Bidirectional Associative Memory,' *IEEE Transactions on Neural Networks*, Vol. 1, No. 1, March 1990, pp. 81–92.

[Wang/Suen 1984] WANG, Q.R., AND C.Y. SUEN, 'Analysis and Design of a Decision Tree Based on Entropy Reduction and Its Application to Large Character Set

Recognition,' *IEEE Transactions on Pattern Analysis and Machine Intelligence*, Vol. 4, 1984, pp. 406–417.

[Watanabe 1985] WATANABE, S., *Pattern Recognition: Human and Mechanical*, John Wiley & Sons, New York, 1985.

[Weizenbaum 1966] WEIZENBAUM, J., 'ELIZA—A Computer Program for the Study of Natural Language Communication between Man and Machine,' *Communications of the Association for Computing Machinery*, Vol. 9, No. 1, 1966, pp. 36–45.

[Weszka 1976] WESZKA, J.S., C.R. DYER, AND A. ROSENFELD, 'A Comparative Study of Texture Measures for Terrain Classification,' *IEEE Transactions on Systems, Man, and Cybernetics*, Vol. SMC-6, No. 4, April, 1976, pp. 269–285.

[White et al. 1988] WHITE, H.J., N.B. ALDRIDGE, AND I. LINDSAY, 'Digital and Analog Holographic Associative Memories,' *Optical Engineering*, Vol. 27, No. 1, 1988, pp. 30–37.

[Widrow/Hoff 1960] WIDROW, B., AND M.E. HOFF, 'Adaptive Switching Circuits,' 1960 IRE WESCON Conv. Record, Part 4, Aug. 1960, pp. 96–104 (reprinted in [Anderson/Rosenfeld 1988]).

[Wieland/Leighton 1987] WIELAND, A., AND R. LEIGHTON, 'Geometric Analysis of Neural Network Capabilities,' *IEEE 1st International Conference on Neural Networks*, June 1987, pp. III385–III392.

[Wiitala 1987] WIITALA, S.A., *Discrete Mathematics, A Unified Approach*, McGraw-Hill, New York, New York, 1987.

[Wilkenson 1971] WILKENSON, J.H., AND C. REINSCH, *Handbook for Automatic Computation, Vol. 2: Linear Algebra*, Springer-Verlag, Berlin, 1971.

[Woods 1970] WOODS, W.A., 'Transition Network Grammars for Natural Language Analysis,' *Communications of the Association for Computing Machines*, Vol. 13, No. 10, 1970, pp. 591–606.

[Young/Calvert 1974] YOUNG, T.Y., AND T.W. CALVERT, *Classification, Estimation and Pattern Recognition*, Elsevier, New York, 1974.

[Yunck 1976] YUNCK, T.P., 'A Technique to Identify Nearest Neighbors,' *IEEE Transactions on Systems, Man and Cybernetics*, Vol. SMC-6, Oct. 1976, pp. 678–683.

[Zadeh 1975] ZADEH, L., ET AL., *Fuzzy Sets and Their Applications to Cognitive and Decision Processes*, Academic Press, New York, 1975.

[Zenzo 1983] ZENZO, S. D., 'Advances in Image Segmentation,' *Image and Vision Computing*, Vol. 1, No. 4, Nov. 1983, pp. 196–210.

[Zuck et al. 1981] ZUCKER, S.W., Y. G. LECLERC, AND J.L. MOHAMMED, 'Continuous Relaxation and Local Maxima Selection: Conditions for Equivalence,' *IEEE Transactions on Pattern Analysis and Machine Intelligence*, Vol. PAMI-3, No. 2, March 1981, pp. 117–127.

Permission Source Notes

Figure 10, Chapter 12, p. 258: Reprinted courtesy of *Research Magazine* ©1990 Eastman Kodak Co.

Figure 6, Chapter 13, p. 281: Carpenter, G., and Grossberg, S., *Applied Optics*, Vol. 26, No. 23, p. 4920, 1987.

Figure 8, Chapter 13, p. 283: Kangas, Kohonen, and Laaksonen, "Variants of Self-Organizing Maps," *IEEE Transactions on Neural Networks*, ©1990 IEEE.

Figure 9, Chapter 13, p. 285: Kohonen, T., Tutorial Notes from ICNN88 (Self-Organizing Maps), ©1987 IEEE.

Index